Science and Technology in International Economic Law

Science and technology play an increasingly important role in the continued development of international economic law. This book brings together well-known and rising scholars to explore the status and interaction of science, technology and international economic law. The book reviews the place of science and technology in the development of international economic law with a view to ensuring a balance between the promotion of trade and investment liberalization and decision-making based on a sound scientific process without hampering technological development.

The book features chapters from a range of experts – including Lukasz Gruszczynski, Jürgen Kurtz, Andrew Mitchell and Peter K. Yu – who examine a wide range of issues such as investment law, international trade law, and international intellectual property. By bringing together these issues, the book asks how international trade and investment regimes utilize, govern and promote science and technology, and whether they do so fairly and in the interest of broader public policies. This book will be of great interest to researchers of international economic law, health law, technology law and international intellectual property law.

Bryan Mercurio is Professor, Vice Chancellor's Outstanding Fellow of the Faculty of Law and Associate Dean (Research) at the Chinese University of Hong Kong.

Kuei-Jung Ni is Professor and former Director of the Institute of Technology Law, National Chiao Tung University, Taiwan.

Routledge Research in International Economic Law

Available:

Recognition and Regulation of Safeguard Measures under GATT/WTO
Sheela Rai

The Interaction between WTO Law and External International Law
The Constrained Openness of WTO Law
Ronnie R.F. Yearwood

Human Rights, Natural Resource and Investment Law in a Globalised World
Shades of Grey in the Shadow of the Law
Lorenzo Cotula

The Domestic Politics of Negotiating International Trade
Intellectual Property Rights in US-Colombia and US-Peru Free Trade Agreements
Johanna von Braun

Foreign Investment and Dispute Resolution Law and Practice in Asia
Vivienne Bath and Luke Nottage (eds)

Improving International Investment Agreements
Armand De Mestral and Céline Lévesque (eds)

Public Health in International Investment Law and Arbitration
Valentina Vadi

The WTO and the Environment
Development of Competence beyond Trade
James Watson

Foreign Direct Investment and Human Development
The Law and Economics of International Investment Agreements
Olivier De Schutter, Johan Swinnen and Jan Wouters

Microtrade
A New System of International Trade with Volunteerism towards Poverty Elimination
Yong-Shik Lee

Science and Technology in International Economic Law
Balancing Competing Interests
Bryan Mercurio and Kuei-Jung Ni

Forthcoming:

Trade Remedies
A Development Perspective
Asif Qureshi

Chinese Perspectives on International Investment Law
Guiguo Wang

Science and Technology in International Economic Law

Balancing Competing Interests

Edited by
Bryan Mercurio and
Kuei-Jung Ni

Routledge
Taylor & Francis Group
LONDON AND NEW YORK

First published 2014
by Routledge
2 Park Square, Milton Park, Abingdon, Oxon, OX14 4RN

and by Routledge
711 Third Avenue, New York, NY 10017

Routledge is an imprint of the Taylor and *Francis Group, an informa business*

British Library Cataloguing in Publication Data
A catalogue record for this book is available from the British Library

Library of Congress Cataloging-in-Publication Data
Science and technology in international economic law: balancing competing
interests/[edited by] Bryan Mercurio, Kuei-Jung Ni.
p. cm. – (Routledge research in international economic law)
Includes bibliographical references and index.
1. Foreign trade regulation. 2. International economic relations.
3. Investments, Foreign – Law and legislation. 4. Science and law.
5. Technology and law. I. Mercurio, Bryan, editor of compilation.
II. Ni, Kuei-Jung, editor of compilation.
K3943.S38 2013
343.08′7 – dc23
2013024909

ISBN: 978-0-415-82996-0 (hbk)
ISBN: 978-0-203-38170-0 (ebk)

Typeset in Garamond
by Florence Production Ltd, Stoodleigh, Devon, UK

MIX
Paper from
responsible sources
FSC
www.fsc.org
FSC® C013604

Printed and bound by CPI Group (UK) Ltd, Croydon, CR0 4YY

Contents

Contributors

Julien Chaisse is Associate Professor at the Faculty of Law, the Chinese University of Hong Kong.

Debashis Chakraborty is Assistant Professor at the Indian Institute of Foreign Trade.

Lukasz Gruszczynski is Assistant Professor of Law at the Institute of Law Studies, Polish Academy of Sciences (Warsaw, Poland).

Andrew Higgins is a Lecturer in Civil Procedure at the Faculty of Law at the University of Oxford.

Arno Hold is a Research Fellow at the World Trade Institute at the University of Berne.

Jia-Xiang Hu is Professor at the Koguan Law School, Shanhai Jiao Tong University.

Naoto Jinji is Associate Professor, Faculty of Economics, Kyoto University.

Animesh Kumar is Researcher at the Indian Institute of Foreign Trade.

Jürgen Kurtz is Associate Professor at Melbourne Law School and Director of the International Investment Law Research Programme of the Institute for International Law and the Humanities at the University of Melbourne, Australia.

Bryan Mercurio is Professor, Vice Chancellor's Outstanding Fellow of the Faculty of Law and Associate Dean (Research) at the Chinese University of Hong Kong.

Kate Miles is Fellow and College Lecturer in Law, Gonville and Caius, University of Cambridge.

Andrew Mitchell is Professor of Law at Melbourne Law School.

James Munro is a PhD candidate at the University of Melbourne. He is currently engaged as a Research Fellow at the University of Melbourne under a grant from the Australian National Preventive Health Agency and is on leave from a position in the Attorney General's Department of the Australian government.

Kuei-Jung Ni is Professor and former Director of the Institute of Technology Law, National Chiao Tung University, Taiwan.

Shin-Yi Peng is Professor and Director of the Institute of Law for Science and Technology at National Tsing Hua University (NTHU), Taiwan, and Deputy Director of NTHU's Research Center for Humanities and Social Sciences.

Richard Li-dar Wang is Associate Professor at the Institute of Technology Law, National Chiao Tung University, Taiwan.

Kimberlee Weatherall is Associate Professor at the Sydney Law School.

Peter K. Yu is Kern Family Chair in Intellectual Property Law and the founding director of the Intellectual Property Law Center at Drake University Law School.

Abbreviations

APEC	Asia-Pacific Economic Cooperation
DDA	Doha Development Agenda
DSB	Dispute Settlement Body
EC	European Communities
EPA	economic partnership agreement
EU	European Union
FAO	Food and Agriculture Organization of the United Nations
FTA	free trade agreement
GATS	General Agreement on Trade in Services
GATT	General Agreement on Tariffs and Trade
GDP	gross domestic product
GPA	Agreement on Government Procurement (WTO)
GSP	generalized system of preferences
HS	Harmonized System
ICTSD	International Centre for Trade and Sustainable Development
IPR	intellectual property rights
ITA	Information Technology Agreement
MFN	most favoured nation
NT	national treatment
OECD	Organization for Economic Co-operation and Development
SPS	Sanitary and Phytosanitary
TBT	Technical Barriers to Trade
TPP	Trans-Pacific Partnership
TRIPS	Trade-Related Aspects of Intellectual Property Rights
WHO	World Health Organization
WIPO	World Intellectual Property Organization
WITS	World Integrated Trade Solution
WTO	World Trade Organization

Cases

1 Index of WTO Dispute Settlement Panel and Appellate Body Reports

Short title	*Full title and citation*
Australia – Apples	Appellate Body Report, *Australia – Measures Affecting the Importation of Apples from New Zealand*, WT/DS367/AB/R, adopted 17 December 2010
Australia – Salmon	Appellate Body Report, *Australia – Measures Affecting Importation of Salmon*, WT/DS18/AB/R, adopted 6 November 1998, DSR 1998:VIII, 3327
Australia – Salmon	Panel Report, *Australia – Measures Affecting Importation of Salmon*, WT/DS18/R and Corr.1, adopted 6 November 1998, as modified by Appellate Body Report WT/DS18/AB/R, DSR 1998:VIII, 3407
Australia – Tobacco Plain Packaging	Request for Consultations by Ukraine, *Australia – Certain Measures Concerning Trademarks and Other Plain Packaging Requirements Applicable to Tobacco Products and Packaging*, WT/DS434 [Panel composition pending]
Brazil – Retreaded Tyres	Panel Report, *Brazil – Measures Affecting Imports of Retreaded Tyres*, WT/DS332/R, adopted 17 December 2007, as modified by Appellate Body Report WT/DS332/AB/R, DSR 2007:V, 1649
Brazil – Retreaded Tyres	Appellate Body Report, *Brazil – Measures Affecting Imports of Retreaded Tyres*, WT/DS332/AB/R, adopted 17 December 2007, DSR 2007:IV, 1527
Canada – Aircraft	Panel Report, *Canada – Measures Affecting the Export of Civilian Aircraft*, WT/DS70/R, adopted 20 August 1999, upheld by Appellate Body Report WT/DS70/AB/R, DSR 1999:IV, 1443
Canada – Continued Suspension	Appellate Body Report, *Canada – Continued Suspension of Obligations in the EC – Hormones Dispute*, WT/DS321/AB/R, adopted 14 November 2008, DSR 2008:XIV, 5373
Canada – Dairy (Article 21.5 – New Zealand and US)	Panel Report, *Canada – Measures Affecting the Importation of Milk and the Exportation of Dairy Products – Recourse to Article 21.5 of the DSU by New Zealand and the United States*, WT/DS103/RW, WT/DS113/RW, adopted 18 December 2001, as reversed by Appellate Body Report WT/DS103/AB/RW, WT/DS113/AB/RW, DSR 2001:XIII, 6865
Canada – Feed-in Tariff Program/Canada – Renewable Energy	Appellate Body Reports, *Canada – Measures Relating to the Feed-in Tariff Program*, WT/DS426/AB/R/ *Canada – Certain Measures Affecting the Renewable Energy Generation*

	Sector, WT/DS412/AB/R, circulated to WTO Members 6 May 2013 [adoption pending]
Canada – Renewable Energy	Panel Report, *Canada – Certain Measures Affecting the Renewable Energy Generation Sector*, WT/DS412/R and Add.1, circulated to WTO Members 19 December 2012 [adoption/appeal pending]
China – Publications and Audiovisual Products	Panel Report, *China – Measures Affecting Trading Rights and Distribution Services for Certain Publications and Audiovisual Entertainment Products*, WT/DS363/R and Corr.1, adopted 19 January 2010, as modified by Appellate Body Report WT/DS363/AB/R, DSR 2010:II, 261
China – Publications and Audiovisual Products	Appellate Body Report, *China – Measures Affecting Trading Rights and Distribution Services for Certain Publications and Audiovisual Entertainment Products*, WT/DS363/AB/R, adopted 19 January 2010, DSR 2010:I, 3
EC – Approval and Marketing of Biotech Products	Panel Reports, *European Communities – Measures Affecting the Approval and Marketing of Biotech Products*, WT/DS291/R / WT/DS292/R / WT/DS293/R, Add.1 to Add.9, and Corr.1, adopted 21 November 2006, DSR 2006:III–VIII, 847
EC – Asbestos	Panel Report, *European Communities – Measures Affecting Asbestos and Asbestos-Containing Products*, WT/DS135/R and Add.1, adopted 5 April 2001, as modified by Appellate Body Report WT/DS135/AB/R, DSR 2001:VIII, 3305
EC – Biotech Products	Panel Report, *EC – Measures Affecting the Approval and Marketing of Biotech Products*, WT/DS291/R, WT/DS292/R, WT/DS293/R, Add.1 to Add.9, and Corr.1, adopted 21 November 2006, DSR 2006:III–VIII, 84
EC – Computer Equipment	Appellate Body Report, *European Communities – Customs Classification of Certain Computer Equipment*, T/DS62/AB/R, WT/DS67/AB/R, WT/DS68/AB/R, adopted 22 June 1998, DSR 1998:V, 1851
EC – Hormones	Appellate Body Report, *EC Measures Concerning Meat and Meat Products (Hormones)*, WT/DS26/AB/R, WT/DS48/AB/R, adopted 13 February 1998, DSR 1998:I, 135
EC – Hormones (Canada)	Panel Report, *EC Measures Concerning Meat and Meat Products (Hormones), Complaint by Canada*, WT/DS48/R/CAN, adopted 13 February 1998, as modified by Appellate Body Report WT/DS26/AB/R, WT/DS48/AB/R, DSR 1998:II, 235
EC – Sardines	Appellate Body Report, *European Communities – Trade Description of Sardines*, WT/DS231/AB/R, adopted 23 October 2002, DSR 2002:VIII, 3359
EC – Sardines	Panel Report, *European Communities – Trade Description of Sardines*, WT/DS231/R and Corr.1, adopted 23 October 2002, as modified by Appellate Body Report WT/DS231/AB/R, DSR 2002:VIII, 3451
EC – IT Products	Panel Reports, *European Communities and its Member States –Tariff Treatment of Certain Information Technology Products*,WT/DS375/R / WT/DS376/R / WT/DS377/R, adopted 21 September 2010, DSR 2010:III, 933-DSR 2010:IV, 1567
Japan – Agricultural Products II	Appellate Body Report,*Japan – Measures Affecting Agricultural Products*, WT/DS76/AB/R, adopted 19 March 1999, DSR 1999:I, 277

Japan – Apples	Panel Report, *Japan – Measures Affecting the Importation of Apples*, WT/DS245/R, adopted 10 December 2003, upheld by Appellate Body Report, WT/DS245/AB/R, DSR 2003:IX, 4481
Mexico – Telecoms	Panel Report, *Mexico – Measures Affecting Telecommunications Services*, WT/DS204/R, adopted 1 June 2004, DSR 2004:IV, 1537
US – Carbon Steel	Appellate Body Report, *United States – Countervailing Duties on Certain Corrosion-Resistant Carbon Steel Flat Products from Germany*, WT/DS213/AB/R and Corr.1, adopted 19 December 2002, DSR 2002:IX, 3779
US – Clove Cigarettes	Panel Report, *United States – Measures Affecting the Productions and Sale of Clove Cigarettes*, WT/DS406/R, adopted 24 April 2012, as modified by Appellate Body Report, WT/DS406/AB/R
US/Canada – Continued Suspension	Panel Report, *United States – Continued Suspension of Obligations in the EC – Hormones Dispute*, WT/DS320/R, adopted 14 November 2008, as modified by Appellate Body Report WT/DS320/AB/R, DSR 2008:XI, 3891-DSR 2008:XIII, 4913
US – Gambling	Panel Report, *United States – Measures Affecting the Cross-Border Supply of Gambling and Betting Services*, WT/DS285/R, adopted 20 April 2005, as modified by Appellate Body Report WT/DS285/AB/R, DSR 2005:XII, 5797
US – Gambling	Appellate Body Report, *United States – Measures Affecting the Cross-Border Supply of Gambling and Betting Services*,WT/DS285/AB/R, adopted 20 April 2005, DSR 2005:XII, 5663 (Corr.1, DSR 2006:XII, 5475)
US – Gasoline	Appellate Body Report, *United States – Standards for Reformulated and Conventional Gasoline*, WT/DS2/AB/R, adopted 20 May 1996, DSR 1996:I, 3
US – Gasoline	Panel Report, *United States – Standards for Reformulated and Conventional Gasoline*, WT/DS2/R, adopted 20 May 1996, as modified by Appellate Body Report WT/DS2/AB/R, DSR 1996:I, 29
US – Shrimp	Appellate Body Report, *United States – Import Prohibition of Certain Shrimp and Shrimp Products*, WT/DS58/AB/R, adopted 6 November 1998, DSR 1998:VII, 2755
US – Shrimp	Panel Report, *United States – Import Prohibition of Certain Shrimp and Shrimp Products*, WT/DS58/R and Corr.1, adopted 6 November 1998, as modified by Appellate Body Report WT/DS58/AB/R, DSR 1998:VII, 2821
US – Tuna II (Mexico)	Panel Report, *United States – Measures Concerning the Importation, Marketing and Sale of Tuna and Tuna Products*, WT/DS381/R, adopted 13 June 2012, as modified by Appellate Body Report, WT/DS381/AB/R
US – Wool Shirts and Blouses	Appellate Body Report, *United States – Measure Affecting Imports of Woven Wool Shirts and Blouses from India*, WT/DS33/AB/R, adopted 23 May 1997, and Corr.1, DSR 1997:I, 323

2 Index of GATT Dispute Settlement Panel Reports

Short title	*Full title and citation*
Thailand – Cigarettes	GATT Panel Report, *Thailand – Restrictions on Importation of and Internal Taxes on Cigarettes*, DS10/R, adopted 7 November 1990, BISD 37S/200
US – Tuna (Mexico)	GATT Panel Report, *United States – Restrictions on Imports of Tuna (Mexico)*, DS21/R, DS21/R, 3 September 1991, unadopted, BISD 39S/155
US – Tuna (EEC)	GATT Panel Report, *United States – Restrictions on Imports of Tuna (EEC)*, DS29/R, 16 June 1994, unadopted

Treaties and international agreements

1 International conventions and multilateral treaties

Short title	*Long title*	*Status*
AIDCP	Agreement on International Dolphin Conservation Program	Adopted in Washington, DC by Belize, Colombia, Costa Rica, Ecuador, El Salvador, European Union, Guatemala, Honduras, Mexico, Nicaragua, Panama, Peru, United States and Venezuela on 21 May 1998; in force February 1999
Basel Convention	Basel Convention on the Control of Transboundary Movement of Hazardous Wastes and their Disposal	Adopted in Basel by the Conference of Plenipotentiaries on 22 March 1989; in force 5 May 1992
CITESWFF	Convention on International Trade in Endangered Species of Wild Fauna and Flora	Adopted in Washington, DC by the World Conservation Union on 3 March 1973; in force 1 July 1975
Kyoto Protocol	Kyoto Protocol to the United Nations Framework Convention on Climate Change	Adopted in Kyoto, Japan by the Diplomatic Conference on 11 December 1997; in force 16 February 2005
CBD	Convention on Biological Diversity	Adopted in Rio de Janeiro by the Diplomatic Conference on 5 June 1992; in force 29 December 1993
WCT	WIPO Copyright Treaty	Adopted in Geneva by the Diplomatic Conference on 20 December 1996; in force 6 March 2002
WPPT	WIPO Performances and Phonograms Treaty (1996)	Adopted in Geneva by the Diplomatic Conference on 20 December 1996; in force 20 May 2002

2 GATT/WTO Agreements

Short title	*Full title*	*Status/Source*
Agreement on Basic Telecom-munications Services	WTO Agreement on Basic Telecommunications Services	Annex 1B of the WTO Agreement
Agriculture Agreement	Agreement on Agriculture	Annex 1A of the WTO Agreement
Antidumping Agreement	Agreement on Implementation of Article VI of the General Agreement on Tariffs and Trade 1994	Annex 1A of the WTO Agreement
DSU	Understanding on Rules and Procedures Governing the Settlement of Disputes	Annex 2 of the WTO Agreement
GATT 1947	General Agreement on Tariffs and Trade 1947	Signed 30 October 1947; in force 1 January 1948
GATT 1994	General Agreement on Tariffs and Trade 1994	Annex 1A of the WTO Agreement
SCM Agreement	Agreement on Subsidies and Countervailing Measures	Annex 1A of the WTO Agreement
SPS Agreement	Agreement on the Application of Sanitary and Phytosanitary Measures	Annex 1A of the WTO Agreement
TBT Agreement	Agreement on Technical Barriers to Trade	Annex 1A of the WO Agreement
TRIMS Agreement	Agreement on Trade-Related Investment Measures	Annex 1A of the WTO Agreement
TRIPS Agreement	Agreement on Trade-Related Aspects of Intellectual Property Rights	Annex 1C of the WTO Agreement
WTO Agreement	Marrakesh Agreement Establishing the World Trade Organization	Signed 15 April 1994; in force 1 January 1995

1 The use of science and technology in international economic law

An introduction

Bryan Mercurio and Kuei-Jung Ni

> The protection and enforcement of intellectual property rights should contribute to the promotion of technological innovation and to the transfer and dissemination of technology, to the mutual advantage of producers and users of technological knowledge and in a manner conducive to social and economic welfare, and to a balance of rights and obligations.
>
> The TRIPS Agreement, Article 7

The contribution and importance of science and technology to our modern society are self-evident. Science and technology continue to shape our life and the future. Given the strength and influence of science and technology, their prudent management, both morally and legally, is highly desirable. Science and technology should be managed in such a way as to advance social welfare and benefit humankind as a whole. From the perspective of national governance and lawmaking, abundant literature exists that addresses the interrelationship between science, technology and law. Much of this comes from the countless intellectual property (IP) disputes relating to the dominance of certain technologies and abuse of market power. Moreover, most regulators are concerned with the issue of whether and to what extent governments should intervene or control the developments of controversial scientific activities, such as stem cell research and human cloning. In these contexts, how these issues are ultimately resolved – usually in the form of intervention or promotion – is wholly subject to national consensus and/or domestic social values as embodied in domestic law.

As the impact of modern science and technology developments has penetrated national boundaries and increasingly affects the global order, the topic of science and technology has firmly reached the realm of the international agenda. In the context of science and technology in relation to IP, the World Intellectual Property Organization (WIPO) has traditionally been the default organization to deal with such issues. For some time, WIPO was the only international institution serving to protect intellectual property rights through the administration of treaties and conventions, such as the prominent Paris (1883) and Berne (1886) Conventions. But the WIPO treaties were often designed more to protect owner rights than to balance societal interests, particularly in such delicate areas as science and technology. In addition, while these treaties have stood the test of time rather well, certain science and technology issues do leave the historical treaties looking somewhat dated. That being the case, WIPO has managed to initiate several recent initiatives. Most notably in relation to science and technology are the Copyright Treaty (WCT) and the WIPO Performances and Phonograms Treaty (WPPT), collectively known as the WIPO Internet Treaties.

The United Nations (UN) is also relevant to the intersection of science and technology and law. Among its recent successes is the adoption of a global accord to prohibit human cloning.[1] The UN has also been successful in promoting multilateral environmental agreements (MEAs), with the Convention on Biological Diversity (CBD) and its Biosafety Protocol becoming the first MEAs to address transboundary movement of gene-related products or substance, including genetically modified organisms (GMOs).[2] Indeed, most MEAs now place the transfer or diffusion of environmentally friendly technologies into one of their mandates.[3] The Codex Alimentarious Commission (CAC), created jointly by the World Health Organization (WHO) and the Food and Agriculture Organization (FAO), is another relevant body, with its mandate to adopt international standards for food safety.[4] Apart from intergovernmental organizations (IGO), the International Organization for Standardization (ISO) is of critical importance – it is the leading non-governmental organization (NGO) affecting the development of science and technology – by setting common standards for products and services.[5]

Turning to the legal side of the international fora, international economic law plays a relatively responsive role in facilitating science and technology developments. It does so through a bifurcated regime, with the World Trade Organization (WTO) and an increasing number of varied free trade agreements (FTAs) addressing the trade side and bilateral investment treaties (BITs) and FTAs covering investment. In contrast to many of the UN-related systems, most trade and investment mandates are of hard disciplines and regulations with legally binding force on contracting parties. Such hard law is enforceable through compulsory jurisdiction with binding decisions. The WTO, FTA and BIT model is rarely applied by other international regimes.

The international economic legal order has developed a rather sophisticated and mutually supportive relationship with science and technology developments. In particular, the WTO heavily relies on science-based evidence when dealing with various forms of non-tariff barriers as a form of protectionism. For instance, the WTO's Agreement on the Application of Sanitary and Phytosanitary Measures (SPS) and the Agreement on Technical Barriers to Trade (TBT) both require science principles to be observed in regulating national health or environmental risks, with deviations to the rules only justifiable on the basis of scientific evidence. Likewise, the WTO's General Agreement on Trade in Services (GATS) promotes the liberalization of technology-related services, including telecommunication and environmental services. Of course, there is also the WTO's Trade-Related Aspects of

Intellectual Property Rights Agreement (TRIPS), which was mainly created to reward and protect technology inventors while at the same time balancing the interests of users. Subsequent FTAs have furthered the interest of inventors through the common addition of so-called TRIPS-plus provisions.

Turning to investment, BITs and FTAs almost always explicitly protect IP as a 'covered investment' as well as protect the management of technologies. In agreements negotiated by developed countries, performance requirements are severely limited if not prohibited, and include a prohibition on the forced transfer of technologies. Science is also increasingly playing a role in international investment agreements, with the recent claims by Philip Morris against Uruguay and Australia for, inter alia, various restrictions on the packaging of tobacco products making this link apparent.

Despite the abundance of legal norms dealing with science and technology issues, science and technology by their nature are not easily accessible by the general public. Instead, their creation and the understanding thereof are mainly dominated by the private sector and often by large multinational companies, most often for the purpose of commercialization. Relevant private sectors thus have more capacity to influence not only the creation of science evidence but also the direction and interpretation of the governing legal framework. In such a context, the question of who speaks for the public interest or countries with lower levels of technology becomes relevant.

Given this backdrop, it is worth engaging in a critical review on pertinent jurisprudence and lawmaking to examine whether competing interests are balanced and harmonized. At the forefront, the question to ask is whether the laws, and perhaps more importantly the interpretation of those laws by the relevant dispute settlement mechanisms, reached interpretations on science or technology related rules so as to encourage continued creativity while at the same time not negating public interest and other concerns. An exploration of the consistency of such laws and interpretations is also warranted, as is an evaluation as to the future direction of such laws and interpretations.

This collection aims to explore these matters through an issues-based approach. The idea for this collection originated at the International Conference on Trade, Science, Technology, and Justice, held at the National Chiao Tung University (NCTU) in Hsin Chu, Taiwan, on 1–2 November 2011. The conference, jointly organized by the NCTU Institute of Technology Law and the Chinese University of Hong Kong (CUHK), Faculty of Law, featured several prominent academics from Asia-Pacific, Europe and the Middle East as well as voices from the local public sector, industries, judicial branches and practitioners. The complementary nature of the discussions was mutually inspiring, and the seed for a collection was sown.

The collection is designed to explore the status and interaction of and between science, technology and international economic law (namely, trade and investment) with a view to seeking a proper balance between promoting trade/investment liberalization and ensuring that decisions are soundly based and that technological advancement is not hampered. The objective of the book is not only to review the place of science and technology in the development of international economic law, and vice versa, but also to add to the understanding of whether and how the trade and investment regimes utilize science and technology, and whether they do so fairly and in the interest of global justice. In so doing, this collection fills a gap in the literature; while science and international economic law issues have been extensively analysed there is a dearth of literature on issues involving technology and international economic law.[6] Moreover, no other collection attempts to bring both science and technology issues together in a coherent manner. This collection is not intended to be a treatise, but rather seeks to provide views and research on contemporary international economic legal issues relating to science and technology. It is our hope that this collection inspires the future research on the issues, all of which can inform future developments of international economic lawmaking, negotiations and interpretations in a manner conducive to a fair balance between promoting science and technology and securing social justice.

This collection features 13 substantive chapters spread over five parts. Part I consists of three chapters discussing the science and health risks of trade in goods. In Chapter 2, Lukasz Gruszczynski of the Polish Academy of Science analyses how scientific criteria were conceptualized in the case law under different WTO agreements. In this context, Gruszczynski argues that the adoption of the SPS Agreement and the corresponding need to ensure a consistent approach of WTO dispute settlement bodies has led to science becoming a point of reference in all health and environment-related trade disputes (irrespectively of the agreement). The chapter also submits that an important element, which influenced the change, is legitimizing the nature of science. In particular, the employment of science and reliance on scientific criteria can be seen a way of improving the legitimacy of panels and Appellate Body decisions, and constitute an answer to accountability dilemmas. Finally, the chapter attempts to assess the importance and origin of the divergences between the standards in various WTO agreements. The chapter concludes with an assessment on the capacity of science to perform such functions (i.e. to provide neutral and objective criteria that would allow to depoliticize trade disputes and facilitate their settlement, to improve the legitimacy of decisions rendered by WTO dispute settlement bodies).

Chapter 3, authored by Kuei-Jung Ni of National Chiao Tung University, discusses the interplay between a science-based approach and its erosion through industrial and political influence, with particular focus on arguments surrounding the appropriateness of the relevant standards (this is especially the case when a member maintains a level of protection that is more stringent than the relevant international standards). The chapter does so by looking at the Appellate Body in *Hormones II* as a starting point in order to analyse the effectiveness of the WTO definition and interpretation of the interaction of science and trade rules, with a particular focus on the response to problematic international science-making.

In Chapter 4, Naoto Jinji of Kyoto University provides an economic theory of the SPS Agreement. More specifically, Jinji examines the role of the SPS Agreement in developing the international trade regime as it relates to agricultural and food products. In particular, the chapter attempts to investigate how the SPS Agreement can or cannot successfully deter the use of SPS measures for disguised protectionist purposes. In contrast to certain criticisms by economists, Jinji demonstrates that the SPS Agreement can play a role of mitigating disguised protectionism and improving welfare in international trade of agricultural and food products. However, Jinji cautions that science as the basis for SPS risk analysis involves uncertainty. Owing to this uncertainty, Jinji concludes that the SPS Agreement may fail to prevent SPS measures from being used for protectionism purposes.

Part II contains two chapters related to technology in the service sector. In Chapter 5, Jia-Xiang Hu of Shanhai Jiao Tong University discusses the principle of technology neutrality – that is, the presumption that the law should have the same application to electronic commerce regardless of its transaction means – in relation to WTO law. Both the panels in *US – Gambling* and *China – Audiovisual Products* accepted and highlighted this issue. While this principle can reasonably be read into the provisions of GATS and the various commitments of members, Hu argues that the principle is not well regarded by members who in reality are unable to foresee the development of relevant technologies or simply ignored this issue while making commitments on trade in services. The chapter concludes by analysing ways to realistically yet meaningfully combine the application of the principle of technology neutrality with the commitments of members.

Chapter 6, authored by Shin-Yi Peng of National Tsing Hua University, deals with the under-studied area of interpretation of member schedules. This issue has been the subject of several panel and Appellate Body reports in recent years, and it is anticipated that the schedules related to information and communication technologies will increasingly be challenged. In the chapter, Peng agrees with the panel in *EC – IT Products* in determining that the Information Technology Agreement is not relevant in determining the object and purpose of the WTO Agreement. However, she argues that the Panel should have elaborated upon the question of how 'technological development' and 'product evolution' should be dealt with in interpreting concessions. In so doing, Peng emphasizes the 'brave' but necessary position the Appellate Body in *China – Publications and Audiovisual Products* took on the issue of whether the definition of 'sound recording distribution services' is alterable and evolutionary through time. Peng concludes by suggesting that this line of reasoning ought to be supported in light of the principle of 'technological neutrality'.

Part III includes three chapters on contemporary issues cross-cutting both trade and investment as they relate to science and technology. In Chapter 7, Andrew Mitchell and James Munro of the University of Melbourne together with Andrew Higgins of the University of Oxford explore the importance of science in determining the outcome of trade and investment claims made against health-related measures. Focusing on Australia's introduction of plain packaging of tobacco products, Mitchell, Higgins and Munro provide a comprehensive analysis of the weighing of such issues as scientific uncertainty and standard of proof in an attempt to provide some clarity to an emerging area of the international economic law.

Chapter 8, authored by Jürgen Kurtz of the University of Melbourne, explores the potential for common disciplines within WTO and investment law to apply to laws and regulations that are non-discriminatory (to foreign goods/services/investors) in design and application. The chapter focuses on the contentious and fractured investor-state arbitral jurisprudence surrounding the scope of the obligation of states to accord foreign investors 'fair and equitable treatment', with a detailed particular emphasis on the manner in which scientific evidence and/or international standards as a condition of regulatory rationality in WTO law (under the WTO SPS and TBT Agreements) might be used productively as a model for determining whether a state has acted fairly and equitably under investment law in a defined category of cases.

In Chapter 9, Kate Miles of the University of Cambridge explores the complex relationship between international economic law and climate-related measures and technology. As the chapter demonstrates, this relationship has both a mutually supportive and conflicting character dependent on the circumstances. Science and technology play and will continue to play a central role in understanding these issues.

Part IV contains two complementary chapters that focus on intellectual property issues. In Chapter 10, Peter K. Yu of Drake University focuses on the 'cat-and-mouse' game being played when trade agreements encounter digital technology. Noting that the interplay between trade agreements and digital technology is under-studied and misunderstood, Yu focuses on copyright and critically analyses the trend of recent bilateral, plurilateral and regional efforts to strengthen the protection and enforcement of intellectual property rights. Yu concludes by calling upon policymakers to develop a 'better and deeper appreciation of the challenges digital technology has posed to trade agreements'.

In Chapter 11, Kimberlee Weatherall of Sydney University looks at what the research into the operation of the IP system, and particularly IP enforcement, tells us about the issues that research-based firms face. In order to complement Yu's chapter, Weatherall focuses on the 'science' side of IP, particularly patents, using research and information about domestic developments to critique the approach taken in the most recent IP negotiations affecting the Asia-Pacific region – namely, the Anti-Counterfeiting Trade Agreement ('ACTA') concluded in late 2010, and the Trans-Pacific Partnership Agreement ('TPPA'), which remains under negotiation. In the chapter, Weatherall summarizes current research, particularly into IP enforcement, to identify what we know about the problems encountered by research-based firms, and considers the relevance of this research for international IP lawmaking efforts, seeking to show how ACTA and the US TPPA IP proposal not only fail to address the issues, but may even be harmful to domestic efforts to promote innovation through the IP system.

Part V looks at science and technology issues as they relate specifically to the developing world. In Chapter 12, Richard Li-dar Wang of National Chiao Tung University examines and reassesses the application of the liability rule in the field of intellectual property. After some theoretical investigation, the chapter proceeds to the specific context of developing countries to see if the liability-style IP protection accommodates their long-felt developmental needs. Developing countries generally suffer from deficiencies of IP utilization, and correspondingly need innovative products and technology transfer to address societal problems – such as the spread of the HIV virus – and to ignite economic growth and industrialization. Wang argues that the liability rule can help those countries to ease the obstacles that IP rights create for them in exploiting new technologies. He then focuses discussion on whether the rule can provide sufficient incentive to local innovation and foreign direct investment.

In Chapter 13, Debashis Chakraborty and Animesh Kumar – both from the Indian Institute of Foreign Trade – together with Julien Chaisse from the Chinese University of Hong Kong analyse to what extent the provision of subsidies in developed countries affect the market access for major developing country exporters. Using science as a means of measuring subsidies and their effects, the chapter begins with a survey on fisheries subsidies in developed countries before highlighting key trends in the WTO discussions on the same. The chapter then highlights fishery exports from developing countries and uses empirical evidence to analyse the exports of select developing countries in their developed counterparts. Finally, on the basis of the findings, conclusions on future policy considerations are drawn.

In the concluding chapter, Arno Hold of the World Trade Institute at the University of Berne and Bryan Mercurio of the Chinese University of Hong Kong investigate ways to link the requirement of developed countries to provide technical and financial assistance to developing countries for implementing the TRIPS Agreement with the obligation of least developed counties (LDC) to comply with the TRIPS Agreement. This suggestion contrasts with the view that LDCs should receive an ongoing waiver from their obligations under the TRIPS Agreement and is viewed by the authors as a more permanent resolution to the issue and more in line with the aims and objectives of the TRIPS Agreement and the WTO.

This collection provides a wide-ranging view of the interaction between and among science and technology in international economic law. The collection is not meant to provide a review of existing literature or to serve as a handbook, but instead to offer analysis and insights into an increasingly important area of the law.

Before concluding, it would be remiss of us not to thank the many individuals who helped to bring this book to fruition. We particularly thank and are indebted to Isabella Ma from the Chinese University of Hong Kong for her invaluable assistance in researching and editing this collection. We would also like to thank Katie Carpenter from Routledge for her unwavering belief in this project as well as Mark Sapwell for his tenacity in bringing this project to a timely conclusion.

Notes

1 The United Nations Declaration on Human Cloning, GA/10333; 49th General Assembly (March 8, 2005), available at www.un.org/News/Press/docs/2005/ga10333.doc.htm.
2 See the Convention on Biological Diversity, art. 19.
3 See the United Nations Framework Convention on Climate Change, art. 4.5.
4 'Statements of Principles Concerning the Role of Science', in Codex Procedural Manual, at 209–10 (20th edn, 2011), available at ftp://ftp.fao.org/codex/Publications/ProcManuals/Manual_20e.pdf.
5 See the ISO website: www.iso.org/iso/home/about.htm.
6 The study of international law and technology has recently been incorporated into the academic setting. See, for instance, the American Society of International Law (ASIL), which has set up an interest group of International Law and Technology: www.asil.org/interest-groups-view.cfm?groupid=66; and the International Law Association (ILA), which has established an International Law and Biotechnology Committee.

Part I

Trade in goods

Science and health risks

2 Science and the settlement of trade disputes in the World Trade Organization

Lukasz Gruszczynski

2.1 Introduction

Different WTO agreements require, implicitly or explicitly, recourse to science and scientific expertise in order to determine (or assist in the determination of) the legality of national health and environmental measures that impact on international trade. GATT (General Agreements on Tarriffs and Trade) 1994 stipulates in Article XX that Members may justify a measure that would be otherwise inconsistent with GATT disciplines if such a measure is, among other things, necessary to protect human, animal or plant life or health or related to the conservation of exhaustible natural resources. Science is used in order to establish necessity, i.e. to show the existence of specific risks and to prove the required relation between a measure and an identified risk. Similarly, the TBT Agreement provides that technical regulations shall not be more trade-restrictive than necessary to fulfil various legitimate objectives, including the protection of human health or safety, animal and plant life or health, or the environment. The necessity requirement is again assessed with the help of scientific evidence and technical data. The most elaborate framework is, however, provided by the SPS Agreement, which openly designates science as a criterion for distinguishing between permitted and prohibited measures.

This chapter submits that science has become, in the context of the WTO, an important element (or even a point of reference) in the assessment of domestic health and environmental measures with respect to their compatibility with WTO obligations. Under current practice, WTO panels and the Appellate Body seem to be concerned not only with external legitimacy (i.e. the absence of alternative less trade-restrictive measures that could meet the health policy objective), but also with the internal legitimacy of domestic measures (i.e. the existence of a scientific basis). This sharply contrasts with the approach taken under GATT 1947, where panels tended to concentrate only on the first element. This chapter also suggests some reasons that could explain such a shift. In particular, it is argued that, besides the need to guarantee the consistency of different WTO agreements and the increased legalization and formalization of the WTO dispute settlement process, the legitimizing character of science is also an important factor.

The chapter proceeds as follows. The first part briefly analyses the relevant provisions of the SPS Agreement, a treaty that introduced science and scientific criteria into the domain of international trade law, as well as the corresponding case law. The second part turns to GATT 1994 and the TBT Agreement, and compares the approach of WTO dispute settlement bodies with the practice under GATT 1947. The last part summarizes the previous discussion and elaborates on the reasons behind the new science-based approach of WTO dispute settlement bodies.

2.2 The SPS Agreement and its scientific obligations

The SPS Agreement establishes certain standards for national SPS regulations. This category is defined by the SPS Agreement as measures adopted for the protection, within the territory of an importing WTO Member, of the life and health of people, animals and plants from enumerated SPS risks.[1] While the SPS Agreement reiterates traditional GATT principles, such as national treatment or most favoured nation status (with some modifications necessary in the SPS context), it also adds science-based obligations that appear to go beyond the mere elimination of discrimination. On one hand, it recognizes the right of each WTO Member to establish any level of protection deemed appropriate and to take all necessary steps to that end. On the other hand, it requires that all domestic measures that do not conform to international standards (in the majority of cases measures aiming at higher levels of protection than those provided by international standards)[2] are to be based on scientific principles and cannot be maintained without sufficient scientific evidence (Articles 3.3 and 2.2). This obligation is further clarified in Article 5.1, which explains that the 'scientific basis' needs to take the form of a formal risk assessment. Such an assessment is of scientific character and aims at evaluating the potential (or probability) for adverse effects resulting from the importation of a particular product – e.g. owing to the presence of contaminants and toxins in food or disease-causing organisms in plant and animal products (Annex A(4)). Although the SPS Agreement does not predetermine any minimum magnitude of risk that can trigger a national response,[3] the risk, which is subject to regulation, needs to be ascertainable, i.e. have some indication of potentiality.[4] Consequently, the identification of a theoretical uncertainty relating to the safety of a specific product is insufficient to justify an SPS measure. It is also worth noting that older SPS jurisprudence was not entirely clear (if not inconsistent) about this issue. For example, one of the panels used the concept of 'negligible risk', which implies the existence of some threshold limit, and refused to recognize such a risk as a legitimate subject of regulation.[5]

Risk may be expressed both in quantitative and qualitative terms.[6] The quantitative measurement provides information on the probability of the occurrence of an adverse effect (e.g. 1:1,000,000), while the qualitative measurement relates only to the possibility of a causal link (e.g. low or medium), without indicating its likelihood. In any case, risk assessment needs to be specific, meaning that it has to evaluate the particular potential (probability) of harm arising from a specific SPS risk (e.g. evaluation of 'entry, establishment, or spread of fire blight through [US] apple fruit as a separate and distinct vector').[7] Consequently, a general discussion of the potentiality/likelihood or assessment of whole categories of hazardous agents is insufficient for the purposes of Article 5.1.[8] The more recent SPS case law, however, has admitted (by making a textual argument that any assessment of risk needs to be performed 'as appropriate to the circumstances') that the specificity requirement is not of an absolute character. This means that an assessment may be influenced by methodological difficulties posed by the nature and characteristics of a particular hazard (e.g. a chemical substance).[9] Consequently, in the *US/Canada – Continued Suspension* dispute, it was not necessary for the EC (European Communities) to show a direct causal link between potential adverse human health effects and residues of oestradiol-17β, because residues of this hormone were only one of the many hormones that humans are exposed to. A more general examination of overall risk resulting from exposure to different hormones, both endogenous and artificial, was considered to be sufficient.[10] This closely corresponds with the finding of the *EC – Biotech Products* Panel, which held that when deciding on a measure Members may account for existing scientific uncertainties to be in evaluation of risk. According to the Panel, the same risk assessment can equally support very different measures, not only because of variations in the relevant levels of protection but also owing to differing assessments of identified uncertainties.[11]

The SPS case law is consistent in holding that risk assessment may be based not only on mainstream science, but also on the opinions of scientists taking a divergent view.[12] In its attempt to eliminate 'junk' science as a possible justification for a measure, the Appellate Body held that such opinions 'must . . . have the necessary scientific and methodological rigour to be considered reputable science'.[13] In other words, minority scientific views need to meet a certain epistemic threshold in order to be qualified as legitimate science. In scientific practice this is normally determined through various mechanisms, such as evaluation of a specific claim against more general theories or established scientific views, the logical coherence of a claim, its methodological soundness, or its ability to explain a particular phenomenon.[14] This means that, at least in theory, the requirement of a scientific basis may be satisfied under the SPS Agreement by one of several rival views.[15] Having said this, it also needs to be noted that some SPS panels have sought to establish the 'best science in the field' rather than to verify the scientific quality of arguments put forward by defendants.[16] Obviously this has the effect of limiting the role of minority scientific opinions. The risk of marginalizing minority opinions is also exacerbated by the specificity requirement discussed above. As noted by Peel, many divergent views are 'based on the kind of suggestive but not definitive scientific evidence' that in turn may result in them having limited value in the eyes of panels.[17]

The SPS Agreement accepts that WTO Members sometimes need to act despite the lack of sufficient scientific evidence (i.e. 'insufficiency of scientific evidence' in the language of the agreement)[18] that would allow them to perform a required risk assessment. The SPS case law has struggled to distinguish this notion from the concept of scientific uncertainty. Although the official position is that the two terms are completely different, with scientific uncertainty not capable of triggering the application of Article 5.7,[19] a deeper analysis shows that at least some forms of scientific uncertainty have been regarded as instances of insufficiency (e.g. practical immeasurability and indeterminacy).[20] Overall, the first condition of Article 5.7 was interpreted rather strictly, with some panels refusing to recognize a normative dimension in the assessment of sufficiency/insufficiency (i.e. subjective aspects of a risk assessor's decision-making that are influenced by the culture of a specific society). In practice this meant that panels considered that the chosen level of protection could not influence the parameters of evaluation of scientific evidence.[21] This was an undesirable development. As noted by a group of eminent scholars, 'evidence deemed reliable enough to generate a sufficient risk assessment in one regulatory context may fail in other contexts because of the different concerns, risk frames, and particular circumstances'.[22] These concerns were recognized and addressed by the Appellate Body in one of its more recent decisions, where it held that the level of protection sought might play a role in the assessment of insufficiency (e.g. by framing the scope and the methods of risk assessment).[23] In a similar vein, it recognized that the spatial aspect of insufficiency (i.e. a concurrent existence of insufficiency and a relevant international standard) is independent from the temporal dimension (i.e. scientific developments that take place after the adoption of a standard).[24]

The remaining part of Article 5.7 requires Members to base their provisional measures on available pertinent data. Moreover, Members are obliged to actively seek additional scientific information in order to perform a more objective assessment of risks, and to review measures within a reasonable period of time.

The SPS Agreement also encourages panels to consult experts on technical and scientific matters, either at the request of a party to a dispute or on their own initiative (Article 11.2). The consultation mechanism is intended to help a panel overcome its epistemic limitations when confronted with complex scientific and technical issues. Although panels may choose, under Article 11, between an advisory experts group and individual experts,[25] in practice all of them have preferred the second option.[26]

An interesting development that has taken place in the context of the SPS Agreement is the progressive intensification of the applicable standard of review with respect to scientific evidence put forward by defendants (as well as a recent shift in *US/Canada – Continued Suspension* in the opposite direction). In theory, such a standard may vary from *de novo* review to full deference. Under *de novo* review, one body is able to review all the factual determinations (including scientific ones) made by another body and substitute them with its own. At the other end of the spectrum, a fully deferential standard restricts the powers of the reviewing body to monitor procedural compliance (i.e. whether the prescribed procedure(s) were followed), and prohibits any inquiry into the substantive merits of factual determinations. Between these two extremes lie a number of less or more deferential types of review.

The SPS case law adopted the so-called 'objective assessment of facts' standard, which in early practice was quite deferential. Subsequent panels, although formally following the 'objective assessment' standard, conducted more intrusive reviews of the scientific basis supporting national measures, inquiring into the quality, persuasive force and correctness of scientific findings made on the domestic level. The panel reports in *EC – Biotech Products* and *US/Canada – Continued Suspension* were probably the culmination points of this trend, with both Panels engaging in an in-depth analysis of the scientific evidence and choosing between competing scientific views. The more recent case law is more ambiguous. The Appellate Body in *US/Canada – Continued Suspension* reverted back to a relatively deferential approach and instructed the Panel to concentrate on the coherence of domestic risk assessment and evaluate whether it contained minimum epistemic value.[27] As a consequence, the Panel was not expected to assess the correctness of the domestic risk assessment. The subsequent case law (i.e. *Australia – Apples*[28]) further obscured the picture. On one hand, the Appellate Body explained that a panel has to only determine whether a specific claim can be regarded as 'legitimate' science (and not 'the best science').[29] This implies a rather deferential approach and follows the principles set out in the *US/Canada – Suspension* report. On the other hand, however, it accepted a rather intrusive examination into the reasoning included in a risk assessment. Consequently, it is not enough for a panel to inquire whether such reasoning falls within a range that could be considered legitimate by the scientific community.[30] This obviously opens up the possibility of a quite intrusive investigation into the reasoning underlying a risk assessment, including its assumptions, intermediate conclusions and final determinations.[31]

Overall, the SPS case law has established a relatively strict science-based framework for assessing national SPS measures. Although the system provides some flexibility (especially when it comes to human health risks), a number of standards are formulated in a strict fashion that may unnecessarily constrain the ability of WTO Members to regulate health and environmental risks (e.g. in terms of specificity of risk assessment and conceptualizing insufficiency of scientific evidence as a quasi-objective category). The applicable standard of review still remains relatively intrusive, with a panel entitled to make an inquiry into the scientific basis underlying a national measure (at least with respect to the methodology used in risk assessment).

2.3 GATT 1994 and the TBT Agreement

The issue of science and scientific evidence is relevant not only under the SPS Agreement, but also in the context of other WTO agreements. Arguably the most important in this context are GATT 1994 and the TBT Agreement. Although other parts of WTO law, such as the TRIPS Agreement or GATS, may also require an assessment of scientific data, until now there has not been any relevant case law with regard to these agreements.[32] As a consequence, they are not discussed in this chapter.

This section summarizes the major science-related developments that have taken place under both GATT 1994 and the TBT Agreement. However, before moving to the analysis of specific provisions, it is worth reviewing the practice under the old GATT 1947.

2.3.1 The traditional approach under GATT 1947

The relevant GATT 1947 case law is very limited. Genuine scientific questions appeared only once, in *Thailand – Cigarettes*, a case concerning Thai restrictions on the importation and sale of foreign cigarettes. The US argued that the ban was inconsistent with Article XI of GATT 1947 (i.e. prohibition of quantitative restrictions) and could not be justified by the exception contained in Article XX(b).[33] One of Thailand's arguments was that the chemicals and other additives contained in US cigarettes (a complainant in the case) might make them more harmful to human health than their Thai counterparts.[34] Moreover, Thailand also submitted that some US cigarettes 'contained nicotine which was extracted from tobacco leaf, resprayed back into the leaf as part of a process called "reconstituting" the tobacco'.[35] According to Thailand, this process might have made US cigarettes more addictive, since it could have resulted in the easier inhalation and absorption of nicotine by the bloodstream and the brain.

The Panel held that the measure violated Article XI of GATT 1947. Although it recognized the priority of human health over trade liberalization, it found the measure to be unnecessary because other methods, which were less inconsistent with GATT 1947 (and thus constituted the least restrictive alternative), could have reasonably been used by Thailand to address its health concerns.[36] These included, among others, a ban on the advertisement of cigarettes of both domestic and foreign origin or the creation of a governmental monopoly for the importation and sale of cigarettes. When deciding the case, the GATT panel took for granted that the Thai measure was backed up by sufficient scientific evidence. At the same time, it did not address the claims of Thailand that US cigarettes were actually more harmful than Thai ones (owing to the presence of additives and the specific process used in their production). Any finding in this respect could arguably have influenced the assessment of available alternatives (i.e. whether a controlled use or a ban on advertisement was really a feasible alternative). On one hand, the Panel's approach appeared to be very deferential by assuming the existence of sufficient scientific evidence supporting the measure. On the other hand, however, it was also very intrusive as it exercised its discretion in substituting the judgment of a national government concerning available alternatives with its own views, without examining the internal legitimacy of alternative measures.

Goh identifies a number of reasons that could explain the Panel's approach. In particular, he argues that the trade effects test used by the Panel (which concentrated on the external legitimacy of the measure) corresponded closely with the character of GATT 1947. As a trade instrument 'it encouraged the development of practical trade effects tests in examining the legitimacy of measures, as opposed to internal or "scientific" tests'.[37] It seems that GATT panels in general were rather reluctant to develop any new tests especially when faced with politically controversial disputes. As Wirth notes, GATT panels tended to be deferential to any substantive determinations (including those that involved scientific elements) made by national governments, and concentrated more on procedural compliance.[38] For example, in the *Tuna* cases[39] – other health/environment-related disputes – the Panels avoided any discussion of the scientific merits of the US importation ban (e.g. whether it was necessary and whether possible alternatives might be sufficiently effective),[40] and concentrated instead on the problem of the extra-territorial application of the US measure and its unilateral character.[41]

2.3.2 GATT 1994

One would expect to see the same approach under GATT 1994. Despite the fundamental institutional changes that took place with the creation of the WTO and the adoption of various new agreements, the text of GATT 1994 remained the same as that of GATT 1947. In addition, the newly-created Appellate Body from the outset recognized GATT 1947 jurisprudence as relevant in the interpretation of WTO agreements. Indeed the first case *US – Gasoline* appeared to confirm the previous approach. The Panel simply assumed the existence of sufficient scientific evidence underlying a measure, noting that air pollution, and in particular ground-level ozone and toxic substances, presented health risks to humans, animals and plants.[42] Thus the Panel concentrated its analysis on available alternatives (non- or less restrictive), but it did not discuss their scientific plausibility. Although the Appellate Body introduced a number of important changes to the Panel report, it did not comment on the Panel's treatment of science and scientific evidence.

The next case with an environmental dimension (*US – Shrimp*) was more ambiguous. Although none of the parties requested consultations with experts, the panel nevertheless decided to consult them on a number of scientific issues, explaining its decision in this respect by the amount of scientific documentation submitted by both parties.[43] In particular, it extensively inquired into two research areas: approaches to sea turtle conservation, and the habitat and migratory patterns of sea turtles.[44] On its face, this significantly differed from the approach of the GATT *US – Tuna* panel, despite many factual similarities between the two cases. As a consequence, one might expect that science would play an important role in deciding the dispute. However, this was not the case. In the end the Panel did not engage in any discussion on the underlying science (e.g. as to the effectiveness of specific turtle conservation policies), and avoided all scientific questions by starting its analysis from the chapeau of Article XX. After finding that the US measure amounted to arbitrary and unjustifiable discrimination (the traditional GATT test), it stopped short of examining specific subparagraphs of the general exception, where scientific issues could be of prime importance.[45] The Appellate Body changed the sequence of analysis, but in its examination, under subparagraph (g),[46] it also did not go into the details of the internal (i.e. scientific) legitimacy of the measure. Although the Appellate Body found that sea turtles could qualify as exhaustible natural resources[47] and that the US measure was related to the conservation of such resources,[48] it came to these conclusions not on the basis of expert opinions or scientific evidence, but by referring to various international environmental instruments (e.g. the Convention on International Trade in Endangered Species of Wild Fauna and Flora).[49] The rest of its analysis was not concerned with the scientific aspects of the US measure, but instead procedural and transparency questions played a central role.

The approach of the WTO dispute settlement bodies changed with the famous *EC – Asbestos* case, which concerned the French ban on the importation of certain asbestos products owing to risks to human health posed by exposure to asbestos fibres. Both the Panel and the Appellate Body engaged in a detailed examination of the internal legitimacy of the measure, including the nature and degree of the risk being addressed. At the same time, there were some important differences between the reasoning of the Panel and that of the Appellate Body. The approach of the former was more market-oriented, as its analysis of the likeness of different products (*in casu* chrysotile fibres (asbestos) and cellulose fibres/PVA/glass fibres) under Article III:4 of GATT 1994[50] concentrated on their competitive relationship. As a consequence, the Panel decided on the issue of likeness in terms of narrowly understood competitive substitutability and did not really consider as relevant the capacity of asbestos to cause cancer.[51] Only after concluding that the French ban was inconsistent with the requirement of Article III:4 of GATT 1994 did it find the scientific evidence pertinent for its analysis under Article XX. This included two specific issues: (i) the existence of a risk to human health for the purpose of determining necessity and (ii) the existence of other measures that are either consistent or less inconsistent with GATT 1994 and achieve the same level of protection.[52] The approach of the Appellate Body, while also concentrating on the internal legitimacy of the measure, was entirely different. The Appellate Body, similar to the Panel, saw the assessment of likeness under Article III:4 in terms of competitive relation, but it also considered the potential health risks posed by one of the products (which was shown by scientific evidence) to be a relevant factor in the final determination as to whether two products are like or not.[53] In particular it found that carcinogenicity constituted one of the defining elements of the physical properties of the products involved, and that it might have influenced consumer preferences.[54]

The approach adopted in *EC – Asbestos* bears many similarities to the SPS standards. Although the panel expressed its reservation about following SPS case law,[55] in fact both the Panel and the Appellate Body relied on various mechanisms developed in the context of the SPS Agreement. Both were also concerned with the internal and external legitimacy of the measure, thus going beyond the traditional GATT 1947 approach. In addition such a change forced the Panel to consult with experts on a number of scientific issues (e.g. the existence of risk resulting from exposure to chrysotile fibres and the efficiency of alternatives identified by Canada in achieving the French health objectives). The Appellate Body recognized, in line with the SPS Agreement standards, that risk as such did not need to be assessed in quantitative terms and that qualitative measurement was also sufficient under GATT 1994.[56] In addition the measure could be supported not only by mainstream scientific research, but also using minority views. As far as the latter category is concerned, a certain quality threshold was introduced, as minority scientific opinions had to come from qualified and respected sources.[57] This corresponded closely with the treatment of minority views under the SPS Agreement. The applicable standard of review was quite deferential and followed the initial approach of the WTO dispute settlement bodies under the SPS Agreement. In this context, the Panel explained that 'it is not its function to settle a scientific debate, not being composed of experts in the field of the possible human health risks posed by asbestos. Consequently, the Panel does not intend to set itself up as an arbiter of the opinions expressed by the scientific community.'[58] Its limited role only required assessing whether the evidence was sufficient to conclude that there was a human health risk, and whether the measure was necessary to achieve France's legitimate goal (and not to determine whether the risk exists 'objectively', e.g. according to the best available science).

The subsequent health/environment-related case law has followed the standards established by *EC – Asbestos*. The Panel in *Brazil – Retreaded Tyres*[59] found the Brazilian measure to be a quantitative restriction in violation of Article XI of GATT 1994, and examined the measure under Article XX. The Panel clarified that a product that is regulated does not need to pose a direct risk in order to fall within the ambit of Article XX(b). This was an important development since in *EC – Asbestos* chrysotile fibres posed direct and immediate risks to human life and health. The situation in *Brazil – Retreaded Tyres* was different, as retreaded tyres as such did not give rise to any risk to human, animal or plant life and health. It was only the accumulation of inappropriately disposed of waste tyres that posed risk. Thus, the Panel was satisfied with the fact that there was a relationship between the risks arising from the accumulation of waste tyres and the ban on importation of retreaded tyres. As far as the substance of the measure was concerned, the Panel concentrated on two issues. First, it examined whether there was a risk to human, animal or plant life or health and, if so, whether the objective of the import ban was to reduce such risk. Although the Panel did not consult experts, in its analysis it frequently referred to scientific evidence. Interestingly, the Panel was satisfied with the evidence, which merely suggested a correlation between the spread of different diseases and the accumulation of used tyres. It did not require any specific evaluation of the risk posed by the improper management of used tyres in Brazil. It accepted evidence of general nature (e.g. the Basel Convention Technical Guidelines on the Identification and Management of Used Tyres), including indirect evidence relating to practices in other countries (e.g. the European Union, the UK).[60] The Panel also explicitly refused to recognize the specificity requirement (i.e. evidence of the actual negative health effects of tyre fires within Brazil).[61] This was definitively a much more liberal approach than the one required by the SPS Agreement. Second, the Panel analysed the necessity of the measure, relying on the process of weighing and balancing different factors. Scientific evidence appeared to be of prime importance in this context, both for the examination of contribution of the measure to realization of the end pursued (i.e. reduction of the risks to human, animal and plant life and health) and the availability of alternatives measures (i.e. whether an alternative is a feasible option). Although the Appellate Body reversed various findings of the Panel, it upheld the entire necessity analysis, including the examination of possible alternatives to the Brazilian measure, its contribution to achievement of the regulatory objective, as well as the weighing and balancing of various relevant factors.[62] As noted above, the necessity test was that part of the Panel's analysis that was dominated by scientific considerations.

2.3.3 The TBT Agreement

The TBT Agreement, similar to its SPS counterpart, openly refers to science. To start with, Article 2.2 requires WTO Members to ensure that their 'technical regulations are not prepared, adopted or applied with a view to or with the effect of creating unnecessary obstacles to international trade'. For this purpose, they cannot be 'more trade-restrictive than necessary to fulfil a legitimate objective, taking account of the risks non-fulfilment would create'. The list of legitimate regulatory objectives is open-ended and includes protection of human health or safety, animal or plant life or health, as well as the environment. When assessing the risks of non-fulfilment, WTO Members are expected to take into account, among other things, available scientific evidence. In addition, Article 14.2 explicitly confirms the right of a panel, in the context of the TBT Agreement, to consult experts on questions of a technical nature.

Considering this explicit reference to science, one should not be surprised to find analyses of the internal legitimacy of TBT measures under Article 2.2. Two recent cases may serve as good examples. The *US – Clove Cigarettes* dispute concerned the US ban on production and sale of flavoured cigarettes (including clove cigarettes), with the exception of the menthol version. The aim of this prohibition was to reduce youth smoking by eliminating cigarettes that, by masking the regular taste of tobacco (which may be unpleasant for beginners), are particularly appealing to young people.[63] Indonesia claimed, among other things, that the ban was discriminatory (Article 2.1) because it treated menthol (mainly domestically produced in the US) and clove cigarettes (all of which were imported) differently, and furthermore that the ban was unnecessary (Article 2.2).[64] Since the case did not concern the relative toxicity of clove, menthol and regular cigarettes (owing to the presence of some specific additives),[65] the Panel was not expected to look at the scientific evidence that would support such a contention. However, under the necessity analysis, the Panel was confronted with the question of the effectiveness of the US measure (i.e. whether banning clove cigarettes would contribute to the achievement of the regulatory objectives sought by the US). In answering this question, the Panel engaged in a detailed analysis of the scientific evidence and ultimately found that extensive scientific research supported the conclusion that banning clove and other flavoured cigarettes could contribute to a reduction in youth smoking.[66] In the context of its analysis, the Panel also indirectly recognized that minority scientific opinion could constitute a sufficient basis for TBT measures.[67] On the other hand, the issue of internal legitimacy was not so visible in the Panel's discussion of available alternatives that might have been employed by the US. This was, however, more connected with the structure of Indonesia's argument rather than an axiomatic stance taken by the Panel.[68] Since Indonesia did not appeal the Panel's findings under Article 2.2, the Appellate Body did not have the opportunity to review this part of the report.

A similar approach was taken in a subsequent TBT dispute, *US – Tuna II (Mexico)*. The case concerned the US measure establishing the conditions for use of 'dolphin safe' labels on tuna products. Mexico argued that the measure was incompatible with certain TBT provisions, in particular Article 2.1 (because Mexican tuna products had received less favourable treatment as compared to products originating in other countries, including the US), as well as Article 2.2 (as being more trade restrictive than necessary to fulfil the legitimate objective(s) sought by the US).[69] The Panel, when assessing the measure under Article 2.2, enquired whether the US measure fulfilled the stated objective (i.e. protection of consumers by ensuring that they are not misled as to the quality of tuna products and protection of dolphins by discouraging certain fishing techniques that harm them), and whether there were other less trade-restrictive alternatives.[70] In this context, it analysed a large amount of scientific data on the impact of purse seine operations on the health of wild aquatic mammals,[71] dolphin mortality rates associated with fishing techniques other than what is referred to as 'setting on' dolphins,[72] and risks of dolphin mortality or injury arising from tuna fishing operations outside the Eastern Tropical Pacific Region.[73] The Panel's examination of available alternative measures was also partially based on its previous scientific determinations. All those endeavours were aimed at assessing the internal (i.e. scientific) legitimacy of the US measure. The Panel also touched upon the standard of review applicable to scientific evidence. Similar to the approach taken under GATT 1994, it was interested in determining whether specific claims were sufficiently substantiated by the relevant party rather than whether they represented the best available science.[74]

The Appellate Body reversed the Panel's findings under Article 2.2. It explained that the relevant test required the Panel to determine: (i) the existence of a legitimate objective(s); (ii) the degree to which a contested measure contributes to such an objective(s); (iii) the trade-restrictiveness of a measure and (iv) the nature of the risks and the gravity of the consequences arising from non-fulfilment of the objective(s) pursued by the Member.[75] The last three elements are used to establish whether a measure is more trade-restrictive than necessary. The Appellate Body also endorsed a comparison of a contested measure with (reasonably) available alternatives as a conceptual tool for ascertaining its relative necessity. Although it disagreed with the Panel that the alternative measure identified by Mexico (i.e. co-existence of the US and AIDCP label[76]) would contribute to the achievement of the regulatory objective to the same extent as the existing US measure,[77] this finding did not alter the approach with respect to its treatment of scientific data. In the context of the analytical framework proposed by the Appellate Body, scientific evidence still seems to be highly relevant to a determination of whether there is a genuine risk that needs to be addressed, the nature of such risk, the contribution of a measure to the achievement of the objective, and the feasibility of identified alternatives.

2.4 Scientific standards and health/environment-related trade disputes

As discussed above, science has become a central benchmark for the assessment of SPS measures. Domestic regulations are tested against science-based criteria with respect to their internal legitimacy. Having said this, it is not clear what drafters had in mind when they decided to introduce such a novel mechanism into the trade regime.[78] A part of the literature argues that science, under the SPS Agreement, is used as a sophisticated instrument for the detection of protectionist regulations. As explained by Sykes, the requirement of scientific justification 'aids in motive review, and helps to sort regulations between those that are protectionists and those that seek to promote some legitimate, non-protectionist regulatory objective'.[79] The scientific obligations, however, seem to go further than a mere detection and elimination of protectionism. Science acts more as a mechanism aimed at the elimination of *all* 'unnecessary' (assessed against some objective standard) restrictions on international trade. Consequently, scientific criteria under the SPS Agreement aim at eliminating obstacles to international trade, irrespective of whether they are motivated by protectionism. Irrespectively from the motives, the SPS Agreement is predominantly concerned with the internal legitimacy of national measures,[80] while assessment of external legitimacy is of secondary importance (e.g. under Article 5.6[81]).[82] The TBT Agreement is similar to some extent. The scope of the TBT Agreement, and particularly Article 2.2, seems to go beyond the mere eradication of protectionism and require that domestic technical regulations maintain a certain standard of internal rationality.[83] Although GATT 1994 remains preoccupied with the problem of discrimination, nevertheless science plays a more important role than under the old rules.

Analysis of the relevant GATT 1994 and TBT case law further reveals a number of similarities to the SPS Agreement. As noted above, science is an important element in all health and environment-related trade disputes, irrespective of which agreement they are brought under, with WTO dispute settlement bodies inquiring into the internal legitimacy of the measures they examine. In line with the SPS Agreement, the existence of risk can be shown both qualitatively and quantitatively; domestic measures may be based on either majority or minority scientific opinions (if they come from qualified and respected sources); there is no requirement of minimum magnitude of risk (although the risk needs to be ascertainable); and the standard of review applied to scientific determinations at the domestic level remains relatively deferential (which corresponds with at least a part of the SPS jurisprudence). Of course there are still important differences between agreements. For example, there is no obligation, neither under the TBT Agreement nor GATT 1994, to have a risk assessment that would support a national measure. Similarly, the specificity requirement is less stringent. This eventually makes the applicable science-based tests under both agreements less demanding. Nevertheless, considering the earlier GATT approach (and despite the differences in the language employed in each of the treaties), the change in overall approach is significant. One may therefore wonder about the reasons behind this shift in the practice of the WTO dispute settlement bodies.

In part this development is probably connected with the overall scientification of various spheres of human activity. This is also reflected in the law, both domestic and international, as well as in the settlement of disputes.[84] Consequently, the shift that occurred in the context of WTO law (in the sense of creating new SPS/TBT rules but also modifying the character of the inquiry under GATT rules) should be seen as a part of the broader process that has taken place in a variety of areas. Another possible reason is the progressive legalization and formalization of the trade dispute settlement system. The WTO, as compared to the old diplomatic-like GATT system, is more legalistic and has a formalized dispute settlement mechanism. This requires the parties to a dispute to elaborate on their legal arguments and comprehensively substantiate all factual claims. In the case of health and environmental disputes, a reference to science seems to be indispensible. Panels also tend to produce longer reports that attempt to fully address all the arguments (including all factual aspects) put forward by the parties, as well as to explain the reasoning behind their interpretative choices and factual conclusions. This is partially because of fear of being overruled by the Appellate Body, and partially because panels act as sole fact-finders in the WTO dispute settlement process (without the possibility to remand a case if the Appellate Body finds a factual determination to be insufficient). The need to ensure the overall consistency of WTO case law is another important factor. Since the SPS Agreement provides the most elaborate set of rules for trade measures that have a health or environmental dimension, it is only natural to treat its standards as a kind of 'guideline' as to how to approach similar situations (i.e. measures addressing health or environmental risks) under other agreements. It should also be noted that the consistency of case law impacts on the overall legitimacy of the dispute settlement system as a whole, as it increases the predictability of decisions and certainty in the law, thus reducing arbitrariness.

Another factor that may explain the shift in GATT 1994 case law (as well as the introduction of scientific criteria to the SPS and TBT Agreements) relates to the legitimizing nature of science. GATT 1947 was predominantly concerned with tariff barriers and quotas. Its success in reducing these types of obstacle has shifted the attention of countries to market access problems caused by internal measures (i.e. non-tariff barriers). In consequence, potential disputes under WTO law have become not only more complex (than tariff barriers and quotas), but also more politically contentious.[85] This has put the WTO dispute settlement bodies under considerable pressure from WTO Members. Both the Appellate Body and panels are accountable to the states that created the WTO system and delegated some of their powers. However, owing to the principle of negative consensus, WTO Members have only a limited control over the outcomes of disputes. This forces both panels and the Appellate Body to ensure that their decisions are recognized as legitimate and as within the scope of their delegated powers.[86]

The recourse to science and scientific expertise may thus be seen as a way of improving the legitimacy of the decisions rendered by dispute settlement bodies. As noted by Peel, '[i]n emerging areas of international law concerned with the regulation of risk, expertise based on scientific and technical knowledge is typically viewed as a plausible basis for legitimating the growing authority exercised by relevant international rules'.[87] Science can, therefore, be regarded as a kind of an objective and value-free benchmark against which national measures can be tested and their legality assessed. Deciding disputes on a technical level, with science playing the central role in the assessment of the legality of national measures, depoliticizes (at least on its face) a particular trade controversy. Such an approach reduces the relevance of political/policy considerations in the dispute settlement process – a specific issue is decided against the objective criterion of science and does not require making difficult normative decisions – while reference to the 'higher' rationality of science shields dispute settlement bodies against the criticism from the governments of WTO Members. In other words, reliance on science can be seen as a form of denial of any policymaking role on the part of dispute settlement bodies and a defence mechanism against charges that they, acting as agents, have exceeded their delegated powers.[88] As rightly summarized by Shaffer 'for legal institutions, it is sometimes thought that the expertise of science can help to resolve competing claims in a neutral manner, evade normative judgements with their distributional implications, and legitimize legal decisions through the authority of science'.[89] It should also be noted that the WTO, as a relatively young international organization, is particularly vulnerable to the accusation of overstepping its mandate. Its limited institutional record, combined with uncertainties as to the exact scope of rights and obligations arising from the WTO agreements,[90] produces a situation whereby both panels and the Appellate Body feel a need to be very careful in establishing and maintaining their authority over trade disputes. This is particularly important when they are confronted with highly sensitive issues involving human health or environmental protection, matters that are at the core of the sovereign prerogatives of each state.

One may rightly ask whether science has fulfilled the above expectations. Two relatively recent rulings (*EC – Biotech Products* and *US/Canada – Continued Suspension*) show that this is not necessarily the case. Disputes that are highly politicized remain contentious irrespective of the criteria that are used to resolve them.[91] Parties tend to disagree about what science actually says in a particular case, highlight or downplay existing uncertainties, and use the complexities involved to further their agendas. Although this is particularly visible in the context of the SPS Agreement where science occupies a special place, real disagreements about specific scientific claims can also occur under GATT 1994 and the TBT Agreement (compare *EC – Asbestos*). At the same time, one has to admit that in less controversial cases (e.g. *Australia – Salmon*, *Japan – Agricultural Products II*, *US – Clove Cigarettes*) science has indeed served as a very useful tool in assisting panels in their assessment of domestic measures.

The inability of science to resolve some trade disputes is probably connected with its nature. Science, as used in assessment of risk, is not an entirely objective criterion. The construction of scientific knowledge is a social process that is culturally dependent,[92] and the assessment of risks relies on a number of normative non-scientific approximations and assumptions (e.g. owing to gaps in the knowledge, with some of them being irreducible). This means that science is not capable of being a fully objective benchmark in international trade disputes. In consequence, the reliance on science and scientific expertise, although sometimes helpful, may also sometimes fail to improve the legitimacy of some WTO dispute settlement decisions.

Notes

1 For the list of relevant risks, see Annex A(1) of the SPS Agreement.
2 Relevant international standards are those that are promulgated by the Codex Alimentarius Commission (food safety), World Organization for Animal Health (animal safety) or under the framework of the International Plant Protection Convention (phytosanitary safety). It is also possible for the SPS Committee to identify other organizations as relevant standard-setting bodies.
3 Appellate Body Report, *EC – Hormones*, para. 186.
4 Appellate Body Report, *US – Continued Suspension*, para. 569.
5 Panel Report, *Japan – Apples*, para. 8.149.
6 Appellate Body Report, *Australia – Salmon*, para. 124.
7 Appellate Body Report, *Japan – Apples*, para. 200.

8 E.g. Appellate Body, *EC – Hormones*, para. 200.
9 For a more detailed discussion, see L. Gruszczynski, *Regulating Health and Environmental Risks Under WTO Law: A Critical Analysis of the SPS Agreement*, Oxford: Oxford University Press, 2010, pp. 120–2.
10 Appellate Body, *US – Continued Suspension*, para. 562.
11 E.g. Panel Report, *EC – Biotech Products*, para. 7.1525.
12 Appellate Body, *EC – Hormones*, para. 194.
13 Appellate Body, *US – Continued Suspension*, para. 591.
14 D. Crawford-Brown, J. Pauwelyn and K. Smith, 'Environmental Risk, Precaution and Scientific Rationality in the Context of WTO/NAFTA Trade Rules', *Risk Analysis* 24(2), 2004, 461 at 465.
15 J. Atik, 'Science and International Regulatory Convergence', *Northwestern Journal of International Law* and *Business* 17, 1996/97, 736 at 742.
16 E.g. Panel Report, *EC – Biotech Products*, para. 7.3300; Panel Report, *US – Continued Suspension*, para. 7.420.
17 J. Peel, 'Risk Regulation Under the WTO SPS Agreement: Science as an International Normative Yardstick', *Jean Monnet Working Paper* No. 2002/04, at 71.
18 On the relationship between disciplines of Articles 2.2/5.1 and 5.7, see Gruszczynski, op. cit. pp. 178–85.
19 E.g. Appellate Body Report, *Japan – Apples*, para. 184.
20 Cf. also, Gruszczynski, op. cit. pp. 188–91.
21 E.g. Panel Report, *EC – Biotech Products*, para. 7.3240; Panel Report, *US – Continued Suspension*, para. 7.612.
22 D. Winickoff, Sh. Jasanoff, L. Busch, R. Grove-White and B. Wynne, 'Adjudicating the GM Food Wars: Science, Risk, and Democracy in World Trade Law', *Yale Journal of International Law* 30, 2004, 80 at 114.
23 Appellate Body, *US – Continued Suspension*, paras 685–6.
24 Ibid. para. 695.
25 Appellate Body Report, *EC – Hormones*, para. 147.
26 With respect to experts in the WTO system, see: G. Marceau and J. Hawkins, 'Experts in WTO Dispute Settlement', *Journal of International Dispute Settlement* 3(3), 2012, 493; more specifically on SPS experts: L. Gruszczynski, 'The Role of Experts in Environmental and Health Related Trade Disputes in the WTO: Deconstructing Decision-Making Processes', in M. Ambrus, K. Arts, H. Raulus and E. Hey (eds), *Irrelevant, Advisors or Decision-Makers? The Role of 'Experts' in International Decision-Making*, Cambridge: Cambridge University Press, 2014.
27 Appellate Body Report, *US – Continued Suspension*, para. 592.
28 Appellate Body Report, *Australia – Apples*.
29 Ibid. para. 225.
30 Ibid. para. 231.
31 For a more detailed discussion, see L. Gruszczynski, 'Standard of Review of Health/Environmental Regulation by WTO Panels', in G. Van Calster and D. Prévost (eds), *Research Handbook on Environment, Health and the WTO*, Cheltenham, UK and Northampton, MA: Edward Elgar, 2013.
32 For example, scientific evidence could be relevant in the context of Article 20 of the TRIPS Agreement. In particular, science may be helpful in deciding whether a specific encumbrance of a trademark use is justifiable. This is actually one of the issues in the currently pending case relating to the Australian plain packaging law (cf. *Australia – Tobacco Products and Packaging (Ukraine)*, WT/DS434).
33 The relevant part of Article XX(b) provides that '[s]ubject to the requirement that such measures are not applied in a manner which would constitute a means of arbitrary or unjustifiable discrimination between countries where the same conditions prevail, or a disguised restriction on international trade, nothing in this Agreement shall be

construed to prevent the adoption or enforcement by any contracting party of measures: . . . (b) necessary to protect human, animal or plant life or health'.

34 Another argument put forward by Thailand was that foreign cigarettes were particularly attractive to local consumers and could contribute to the increased consumption of tobacco products. In this context, Thailand also argued that various marketing techniques used by foreign companies would have the same effect.

35 Ibid. para. 28.

36 Ibid. para. 81.

37 G. Goh, 'Precaution, Science and Sovereignty Protecting Life and Health under the WTO Agreements', *Journal of World Intellectual Property* 6(3), 2003, 441 at 445.

38 David A. Wirth, 'The Role of Science in the Uruguay Round and NAFTA Trade Disciplines', *Cornell International Law Journal* 27, 1994, 817 at 844.

39 GATT Panel Report, *US –Tuna (Mexico)*; GATT Panel Report, *US – Tuna (EEC)*.

40 Note that Mexico claimed in the first *Tuna* dispute that dolphins could be regarded as exhaustible natural resources only if this were shown by scientific evidence (para. 3.44), while the US argued that 'if a party's measures were based on scientific information evaluated using recognized scientific approaches, a dispute settlement panel in the GATT should not substitute its own judgment for that of the contracting party whose measure is challenged'. The Panel did not address either of these arguments.

41 GATT Panel Report, *US – Tuna (Mexico)*, para. 5.28 (finding that the US did not demonstrate that 'it had exhausted all options reasonably available to it to pursue its dolphin protection objectives through measures consistent with the General Agreement, in particular through the negotiation of international cooperative arrangements').

42 Panel Report, *US – Gasoline*, para. 6.21 (note that the approach of the Panel might have been influenced by the arguments used by Brazil and Venezuela).

43 Panel Report, *US – Shrimp*, para. 7.9.

44 Ibid. para. 5.1.

45 Ibid. para. 7.29.

46 Subparagraph (g) concerns measures 'relating to the conservation of exhaustible natural resources if such measures are made effective in conjunction with restrictions on domestic production or consumption'.

47 Appellate Body Report, *US – Shrimp*, para. 134.

48 Ibid. para. 142.

49 J. Peel, *Science and Risk Regulation in International Law*, Cambridge: Cambridge University Press, 2010, p. 272. Note that to some extent the approach of the Appellate Body could have been influenced by the wording of the relevant provisions. Both cases (*US – Gasoline* and *US – Shrimp*) were decided under subparagraph (g), which only requires that a measure is related to a regulatory objective. This is a weaker requirement than the necessity test envisaged by subparagraph (b), and arguably it gives more flexibility to dispute settlement bodies as to choice of the appropriate methodology.

50 The relevant part of Article III:4 of GATT 1994 provides that: 'The products of the territory of any contracting party imported into the territory of any other contracting party shall be accorded treatment no less favourable than that accorded to like products of national origin in respect of all laws, regulations and requirements affecting their internal sale, offering for sale, purchase, transportation, distribution or use.'

51 Panel Report, *EC – Asbestos*, para. 8.122.

52 Ibid. para. 8.179.

53 Appellate Body Report, *EC – Asbestos*, para. 125.

54 Ibid. paras 113–14.

55 Panel Report, *EC – Asbestos*, para. 8.180.

56 Appellate Body Report, *EC – Asbestos*, para. 167.
57 Ibid. para. 178.
58 Panel Report, *EC – Asbestos*, para. 8.181.
59 Panel Report, *Brazil – Retreaded Tyres*.
60 Ibid. paras 7.61, 7.68 and fn. 1118.
61 Ibid. para. 7.77.
62 Appellate Body Report, *Brazil – Retreaded Tyres*, paras 134–83.
63 Panel Report, *US – Clove Cigarettes*, paras 2.7–8.
64 Ibid. para. 3.1.
65 Ibid. para. 7.154.
66 The Panel also discussed scientific evidence in the context of Article 2.1 in order to establish whether clove and menthol cigarettes were like products (e.g. para. 7.229). Although the Appellate Body reversed the Panel with respect to some of its findings under this article, this did not concern the treatment of scientific data.
67 Ibid. para. 7.401 and fn. 715 (finding that there was scientific consensus on the connection between flavoured cigarettes and smoking rates in younger groups of consumers, but also referring to the relevant SPS law on minority scientific opinions).
68 Ibid. paras 7.418–28.
69 Panel Report, *US – Tuna II (Mexico)*, para. 3.1.
70 Ibid. para. 7.473.
71 Ibid. para. 7.496.
72 Ibid. para. 7.517 and subsequent.
73 Ibid. para. 7.529.
74 Ibid. para. 7.504.
75 Appellate Body Report, *US – Tuna II (Mexico)*, para. 322.
76 A label that was created within the context of the Agreement on International Dolphin Conservation Program (1998).
77 Appellate Body Report, *US – Tuna II (Mexico)*, para. 330.
78 Cf. R. Hudec, 'Science and Post-discriminatory WTO Law', *Boston College International and Comparative Law Review* 26, 2003, 186.
79 A. O. Sykes, 'Domestic Regulation, Sovereignty and Scientific Evidence Requirements: A Pessimistic View', *Chicago Journal of International Law* 3, 2002, 355.
80 Goh, op. cit. p. 447.
81 Article 5.6 provides: '[W]hen establishing or maintaining sanitary or phytosanitary measures to achieve the appropriate level of sanitary or phytosanitary protection, Members shall ensure that such measures are not more trade-restrictive than required to achieve their appropriate level of sanitary or phytosanitary protection, taking into account technical and economic feasibility.'
82 For comprehensive review of the advantages and disadvantages of having scientific evidence requirements, see A. Green and T. Epps, 'The WTO, Science, and the Environment: Moving Towards Consistency', *Journal of International Economic Law* 10(2), 2007, 285, at 302–7.
83 But, see the Appellate Body Report, *US – Clove Cigarettes*, para. 96 (noting that 'the balance set out in the preamble of the TBT Agreement between, on the one hand, the desire to avoid creating unnecessary obstacles to international trade and, on the other hand, the recognition of Members' right to regulate, is not, in principle, different from the balance set out in the GATT 1994, where obligations such as national treatment in Article III are qualified by the general exceptions provision of Article XX').
84 Cf. House of Lords Science and Technology Committee, *Sciences and Treaties, Vol. 1: Report*, London: 2004; J. E. Alvarez, 'Are International Judges Afraid of Science? A Comment on Mbengue', *Loyola of Los Angeles International and Comparative Law Review* 34, 2011, 81. On the relationship between science and law on the domestic

level, see: R. Feldman, *The Role of Science in Law*, New York: Oxford University Press, 2009.

85 S. Picciotto, 'The WTO's Appellate Body: Legal Formalism as a Legitimation of Global Governance', *Governance: An International Journal of Policy, Administration, and Institutions* 18(3), 2005, 477 at, 483.

86 Since the WTO is an intergovernmental organization, the Appellate Body and panels arguably tend to legitimize their judgments vis-à-vis governments rather than other actors.

87 Peel, op. cit. p. 14.

88 Picciotto, op. cit. p. 481 (discussing this argument in the context of legalistic formalism used by the Appellate Body).

89 G. Shaffer, 'Risk, Science, and Law in the WTO: The Centrality of Institutional Choice', *Proceedings of the Annual Meeting*, Vol. 104, (March 24–7, 2010), 19.

90 WTO agreements can be seen as a type of unfinished contract. Specific provisions are formulated in very general and sometimes ambiguous language, while the system as such has numerous gaps that have to be filled in by the WTO dispute settlement bodies when interpreting and applying WTO law.

91 Cf., T. Epps, *International Trade and Health Protection. A Critical Assessment of the WTO's SPS Agreement*, Cheltenham, UK and Northampton, MA: Edward Elgar, 2008, pp. 92–100 (distinguishing between 'green' and 'amber' (difficult) cases).

92 See, generally, S. Jasanoff, *Designs on Nature: Science and Democracy in Europe and the United States*, New York: Princeton University Press, 2005.

3 Does science speak clearly and fairly in trade and food safety disputes?

The search for an optimal response of WTO adjudication to problematic international standard-making

Kuei-Jung Ni[1]

3.1 Introduction

Harmonization of national sanitary and phytosanitary measures is considered a useful means to promote trade liberalization of agricultural and food products.[2] In effect, the SPS Agreement requires that WTO members base their sanitary and phytosanitary measures on relevant international standards,[3] which are established not by the trade regime itself, but by other professional international institutions.[4] With respect to food safety, it is the Codex Alimentarius Commission ('Codex') that has the competence to set the relevant standards. The standards adopted by the Codex are not binding on members. Yet, by the explicit incorporation of such an international standard-setting mechanism into the trade system, since its inception the WTO has drastically changed the status of the Codex to the extent that theoretically voluntary standards have gained greater force and significance in deciding whether a national measure is consistent with SPS obligations.

Codex standard-setting should be done on a scientific basis, and, indeed, scientists used to play a major role in standard-making. However, linkages between trade interests and the Codex's standard-setting have made the institution susceptible to non-scientific influences, and the intervention of political and industrial forces into the operations of the Codex are evident.[5] The Codex has resorted to voting[6] to determine standards instead of endeavouring to reach a decision by consensus, especially when dealing with controversial or uncertain scientific findings on food safety.

The adoption of Codex standards may trigger complaints to be addressed through the WTO dispute settlement mechanism. For instance, soon after the standards on growth promoting hormones – which favoured the position of the United States ('US') – were approved by the Codex, the US filed a suit against the European Communities' ('EC') measures as distinct from those of the Codex. After a lengthy debate on international standards for ractopamine,[7] the Codex finally approved the standards in July 2012.[8] The US, which permits the use of ractopamine, complained that some countries have imposed unjustified trade restrictions on the importation of US pork and beef.[9] It is to be expected that the new Codex standards may bring pressure on China, Europe and other countries that prohibit the use of this veterinary drug and take different positions with the Codex.

As the legitimacy of Codex standard-making has been criticized,[10] the question arises whether the WTO should be more proactive in addressing problems with Codex standard-setting. The *EC – Hormones and EC – Sardine* cases[11] showed that the WTO has adopted a policy of deference to Codex standards, rejecting challenges raised by the EC against the problematic operations of the institution. Not until the WTO adjudication of *US – Continued Suspension*[12] did the Appellate Body take a relatively flexible approach regarding the extent of an importing country's obligation to comply with scientific principles of the SPS Agreement. Further, the Appellate Body did not agree with the Panel's selection of Codex experts to opine on the EC's new measures. The WTO jurisprudence should be welcomed by members adopting higher levels of public health protection than that embraced by the Codex. Yet, the soft stance over measures distinctive from the Codex formula also leaves some questions unanswered.

The SPS Agreement encourages members to follow international standards, but how should WTO adjudicators respond to a flawed international standard-making mechanism? As complaints about the legitimacy of the approval process continue to arise, to what extent and on what legal basis should adjudicators evaluate the standards in question?

WTO adjudicators do not set scientific standards, but rely on technical experts to advise them on SPS requirements, such as the sufficiency of scientific evidence specified in Article 5.7. In *US – Continued Suspension*, the Appellate Body rejected the ruling of the Panel, which fully deferred to the opinion of the experts who were previously involved in setting the food standards in question.[13] Yet, no clear rationale sustaining the rejection has been provided. Should such opinion not be taken into account simply because it stemmed from a prior international standard-making decision?

As international food safety standards have become increasingly important to WTO judicial activities, it is essential that their legitimacy be vigorously reviewed. The emergence of some justifiable basis for the interactions between these two institutions appears imminent. This chapter aims to explore how the WTO adjudication should address the problems associated with Codex international standard-making. The second section of the chapter reveals the uncertainties and limits of science in determining food safety standards so as to acknowledge the controversy behind the application of an alleged scientific approach in setting international standards. In the third section, the chapter will analyse the defects in the functioning of the Codex. Section 4 proposes an optimal response for the WTO to flawed standard-making like that of the

Codex following a critical examination of relevant scholarly works and WTO case law. The final section offers concluding remarks.

3.2 The uncertainties and limitations of science in the determination of food safety standards

Scientific evidence and findings should speak powerfully in the determination of food safety-related standards, especially in the risk analysis of food products in question. Not surprisingly, the professional language and expertise of the Joint Expert Committee on Food Additives ('JECFA'),[14] which is responsible for performing risk assessments and providing scientific advice to the Codex, is fairly scientific.[15] Yet, a critical review of the JECFA risk analysis process reveals the limits and uncertainties of science in assessing risk.

Prior to discussing the deliberations of the JECFA, it may be necessary to discuss certain limitations inherent in scientific studies of food safety. First, it is pointed out that most scientific surveys are subject to uncertainty, and that the findings are usually inconclusive.[16] Such uncertainties could be the result of deviations in the experimental process, misinterpretation of experimental data and insufficient evidence. Even a process that makes use of identical materials may produce different results owing to a variety of factors, including, inter alia, differences in animal test results, human populations, geographic location and timing.[17]

Moreover, much data to be used falls short of the information concerning field trials. Evidence and data collected from the laboratory may not carry the same implications as field tests – the variations occur owing to factors in the natural environment that are beyond laboratory controls. Some natural factors associated with disease-causing organisms may, or may not, accelerate the progress of an effect.[18] Theoretically, gathering sufficient data from field tests will serve as a warranty behind a sound science-based standard. But, in reality, it has been observed that such tests usually appear politically and economically infeasible.[19]

The major task of the JECFA is to decide upon acceptable maximum residue levels ('MRL's) for veterinary drugs, pesticides, additives and contaminants. Lacking field test information[20] for a given proposed MRL underscores the fact that there is often insufficient information available to reach a scientific conclusion on an MRL. Applying MRLs as food safety standards is an assumption that certain levels of risk can be acceptable to human beings. In effect, the policy that invokes MRLs as a benchmark rules out the zero risk tolerance position arising from food contaminants.[21] As observed, the scientific basis for deciding upon an MRL may be incomplete or not entirely solid. Thus the data collected may not guarantee the complete safety of food products. Rather, only as a result of risk assessments will the information disclose apparently acceptable effects on human health. The uncertainty and evolving nature of the science concerning food safety thus may help explain why Codex standards are of voluntary basis per se.

3.3 The problematic operation of international standard-setting involving food safety

Since Codex standards have attained a greater influence in settling food trade disputes, the standard-setting and decision-making of the institution have drawn greater and more serious attention and criticism. The complaints are mainly of two types: first, the scientific approach of Codex expert bodies has been, to some extent, diluted by non-scientific factors. Second, the process of setting food safety standards generally falls short of due process, and thus constitutes a major challenge to the legitimacy of its operations.

3.3.1 The dilution of a science-based approach in the standard-setting process

The Codex explicitly requires that relevant food standards and recommendations be based on sound scientific principle.[22] Indeed, the major task of evaluating and analysing the risk of food processing should be on the shoulders of scientists and competent experts. Of the Codex's eight steps to set a food safety standard,[23] Step 2 deals with serious risk assessment and analysis; when dealing with highly contested standards for residues, this depends on the risk assessments of independent expert bodies of two joint FAO/WHO committees: the Joint Meeting on Pesticide Residues ('JMPR') and the JECFA.

However, sceptics of the JECFA have raised concerns over the independence and impartiality of its deliberations. Of course, JECFA members should be professionals of high qualifications.[24] However, the experts do not always conduct scientific experiments themselves to produce the relevant data. Instead, the making of an MRL standard hinges on the review of available scientific data.[25] Normally, the body relies heavily on data provided by the industries concerned.[26] The risk assessment usually proceeds by reviewing the information submitted by pharmaceutical companies, the findings of which influence the assessment of the JECFA.[27]

The JECFA has also been criticized because its data collecting and findings fail to cover the information that reflects a worldwide basis.[28] Thus, for example, the MRLs for pesticides were mainly finalized as a result of counting information provided by developed countries like the US and the EU (European Communities).[29] Further, it is observed that most data was collected mainly from animal tests.[30] It should be noted that Codex standards for food safety are set to ensure public health as food products are consumed by human beings. Nevertheless, the data to support a given MRL rarely comes from human tests. For example, a competent European authority found that little data collected concerning the adverse effects of ractopamine is derived from human tests,[31] and China considers the current data on ractopamine incomplete owing to a lack of information on the impact on human livers and risks to certain people.[32]

Further, the function and operations of the JECFA in particular arouses more concern as the JECFA has constantly determined certain controversial MRLs for additives or veterinary drugs in food. For instance, in the middle of the 1990s, it recommended MRLs for growth promoting hormones in beef, which were not based purely on scientific considerations. The MRLs of hormones, apart from being a result of pure scientific studies, have been blended with other risk management factors. The MRLs have actually incorporated the idea of Good Agriculture Practices ('GAP'),[33] which is yet to be endorsed by all countries.[34] But, it appears that the calculated risk would be subject to whether, and to what extent, farmers follow established good practices on the use of drugs. Thus, at least in this case, the scientific approach has been compromised by non-science factors.

As a particular risk assessment is being finalized by the JECFA, a proposed standard is forwarded to Codex subsidiary bodies for deliberations.[35] The subsequent formulation of risk management is relatively political[36] and has proven problematic and subject to criticism. The composition of participants at the current Codex deliberation is diverse. The Codex used to be a club for scientists, who were the major players in the institution. Nowadays, in addition to member states represented by government officials, a variety of non-governmental organizations ('NGO's), including industry, consumer and environmental groups, can be present as observers at Codex meetings.[37] Yet, the participation and influence of each non-state group falls short of equality. Food industry groups have traditionally been deeply involved in the standard-setting and have become the primary constituent of NGOs. By contrast, the portion of non-commercial interested groups, though increased, still falls behind that of industry groups.[38]

Compared with NGOs, states enjoy far greater powers and privileges during Codex deliberations. In terms of forming national delegations and setting positions, industry voices have disproportionately prevailed over those of consumers and environmental groups.[39] Given the close institutional linkages between the Codex and the WTO/SPS, industries have been more active at the Codex, joining with governmental delegates to influence national positions and Codex operations.[40] If an adopted Codex standard favours a domestic food-related industry, the move may help open global markets.[41] The Codex standards on growth promoting hormones are illustrative in this regard. A newly adopted standard on ractopamine may open doors to new food markets. Thus, those likely to benefit, or concerned that they might be harmed by new players in local markets, are motivated to shape Codex standards in ways not exactly reflective of scientific findings, but that rather serve the interests of industry.

3.3.2 Lack of consensus in adopting international food safety standards

3.3.2.1 The significance of engaging in international rule-making by consensus

A critical criterion in evaluating the legitimacy of an international lawmaking process is by the extent of democratisation.[42] Apart from ensuring universal participation, especially in rule-making processes, it has been widely accepted that democratisation would be squarely fulfilled if a rule or standard-making would be engaged 'by consensus negotiating procedure'.[43] Such procedures may allow countries, regardless of how strong or weak they may be, to leverage their bargaining power.[44]

In contrast to resorting to voting, decision-making by consensus discards the use of voting and circumvents the taking of clear positions in favour, against, or abstaining. For instance, the UN Convention on the Law of the Sea defines consensus as 'the absence of any formal objection'.[45] Some commentators suggest that the merit of governing by consensus is that it avoids introducing divisions between members so as to prevent creating hostility publicly.[46] For countries that do not have a clear interest on certain issues, this manner of decision-making can help avoid the jeopardy that comes with being forced to choose sides.[47]

Of course, seeking consensus is not always flawless. For instance, the UN Fishery Conservation Agreement[48] was the product of a package deal between coastal and fishing countries, which was negotiated and concluded by consensus. At the forum, some countries opted not to object explicitly to avoid being condemned for obstructionism. Yet, Boyle and Chinkin observe that a number of states later expressed dissent, and some in fact declined to ratify or accede to the treaty.[49]

Regardless of the advantages of consensus, it is not always an ideal decision-making model for all international rule-setting procedures. A consensual deal is suitable for the issue that is of compromising nature. Nations with conflicting interests have to make concessions and compromises to reach consensus. However, negotiations may not guarantee that a compromise or consensus is reached, or may result in a weaker or vague commitment.[50] Normally, decision-making by consensus will not be suitable for agendas that are beyond compromise, or where a package deal is not possible.[51] For instance, international legislation on human rights is normally finalized by majority voting[52] and allows for parties to register their reservations. In contrast, some contend that reaching a decision by voting is not suitable to regimes built on the 'politics of interdependence', such as those governing international trade, the oceans, or global environment protection.[53]

The matters governed by the Codex relate to public health and fair trade in food. Therefore, its decision-making is not suitable for voting. The approval of a controversial standard by voting may lead to serious antagonism and mistrust among members. Furthermore, it should be noted that the WTO itself practically engages in rule-making by consensus, instead of voting.[54] In terms of regulating global trade in food, it is essential that the WTO and the Codex operate in a coherent manner, especially concerning their decision-making processes. At the Codex, resorting to voting to approve a standard would result in irregularities between these two international institutions, which are supposed to act in harmony with one another. Hence the standard-setting process of the Codex should be run based on consensus as far as possible.

3.3.2.2 The procedural defect in the Codex standard-setting process

The Codex used to set voluntary standards by consensus. There seemed no need to resort to voting, which allowed Codex members to engage in deliberations with greater patience. Prior to the establishment of the WTO, there was no history of resorting to voting in Codex decision-making.[55]

That the SPS Agreement pressures WTO members to stick to international standards, including those adopted by the Codex, has significantly changed the attitudes of participants in Codex deliberations. Nowadays, Codex standards carry legal weight and are economically important in the global trading system. Securing a standard that matches national or regional regulations may convey a two-fold advantage. For importing countries, a Codex standard that endorses and reflects national regulations may make trading partners' challenges of WTO inconsistency relatively difficult.[56] For exporting countries, if the Codex sides with their national standards, the situation will impose much pressure and cost on countries that adopt a standard higher than that of the Codex.[57]

Decision-making by consensus normally involves a lengthy process, and has become unpopular and difficult in the Codex community as the number and diversity of stakeholders have increased.[58] Also, Codex members are increasingly unwilling to make compromises and offer concessions as their respective national standards are quite different.[59] Thus, the usual consensual approach of Codex decision-making is fading and becoming less dominant, especially on highly controversial issues. If a majority of Codex members find themselves taking the same position, they will be motivated to push for a vote to secure the adoption of those standards they favour in order to serve their national interests.

Since 1995, the Codex has approved several contentious standards, not by consensus, but by a majority vote. Indeed, the approval of MRLs for five growth hormones in 1995 proved to be extremely controversial. These standards were adopted by a simple, closely contested, majority vote.[60] Another deficiency of the procedure is that it employs a secret ballot instead of open, public vote.[61] The EC, which opposed these standards, heavily criticized this voting method for lacking transparency.[62]

The adoption of a commodity standard on natural mineral waters by a narrow majority vote[63] also aroused resentment. The standard actually echoes the EC national policy that requires the bottling of mineral waters at their source.[64] As mentioned above, adopting such a standard would make it difficult for exporting countries whose mineral water bottling methods fail to comply with the EU law to challenge the WTO/SPS inconsistency of such measure successfully. The US, which applies less stringent bottling regulations, expressed strong objections to the standard on the grounds that the criterion does not serve to further the protection of public health.[65]

The tendency to resort to voting in an attempt to break deadlocks disturbs most of those Codex members who still favour setting standards by consensus.[66] As a result, the Codex was pressured to revise its procedural rules. Thus the amended Rule XII specifies that 'The Commission shall make every effort to reach agreement on the adoption or amendment of standards by consensus. Decisions to adopt or amend standards may be taken by voting only if such efforts to reach consensus have failed.'[67]

The revision does verify the supreme status of consensual decision-making. Nevertheless, the statement does not rule out the possibility of resorting to voting. In addition, it is observed that the above simplification cannot resolve problems currently facing the Codex. First, the rule does not provide a clear definition of 'consensus'. During the 2001 session, as deliberations over the idea of insufficient scientific information took place, the Chairperson and members disagreed on the definition of 'consensus'. Further, the revision does not clarify what circumstances constitute failed efforts to reach consensus. Nor does the rule stipulate when voting should proceed and who has the authority to initiate the voting.[68]

Moreover, Codex subsidiary committees are likely to ignore efforts to seek consensus so as to rush to voting. It is submitted that individual committees should play the role of consensus-builders.[69] Yet, 'The Guidelines for Committees' simply state that 'the Chairpersons should always try to arrive at a consensus and should not ask the Committee to proceed to voting if agreement on the Committee's decision can be secured by consensus'. In contrast to the procedural rule mentioned above, the Guidelines use a relatively weaker expression, which does not express the same resolve to pursue consensus. The Committees would thus encounter problems similar to those faced by the Commission.[70]

Unfortunately, after a long debate among Codex members on the MRLs for ractopamine, the Codex again failed to reach a decision by consensus. The eventual adoption of the veterinary drug standards by a very close vote mirrors the earlier hormone scenario. Such moves are indicative of how hard it is, in practice, for the Codex to resist the temptation of using voting to resolve differences.

3.4 Search for an optimal response by the WTO to defective international standard-setting

The previous section of this chapter revealed deficiencies in standard-making at the Codex. Although the organization responsible for setting global food standards has been under reform, there is no guarantee that the flaws in its operations will be remedied in the short term. Science should have been the core element in making Codex standards, regardless of its limitations. Yet the role and voice of science have been eclipsed by those of the industries. The rush to voting further diminishes the credibility of the Codex. Unsurprisingly, critique has arisen to challenge the legitimacy of current Codex operations.

Through the incorporation of international standards set by organizations like the Codex into WTO agreements, the multilateral trade regime cannot avoid encountering the legitimacy issue, at either the diplomatic or the dispute settlement forum. Indeed, at the inception of the WTO, trade negotiators had no way of knowing whether, or to what extent, the WTO would rectify this flaw in making Codex standards. However, the accountability of the WTO will be diminished if it simply turns a blind eye to Codex deficiencies. It is worth examining approaches that would offer a more positive role to the WTO in this balancing act. What follows provides a critical review of proposals to allow WTO adjudicators to engage in judicial review of Codex standard-setting. Further, it may be interesting to analyse how the recent WTO ruling on the *US – Continued Suspension* dispute dealt with the credibility of technical experts that had been involved with the previous Codex standard-setting on hormones.

3.4.1 Whether, and to what extent, WTO adjudicators may conduct judicial review of flawed international standard-setting

3.4.1.1 The status of play for WTO adjudicators in reviewing Codex standards

It is observed that the Understanding on Rules and Procedures Governing the Settlement of Disputes ('DSU') of the WTO does not explicitly extend to either the Panel or the Appellate Body the authority to conduct judicial review of international standards.[71] Neither do trade agreements, like the SPS Agreement, authorize such competence. Nonetheless, in the WTO dispute settlement proceedings, it would be desirable for disputant parties to argue the legitimacy of making the controversial Codex standards. Parties that lost certain Codex battles may wish that the trade regime take a sceptical stance towards Codex standard-setting. They may persuade adjudicators to review such standards so as to negate their validity in a trade dispute. Upon refusal to apply the standards or to recognize their validity, the responding party would be exposed to little risk of being found to violate the harmonization principle embodied in the SPS Agreement.[72]

Although, at least morally, the legitimacy of an international standard-making should be scrutinized, the present WTO adjudication bodies have yet to meet that expectation. For instance, in the dispute over hormone beef between the US, Canada and the EC, the EC managed to challenge the validity of hormone standards by reminding adjudicators that the MRLs for hormones were adopted without universal support, and reflected the opinions of only some members.[73] The EC argued that the adoption was a departure from the normal Codex practice of making decision by consensus.[74] However, the Panel did not respond to the appeal of the EC in a positive manner. Rather, the Panel clearly ruled that it only has to examine whether a standard exists in order to decide the compatibility of members' measures with Article 3.1 of the SPS Agreement.[75] The Panel was not convinced that it needed to consider whether or not the standards were adopted according to a particular methodology.[76]

In the later *EC – Sardine* dispute, the conservative approach of WTO adjudicators remained unchanged. The EC contended that the process by which the Codex standards in question were set did not comply with its procedural rules. According to the Codex standard-making rule, at Step 8, any submitted standard that needs a substantial revision must be remanded to relevant committees for further comment. In fact, the standards under challenge failed to observe that regulation. Thus, as the EC claimed, the standard does not meet the definition of 'relevant standards' specified in Article 2.4 of the TBT Agreement.[77] Yet again the Panel failed to endorse the argument of the EC, saying simply that an alleged 'standard' in Annex 1.2 of the TBT Agreement does not cover considerations of whether the process to set the standard met the procedural requirements. Thus, it declined to review whether the process satisfied the requirements of due process.[78]

The EC also argued that the standard was not adopted on the basis of consensus. The EC maintained that, in this instance, Codex practices were at odds with the principles[79] adopted by the TBT Committee requiring consensus in developing standards.[80] However, the Panel did not recognize that the TBT document should play a vital role in deciding the validity of such a standard. Instead, it found that the consensus approach revealed by the TBT Committee is not mandated in the text of the TBT Agreement, but is 'a policy statement of preference'.[81] In addition, the Panel did not agree with the EC that standards must be approved by consensus to satisfy the definition of a 'standard' in the TBT Agreement. It referred to the last two sentences of the Explanatory Note of Annex 1.2 to the TBT Agreement, concluding that 'even if not adopted by consensus, an international standard can constitute a relevant international standard'.[82] The Appellate Body agreed with the Panel and confirmed that a standard recognized in the TBT Agreement 'does not require approval by consensus'.[83]

The present passive stance of WTO adjudication may indicate its unwillingness to challenge or review the legitimacy of an international standard-setting process. The deferential approach certainly provokes criticism, not only from academics,[84] but also from WTO members.[85] Although judicial review should be expected, at least on moral grounds, it is worth analysing whether solid legal grounds exist to underpin such trans-institutional activity.

3.4.1.2 A critique on the proposals to advocate judicial review of the WTO on international standard-making

Judicial review has been regarded as a democratic mechanism ensuring the rule of law in the domestic constitutional structure.[86] A national court, especially at the highest level, has the power to invalidate measures approved by the legislative or executive branch. The well-established domestic norm aims to protect individuals from acts ultra vires that thus fall short of legitimacy. Nowadays, strong arguments have been made for the necessity of applying the mechanism to constrain the acts of international organizations on the ground that the decisions of respective international institutions increasingly affect not only states but also individuals.[87] Thus international courts should be permitted to perform the review.

From a theoretical perspective, the desirability of extending the power of judicial review to international tribunals proves quite solid. Yet, in practice, consistent and positive developments have still to become a reality. Indeed, the International Court of Justice ('ICJ') has had opportunities to exercise review over the decisions of other UN organs such as the General Assembly or the Security Council when an advisory opinion was being sought, and the World Court could review several decisions of the Security Council in the *Lockerbie*[88] or the *Bosnia*[89] cases. Yet the Court refrained from deciding the legal effect of the decisions.[90]

As indicated, the WTO itself has no power to set international standards in terms of SPS-related issues. Rather, it recognizes the lawmaking competence of relevant international organizations like the Codex, and is entitled to enforce and apply such standards. The respective functions of the WTO and the Codex alike are classified as reflective of the separation of powers under a domestic constitutional structure.[91] As such some commentators argue that WTO judicial bodies should exercise the power to judicially review Codex decisions.[92] Livermore contends that a review conducted by WTO judicial organs may provide process protection for stakeholders whose interests have not been properly taken into account during Codex operations. In addition, the review he considers would be able to mitigate some of the problems with Codex decision-making, such as the insufficiency of representation and equity.[93]

Yet the counter-argument is not without force. Masson-Matthee is sceptical of the approach on the ground that there is no explicit authorization by the DSU to do so.[94] Seeing that the Codex is not part of WTO agreements, Masson-Matthee does not consider that Codex decisions should be part of WTO applicable law in proceedings.[95] Even though she admits that the WTO adjudicative bodies have the experience of examining and adjudicating non-covered agreements,[96] Masson-Matthee argues that WTO adjudicators should refrain from reviewing Codex standards without a legal basis.[97] Otherwise, such acts may run the danger of being at odds with the meaning, purpose and function of Codex agendas. Further, without clearly delineating the scope of the applicable law in question, it would be difficult to ensure the legitimacy of exercising such a review.[98]

Irrespective of concerns about an unclear delimitation between applicable law and judicial review, the risks associated with reviewing Codex standards without proper limits have been recognized. From a practical point of view, Livermore holds that the WTO is incompetent in undertaking reviews of substantial aspects of Codex standards because Codex expertise and professionalism extend beyond those of the WTO.[99] Nevertheless, he contends that the WTO should be allowed to review the procedural requirements of Codex decision-making, and proposes that certain procedure rules of national administrative law be applied to assist the WTO in fulfilling this duty.[100]

In *US – Shrimp*, he observes that the Appellate Body has actually invoked certain principles of due process of law to determine the WTO consistency of the US measures in dispute.[101] In addition, certain administrative principles embodied in WTO agreements, for instance transparency and consultation, can be invoked in deciding the legitimacy of the Codex lawmaking process.[102] Further, the practices and operations of other international organizations, such as the International Organization of Standardization ('ISO'), may be instrumental in assessing Codex standard-setting.[103] Overall, he concludes that such a review, even if desirable, must be based on principles of international law, WTO merits, and the practices of other international institutions so as to ensure its legitimacy.[104]

As mentioned, the Codex has been under reform. Yet there is no guarantee that a satisfactory result will be produced through internal change. As indicated, there has been a strong argument in favour of turning to an external force to rectify these flaws. Judicial review by the WTO has been hailed as an optimal corrective mechanism, and commentators have proposed novel and constructive ideas. Yet, other approaches may also provoke further controversy. The legitimacy of undertaking such a review through WTO adjudication is worth examining.

In contrast to the ICJ and the Security Council, both of which are UN organs, the WTO and the Codex were not created under the same roof. The WTO is independent of the UN system, which includes the Codex. It should be noted that no hierarchy is established between international legal branches. The WTO and the Codex are arguably on an equal footing under international law, but justification for the review can be sustained if a decent basis for such trans-institutional activities can be established. Therefore, theoretically, it would be highly inappropriate, in political and legal terms, for the WTO to intervene unless a consensus or deal could be reached between the two organs regarding such a review. It is true that the SPS Committee has the competence and duty to coordinate efforts with the Codex.[105] But it may be beyond the mandate and level of the Committee to seek a deal with the Codex on the matter of judicial review. Thus, certain solutions need to be formulated to help overcome the legal barriers for the review and make the function attain a greater degree of legitimacy, if no consensus between them would be plausible.[106]

First, consensus-building within the WTO community is essential to reduce misunderstandings and tensions between the legislative and judicial branches. To avoid judicial activism[107] in exercising the review especially when WTO members have yet to give explicit authorization, it is suggested that revisions of WTO agreements such as the SPS Agreement, or the DSU, be undertaken to the extent that a well-structured review framework can be formulated.[108] The added rules may provide a clearer road map for adjudicators to fulfil their duties in a right direction. If it is difficult to realize such a revision, the General Council or the Ministerial Conference can alternatively adopt a decision of authoritative interpretation[109] to endorse the power of judicial review. Of course, both solutions would require strong political will to make it happen.

Moreover, it may be interesting to explore whether WTO adjudicators still have the discretion to exercise such a review even if no political will materializes in forming a binding instrument. Indeed, as observed, no DSU provision explicitly provides for such a review mechanism. Nevertheless, I argue that the issue should be decided on a case-by-case basis.

In terms of trade and food safety arrangements, in the context of the SPS Agreement and Codex standard-making system, I favour leaving some room for discretion to the WTO judicial system. In the context of the SPS Agreement, it is obvious that the health-related agreement not only recognizes the authority of the Codex in making relevant standards, but actually brings to life the non-trade standards of science into the WTO regime. In essence, for the sake of harmonization on global food safety standards, Codex standards have become inextricably bound up with the WTO. This close and dynamic relationship means that the boundaries between the WTO and the Codex are different from those of other international institutions.

If Codex standard-making activities, especially their procedures, have inherent or inadmissible flaws, this would render WTO adjudicators' neglect of the problem illegitimate. It should be noted that the SPS Agreement highly values scientific principles. If the making of a contested Codex standard failed to comply with the Codex's own scientific and/or due process requirements, it would seriously undermine the SPS mandate if there were no such review.

Upon reviewing Codex standards, a critical issue may arise concerning the legal consequences of the review. From the viewpoint of international law in general, Klabbers proposes three options concerning the effect of judicial review, namely invalidating decisions, rendering relevant decisions inapplicable, and making a statement of inconsistency. She considers the second choice relatively more appropriate in dealing with international relations given that the first is too strong and the third too weak.[110] The argument applies in the context of the WTO/Codex. In effect, a hypothetical WTO announcement invalidating a Codex standard would be too intrusive while a mere statement of inconsistency would not send a strong enough signal to the Codex.

3.4.2 Whether consulting technical experts involved in a prior standard-setting procedure should be permissible

Transatlantic trade disputes over hormones in beef have resulted in extremely contested and lengthy WTO adjudication. Even though the US won the case against the EC's ban on US hormone beef in 1998, the EC failed to lift the trade measure. According to Article 22.6 of the DSU, the US was authorized to terminate its concessions and obligations towards the EC by imposing higher tariffs on the importation of EC products.[111] Under the US trade retaliation, the EC continued to work on science investigations to prove the health risk caused by the consumption of hormone beef. In 2008, based on new findings, the EC brought a suit to challenge the continued suspension of the US's trade obligations. The issue arose as to how WTO adjudicators should treat the technical advice of experts previously involved in making the Codex standards so as to fulfil the responsibility of making an objective assessment.[112] As the contested international hormone standards remain valid and there is no clear precedent for WTO adjudicators to conduct judicial review of such standards, this dispute may offer a good opportunity to examine whether WTO adjudicators have adopted an appropriate and balanced approach towards the use of technical experts.

3.4.2.1 EC elaboration of a new scientific study on hormones and the inclination of the Panel to heed the advice of scientists involved in making Codex standards in questions

In response to the 1998 WTO verdict that confirmed the violation of EC obligations under the SPS Agreement, the EC endeavoured to conduct research on the effect of hormones by providing definite risk assessments and offering more convincing scientific evidence. Based on the three new scientific opinions issued by the Scientific Committee on Veterinary Measures relating to Public Health ('SCVPH') in 1999, 2000 and 2002,[113] the EC adopted Directive 2003/74/EC as an amendment of the previous Directive 96/22/EC.[114] The EC contended that the new regulations on hormone control have implemented the verdict of the original adjudication, and thus appealed the termination of the retaliation imposed by the US and Canada. As no consensus about the lifting of trade sanctions was reached between disputants, the EC decided to bring the dispute to the WTO.

The Panel had to decide whether the new European measures resulted from an updated analysis of the risks associated with hormones, and could thus be justified. Under the circumstances, the SPS Agreement provides that the Panel should seek advice from technical experts, and that it has the competence to select experts under consultation with disputant parties. Further, the Panel enjoys the discretion to establish an advisory technical experts group.[115] The DSU also specifies the rules for the establishment of such a group and its procedures.[116] The 'Rules of Conduct' adopted by the DSB (Disputes Settlement Body) underline the requirements of independence and impartiality for expert advisors.[117]

Against the objection of the EC, the Panel selected six experts, including two scientists who had been directly involved in the drafting and adoption of previous JECFA reports on the MRLs for growth promoting hormones. The EC questioned the independence and impartiality of Dr Boisseau and Dr Boobis because they were co-authors of the reports that had disfavoured the EC approach towards the hormones in question. The EC argued that the selection of these doctors to give advice on the new European scientific studies 'would amount to asking them to review and criticize their proper work'.[118]

Nevertheless, the Panel disagreed with the EC's objection. It was not convinced that previous experience with the JECFA would prevent these experts from providing an unbiased evaluation of new scientific evidence and findings that may contradict the previous JECFA decision on hormone standards.[119]

Further, given that the arguments of the disputant parties were all related to the previous work of the JECFA,[120] the Panel felt that the experts who had participated in the JECFA deliberations might be in a better position to help the Panel comprehend the operations of the group.[121] That the SPS Agreement recognizes the international standard-making status of the Codex seems to provide the Panel the justification for relying on experts that had substantially contributed to the findings in questions. Thus, the Panel's selection of JECFA members as experts seems to indicate its strong commitment to honouring the harmonization principle of the SPS Agreement.

3.4.2.2 *The Appellate Body rejects the Panel's selection and use of technical experts involved in international standard-setting*

In reviewing whether the Panel's selection of two JECFA scientists as technical experts infringed on the due process rights of the EC,[122] the Appellate Body largely sided with the EC. The appeal provides a good opportunity to examine the process of selecting and consulting with experts who have been deeply involved in setting an international standard.

The Appellate Body first looked into the affiliation of the two experts with the JECFA, and found that Drs Boisseau and Boobis took key positions in the JECFA respectively when the six hormones at issue were evaluated.[123] Further, in response to questions raised by the Panel, the selected experts, as observed by the Appellate Body, evaluated the risk assessments of the EC by applying the findings and conclusions of the JECFA as a benchmark.[124] The Appellate Body applied the term 'natural inclination' to illustrate the tendency of such experts to favour or defend the approach of the JECFA, but not 'to assess whether the science relied upon by the European Communities can support the conclusions it reached'.[125]

The Appellate Body found reason to question the impartiality of these experts in assessing EC new scientific findings, especially as the EC has repeatedly questioned the validity of the previous JECFA risk assessments and refused to follow them.[126] Accordingly, the Appellate Body found that the Panel's selection and consultations with Drs Boisseau and Boobis failed to meet the independence and impartiality requirements for serving technical experts.[127]

3.4.2.3 *Overall assessment and need for a better solution*

It is likely that the Panel's deference to the authority of the JECFA and respect for the text of the SPS Agreement that recognizes the Codex's status will make it hard to exclude JECFA members from its consulting list. Apparently, the reasoning by which the Panel rebutted the EC's challenge about the lacking of impartiality or independence of the two experts seems quite weak. Similarly, the Appellate Body provided a barely sufficient rationale for why these two JECFA experts were unfit to give an objective assessment of the EC's updated studies on hormone risks. It may be premature to assume that the Appellate

Body would regularly be sceptical of the operations of the JECFA/Codex. Yet, the Appellate Body seems to have distanced itself from the international institutions when it had to judge a risk assessment conducted by a member who had established safety levels that exceed international standards.

Notwithstanding the legitimacy of standard-making processes in the Codex, the WTO judicial system cannot avoid dealing with Codex standards, especially if a member adopts a different benchmark from that of the Codex. As the Appellate Body has yet to judicially review Codex standards, the *US – Continued Suspension* simply reveals that it will not defer to any reference related to Codex activities without reservation. In effect, previous Codex scientific evaluation may not always play a critical role in deciding the consistency of measures that depart from Codex standards with the SPS Agreement. It may be an overstatement that the Appellate Body approach has undermined the influence of international standard-making. But by the disconnection of Codex experts from the appraisal of national risk assessments, members are likely to survive the test of complying with SPS obligations when they refuse to comply with Codex standards.[128]

In *US – Continued Suspension*, the Appellate Body's deference to national health regulations was quite obvious. Yet a decent basis and rationale to denounce the selection of JECFA/Codex experts to review measures that are at odds with international standards remains wanting.[129] As honouring international standard-setting is intact under the SPS Agreement, an objective and systematic mechanism needs to be built into the WTO dispute settlement system by which the real independence and impartiality of experts can be gauged. It does not seem convincing to discount the competence of Codex experts merely because of previous connections with Codex activities. There is a strong demand to establish fair criteria for expert selection as the process has proved crucial to arriving at fair judgments on international inconsistent national standards.

3.5 Concluding remarks

This chapter has revealed that the Codex standard-setting process has not always adhered to a scientific orientation. The dilution of science in the standard-making process increases as proposed standards involve huge trade and industry interests. Politics and the industrial sector now play a greater role in shaping Codex decision-making. As the progress of Codex reform remains uncertain and unpredictable, this chapter has explained that the WTO should deal with Codex standards in a proper manner. It is submitted that the WTO adjudication may become an optimal vehicle for rectifying the injustice arising from an undesirable Codex standard.

Judicial review is well established in domestic constitutional structures, and should be extended to the relations between international regimes. As the WTO and the Codex are separate and equal bodies in the international legal system, it is better for the two organs to reach an agreement on the use of judicial review. Yet, the difficulty of reaching a consensus about the matter should not prevent WTO adjudicators from exercising that function. To avoid excessive judicial intrusion into the operations of the Codex, it is suggested that the effect of such judicial review should be limited to a declaration of inapplicability of the standard in question in the relation between disputants, but not to nullification of the standards.

Finally, though WTO judicial review on international food safety standards has yet to happen, the *US – Continued Suspension* ruling by the Appellate Body has indicated that it would not uphold consultations with the experts who played a substantial and critical role in international standard-making to assess national findings distinct from international standards in questions. However, objective criteria and grounds to exclude, or include, JECFA experts need to be formulated. It remains to be seen whether the *US – Continued Suspension* adjudication that hesitates to embrace international science makers may make it difficult, or even impossible, for the Panel to select experts involved in a previous standard-making process. Nevertheless, the Appellate Body's approach, of course, would please members who decline to observe such international standards.

Notes

1 Professor of Law and Director, Institute of Technology Law, National Chiao Tung University, Taiwan. Email: kjni@mail.nctu.edu.tw. An earlier version was delivered at the International Conference on Trade, Science, Technology, and Justice, organized by the Institute of Technology Law, National Chiao Tung University, in Hsin Chu, Taiwan, on 1 November 2011. This chapter originally appeared in *Food and Drug Law Journal* 68, 2013, 97–114, and is reprinted with permission of the Food and Drug Law Institute. The author thanks Min-Chao Sun and Kai-Chih Chang for research assistance.

2 See recitals 5 and 6 of the Preamble to the SPS Agreement.

3 The SPS Agreement Article 3.1. Apart from harmonization, the SPS Agreement underlines several principles to be observed, including scientific principle, mutual recognition, transparency, etc.

4 E.g. Codex Alimentarius Commission ('Codex'), the International Office of Epizootics ('OIE') and the International Convention on Plant Protection ('IPPC') are explicitly recognized by the SPS Agreement as international standard-setters. Paragraph 3 of Annex A to the SPS Agreement.

5 See Section 3.3.1 of this chapter.

6 See Section 3.3.2 of this chapter.

7 Ractopamine, a veterinary drug administered as a feed additive, is used to increase leanness in pork and beef. See Food and Agriculture Organization of the United Nation, 'UN food safety body sets limits on veterinary growth promoting drug', available at www.fao.org/news/story/en/item/150953/icode/ (accessed 20 October 2011).

8 At the previous Codex sessions, no consensus was reached concerning the approval of a residue standard for ractopamine. The US and Canada favoured the proposed draft standard, but European countries opposed the adoption of such a standard. Eventually, the Codex adopted a standard at the 35th session, held in Rome on 6 July 2012, by a very close vote: 69 in favour, 67 against, with 7 abstentions. See

Food and Agriculture Organization, op. cit. The move was seen as a triumph by countries that approve the use of the drug in meat production. See Helena Bottemiller, 'Codex Adopts Ractopamine Limits for Beef and Pork', *Food Safety News*, 6 July 2012, available at www.foodsafetynews.com/2012/07/codex-votes-69-67-to-advance-ractopamine-limits-for-beef-and-pork/ (accessed 9 August 2013).

9 See the statement of the US Trade Representative at USTR website: www.ustr.org (accessed 1 August 2011). For the official statement of the US government on the adoption of the standards, see www.usda.gov/wps/portal/usda/usdahome?contentid=2012/07/0222.xmlandnavid=NEWS_RELEASEandnavtype=RTandparentnav=LATEST_RELEASESandedeployment_action=retrievecontent (accessed 25 July 2012).

10 M. A. Livermore, 'Authority and Legitimacy in Global Governance: Deliberation, Institutional Differentiation and the Codex Alimentarius', *NYU Law Review* 81, *2006*, 766 at 777–89; R. A. Pereira, 'Why Would International Administrative Activity be Any Less Legitimate? – A Study of the Codex Alimentarius Commission', *German Law Journal* 9, 2008, 1693 at 1713–18.

11 Appellate Body Report, *EC – Hormones*; Appellate Body Report, *EC – Sardines.*

12 Appellate Body Report, *US – Continued Suspension.*

13 Ibid. paras 421–2, 467, 472, 477, 479, 481–2.

14 The JECFA was established in 1956 under the auspice of the FAO/WHO, which is run independently of the Codex. See Codex, 'JECFA – Joint FAO/WHO Expert Committee on Food Additives', available at www.codexalimentarius.org/scientific-basis-for-codex/jecfa/en/ (accessed 7 January 2013).

15 J. Peel, *Science and Risk Regulation in International Law*, Cambridge: Cambridge University Press, 2010, p. 294; Panel Report, *US – Continued Suspension.*

16 A. Eliason, 'Science Versus Law in WTO Jurisprudence: The (Mis)Interpretation of the Scientific Process and the (In)Sufficiency of Scientific Evidence in EC – Biotech', *NYU Journal of International Law and Policy* 41, 2009, 342 at 353.

17 Peel, op. cit. at 98–103 (elaborating works of social scientists regarding uncertainty in science).

18 The case of *E. coli* alarmed by the EC provides a good example. See Panel Report, *EC – Hormones (Canada).*

19 M. D. Masson-Matthee, *The Codex Alimentarius Commission and Its Standards*, The Hague: T.M.C. Asser Press, 2007, p. 69, n. 91 (explaining the lacking of national regulations for field test requirement and the reluctance of local industry to accept the requirement).

20 Ibid. at 68.

21 Cf. It is argued that every product implies differential risk. To require a zero risk is impracticable. However, according to the ruling in Appellate Body Report, *Australia – Salmon*, the Appellate Body recognizes the right of WTO members to use zero risk as an appropriate level of protection.

22 'Statements of Principles Concerning the Role of Science', in Codex Procedural Manual, at 209–10 (20th edn, 2011), available at ftp://ftp.fao.org/codex/Publications/ProcManuals/Manual_20e.pdf (accessed 31 July 2011) ('Codex Procedural Manual').

23 According to Codex Procedural Manual, the procedure to conclude a food standard consists of eight steps. See 'Uniform Procedure for the Elaboration of Codex Standards and Related Texts', in Codex Procedural Manual, ibid. at 31–2.

24 Peel, op. cit. at 294.

25 Masson-Matthee, op. cit. at 68; Pereira, op. cit. at 1701.

26 Masson-Matthee, op. cit. at 68.

27 G. G. Moy and J. R. Wessel, 'Codex Standards for Pesticides Residues' in N. Rees and D. Watson (eds), *International Standards for Food Safety*, Gaithersburg, MD: Aspen Publishers, 2000, p. 215.

28 Masson-Matthee, op. cit. at 68.

29 Ibid. at 69.

30 D. G. Victor, 'The Sanitary and Phytosanitary Agreement of the WTO: An Assessment After Five Years', *NYU Journal of International Law and Policy* 32, 2000, 865 at 889 (explaining the determination of MRLs to rely on the 'no effect' level in tested animals, but questioning that 'how it translates to human effects has not been rigorously defined or quantified').

31 It is observed that there are only six test persons that have been studied concerning ractopamine's effect. See European Food Safety Authority's scientific opinion on 'Safety Evaluation of Ractopamine: Scientific Opinion of the Panel on Additives and Products or Substances Used in Animal Feed', adopted on 2 April, 2009, 1041 *The EFSA Journal*, 2009, 7, available at www.efsa.europa.eu/en/efsajournal/pub/1041.htm (accessed 1 May 2012).

32 Many Asians preferentially consume the organs of livestock. China has raised concerns about the higher concentrations of ractopamine residues in pig organs. Botemiller, op. cit.

33 Codex Procedural Manual, op. cit. at 25.

34 Masson-Matthee, op. cit. at 172.

35 See Steps 4, 5 of Uniform Procedure for the Elaboration of Codex Standards and Related Texts, Codex Procedural Manual, op. cit. at 31, 32.

36 Pereira, op. cit. at 1700–1. A risk assessment as observed is to decide what level of risk is acceptable, which usually subjects to non-science factors. Although risk managers are expected to base their judgment on risk assessments, they need to consider other factors relating to the protection of consumers' health and the promotion of fair food trade. Ibid.

37 Livermore, op. cit. at 784–5; Lucinda Sikes, 'FDA's Consideration of Codex Alimentarius Standards in Light of International Trade Agreements', *Food and Drug Law Journal* 53, 1998, 327 at 330.

38 Livermore, op. cit. n.90.

39 The voice of consumer groups remains less influential than that of groups of industry. Ibid. at 785–6.

40 L. M. Wallach, 'Globalization and Sovereignty: Accountable Governance in the Era of Globalization: The WTO, NAFTA and International Harmonization of Standards', *Kansas Law Review* 50, 2002, 823 at 836.

41 It has been rightly pointed out that 'industry representatives are seeking to use the international harmonization process as a vehicle for global deregulation'. B. A. Silverglade, 'The Impact of International Trade Agreements on US Food Safety and Labelling Standards', *Food and Drug Law Journal* 53, 1998, 537 at 540.

42 A. Boyle and C. Chinkin, *The Making of International Law*, Oxford: Oxford University Press, 2007 p. 101; J. Klabbers, A. Peters and G. Ulfstein, *The Constitutionalization of International Law*, Oxford: Oxford University Press, 2009, p. 55.

43 Boyle and Chinkin, op. cit. at 101–2.

44 Ibid.

45 The United Nations Convention on the Law of the Sea, Article 161, UN Doc. A/CONF.62/122 (1982), 21 I.L.M. 1261 (entered into force 16 November 1994).

46 Boyle and Chinkin, op. cit. at 158.

47 Ibid. at 158.

48 Agreement for the Implementation of the Provisions of the United Nations on the Law of the Sea of 10 December 1982 relating to the Conservation and Management of Straddling Fish Stocks and Highly Migratory Fish Stocks, UN Doc. A/CONF.164/37 (1995), 34 I.L.M. 1542 (entered into force 11 November 2001).

49 Boyle and Chinkin, op. cit. at 158.

50 Ibid. at 159.

51 Ibid.

52 For instance, the 2007 UN Declaration on the Rights of Indigenous Peoples was adopted by voting. The UN Declaration was adopted by a majority of 143 states in favour, with 4 votes against (Australia, Canada, New Zealand and the United States) and 11 abstentions (Azerbaijan, Bangladesh, Bhutan, Burundi, Colombia, Georgia, Kenya, Nigeria, Russian Federation, Samoa and Ukraine). See Office of the United Nations High Commissioners for Human Rights, available at www2.ohchr.org/english/issues/indigenous/declaration.htm (accessed 10 August 2012).

53 B. Buzan, 'Negotiating by Consensus: Developments in Technique at the UN Conference on the Law of the Sea', *American Journal of International Law* 75, 1981, 324 at 329.

54 Since the inception of the WTO in 1995, the trade regime has constantly engaged in negotiation and decision-making based on consensus. The WTO never resorts to a voting process. Otherwise, the major members that are developing countries would have dominated the decision-making of the regime. Yet, it is also true that the current Doha negotiation almost collapsed mainly because no consensus could be reached among WTO members.

55 Livermore, op. cit. at 787.

56 The SPS Agreement Article 3.2 (the conformity of national SPS measures with international standards will lead to a presumption of consistency with the SPS Agreement).

57 Ibid. Article 3.3 (WTO members need to provide scientific justification if they deviate from international standards).

58 T. P. Stewart and D. S. Johanson, 'The SPS Agreement of the World Trade Organization and International Organizations: The Roles of the Codex Alimentarius Commission, the International Plant Protection Convention, and the International Office of Epizootics', *Syracuse Journal of International Law and Commerce* 26, 1998, 27 at 45.

59 Victor, op. cit. at 931; Livermore, op. cit. at 789. Countries such as America and the European nations have adopted a differential policy on growth promoting hormones. The use of hormones would be legal in North America if farmers comply with regulations. By contrast, the EC directives prohibit the use of hormones as veterinary drugs.

60 There were 33 votes in favour, 29 against and 7 abstentions. Report of the 21st Session of the Joint FAO/WHO Codex Alimentarius Commission, Rome, 3–8 July 1995 ALINORM 95/37, para. 45 ('Codex 21st Session Report').

61 Rules of Procedure, Rule VIII, para.5, in Codex Procedural Manual, op. cit. at 11.

62 Codex 21st Session Report, op. cit. para. 46; Stewart and Johanson, op. cit. at 42.

63 There were 33 votes in favour, 31 against and 10 abstentions. Report of the 22nd Session of the Joint FAO/WHO Codex Alimentarius Commission, Geneva, 23–8 June 1997 ALINORM 97/37, para. 69 ('Codex 22nd Session Report').

64 Victor, op. cit. at 887.

65 The US objected to the standard by stating that '[this] standard ignores public health protection by prohibiting any antimicrobial treatment and creates a barrier to international trade by including unnecessary and inappropriately restrictive requirements which are contrary to the General Principles of Codex Alimentarius, adopted by the Commission to protect public health and facilitate international trade'. Codex 22nd Session Report, op. cit. para. 91.

66 Ibid. para. 93; according to an evaluation initiated by the FAO in 2002, the majority of Codex members objected an increase of resorting to vote in standard-making. W. Bruce Traill, R. Bedouin, K. Gourlie, J. Husch and A. Lustre plus Independent Expert Panel, Report of the Evaluation of the Codex Alimentarius and Other FAO and WHO Food Standards Work, 2002, at § 4.4.3.7.

67 Rules of Procedure, Rule XII, para. 2, in Codex Procedural Manual, op. cit. at 14.
68 Masson-Matthee, op. cit. at 233.
69 Ibid. at 236.
70 Ibid.
71 Masson-Matthee, op. cit. at 185.
72 The SPS Agreement Article 3.
73 Panel Report, *EC – Hormones*, op. cit. para. 9.72.
74 Ibid.
75 Ibid.
76 Ibid.
77 Panel Report, *EC – Sardines*.
78 Ibid.
79 Decision of the Committee on Principles for the Development of International Standards, Guides and Recommendations With Relation to Articles 2, 5 and Annex 3 of The Agreement, Committee on Technical Barriers to Trade, WTO Doc. G/TBT/9, para. 9 (13 November 2000).
80 Panel Report, *EC – Sardines*, para. 4.33.
81 Ibid. para. 7.91.
82 Ibid. para. 7.90.
83 Appellate Body Report, *EC – Sardines*, para. 227.
84 H. Horn and J. H. H. Weiler, 'European Communities – Trade Description of Sardines: Textualism and Its Discontent', in H. Horn and P. C. Mavroidis (eds), *The WTO Case Law of 2002*, The American Law Institute Reporters' Studies, Cambridge: Cambridge University Press, 2005, p. 255.
85 For instance, Chile worried about the adverse effect of the Appellate Body ruling. See Dispute Settlement Body, WTO Doc. WT/DSB/M/134, at 12, para. 41 (23 October 2002).
86 Klabbers *et al.*, op. cit. at 64.
87 Ibid. at 64–6.
88 Questions of Interpretation and Application of the 1971 Montreal Convention arising from the Aerial Incidents at Lockerbie (preliminary objections) 1988 I.C.J. 9 ('Lockerbie').
89 Application of the Convention on the Prevention and Punishment of the Crime of genocide (*Bosn. and Herz. v. Serb. and Montenegro*) (request for the indication of provisional measures), 1993 I.C.J. 3.
90 Lockerbie, op. cit. at 15.
91 Livermore, op. cit. at 790.
92 Ibid. at 790–6; J. Scott, 'International Trade and Environmental Governance: Relating Rules (and Standards) in the EU and the WTO', *European Journal of International Law* 15, 2004, 307 at 330–3; Pereira, op. cit. at 1711–12.
93 Livermore, op. cit. at 790–1.
94 Masson-Matthee, op. cit. at 190–1.
95 Ibid. at 191.
96 Ibid. at 190. (For instance, Masson-Matthee observes that the Lome Convention had been reviewed in the WTO *EC – Bananas* Appellate Body Report, European Communities – Regime for the Importation, Sale and Distribution of Bananas, WT/DS27/AB/R, adopted on 25 September 1997).
97 Ibid.
98 Ibid. at 191.
99 Livermore, op. cit. at 792. Cf. From a general perspective of international law, Klabbers, Peters and Ulfstein submit that the scope of matters to be reviewed should also cover the content of the decisions so as to ensure respect of general international law, of course, including *erga omnes*. Klabbers *et al.*, op. cit. at 67.

100 Livermore, op. cit. at 794–5.

101 The Appellate Body considered that the lack of a proper appeal mechanism provided for importing countries as such was of arbitrary discrimination, and thus violated US obligations under the chapeau of Article XX of the GATT 1994. Appellate Body Report, *US – Shrimp*. For a discussion on the principle of due process in the WTO dispute settlement proceedings, see A. Mitchell, *Legal Principles in WTO Disputes*, Cambridge: Cambridge University Press, 2008, pp. 145–76.

102 Livermore, op. cit. at 795.

103 Ibid.

104 Ibid. at 796.

105 The SPS Agreement Article 3.5.

106 It should be understandable that a Codex member will oppose such review if a presumed Codex standard favouring its position would be so applied as to push the lift of trade restrictions of other countries.

107 R. H. Steinberg, 'Judicial Lawmaking at the WTO: Discursive, Constitutional, and Political Constraints', *American Journal of International Law* 98, 2004, 257 (addressing concerns about expansive judicial lawmaking at the WTO); Boyle and Chinkin, op. cit. at 263–311(providing a general discussion on lawmaking activities of international courts).

108 It is proposed that a structure of international judicial review should encompass issues of scope, matters to be covered, standing and effects, etc. Klabbers *et al.*, op. cit. at 66–7.

109 WTO Agreement, Article IX, para. 2.

110 J. Klabbers, 'Straddling Law and Politics: Judicial Review in International Law', in R. St.J. MacDonald and D. M. Johnston (eds), *Towards World Constitutionalism: Issues in the Legal Ordering of the World Community*, Leiden: Martinus Nijhoff, 2005, pp. 809–33.

111 See Appellate Body Report, *US – Continued Suspension*, paras 8–9.

112 Article 11 of the DSU requires the Panel to conduct an objective assessment of the matter before it.

113 Appellate Body Report, *US – Continued Suspension*, paras 10–11.

114 Ibid. para. 11.

115 The SPS Agreement Article 11.2.

116 Appendix 4 to the DSU.

117 'Rules of Conduct for the Understanding on the Rules and Procedures Governing the Settlement of Disputes', WTO Doc. WT/DSB/RC1, Section II: para. 1 (3 December 1996).

118 Letter from the European Communities to the Panel dated 16 January 2006 (quoted in Appellate Body Report, *US – Continued Suspension*, para. 417).

119 Panel Report, *US – Continued Suspension*, para. 6.22.

120 Ibid. para. 7.84.

121 Ibid. para. 7.85.

122 The Appellate Body held that due process protection covers the selection and consultations with experts. See Appellate Body Report, *US – Continued Suspension*, para. 436.

123 The two doctors were not only members of the JECFA, but also played a significant role in hormone discussions by serving Chairman, Vice-Chairman, and Joint-Rapporteur. See ibid. para. 460.

124 Ibid. paras 462–8, 477.

125 Ibid. para. 469.

126 Ibid. paras 458, 477, 479 (the EC argued the limitations in JECFA's assessments and pointed out that the data used by JECFA was outdated).

127 Ibid. para. 481.

128 S. Cho, 'Case Report on United States – Continued Suspension of Obligations in the EC – Hormones Dispute', *American Journal of International Law* 103, 2009, 299 at 303.

129 J. Pauwelyn, 'US-EU Hormone Case Limits WTO Role in Reviewing SPS Measures', *Inside US Trade*, 24 October 2008; M. M. Du, 'Standard of Review under the SPS Agreement after Hormones II', *International and Comparative Law Quarterly L.Q.*59, 2010, 441 at 459.

4 An economic theory of the SPS Agreement

Naoto Jinji

4.1 Introduction

Regulating food safety in the domestic food market is an important role of the government. As international movements of goods and people continue growing, protecting the domestic ecological system from 'biological invasions' of non-indigenous or 'exotic' species and pests has also become an important policy issue. In the face of these issues, sanitary and phytosanitary ('SPS') measures are necessary to protect human, animal and plant life or health from diseases, pests and contaminants.[1] However, these measures may also be used simply to protect domestic producers from international competition. As tariffs and other traditional forms of trade barrier are progressively dismantled through multilateral, regional and bilateral negotiations over trade liberalization, the temptation to use SPS measures for protectionist purposes has become even stronger.

There are a number of prominent trade disputes over SPS measures used potentially for such disguised protectionist purposes. A famous example is the dispute over hormone-treated beef between the United States ('US') and the European Communities ('EC'). In the 1980s, the EC banned the use of growth promoting hormones in cattle and all imports of meat and meat products from animals that had been supplemented with growth promoting hormones. In 1996, the US and Canada appealed to the Dispute Settlement Body of the WTO. In 1997, the Panel ruled against the EC, finding the import ban not justified.[2] Other such examples include the cases *Japan – Apples*[3] and *Australia – Salmon*.[4]

The SPS Agreement prevents WTO members from using SPS measures discretionarily and arbitrarily. The significance of the SPS Agreement in GATT/WTO disciplines is to establish a *scientific basis* for policies related to SPS. Thus, even if a policy is implemented according to the principle of non-discrimination (that is, the most favoured nation (MFN) and national treatment (NT) principles of GATT), it may be found to have violated the SPS Agreement if such a policy lacks scientific basis. Under the SPS Agreement, a scientifically 'rational relationship' is required between policy measures and their intended goals. The requirement of scientific justification is expected to contribute to mitigating disguised protectionism.

The SPS Agreement also requires harmonization of the respective SPS policies of members with international standards, as well as minimization of their negative impacts on trade. On the other hand, the SPS Agreement respects members' sovereignty on the choice of their own acceptable levels of risk, or the appropriate level of protection ('ALOP'), which can be more stringent than international standards as long as a sufficient scientific justification is demonstrated.[5] Even setting the ALOP at 'zero risk' can be allowed.

Economists have criticized the SPS Agreement for lacking economic considerations in regulating SPS measures. Calvin and Krissoff (1998) argue that the SPS Agreement, which is rooted more in a risk analysis approach, focuses only on losses to producers and ignores the additional costs and benefits resulting from SPS measures. An economic cost–benefit analysis, however, would be able to take these variables into account.[6] James and Anderson (1998) contend that a policy assessment under the SPS Agreement is 'about where environmental policy assessment was two or three decades ago',[7] looking only at direct effects and using command and control measures. The SPS Agreement pays 'virtually no attention to the impact of SPS trade restrictions on consumer prices'.[8]

The main purpose of this chapter is to examine the role of the SPS Agreement in developing the international trade regime of agricultural and food products. In particular, this chapter attempts to investigate how the SPS Agreement can or cannot successfully deter the use of SPS measures for disguised protectionist purposes.

To answer the above questions, I employ a simple two-sector, two-country, perfectly competitive general equilibrium trade model developed by Bagwell and Staiger (1999, 2001).[9] Governments frequently use tariffs and SPS measures to implement policy objectives. The use of tariffs is restricted by international agreements, which correspond to GATT/WTO disciplines. The SPS Agreement is captured as a set of restrictions on SPS measures. To clarify the role of the SPS Agreement, I compare the equilibrium under the SPS Agreement with the equilibrium without the SPS Agreement.

The main findings of the chapter are as follows. In contrast to criticisms by economists that the SPS Agreement lacks economic considerations, I demonstrate that the SPS Agreement can play a role of mitigating disguised protectionism and improving welfare in international trade of agricultural and food products. Requiring a scientific basis is effective in guiding SPS policies to an economically sound direction. However, science as the basis for SPS risk analysis involves uncertainty.[10] For instance, the scientific community may fail to reach a consensus in this area, as a number of opposing but equally plausible views may exist. Owing to this uncertainty, the SPS Agreement may fail to prevent SPS measures from being used for protectionism purposes.

There are a number of studies related to this chapter. First of all, Bagwell and Staiger (1999, 2001) analyse the role of GATT/WTO from an economic point of view. In particular, Bagwell and Staiger (2001) extend the framework of Bagwell and Staiger (1999) to examine the interaction between tariff policies that are directly restricted by GATT/WTO, and domestic policies regarding labour and environmental standards. They show that when the terms-of-trade effect is the only cross-border externality, the current GATT/WTO rules could enable governments to achieve efficient policy combinations of trade and domestic policies with only tariff negotiations, provided that the market access commitments negotiated in the WTO are not eroded by unilateral choices of domestic labour and environmental standards. They demonstrate that the right to bring the 'non-violation' complaints provided in GATT Article XXIII is the key to ensuring that governments achieve efficient trade and domestic policy outcomes by tariff negotiations. Their results imply that GATT/WTO rules need not be broadened to directly regulate the issues of labour and environmental standards in order to achieve a globally efficient outcome. In this chapter, I extend their analysis to clarify the role of the SPS Agreement.

Similar to Bagwell and Staiger (2001), Copeland (1990) explores the interaction between negotiable and non-negotiable trade barriers. He shows that trade negotiations contain loopholes that can be exploited by protectionist governments, but are nevertheless welfare-improving.[11]

The linkage between trade and non-trade issues in the context of self-enforcing international agreements has been analysed by Ederington (2001, 2002) and Limão (2005).[12] Unlike Copeland (1990), Ederington (2001) investigates cooperation over two negotiable instruments of protection. He focuses on the differential treatment of domestic policies and tariffs in GATT/WTO rules. In GATT/WTO rules, the use of domestic policies as a 'disguised' trade barrier is prohibited, while tariff protection is limited only by 'binding levels' that member countries may agree on and to be non-discriminatory. In the framework of an infinitely repeated game in which any deviation in either trade or domestic policy triggers, he shows that differential treatment is efficient if the supply and demand functions are approximately linear in local prices, because there is no gain from trade-distorting domestic policies. Since implementing trade policies is the most efficient means of pursuing terms-of-trade gains, it is also the most efficient means of countering any deviation from cooperation. Thus, under the limited enforcement power that prevents implementation of a fully efficient set of trade and domestic policies, an agreement that requires countries to cooperate fully over domestic policy and to adjust tariffs to satisfy constraints is self-enforcing.

Ederington (2002) compares the linkage and non-linkage of trade and domestic policies in self-enforcing agreements. In a 'linked agreement', any deviation in either trade or domestic policies is punished by infinite reversion to a Nash equilibrium in both policies, whereas in a 'non-linked agreement' punishment is restricted to the policy that is violated. It is commonly viewed that policy linkage strengthens the punishment on deviation. However, he shows that a non-linked agreement can support the 'most-cooperative equilibrium' just as a linked agreement can, which implies that linkage does not necessarily lead to more cooperation. The main reason is that the tariff is the most efficient instrument to address the terms-of-trade effect, which is the only cross-border externality in his model.

Limão (2005) analyses whether linkage of trade and non-trade policies promotes better cooperation in both policies when there are cross-border, non-pecuniary externalities as well as the terms-of-trade externality. In the context of self-enforcing agreements, he shows that if trade and domestic policies are strategic complements, linkage can sustain more cooperation in both policies than non-linkage. When two policies are strategic complements, a country incurs an extra cost when it deviates from both policies, which does not exist if it deviates only in one policy. Consequently, linkage lowers the incentive to deviate in any given policy and hence leads to self-enforcement. He demonstrates that any cross-border negative externality is essential for policies to be strategic complements.

Empirical studies on the economic effects of SPS measures include Otsuki *et al.* (2001a, b), Wilson *et al.* (2003) and Yue *et al.* (2006).[13] For example, Otsuki *et al.* (2001a, b) examine the trade impact of an EC regulation introduced in 1998 that reduced the maximum permissible level of a certain type of aflatoxin (a toxic substance) in food to a lower level than international standards specified by the Codex Alimentarius. Their study shows that EU standards, which would reduce health risk by approximately 1.4 deaths per billion a year, would reduce exports of cereals, dried fruits and nuts from African countries by 64 per cent or US$670 million, as compared with regulations based on the Codex standards.

The remainder of the chapter is organized in the following way. Section 4.2 briefly discusses the background and the main features of the SPS Agreement. Section 4.3 illustrates the structure of the SPS Agreement from an economic point of view. Section 4.4 examines the economic effect of the SPS Agreement in the framework of general equilibrium. Section 4.5 provides some concluding remarks.

4.2 Background

4.2.1 Before the SPS Agreement

Prior to the SPS Agreement, the original GATT, primarily Article XX, and the TBT Agreement, which was known as the Standards Code, established multilateral regimes for regulating the use of SPS measures.[14] However, the consensus view was that GATT and the Standards Code were not enough to deter disruptions of trade in agricultural and food products.

A typical example to illustrate the fallacies of the pre-SPS Agreement legal regime is the unresolved dispute between the US and the EC over the EC's ban on imports of hormone-treated meat and meat products during the 1980s. In March 1987, the US raised the issue of the EC ban under the Standards Code. After six months of fruitless bilateral negotiations, the US requested the establishment of a technical experts group to evaluate the scientific basis for the ban. This request was blocked by the EC, which contended that the use of hormonal growth promotants in beef production was a process and production method ('PPM') rather than a product characteristic and hence did not violate the Standards Code. The EC prohibited the import of meat from animals that had been administered growth hormones but did not refer to the import prohibition of meat containing growth hormones.[15]

4.2.2 The SPS Agreement

The SPS Agreement was negotiated during the Uruguay Round and entered into force in January 1995. It created new WTO disciplines on permissible trade-restricting measures related to protection of human, animal and plant life or health from risks.[16] The TBT Agreement also contains language that refers to protection of human health and the environment. The TBT Agreement covers 'all technical regulations and conformity assessment procedures',[17] except for SPS measures defined by the SPS Agreement. 'The objective of a measure is thus crucial to the determination whether it is subject to the disciplines in the TBT or SPS Agreement.'[18]

The main provisions of the SPS Agreement are as follows. Article 2 (Basic Rights and Obligations) stipulates that members have the right to take SPS measures necessary for the protection of human, animal or plant life or health and that any SPS measure shall be 'applied only to the extent necessary', 'based on scientific principles' and 'not maintained without sufficient scientific evidence'.[19]

Article 3 (Harmonization) states that members are encouraged to base their SPS measures on international standards, where they exist.[20] SPS measures that conform to international standards 'shall be deemed to be necessary to protect human, animal, or plant life and health, and presumed to be consistent with the relevant provisions' of the SPS Agreement and of GATT 1994[21]. However, members can adopt a measure to provide a higher level of SPS protection than that provided by an existing international standard 'if there is a scientific justification'.[22]

Article 4 (Equivalence) states that an importing country must recognize an SPS measure, which differs from its own, as equivalent to its own if the exporting country's measure provides the same level of SPS protection.

Article 5 (Assessment of Risk and Appropriate Level of SPS Protection) requires that any SPS measures be based on a risk assessment, taking into account 'risk assessment techniques developed by the relevant international organizations';[23] Article 5.5 requires internal consistency in ALOP, avoiding 'arbitrary or unjustifiable distinctions in the levels it considers to be appropriate in different situations, if such distinctions result in discrimination or a disguised restriction on international trade'; Article 5.6 stipulates that SPS measures are 'not more trade-restrictive than required' to achieve their ALOP; Article 5.7 states that 'if relevant scientific evidence is insufficient', members may adopt SPS measures on a provisional basis.

Article 7 (Transparency) and Annex B state that members are obliged to ensure that all SPS measures and proposals for change are notified in a transparent manner and to establish a single national enquiry point that is 'responsible for the provision of answers to all reasonable questions from interested Members'.

4.2.3 Agri-food trade disputes

For the subsequent analysis of the role of the SPS Agreement, it would be important to look at the cases involving agriculture and food products, in which the DSB found that articles of the SPS Agreement had been violated. Here, I look at four major cases.

In the *EC – Hormones* dispute,[24] the Appellate Body found that the EC's import ban was not based on a risk assessment, in violation of Article 5.1, and that the EC did not provide scientific evidence to support a higher level of protection than the Codex international standards, in violation of Article 3.3.

In the *Japan – Agricultural Products II*[25] dispute complaint by the US, the Appellate Body found that Japan's quarantine measures affecting imports of certain agricultural products were not based on sufficient scientific evidence, in violation of Article 2.2, nor based on a risk assessment, in violation of Article 5.1.

In the *Australia – Salmon*[26] dispute complaint by Canada, the Panel found that Australia's import ban of fresh, chilled and frozen salmon was not based on sufficient scientific evidence, in violation of Article 2.2, nor based on a risk assessment, in violation of Article 5.1, and was not least trade-restrictive, in violation of Article 5.6.

In the *Japan – Apples*[27] dispute complaint by the US, the Panel found that Japan's import restrictions on US apples were not based on sufficient scientific evidence, in violation of Article 2.2, nor based on a risk assessment, in violation of Article 5.1, and were not least trade-restrictive, in violation of Article 5.6.

In summary, all of the four cases violated Article 5.1 (risk assessment) and three out of the four cases violated Article 2.2 (scientific principles). Moreover, two cases violated Article 5.6 (least trade-restrictive).

4.3 The structure of the SPS Agreement

In this section, I illustrate the structure of the SPS Agreement from an economic point of view. In particular, I show how the usual economic analysis of price and quantity is transformed into food risk in the evaluation of SPS policy under the SPS Agreement.

Consider that a country imports good x, or food, which is subject to SPS policy. Let D, S and S^* be domestic demand for, domestic supply of, and import supply of good x, respectively.

Good x may contain some 'hazard', which is a 'biological, chemical or physical agent in, or condition of, food with the potential to cause an adverse health effect' (Codex, 2003: 51).[28] Thus, a possible contamination of a hazard in good x causes a health risk to consumers. In this situation, some SPS policy is required to achieve a certain level of sanitary or phytosanitary protection (which means the protection of human, animal or plant life or health), or SPS protection. I assume that the SPS protection level that is attained by some SPS policy is measured by the corresponding risk level R. A smaller R means a lower risk. The SPS protection level in this country depends on the total amount of hazard intake. Suppose that consumers in this country take the total amount of H of hazard by consuming good x. Then, the risk level R can be expressed as a function of H, $R(H)$. Let h be per unit hazard intake. Then, $H = h \times x$ holds.

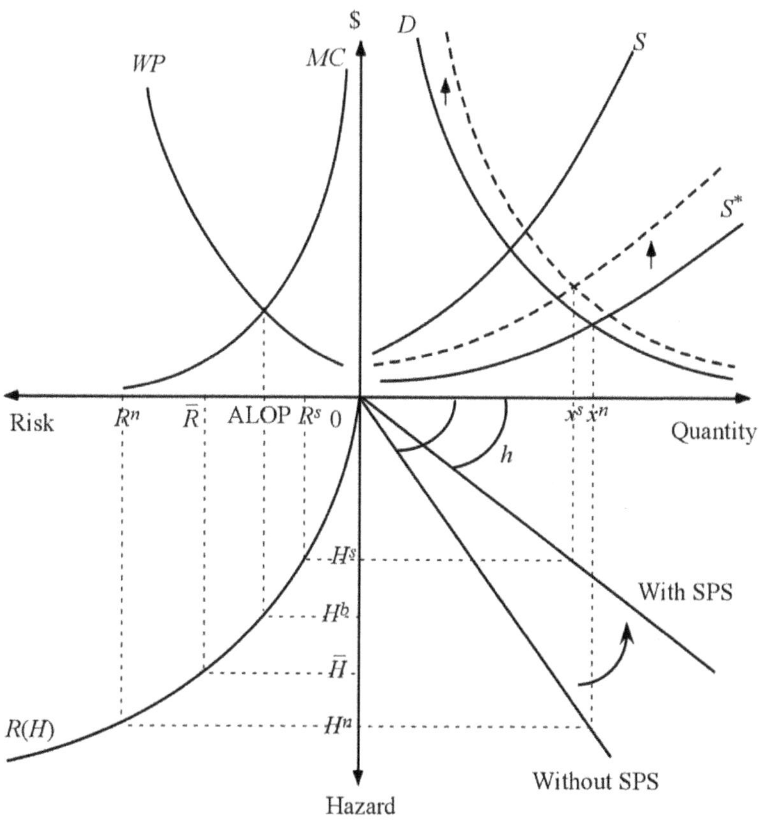

Figure 4.1 Food consumption, hazard and risk

Source: This figure is constructed by modifying and extending the framework developed by Jinji (2008).[29]

Figure 4.1 depicts the relationship among food consumption, hazard intake and risk. In it, the right-hand side of the horizontal axis measures quantity of food consumption and production. The upper side of the vertical axis measures the monetary value and price. Thus, the first quadrant shows the usual relationship between price and quantity of the consumption good. The domestic demand curve, D, the domestic supply curve, S, and the foreign supply curve, S^*, are depicted. The implementation of SPS measures could shift the domestic supply and the foreign supply. It may also shift the domestic demand, because the implementation of SPS measures may alter consumers' assessment of the safety of food. The lower side of the vertical axis measures the level of hazard intake H, and hence the fourth quadrant shows the relationship between the amount of food consumption and hazard intake. The slope of the line in the fourth quadrant is per unit hazard intake h. This line could be rotated by the implementation of SPS measures. The risk level R is measured along the left-hand side of the horizontal axis. The third quadrant shows the relationship between hazard intake and the risk level. Thus, the curve in the third quadrant is the function $R(H)$. Finally, the second quadrant indicates the relationship between the risk level and cost and benefit of attaining a certain level of risk. The *MC* curve indicates the marginal cost of attaining a certain level of risk in the domestic economy, whereas the *WP* curve represents the domestic consumers' willingness to pay for a marginal reduction in risk from a certain level. Thus, the intersection of the two curves gives the optimal level of risk for this country. The government may choose this level as the 'ALOP' of the country. In this way, under the SPS Agreement an SPS policy is assessed by transforming the market outcome (i.e. a combination of price and quantity) into the risk level through taking hazard intake into account. At the same time, the assessment of an SPS policy is conducted by taking into account the ALOP of the country.

Moreover, the relationship between the SPS protection level implied by international standards and the ALOP of the country is also depicted in Figure 4.1. Hazard intake under international standards and the corresponding risk level are indicated as $H = \bar{H}$ and $R = \bar{R}$, respectively. The acceptable level of risk chosen by the government of the country is indicated as 'ALOP'. I consider a case in which the government chooses the optimal level of risk determined by the intersection of the *MC* and *WP* curves in the second quadrant as ALOP. Figure 4.1 indicates a case in which ALOP is more stringent than $\bar{R}$. $H = H^b$ is the level of hazard intake to attain the ALOP. In the fourth quadrant, the line labelled 'Without SPS' depicts the case of no SPS measure being implemented. On the other hand, the line labelled 'With SPS' depicts the case of an SPS measure being implemented. Thus, without SPS measure, the domestic consumption is $x = x^n$, resulting in hazard intake of $H = H^n$. The attained risk level is $R = R^n$, which is higher than the international standard $R = \bar{R}$. If an introduced SPS measure rotates up the line in the fourth quadrant to the line labelled 'With SPS', the domestic consumption is decreased to $x = x^s$ and the corresponding hazard intake is decreased to $H = H^s$. This level of hazard intake achieves the risk level of $R = R^s$, which is lower than ALOP. Thus, in this case the SPS measure is excessive.

4.4 The role of the SPS Agreement in international trade

In this section, I extend the framework in the previous section and analyse the role of the SPS Agreement in international trade. A rigorous analysis of the statements in this section is provided in the Appendix.

4.4.1 The basic framework

Consider a world that consists of two countries. Call them the home and foreign countries. Suppose there are two sectors. One sector produces good x and the other sector produces good y. Assume that all markets are perfectly competitive. Without loss of generality, let good x be the natural import of the home country and good y be the natural import of the foreign country. Each country imposes a tariff on imports. But, the upper bound of tariffs is set by the tariff negotiations.

Assume that both goods are potentially affected by SPS measures.[30] To focus on the situation in which trade disputes occur in the real world, I consider only SPS measures with regard to import goods.[31] Consider a situation in which the government of each country implements some SPS measures. A country's SPS measures could potentially affect both its import demand and the other country's export supply. For example, from December 2005 to February 2013 Japan allowed imports of beef from the US and Canada only from cattle aged 20 months or younger in order to address the issue of bovine spongiform encephalopathy (BSE). This type of SPS measure affects import demand. On the other hand, Japan introduced standards on residue of pesticide, feed additives and veterinary drugs in May 2006. The standards could particularly affect Japan's imports of food from China. This type of SPS measure not only affects Japan's import demand but could also affect China's export supply. Actually, SPS measures affecting export supply and those affecting import demand have quite different effects. Here, I focus on the SPS measures that affect import demand.

Furthermore, I assume the following conditions: (1) trade is balanced; (2) an inward shift of the home (respectively, foreign) import demand curve will result in a lower (respectively, higher) equilibrium world price; (3) an increase in SPS measures reduces import demand; and (4) holding local prices and SPS measures fixed, an improvement in the terms of trade is beneficial to social welfare of the country, which is measured by the real GDP (gross domestic product).

Let R and R^* be the acceptable level of risk or the *SPS protection level from risk to human, animal or plant life or health* that will be achieved by implementing an SPS measure in the home and the foreign countries, respectively. A higher value of R means a higher risk. An increase in the stringency of an SPS measure reduces or does not change R.

4.4.2 GATT/WTO disciplines with the SPS Agreement

Suppose now that the SPS Agreement is entered into force. In this case, in addition to the tariff negotiation, choices of SPS measures are also restricted by the SPS Agreement.

First, the SPS Agreement requires each country to set its own ALOP. The SPS Agreement also requires harmonization of ALOPs to international standards, which are the SPS protection levels set by the relevant international organizations, such as the Codex, the OIE and IPPC. However, it also allows ALOPs to be more stringent than the international standards, if there is a scientific justification. Second, the SPS Agreement requires scientific basis and appropriate risk analysis for SPS measures. This implies that each country is responsible for demonstrating a 'rational relationship' between ALOPs and SPS measures. I define the following three cases: (a) the actual SPS protection level resulting from implementing an SPS measure is higher than the ALOP set by the government (an *overprotective* case); (b) an SPS measure is just enough to achieve the ALOP (a *just protective* case); (c) the actual SPS protection level resulting from implementing an SPS measure is lower than the ALOP set by the government (a *underprotective* case). The SPS Agreement requires that (b) is the case. Finally, the SPS Agreement requires SPS measures to be least trade-restrictive.

Then, given the above conditions, it can be shown that the SPS Agreement, which induces reciprocal reductions in SPS measures from the initial levels, improves the social welfare of both countries, as compared to the case without an SPS Agreement. Thus, the SPS Agreement actually has a positive economic effect, provided that at the equilibrium without SPS Agreement each country would be hurt by a unilateral increase in its trading partner's tariff. The SPS Agreement reduces SPS measures that would be otherwise set at a higher level for manipulating terms of trade, contributes to freer trade and improves welfare in the world, compared to the case without an SPS Agreement.

However, the SPS Agreement in its current form is not enough to guarantee an efficiency gain. The reason is that a country has an incentive to unilaterally increase its actual SPS protection level from international standards. There are two ways to achieve this: the first option is to set its ALOP higher than international standards; and the second option is to make its ALOP conform to international standards but implement SPS measures that will realize a higher level of SPS protection than the ALOP. Although the second option is prevented by the SPS Agreement, the first option may be feasible under the SPS Agreement.

Article 3.3 of the SPS Agreement allows each country to set its ALOP higher than the SPS protection levels set by the relevant international organizations, as long as a scientific justification is provided. However, the state of science for SPS risk assessment is highly uncertain.[32] The AB in *EC – Hormones* case argued that the scientific evidence to support a particular SPS measures is not necessarily based on the 'mainstream' scientific opinion.[33] Governments can base their SPS measures on 'a divergent opinion coming from qualified and respected sources'.[34] It would be sufficient for a country to demonstrate a 'rational relationship' between the SPS measure and the risks it mitigates in order to justify a particular SPS measure.[35] The Appellate Body clarified that even minority opinions could provide this 'rational relationship'.[36] This implies that various ALOPs and SPS measures can be justified by different scientific evidence.[37] Thus, scientific uncertainty might be exploited by disguised protectionism.

4.5 Concluding remarks

In this chapter, I have analysed the role of the SPS Agreement of the WTO, which is aimed at preventing WTO members from using SPS measures discretionarily and arbitrarily, from an economic point of view. The SPS Agreement relies mainly on the risk analysis paradigm, which is based on scientific justification, rather than on the economic paradigm. For that reason, economists have often criticized the SPS Agreement for lacking economic sense.

The analysis in this chapter, however, has demonstrated that the SPS Agreement could play a role in improving social welfare in the world. As long as the SPS protection is set at some proper levels by the relevant international organizations, the SPS Agreement induces reciprocal reductions in SPS measures of both countries from their unilaterally optimal levels, leading to an improvement in economic welfare of both countries.

However, a potential drawback of the SPS Agreement arises from its reliance on the risk analysis paradigm. Science involves uncertainty. Owing to the uncertainty of science, the SPS Agreement leaves room for countries to use SPS measures for disguised protectionist purposes or they may become an obstacle to implementation of welfare-improving SPS measures.

Acknowledgements

I thank Katsuhiko Suzuki, Tsuyoshi Toshimitsu, seminar participants at Chukyo University, Hitotsubashi University, Kwansei Gakuin University, Osaka University and Osaka City University, and members of a research project 'Trade and Food Safety' at the Research Institute of Economy, Trade and Industry (RIETI) for helpful comments and suggestions on earlier versions of the chapter. The usual disclaimer applies.

Appendix: A general equilibrium analysis

In this Appendix, I provide a rigorous analysis of the statements in Section 4.4. The basic framework follows the model constructed by Bagwell and Staiger (1999, 2001). There are two countries: home and foreign. Variables of the foreign country are indicated by an asterisk (*). There are two goods: x and y. All markets are perfectly competitive. Good x (y) is the natural import of the home (foreign) country. Let $p \equiv p_x / p_y$ and $p^* \equiv p_x^* / p_y^*$ be local relative prices in the home and foreign countries, respectively. Let t and t^* be ad valorem import tariffs imposed by the home and foreign governments, respectively. Define $\tau \equiv 1 + t$ and $\tau^* \equiv 1 + t^*$. Then, I have $p = \tau p^w \equiv p(\tau, p^w)$ and $p^* = p^w / \tau^* \equiv p^*(\tau^*, p^w)$, where $p^w \equiv p_x^* / p_y$ is the world relative price.

Let S be a set of SPS measures. Let s_x and s_y^* be SPS measures imposed by the home and foreign governments with regard to their import good, respectively, where $s_x, s_y^* \in S$.

For the home country, imports of x are represented as $M_x(s_x, p(\tau, p^w), p^w)$ and exports of y, are denoted as $E_y(p(\tau, p^w), p^w)$. Foreign imports of y, M_y^* and foreign exports of y, E_x^*, are defined analogously. In these import demand and export supply functions of the home and foreign country, s_x and s_y^* act as shift parameters. From the conditions of balanced trade, I have

$$p^w M_x\left(s_x, p\left(\tau, p^w\right), p^w\right) = E_y\left(p\left(\tau, p^w\right), p^w\right) \tag{A1}$$

$$M_y^*\left(s_y^*, p^*\left(\tau^*, p^w\right), p^w\right) = p^w E_x^*\left(p^*\left(\tau^*, p^w\right), p^w\right) \tag{A2}$$

The equilibrium world price $\tilde{p}^w(\tau, s_x, \tau^*, s_y^*)$ is determined by the x market clearing condition:

$$M_x\left(s_x, p\left(\tau, \tilde{p}^w\right), \tilde{p}^w\right) = E_x^*\left(p^*\left(\tau^*, \tilde{p}^w\right), \tilde{p}^w\right) \tag{A3}$$

with market clearing for y. I assume that the Marshall-Lerner stability conditions are satisfied, so that an inward shift of the home (respectively, foreign) import demand curve will result in a lower (respectively, higher) equilibrium world price. I also assume that $dp/d\tau > 0 > dp^*/d\tau^*$ to avoid the Metzler paradox and $\partial\tilde{p}^w/\partial\tau < 0 < \partial\tilde{p}^w/\partial\tau^*$ to avoid the Lerner paradox. Furthermore, I assume that

$$\frac{\partial M_x\left(s_x, p\left(\tau, p^w\right), p^w\right)}{\partial s_x} < 0 \text{ and } \frac{\partial M_y^*\left(s_y^*, p^*\left(\tau^*, p^w\right), p^w\right)}{\partial s_y^*} < 0 \tag{A4}$$

These assumptions together with the stability assumptions imply

$$\frac{\partial \tilde{p}^w\left(\tau, s_x, \tau^*, s_y^*\right)}{\partial s_x} < 0 \text{ and } \frac{\partial \tilde{p}^w\left(\tau, s_x, \tau^*, s_y^*\right)}{\partial s_y^*} > 0. \quad \text{(A5)}$$

I represent social welfare of the home and foreign country by general functions

$$W\left(s_x, p\left(\tau, \tilde{p}^w\right), \tilde{p}^w\right) \text{ and } W^*\left(s_y^*, p\left(\tau^*, \tilde{p}^w\right), \tilde{p}^w\right)$$

respectively. I assume that

$$\frac{\partial W\left(s_x, p, \tilde{p}^w\right)}{\partial p^w} < 0 \text{ and } \frac{\partial W^*\left(s_y^*, p^*, \tilde{p}^w\right)}{\partial p^w} > 0. \quad \text{(A6)}$$

The SPS protection level in the home and foreign countries are denoted as

$$R = f\left(s_x\right) \text{ and } R^* = f\left(s_y^*\right) \text{ respectively, where } R, R^* \in \left[0, R^{Max}\right]$$

and $f(\cdot)$ is non-increasing in its argument.

Efficient policy choices are identical to those shown by Bagwell and Staiger (2001). That is, any efficient policies (τ^E, s_x^E, τ^{*E}, s_y^{*E}) solve

$$\begin{aligned} &\max_{\tau, s_x, \tau^*, s_y^*} W\left(s_x, p\left(\tau, p^w\right), \tilde{p}^w\right) \\ &\text{subject to } W^*\left(s_x, p\left(\tau^*, \tilde{p}^w\right), \tilde{p}^w\right) \geq \tilde{W}^{*E} \end{aligned} \quad \text{(A7)}$$

where

$$\tilde{W}^{*E} \equiv W^*\left(s_y^{*E}, p\left(\tau^{*E}, \tilde{p}^{wE}\right), \tilde{p}^{wE}\right) \text{ and } \tilde{p}^{wE} \equiv \tilde{p}^w\left(\tau^E, s_x^E, \tau^{*E}, s_y^{*E}\right).$$

The first-order conditions (FOCs) are given by

$$W_s\left(\frac{1}{\partial \tilde{p}^w / \partial s_x}\right) = W_p\left(\frac{\tilde{p}^w}{\partial \tilde{p}^w / \partial \tau}\right), \quad \text{(A8)}$$

$$W_{s_y^*}^*\left(\frac{1}{\partial \tilde{p}^w / \partial s_y^*}\right) = W_{p^*}^*\left(\frac{-p^* / \tau^*}{\partial \tilde{p}^w / \partial \tau^*}\right), \quad \text{(A9)}$$

and

$$\left(1-AW_{p}\right)\left(1-A^{*}W^{*}_{p^{*}}\right)=1 \tag{A10}$$

where subscripts mean partial derivatives and

$$A\equiv\frac{\left(1-\tau\lambda\right)}{\left(W_{p}+\lambda W_{p^{w}}\right)} \text{ and } A^{*}\equiv\frac{\left(1-\lambda^{*}/\tau^{*}\right)}{\left(W^{*}_{p^{*}}+\lambda^{*}W^{*}_{p^{w}}\right)}$$

where

$$\lambda\equiv\frac{\partial\tilde{p}^{w}/\partial\tau}{dp/d\tau}<0 \text{ and } \lambda^{*}\equiv\frac{\partial\tilde{p}^{w}/\partial\tau^{*}}{dp^{*}/d\tau^{*}}<0.$$

The *efficient SPS protection level*, R^{E} and R^{*E}, is also given by

$$R^{E}=f\left(s_{x}^{E}\right) \text{ and } R^{*E}=f\left(s_{y}^{*E}\right). \tag{A11}$$

I now turn to the case in which the SPS Agreement is entered into force. Let $\bar{R}$ and $\bar{R}^{*}$ be ALOPs of the home and foreign country, respectively. Let $\bar{R}_{x}^{w}$ and $\bar{R}_{y}^{w}$ be the SPS protection levels with regard to x and y, respectively, set by the relevant international organizations, such as the Codex, the OIE and IPPC. Then, the SPS Agreement requires $\bar{R}\geq\bar{R}_{x}^{w}$ and $\bar{R}^{*}\geq\bar{R}_{y}^{w}$. However, it also allows ALOPs to be more stringent than $\bar{R}_{x}^{w}$ or $\bar{R}_{y}^{w}$, if there is a scientific justification. Moreover, since the SPS Agreement requires SPS measures to be least trade-restrictive, if there exist $s_{x}', s_{x}''\in S$ such that

$$R'=f(s_{x}') \text{ and } R''=f(s_{x}'') \text{ and } R'=R''\equiv\hat{R},$$

then the home country has to choose s_{x}' such that

$$M_{x}\left(s_{x}',p,p^{w}\right)\geq M_{x}\left(s_{x}'',p,p^{w}\right).$$

for all s_{x}'' such that $\hat{R}=f(s_{x}'')$.

A similar proposition rule applies to the foreign country.

Let $(\bar{\tau},\bar{\tau}^{*},s_{x}^{u},s_{y}^{*u})$ be a combination of policies in Nash equilibrium without the SPS Agreement. Denote $R^{u}=f(s_{x}^{u})$ and $R^{*u}=f(s_{y}^{*u})$. Then the following propositions are obtained.

Proposition 1. Assume that there is a negotiated pair of tariff bindings $(\bar{\tau}, \bar{\tau}^*)$. Suppose that $\bar{R}$ and $\bar{R}^*$ conform to $\bar{R}^w_x$ or $\bar{R}^w_y$. (i) Consider $\bar{R}^w_x$ or $\bar{R}^w_y$ such that $R^u < \bar{R}^w_x \leq R^E$ and $R^{*u} < \bar{R}^w_y \leq R^{*E}$. If $dW/d\tau^* < 0$ and $dW^*/d\tau < 0$ hold at the non-cooperative choices of SPS measures, then the SPS Agreement, which induces reciprocal reductions in s_x and s^*_y from (s^u_y, s^{*u}_y), improves the social welfare of both countries, compared to the case without an SPS Agreement; (ii) If $(\bar{\tau}, \bar{\tau}^*) = (\bar{\tau}^E, \bar{\tau}^{*E})$ and $\bar{R}^w_x = R^E$ and $\bar{R}^w_y = R^{*E}$ hold, the SPS Agreement together with tariff negotiations achieves efficient outcomes.

Proof. (i) Let s^w_x and s^{*w}_y be SPS measures satisfying $\bar{R}^w_x = f(s^w_x)$ and $\bar{R}^w_y = f(s^{*w}_y)$, respectively. Then, although s^w_x and s^{*w}_y may not be uniquely determined, under the SPS Agreement $s^w_x < s^u_x$ and $s^{*w}_y < s^{*u}_y$ must hold for any s^w_x and s^{*w}_y such that $\bar{R}^w_x = f(s^w_x)$ and $\bar{R}^w_y = f(s^{*w}_y)$. Since $(\bar{\tau}, \bar{\tau}^*)$ is binding, governments cannot increase tariffs in response to decreases in s_x and s^*_y.

Given the partner country's SPS measure, the best responses of the home and foreign government are respectively defined by the FOCs:

$$W_s\left(\frac{1}{\partial\tilde{p}^w/\partial s_x}\right) = -\left(\tau W_p + W_{p^w}\right) \tag{A12}$$

$$W_{s^*_y}\left(\frac{1}{\partial\tilde{p}^w/\partial s^*_y}\right) = -\left(\frac{1}{\tau}W^*_{p^*} + W^*_{p^w}\right). \tag{A13}$$

Let

$$s^{BR}_x\left(s^*_y, \bar{\tau}, \bar{\tau}^*\right) \text{ and } s^{*BR}_y\left(s_x, \bar{\tau}, \bar{\tau}^*\right)$$

be the best-responses of the home and foreign country, respectively, which satisfy (A12) and (A13), respectively. By assumption (A6), the following inequalities hold:

$$\tilde{p}^w\left(\bar{\tau}, s^{BR}_x\left(s^{*W}_y\right), \bar{\tau}^*, s^{*W}_y\right) \leq \tilde{p}^w\left(\bar{\tau}, s^W_x, \bar{\tau}^*, s^{*W}_y\right);$$
$$\tilde{p}^w\left(\bar{\tau}, s^W_x, \bar{\tau}^*, s^{*BR}_y\left(s^W_x\right)\right) \geq \tilde{p}^w\left(\bar{\tau}, s^W_x, \bar{\tau}^*, s^{*W}_y\right).$$

Then, from (A5) these inequalities imply that

$$s^{BR}_x\left(s^{*w}_y\right) \geq s^w_x \text{ and } s^{*BR}_y\left(s^w_x\right) \geq s^{*w}_y.$$

At the point where s_x and s_y^* satisfy (A12) and (A13), respectively, a marginal change in s_x (respectively, s_y^*) has no first-order impact on W (respectively, W^*). The impacts of a change in the partner country's SPS measure on domestic welfare are given by

$$\frac{dW}{ds_y^*} = \left(\tau W_p + W_{p^w}\right)\frac{\partial \tilde{p}^w}{\partial s_y^*}, \text{ and } \frac{dW^*}{ds_x} = \left(\frac{1}{\tau^*}W_{p^*}^* + W_{p^w}^*\right)\frac{\partial \tilde{p}^w}{\partial s_x}.$$

Since

$$\frac{dW}{d\tau^*} = \left(\tau W_p + W_{p^w}\right)\frac{\partial \tilde{p}^w}{\partial \tau^*}, \text{ and } \frac{dW^*}{d\tau} = \left(\frac{1}{\tau^*}W_{p^*}^* + W_{p^w}^*\right)\frac{\partial \tilde{p}^w}{\partial \tau},$$

the assumptions of $dW/d\tau < 0$ and $dW^*/d\tau < 0$ with the assumption of $\partial\tilde{p}^w/\partial\tau < 0 < \delta\tilde{p}^w/\delta\tau^*$ imply that

$$\left(\tau W_p + W_{p^w}\right) < 0 \text{ and } \left(\frac{1}{\tau^*}W_{p^*}^* + W_{p^w}^*\right) > 0.$$

Then, from (A5) $dW/ds^* < 0$ and $dW/ds < 0$ hold, which establishes the intended result.

(ii) If $(\bar{\tau}, \bar{\tau}^*) = (\tau^E, \tau^{*E})$, $\bar{R}_x^w = R^E$ and $\bar{R}_y^w = R^{*E}$ hold, then $s_x \le s_y^E$ and $s_y^* \le s_y^{*E}$ must hold. By Article 5.6 of the SPS Agreement, s_x and s_y^* must satisfy respectively the following restrictions:

$$M_x\left(s_x, p\left(\tau^E, \hat{p}^w\right), \hat{p}^w\right) \ge M_x^E, \tag{A14}$$

$$M_y^*\left(s_y^*, p^*\left(\tau^{*E}, \hat{p}^w\right), \hat{p}^w\right) \ge M_y^{*E}, \tag{A15}$$

where M_x^E and M_y^{*E} denote home and foreign import volumes associated with a combination of the efficient policies $(\tau^E, s_x^E, \tau^{*E}, s_y^{*E})$. Then, conditions (A1) through (A3) together with stability assumptions imply that (A14) and (A15) can be rewritten as

$$\hat{p}^w\left(\tau^E, s_x, \tau^{*E}, s_y^*\right) \ge \tilde{p}^{wE}, \tag{A16}$$

$$\hat{p}^w\left(\tau^E, s_x, \tau^{*E}, s_y^*\right) \le \tilde{p}^{wE}, \tag{A17}$$

respectively, where $\tilde{p}^{wE}$ denotes the equilibrium world price associated with a combination of the efficient policies $(\tau^E, s_x^E, \tau^{*E}, s_y^{*E})$. Under assumption (A6), for a given s_y^*, the home government will choose s_x such that $\hat{p}^w(\tau^E, s_x^E, \tau^{*E}, s_y^{*E}) = \tilde{p}^{wE}$. Similarly, for a given s_x, the foreign government will choose s_y^* such that $\hat{p}^w(\tau^E, s_x^E, \tau^{*E}, s_y^{*E}) = \tilde{p}^{wE}$. This implies that the combination of (s_x, s_y^*) in Nash equilibrium is (s_x^E, s_y^{*E}). Q.E.D.

Proposition 2. Given a negotiated pair of tariff bindings $(\bar{\tau}, \bar{\tau}^*)$, if $\bar{R}_x^w$ and $\bar{R}_y^w$ are such that $R^u < \bar{R}_x^w \leq R^E$ and $R^{*u} < \bar{R}_y^w \leq R^{*E}$, a country has an incentive to set its ALOP at a level that is more stringent than $\bar{R}_x^w$ or $\bar{R}_y^w$, or to implement an overprotective SPS measure.

Proof. Given $(\bar{\tau}, \bar{\tau}^*)$ and $\bar{R}^* = \bar{R}_y^w$, if the home government sets $\bar{R} < \bar{R}_x^w$, under the assumption (A4) an SPS measure that corresponds to $\bar{R} = f(s_x)$ yields

$$M_x\left(s_x, p\left(\bar{\tau}, \tilde{p}^w\left(\bar{\tau}, s_x, \bar{\tau}^*, s_y^{*W}\right)\right), \tilde{p}^w\left(\bar{\tau}, s_x, \bar{\tau}^*, s_y^{*W}\right)\right) \qquad \text{(A18)}$$
$$< M_x\left(s_x^W, p\left(\bar{\tau}, \tilde{p}^{wR}\right), \tilde{p}^{wR}\right)$$

where

$$\tilde{p}^{wR} \equiv \tilde{p}^w\left(\bar{\tau}, s_x^W, \bar{\tau}^*, s_y^{*W}\right).$$

Then, under the stability assumptions, (A18) implies that

$$\tilde{p}^w\left(\bar{\tau}, s_x, \bar{\tau}^*, s_y^{*W}\right) < \tilde{p}^{wR}.$$

Thus, under assumption (A6),

$$W\left(s_x, p\left(\bar{\tau}, \tilde{p}^w\right), \tilde{p}^w\right) > W\left(s_x^W p\left(\bar{\tau}, \tilde{p}^{wR}\right), \tilde{p}^{wR}\right)$$

holds. When $\bar{R} < \bar{R}_x^w$, an overprotective s_x, which yields $f(s_x) < \bar{R}$ produces the same result. The case of the foreign country is proved in an analogous way. Q.E.D.

Notes

1 D. Roberts, 'Preliminary Assessment of the Effects of the WTO Agreement on Sanitary and Phytosanitary Trade Regulations', *Journal of International Economic Law* 1(3), 2004, 377–405. SPS measures are defined as measures that 'protect human, animal, or plant life and health within the territory of the Member from risks related to diseases, pests, and disease-carrying or -causing organisms, as well as additives, contaminants,

toxins or disease-causing organisms in food, beverages, or feedstuffs'. Roberts points out that SPS measures are defined with respect to the regulatory goal of a measure rather than the policy instrument itself. Thus, SPS measures cover any policy instrument affecting degrees of trade restriction, such as complete import bans, product and PPM standards, and labelling for informing the potential allergenicity of products.

2 Roberts, op. cit.

3 Panel Report, *Japan – Apples*. Japan restricted imports of US apples because Japan was concerned with the spread of fire blight, a bacterial disease that affects apple trees and other plants in the rose family. However, the Panel found that Japan's phytosanitary measures were inconsistent with Japan's WTO obligations.

4 Panel Report, *Australia – Salmon*. In 1975, Australia introduced a quarantine measure requiring salmon products to be heat-treated for certain prescribed durations and temperatures prior to importation. The reason was to prevent the introduction of pathogens that could be responsible for various fish diseases. In 2000, the WTO Panel found that Australia's measures affecting imports of Canadian salmon were inconsistent with Australia's WTO obligations.

5 For example, Australia, Japan, Mexico and the US inspect some import goods at the point of export in trading partner countries to reduce their risks, whereas the United Kingdom ('UK') inspects at the point of delivery in most cases. Although the inspection costs are much higher in the former system, it is accepted as appropriate to the risks faced, and reduces subsequent control costs of diseases and pests. See J. D. Mumford, 'Economic Issues Related to Quarantine in International Trade', *European Review of Agricultural Economics* 29(3), 2002, 329–48.

6 L. Calvin and B. Krissoff, 'Technical Barriers to Trade: A Case Study of Phytosanitary Barriers and US–Japanese Apple Trade', *Journal of Agricultural and Resource Economics* 23(2), 1998, 351–66.

7 S. James and K. Anderson, 'On the Need for More Economic Assessment of Quarantine Policies', *Australian Journal of Agricultural and Resource Economics* 42(4), 1998, 425–44 at 426.

8 Ibid.

9 K. Bagwell and R. W. Staiger, 'An Economic Theory of GATT', *American Economic Review* 89(1), 1999, 215–48. K. Bagwell and Robert W. Staiger, 'Domestic Policies, National Sovereignty, and International Economic Institutions', *Quarterly Journal of Economics* 116(2), 2001, 519–62.

10 M. Powell, 'Science in Sanitary and Phytosanitary Dispute Resolution', Resources for the Future, Washington, DC Discussion Paper 97–50, 1997. T. Christoforou, 'Settlement of Science-Based Trade Disputes in the WTO: A Critical Review of the Developing Case Law in The Face Of Scientific Uncertainty', *New York University Environmental Law Journal* 8(3), 2000, 622–48.

11 B. R. Copeland, 'Strategic Interaction among Nations: Negotiable and Non-Negotiable Trade Barriers', *Canadian Journal of Economics* 23(1), 1990, 84–108.

12 J. Ederington, 'International Coordination of Trade and Domestic Policies', *American Economic Review* 91(5), 2001, 1580–93. J. Ederington, 'Trade and Domestic Policy Linkage in International Agreements', *International Economic Review* 43(4), 2002, 1347–67. N. Limão, 'Trade Policy, Cross-Border Externalities and Lobbies: Do Linked Agreements Enforce More Cooperative Outcomes?', *Journal of International Economics* 67, 2005, 175–99.

13 T. Otsuki, J. S. Wilson and M. Sewadeh, 'What Price Precaution? European Harmonisation of Aflatoxin Regulations and African Groundnut Exports', *European Review of Agricultural Economics* 28(3), 2001, 263–83. T. Otsuki, J. S. Wilson and M. Sewadeh, 'Saving Two in a Billion: Quantifying the Trade Effect of European Food Safety Standards on African Exports', *Food Policy* 26(5), 2001, 495–514.

J. S. Wilson, T. Otsuki and B. Majumdar, 'Balancing Food Safety and Risk: Do Drug Residue Limits Affect International Trade in Beef?', *Journal of International Trade and Economic Development* 12(4), 2003, 377–402. C. Yue, J. C. Beghin and H. H. Jensen, 'Tariff Equivalent of Technical Barriers to Trade with Imperfect Substitution and Trade Costs', *American Journal of Agricultural Economics* 88(4), 2006, 947–60.

14 Roberts, op. cit.

15 D. Vogel, *Trading Up: Consumer and Environmental Regulation in a Global Economy.* Cambridge, MA: Harvard University Press, 1995, Chapter 5. Roberts, op. cit.

16 Roberts points out that animals and plants in the definition include natural fauna and flora as well as commercial livestock and crops. Thus, the regime of the SPS Agreement applies to measures intended to protect the natural environment from the risks associated from harmful exotic species.

17 Roberts, op. cit. p.383.

18 Roberts, op. cit. p.383.

19 Article 2.2.

20 Article 3.1. Annex A of the SPS Agreement makes specific reference to three international standard setting agencies. For food safety, it is the 'standards, guidelines and recommendations established by the Codex Alimentarius Commission relating to food additives, veterinary drug and pesticide residues, contaminants, methods of analysis and sampling, and codes and guidelines of hygienic practice' that are relevant. For animal health and zoonoses, 'the standards, guidelines and recommendations developed under the auspices of the International Office of Epizootics' (or the Office International des Epizzoties: OIE) apply. For plant health it is those developed 'under the auspices of the Secretariat of the International Plant Protection Convention ('IPPC')' in cooperation with its regional organizations. For any matters not covered by the Codex, the OIE or the IPPC, the SPS Committee has the authority to identify 'other relevant international organizations open for membership to all Members'.

21 Article 3.2.

22 Article 3.3.

23 Article 5.1.

24 Appellate Body Report, *EC – Hormones.*

25 Appellate Body Report, *Japan – Agricultural Products II.*

26 Panel Report, *Australia – Salmon.*

27 Panel Report, *Japan – Apples.*

28 Codex Alimentarius Commission. 2003. *Procedural Manual, 13th edition.*

29 N. Jinji, 'On the Economic Significance of the SPS Agreement', in K. Yamashita (ed.), *Food Safety and Trade: Law and Economics on the SPS Agreement of the WTO*, Tokyo: Nihon-Hyoronsha, 2008, pp. 231–56 (in Japanese).

30 For example, in the case of hormone beef dispute in the period of the pre-Uruguay Round, when a ban imposed by the EC on imports of hormone-treated beef went in force in 1989, the US implemented retaliatory measures in the form of 100 per cent duties on some EC products, such as beef, tomatoes and fruit juices.

31 Some SPS measures are also employed towards export goods. However, trade disputes involving SPS measures usually occur when importing countries impose more stringent SPS measures than exporting countries do. Thus, it is not the focus of this chapter to analyse SPS measures with regard to exporting goods. I assume that SPS measures with regard to export goods are set at some basic level.

32 This is particularly true for biological stressors. It is argued that 'there may be large, irreducible uncertainties in predicting the effects of biological stressors' because, unlike chemical stressors, biological organisms grow, reproduce, disperse both actively and passively, interact with ecosystems in ways that are hard to predict, and evolve largely

randomly. Powell, op. cit. pp.5. See D. Simberloff and M. Alexander, 'Biological Stressors' in Ecological Risk Assessment Issue Papers, 1994, EPA/630/R-94/009, Washington, DC: US Environmental Protection Agency.

33 See, for instance, J. Pauwelyn, 'The WTO Agreement on Sanitary and Phytosanitary (SPS) Measures as Applied in the First Three SPS Disputes: *EC – Hormones, Australia – Salmon* and *Japan – Varietals*', *Journal of International Economic Law* 2(4), 1998, 641–64; B. Mercurio and D. Shao, 'A Precautionary Approach to Decision Making: The Evolving Jurisprudence on Article 5.7 of the SPS Agreement', *Trade, Law and Development* 2(2), 2010, 195–223, at 215–16.

34 Appellate Body Report, *Australia – Salmon.* Appellate Body Report, *EC – Hormones.*

35 Roberts, op. cit.

36 Pauwelyn, op. cit. pp. 649.

37 Christoforou argues there are potential procedural issues at the Dispute Settlement Body ('DSB') of the WTO when science-based trade disputes are dealt with. He points out that the procedural rules of the DSB may contribute to multiple or biased views over scientific information.

Part II

Trade in services

Technology

5 When trade encounters technology

The role of the technological neutrality principle in the development of WTO rules

Jia-Xiang Hu[1]

5.1 Introduction

The principle of technological neutrality originates from electronic commerce, referring to the presumption that the law should have the same application to electronic commerce regardless of what the transaction means. Paragraph 4 of the Work Program on Electronic Commerce-Progress Report to the General Council adopted by the WTO Council for Trade in Services on 19 July 1999 provides that '[i]t was also the general view that the GATS is technologically neutral in the sense that it does not contain any provisions that distinguish between the different technological means through which a service may be supplied'.[2]

The principle of technological neutrality was first formally raised in the dispute settlement of *US – Gambling*. While in defining the sphere of 'cross-border service supply', the Panel assumed that mode 1 under the GATS encompassed all possible means of supplying services from the territory of one WTO member into the territory of another. Therefore, a market access commitment of mode 1 implies the right for other members' suppliers to supply a service through all means of delivery, whether by mail, telephone, Internet, etc., unless otherwise specified in a member's schedule.[3] Based on this reasoning, the Panel concluded that the US Wire Act, which prohibited the service suppliers from supplying gambling and betting services through telephone, Internet and other means of delivery using wire communication, contained a limitation to the service 'in the form of numerical quotas' within the meaning of Article XVI:2 (a) and a limitation to the service 'in the form of quotas or requirement of an economic needs test' within the meaning of Article XVI:2 (c) of the GATS.[4]

This principle was quoted once more during the dispute settlement of *China – Publications and Audiovisual Products*. With regard to the US arguments, the Panel provided that 'we have already found that the core meaning of China's commitment on these services includes the distribution of audio content on non-physical media. The principle of technological neutrality might have come into play had we found that China's commitment covered distribution on physical media and that there was doubt about whether it also covered the distribution of content on non-physical media. But this was not the case here.'[5] In other words, the Panel did not deny the applicability of this principle in defining the means of supplying services. As a matter of fact, it basically accepted the Panel's conclusions of the *US –Gambling* case on the relevant issue that a commitment including all means of delivery was in line with the principle of technological neutrality.[6]

5.2 The applicability of the principle of technological neutrality in electronic commerce

The Internet has brought people together from different parts of the world. It has changed the way of modern communications and even our daily lives in many respects. People can now purchase what they need on the Internet instead of going to the markets in person.[7] They can receive online education and professional consultancy. A substantial part of the current electronic commerce sites on the Web are in English, although sites in other languages and in multiple languages are appearing with increasing frequency. Once the language barrier is overcome, the technology exists for any business to conduct electronic commerce with any other business and for consumers anywhere in the world.

A number of competing definitions of electronic commerce are found in the literature with some suggesting that it encompasses all forms of electronic interaction between businesses. This definition tends to overlook the role of consumers in the exchanges through electronic means. Similarly, the International Data Corporation ('IDC') claims that 'electronic commerce is broadly defined as the exchange of business documents in an electronic format', which limits electronic commerce to office work.[8] Another definition is that electronic commerce is 'a broad term describing business activities with associated technical data that are conducted electronically'. A wider definition is that 'the goal of electronic commerce is to mould the vast network of small businesses, government agencies, large corporations, and independent contractors into a single community with the ability to communicate with one another seamlessly across any computer platform'.[9]

While there are many more definitions of electronic commerce in theory, there are also different types of electronic commerce in practice. For example, Kalakota and Whinston listed three types of it as follows: (1) inter-organizational-business to business, i.e. from one company to another company; (2) intra-organizational-within business, i.e. exchanges in the same company; and (3) extra-organizational-business to customer, i.e. the provision of service.[10] At the most basic level, electronic commerce is about doing business electronically. It is based on the electronic processing and transmitting of data, including text, sound and video.

Electronic commerce includes activities such as electronic trading of goods and services, online delivery of digital content, online education and professional consultancy, electronic fund transfers, electronic share trading, electronic bills of lading, electronic ticket booking and hotel reserving, commercial auctions, collaborative design and engineering, online sourcing, public procurement, direct consumer marketing and after-sales service. It involves both products (e.g. consumer goods, specialized medical equipment) and services (e.g. information services, financial and legal services); traditional activities (e.g. health care, education) and new activities (e.g. virtual malls).[11]

Electronic commerce is not new to many of us. Companies have exchanged business data over a variety of communication networks for many years. The media prefer the Internet to newspapers and magazines in providing news. Even broadcasting and TV stations send their programmes through digital means. The services of search engines provided by companies like Google and Baidu have become a big business. There is now accelerated expansion and radical changes are being driven by the exponential growth of the Internet. In terms of trading, the most obvious advantage of electronic commerce is to increase sales and decrease costs. Advertising done well on the Web can get even a small company's promotional message out to the potential customers in every country in the world. A company can use electronic commerce to reach narrow market segments that are geographically scattered. With the help of the Internet, students in remote areas can receive their education at home without bothering to attend schools. The Web is particularly useful in creating virtual communities that have become ideal target markets for specific types of product or service.

Just as electronic commerce increases business opportunities for the sellers, it also provides the buyers with a wider range of choices than traditional commerce because they can consider more offers of different products and services from sellers. Electronic commerce saves time for customers and is available for them to access 24 hours a day, every day, without worrying about the closing time of the 'shops'. Some buyers prefer to gather a great deal of information before deciding on a purchase. Electronic commerce helps them to easily compare the details from the information they obtain about a prospective purchase.

In spite of the above advantages, many businesses are still facing legal and cultural obstacles in conducting electronic commerce. Some customers are fearful of releasing their private information by sending credit card numbers over the Internet. Others are simply resistant in changing their way of shopping and feel uncomfortable with viewing merchandise on a computer screen rather than communicating with the sellers in person. The legal environment in which electronic commerce is conducted is full of unclear and conflicting laws. The Internet has united customers of different countries that still hold different attitudes towards electronic commerce. In many cases, government regulators have not kept up with the development of new technologies.[12] This is a particularly demanding issue in some developing countries.

While the Internet provides developed countries with opportunities to delocalize services that require heavy labour in developing countries, the electronic commerce revenue in many developing countries is miniscule in comparison with that in developed countries. Many factors may be used to explain this phenomenon. Government policies, shopping habits and basic facilities may all be accountable. But most of all is the lack of technology. The current electronic commerce transactions mainly occur between customers and sellers in developed countries like the United States, Canada and Western Europe. As for many developing countries, the majority of the population sticks to the traditional way of trading either out of cultural customs or owing to technology limits. Even in mainland China where the information technology is comparatively advanced, the merchandise purchased through the Internet in 2010 is only RMB 513.1 billion, which is around 3 per cent of the national total retailing volume.[13]

The current state of electronic commerce in many developing countries is similar to what it was in the United States in the late 1990s. Owing to the lack of professional expertise and incomplete regulations, the uncertainties of the legal environment in these countries are so significant during financial transactions that financial embezzlement is a real risk with electronic commerce. Such fraudulent activities can cause companies' financial losses, either in monetary terms or in equipment or goods. Customers may be cheated without getting any compensation. This is a crucial factor that can heavily discourage developing countries' businesses to join the electronic commerce market. For electronic commerce to be truly a tool for trade in developing countries, a 'secure infrastructure' that makes the electronic exchange of financial transactions safe is a necessary prerequisite.[14] This, however, can be realized only with efforts from both the relevant countries and the international community.

Electronic commerce is by its nature 'international'. This means that its efficient regulation needs the cooperation of different countries. International organizations, particularly trade organizations, are among the first to recognize the significance of the electronic commerce revolution and the corresponding need to provide rules and guidance. Several of these organizations' responses have become international practice or law. In 1996, the UN Commission on International Trade Law released what is now the most popular model for customer protection in an electronic transaction. The UNCITRAL Model Law on Electronic Commerce (the 'Model Law') is intended to provide national legislatures with a template of internationally acceptable rules that remove existing legal obstacles and create a more secure legal environment for electronic commerce.[15] It has provided a general guideline for national governments to supervise transactions through the Internet, including standard ways to assess the legal value of electronic messages and legal rules for electronic commerce in specific areas such as carriage of goods.[16]

Electronic commerce, by its physical characteristics, is the transaction achieved through non-physical media. The rapid development of information technology has made it possible to improve transaction means e.g. from the Internet to the IOT ('Internet of Things'). Based on the connection of different websites, people trade with each other on the Internet. They sign their contracts and pay for their purchases electronically regardless of any specific instrumentality. In this regard, the media through which their transactions are realized have no fundamental difference. With the general guidance of the Model Law and the respective regulation of the national legislations, the principle of technological neutrality may be applicable to electronic commerce in some countries.

5.3 The relevance of the principle of technological neutrality in WTO rules on trade of services

In March 1998, the World Trade Organization released a research paper titled '*Electronic Commerce and the Role of the WTO*'. This paper recognizes the benefits of the use of the Internet to international trade, and asserts that the Internet, as an instrument for international trade, will fall under regulation by the GATS. The stated goal of the WTO, according to this paper in regard to electronic commerce, is not to create a set of new rules to govern the electronic marketplace, but to use the existing frameworks to regulate it. The WTO agreements that deal with electronic commerce issues operate in conjunction with the GATS, the TRIPS and the Agreement on Basic Telecommunications Services. Under the guidelines of these multilateral agreements, the commitments on market accession to trade of service delivered by WTO members are also relevant.

The Progress Report on Electronic Commerce prepared in 1999 by the WTO Council for Trade in Services for the General Council provided that

> [t]he electronic delivery of services falls within the scope of the GATS since the Agreement applies to all services regardless of the means by which they are delivered. . . . Measures affecting the electronic delivery of services are measures affecting trade in services and would therefore be covered by the GATS obligations. All GATS provisions, whether relating to general obligations (e.g. MFN, transparency, domestic regulation, competition, payments and transfers, etc.) or specific commitments (market access, national treatment or additional commitments) are applicable to the supply of services through electronic means. . . . There is still a need to clarify whether certain products delivered electronically might be classified as goods, and therefore subject to GATT disciplines, rather than as services.

The WTO is often stymied in its attempt to push a reformist agenda owing to the *realpolitik* of international trade negotiations, and its work in the *milieu* of electronic commerce is no different.[17] The negotiations during the Uruguay Round on trade of service only resulted in a basic GATS document. The WTO permitted its members to delineate their specific commitments on market access in this area. Even so, WTO members tend to have different views on the means of delivery of service within the commitments owing to the innovations of technology.

With strong regional and domestic factors as considerations, WTO members often find themselves in a position struggling to find consensus even on small issues of trade. Therefore, it is largely unsurprising that only limited progress has been made in the ongoing process of developing agreements on electronic commerce. The difficulties of developing a sound policy are increased by the plethora of competing interests and contradictory objectives and the huge gap of computer technology development among WTO members. Having experienced the unhappy time of the Doha Round negotiations, which dealt with the trade of the tangibles, WTO members may well predict that the difficulties arising from the intangible realm of the Internet are unlikely to be overcome in near future.

Apart from the technology factor, the compatibility of the law and principles applicable in electronic commerce with the WTO rules on trade in services is another issue that deserves further debate. Unlike trade of goods, trade of services is a new area regulated by multilateral trade agreements and the impact of WTO rules on members in this area is different because of different commitments. Furthermore, the means to deliver services are different from those of delivering goods, which are more likely to be affected by the development of technology, including the Internet. The difference of realizing the importance of the Internet among WTO members is obvious, not to mention their domestic laws and regulations.

The WTO is acting as the government of member governments in regulating measures on trade in goods, trade in services and the trade-related aspects of intellectual property right protection. The 159 WTO members range from the most developed countries to the least developed countries. The WTO Agreement and those annexed under it bind all the members. Any new rules or interpretations should help to preserve the rights and obligations of members, and to clarify the provisions of WTO agreements in accordance with customary rules of interpretation of public international law.[18]

In the case of *US – Gasoline*, the Appellate Body noted that 'the general rule of interpretation' set out in Article 31 of the Vienna Convention on the Interpretation of Treaties has been relied upon by all contesting parties and third parties in the WTO dispute settlement procedures, although not always in relation to the same issue. As such, it forms part of the 'customary rules of interpretation of public international law' as defined in paragraph 2 of Article 3 of DSU.[19] Furthermore, the Appellate Body, in doing so, acknowledged that the WTO is not a hermetically closed regime,[20] impermeable to the other rules of international law. In other words, the Appellate Body has 'connected' the GATT/WTO sub-system of law to the rest of the international legal order and imposed on panels and WTO members the obligation to interpret the WTO agreements as any other international treaty, thereby putting an end to what Kuyper has termed 'GATT panels' ignorance'[21] of the basic rules of treaty interpretation. In other words, WTO rules are just part of the international law regime.

With the help of the technological innovations of the Internet, international trade in services is currently conducted to a very large and increasing extent through electronic means. The revolution in information technology has caused many services that were previously regarded as essentially non-tradable to be recognized as eminently tradable as potentially important contributors to international trade and development. More than any other factor, this has overturned the old misconception of 'trade in services' as a contradiction in terms. Cross-border trade of services in particular can be greatly facilitated by the availability of electronic means of delivery and the ease with which service products can be converted into digitized information flow,[22] which should be distinguished from the supply of other services through the medium of the Internet. The digitized form of service products is the updated type of service, which is different from its previous type both in the form of expression and in the form of delivery.

Trade in services became one of the areas regulated with multilateral trade agreements only after the WTO was set up in 1995. As the basic legal document of trade in services, the GATS itself makes no distinction between the different technological means by which a service may be delivered, whether in person, by mail, by telephone or across the Internet. Although the development of information technology during the Uruguay Round negotiations was capable of supporting the supply of some services through electronic means, it did not necessary mean that this technology was widely used in international trade at that time. While the computer and the Internet have become household necessities in many developed countries, they are still unreachable to many families in some underdeveloped countries. Therefore, it still remains debatable whether delivery of service by electronic means is covered by the GATS in the same way as all other means of delivery.

The regime of trade in services is different from that of trade in goods, which has evolved for more than six decades and has a complete set of rules covering both tariff and non-tariff issues. The GATS was the only legal instrument available when the Uruguay Round negotiations came to an end. Although the WTO rules have covered all service sectors except those supplied in the exercise of governmental authority, the scope of binding commitments under it is different for different members. Each member is obliged to keep its measures on trade in services in accordance with the WTO rules to the extent of its commitments. The market access of trade in services is regulated with the general rules of the GATS together with the specific commitments of each member. The multilateral trade agreements in specific service sectors like basic telecommunications can only be reached with further negotiations.

Contrary to this, the 12 multilateral trade agreements affiliated with Annex 1A of the WTO Agreement, under the guidelines of GATT 1994, provide the specific rules on regulating the relevant sectors of trade in goods. Some of them, like the Anti-dumping Agreement and the SCM Agreement, contain substantial and procedural rules directing WTO members to be consistent in both lawmaking and the measures taken. Since the trading goods are 'tangible', people tend to care more about the market access with tariff rates and those non-tariff measures. When the services are 'intangible' in nature, people are more concerned with the technological means of delivering services and the qualifications of the service suppliers.

In the post-Uruguay negotiations on basic telecommunications, the Chairman proposed in January 1997 an interpretative note, which was adopted by the Special Group on Basic Telecommunications and attached to its report to the Council for Trade in Services. This note confirmed the principle that commitments undertaken in basic telecommunications were technologically neutral, i.e. in the absence of an indication to the contrary, any commitment would be assumed to cover local, long distance and international services for public and non-public use, on a facilities or resale basis, and using any technological means of supply (cable, radio, satellite, Internet, etc.). This list may even be extended with the development of technology.

Telecommunication services are an essential part of the infrastructure for electronic commerce. The GATS commitments on telecommunication services have great value in ensuring access to this infrastructure. The Internet, while originally viewed as a computer service, has developed with the convergence of telecoms and computer technology and is widely considered a telecoms service. There are also several others among the services that can be delivered across the Internet. According to the above-mentioned note, if the interpretation on the technological neutrality of basic telecommunications commitments is acceptable, then the commitments on voice, fax and data, for example, would all be included in the provision of such services over the Internet, unless it is stipulated to the contrary in the schedule. This deserves a wider consensus among WTO members as many of them did not think about these issues in making their commitments during the Uruguay negotiations.

The commitments made by WTO members on basic telecommunications are an ad hoc area under the GATS legal framework. Although there is no interpretation in Annex 1B like the general interpretative note to Annex 1A[23] on the relationship between GATS and other agreements made afterwards, it is still not difficult to conclude that the legal effect of the interpretative note proposed by the Chairman of the Special Group on Basic Telecommunications is only limited to the basic telecommunications commitments, and is not yet extended to other sectors in the same regime. Furthermore, the Agreement on Basic Telecommunications Services has been accepted only by some WTO members. It cannot be claimed that the technological neutrality principle is applicable to all service sectors.

The WTO Agreement contains one article that delineates the basic rules on the amendments of multilateral trade agreements. Paragraph 3 of Article X provides that

> [a]mendments to provisions of this (WTO) Agreement, or of the Multilateral Trade Agreements in Annexes 1A and 1C . . . of a nature

> that would alter the rights and obligations of the Members, shall take effect for the Members that have accepted them upon acceptance by two thirds of the Members and thereafter for each other Member upon acceptance by it.

This provision excludes Annex 1B (GATS) from the applicability of this paragraph. This is owing to the fact that GATS binds the WTO members through their specific commitments. Unlike Annexes 1A and 1C, WTO members have not made uniform commitments under Annex 1B. Therefore, the conclusions on the relationships between the GATS provisions and the commitments made by those WTO members in specific sectors can only be derived from the relevant articles of GATS.

Paragraph 1 of GATS Article XIX (Negotiation of Specific Commitments) partly provides that:

> Members shall enter into successive rounds of negotiations . . . with a view to achieving a progressively higher level of liberalization. Such negotiations shall be directed to the reduction or elimination of the adverse effects on trade in services of measures as a means of providing effective market access. This process shall take place with a view to promoting the interests of all participants on a mutually advantageous basis and to securing an overall balance of rights and obligations.

In view of the bigger gap in trade of services than in trade of goods, it is predictable that there is still a long way to go before WTO members achieve this goal.

Following the vein of Article XIX of the GATS, we can conclude that the definition of GATS obligations of each member should be based on the textual expressions in its commitments schedule. The principle of technological neutrality referred to by the Panel in *US – Gambling* as 'largely shared among WTO Members' has never appeared on any WTO agreements or official documents. Since the attitudes of WTO members to this issue are obviously diverse, it is hard to declare that this principle has received consensus from WTO members. The Progress Report on the Work Program on Electronic Commerce admitted at the end of it that 'some delegations expressed a view that these issues were complex and needed further examination'.[24] In view of this, the statement made by the Progress Report cannot be considered as to 'promote the interests of all participants on a mutually advantageous basis and to secure an overall balance of rights and obligations'.

5.4 The principle of technological neutrality in the practice of the WTO dispute settlement

While interpreting 'mode 1' (from the territory of one member into the territory of any other member) defined by Article 1:2(a) of the GATS, the Panel of *US*

– *Gambling* considered that this definition did not contain any indication as to the means that could be used to supply cross-border services. In the view of the Panel, this indicated that the GATS, by its nature, did not limit the various technologically possible means of delivery under mode 1.[25] Paragraph 19 of the Scheduling Guidelines defines 'cross-border supply' as 'International transport', and states that

> the supply of a service through telecommunications or mail, services embodied in exported goods (e.g. a computer diskette, or drawings) are all examples of cross-border supply since the service is not present within the territory of the Member where the service is delivered.

The Panel then concluded that mode 1 under GATS encompasses all possible means of supplying services from the territory of one WTO member into that of another. Therefore, a market access commitment under mode 1 implies the right of other members' suppliers to supply a service through all means of delivery, whether by mail, telephone, Internet, etc., unless otherwise specified in a member's schedule.[26]

According to the Panel of *US – Gambling*, if one, several or all means of delivery of cross-border services are prohibited, the opportunities for foreign markets are clearly reduced, if not nullified. If a member desires to exclude market access with respect to the supply of a service through one, several or all means of delivery included in mode 1, it should do so explicitly in its schedule.[27] The Panel considered that any other interpretation would result in the nullification of benefits of a commitment made for mode 1 as members could, through regulations, impose restrictions or prohibitions essentially on one, several or all means of delivery.

The Panel's explanation was that since WTO members were not required to provide the same level of market access in services, each of them defined its specific commitments before entering the WTO. When a member inscribed the word 'None' in a specific market access column of its schedule for mode 1, it was more often regarded as committing itself not to maintain measures that would prohibit the use of one, several or all means of delivery under mode 1 in the relevant sector or subsector. This was especially so in sectors and subsectors where the delivery means, like the cross-border supply, were effected essentially if not exclusively through the Internet.[28]

Based on the above analysis, the Panel of *US – Gambling* concluded that the United States' schedule under GATS included specific commitments on gambling and betting services under subsector 10.D. By maintaining the measures that, on their face, prohibited one, several or all means of delivery included in mode 1, contrary to its specific market access commitments for gambling and betting services for mode 1, the United States failed to accord services and service suppliers of Antigua treatment no less favourable than that provided for under the terms, limitations and conditions agreed and specified in its schedule, contrary to Article XVI:1 and Article XVI:2 of the GATS.[29]

The controversial issue in *China – Publications and Audiovisual Products* is the means of supplying services (including sound recording distribution services) for audiovisual home entertainment products. The United States argued that any practical differences existing between the supply of sound recordings in physical and non-physical forms were simply differences with respect to the 'means of delivery' as elaborated by the *US – Gambling* Panel. According to the principle of technological neutrality, these differences were not relevant to the interpretation of the scope of a GATS commitment unless they were specified in a member's schedule. The United States further pointed out that the principle of technological neutrality was supported by the Panel of *US – Gambling*.[30]

China argued that the principle of technological neutrality had never been formally accepted by WTO members. Even if the principle had been supported by the Panel of *US – Gambling*, China claimed that it only applied to different technologies used in the supply of the same service, which was not the case with respect to the distribution of sound recordings in non-physical as compared to physical form. For China, the services that were distributed on a non-physical medium were different services ('network music services') and not 'sound recording distribution services' as it made the commitments in its schedule.

Furthermore, China argued that it was necessary to examine the following factors with respect to the two service activities in order to determine whether they constituted the same or different services: (1) essential operational characteristics; (2) perception of the end-users; (3) international classification; and (4) the applicable internationally recognized legal framework. In the view of China, these factors varied case by case, with no single one being decisive.[31] The listed four factors, applied to the services at issue, were sufficiently divergent from the distribution of sound recordings using physical media. Thus, according to China, the services at issue, which involved the use of non-physical media, did not fall within China's commitment on sound recording distribution services. The 'network music services' were different, and for that reason the principle of technological neutrality was not applicable.[32]

The Panel first pointed out that China did not specify the medium through which the audio content was distributed when it chose to inscribe in its schedule 'sound recording distribution services'. According to the Panel, a member is free on whether it would add precision to its schedule by qualifying the terms of the commitment. A member might add descriptive terms that specifically exclude a service supplied in a certain way, or include that service under a different heading with different commitments. It might also add precision by referring directly to a product classification system such as that contained in WTO document (W/120) or CPC, but China had not done so. In the view of the Panel, a reference to an external classification system was in fact recommended in the Schedule Guidelines.[33]

With regard to the principle of technological neutrality raised by the United States, the Panel provided that

> in interpreting China's commitments on 'sound recording distribution services', we have no need to invoke a principle of technological neutrality. We have already found that the core meaning of China's commitment on these services includes the distribution of audio content on non-physical media. The principle of technological neutrality might have come into play, had we found that China's commitment covered distribution on physical media and that there was doubt about whether it also covered the distribution of content on non-physical media. But this was not the case here.[34]

In other words, the Panel did not deny the applicability of this principle in defining the means of delivering services. As a matter of fact, it basically accepted the Panel conclusions of *US – Gambling* on the concerned issue, i.e. that a commitment including all means of delivery was in line with this principle.

From the perspective of technological development, it might be reasonable to derive the principle of technological neutrality from elaborating the implementation of the GATS commitments for each WTO member. The development of information technology has changed all respects of our lives, including the means of delivering services. People may sell or buy publications and music products in a 'non-physical form' through the Internet. Customers can consume online services such as professional consultation, medical treatment or education without bothering to meet the service supplier in person. International trade in services is currently conducted to a very large and increasing extent through electronic means. Indeed, the revolution appearing in information technology has caused the delivery of many services, previously regarded as essentially in physical form, to be recognized as eminently in non-physical form and as potentially important contributors to international trade and development.

Meanwhile, in regard to the interpretation of law, the principle of technological neutrality remains to be debated. Article 3(3) of the DSU provides that WTO members recognize that one of the functions for dispute settlement is to 'clarify the existing provisions of those agreements in accordance with customary rules of interpretation of public international law'. The 'customary rules' are normally referred to the provisions of the Vienna Convention on the Law of Treaties. In spite of the fact that some WTO members, including the United States, have not accepted the Vienna Convention, this convention has widely been used by international dispute settlement institutions including the WTO Dispute Settlement Body. According to Article 31 of the Vienna Convention, a treaty shall be interpreted in good faith in accordance with its text, relevant instruments, and any subsequent agreement, practice or relevant rules of international law. Without these materials, a special meaning shall be given to a term if it is established that the parties so intended.

The implementation of one's commitments concerning trade in goods is different from that concerning trade in services. WTO members are required to fix tariff rates in accordance with their concessions on market accession for trade in goods. As for trade in services, they usually choose to define the specific sectors open for foreign services and service suppliers with a list annexed to the schedule of their commitments under GATS. China did include in Item 2-D (Audiovisual Services) of the Schedule of Specific Commitments on Services the following three sectors that are available for foreign services and service suppliers: (1) audiovisual services; (2) videos, including entertainment software and (CPC 83202) distribution services; and (3) sound recording distribution services. Nevertheless, China did not specify the means of delivering 'sound recording distribution services'. The United States contended that the means of delivery for sound recording distribution services included physical and non-physical forms. Although the Panel concluded on other bases that China's measures were inconsistent with its commitments, the implication was clear that the Panel would accept the principle of technological neutrality if necessary.[35]

5.5 Conclusion

Paragraph 2 of Article XIX of the GATS provides that

> [t]he process of liberalization shall take place with due respect for national policy objectives and the level of development of individual Members, both overall and in individual sectors. There shall be appropriate flexibility for individual developing country Members for opening fewer sectors, liberalizing fewer types of transactions, progressively extending market access in line with their development situation and, when making access to their markets available to foreign service suppliers, attracting to such access conditions aimed at achieving the objectives referred to in Article IV.

It seems clear that the Panel of *US – Gambling* was aware of the stipulations of GATS Article XIX when it made the conclusions by noting:

> We also wish to emphasize what we have *not* decided in this case. We have not decided that WTO Members do not have a right to regulate, including a right to prohibit, gambling and betting activities. In this case, we came to the conclusion that the US measures at issue prohibit the cross-border supply of gambling and betting services in the United States in a manner inconsistent with the GATS. We so decided, not because the GATS denies Members such a right but, rather, because we found, *inter alia*, in the particular circumstances of this case, the measures at issue were inconsistent with the United States' scheduled commitments and the relevant provisions of the GATS.[36]

Both the Panel and the Appellate Body of *China – Publications and Audiovisual Products* accepted the US allegation that China's measures to distinguish the means of service distribution through physical and non-physical forms were inconsistent with certain provisions of its Accession Protocol, GATS, and GATT 1994. This is really too bad for China's implementation of its service commitments. What makes things worse is that the impact of the precedent set in this case will remain for future dispute settlement. Since China has not specified most of its commitments concerning trade in services by referring directly to a product classification system, there will be more disputes arising out of the implementation of the GATS commitments. From that point of view, the principle of technological neutrality might be a panacea for others, but Pandora's box for China.

Notes

1 Professor of Law School, Shanghai Jiao University. No. 1954 Hua Shan Road, Shanghai, P. R. China, 200240. PhD, the University of Edinburgh (UK). This chapter is part of the research programme supported by Shanghai Jiao Tong University (11JCY01). Email: jxhu@sjtu.edu.cn.

2 See S/L/74, 27 July 1999.

3 Panel Report, *US – Gambling*, para. 6.285.

4 In view of the sensitivities associated with the subject matter of the *US–Gambling* case, the Panel emphasized that its conclusion was directly linked to the particular circumstances of this dispute and that its role was to interpret and apply GATS in light of the facts and evidence, not to second-guess the intentions of the United States at the time the commitment was scheduled. Ibid. para. 7.3.

5 See Panel Report, *China – Publications and Audiovisual Products*, para. 7.1258.

6 Following the reasoning of the *US – Gambling* Panel, the Panel in *China – Publications and Audiovisual Products* considered that the principle of technological neutrality had established that any differences between the supply of the sound recording distribution services on physical, as compared to non-physical, media were merely 'technological', and thus should not, unless specified in China's schedule, serve to narrow the scope of China's commitment. Ibid. at para. 7.1256.

7 Relationships of a commercial nature include, but are not limited to, the following transactions: any trade transactions for the supply or exchange of goods or services; distribution agreement; commercial representation or agency; factoring; leasing; construction of works; consulting; engineering; licensing; investment; financing; banking; insurance; exploitation agreement or concession; joint venture and other forms of industrial or business cooperation; carriage of goods or passengers by air, sea, rail or road.

8 International Data Corporation, 'Analytic Applications: 1988 Worldwide Markets and Trends' (IDC No. 17524).

9 Electronic Commerce Resource Center, 1996.

10 R. Kalakota and A. B. Whinston, *Electronic Commerce – A Manager's Guide*, Indianapolis, IN: Addison-Wesley, 1997 at 18.

11 W. Currie, *The Global Information Society*, Chichester: John Wiley & Sons, 2002, at 7.

12 G. P. Schneider and J. T. Perry, *Electronic Commerce*, 2nd edn, Stamford, CT: Thomson Learning, 2001, at 12–14.

13 See the Monitor Report on the China's Electronic Commerce Market 2010 published by the China e-Business Research Center, available at http://b2b.toocle.com/zt/2010bgdz/ (accessed 21 September 2011).

14 S. A. Becker, *Electronic Commerce: Concepts, Methodologies, Tools, and Applications*, Volume I, Hershey, PA: Information Science Reference (an imprint of IGI Global), 2008, at 63.
15 General Assembly Resolution 51/162 of 16 December 1996, amended in 1998, available at www.uncitral.org/pdf/english/texts/electcom/05-89450_Ebook.pdf (accessed 6 August 2013).
16 A. Davidson, *The Law of Electronic Commerce*, Cambridge: Cambridge University Press, 2009, at 25–6.
17 Ibid. at 335.
18 See Article 3 (2) of the DSU.
19 Appellate Body Report, *US – Gasoline*, 17 (Original note omitted).
20 The original words in the Appellate Body Report are 'the *General Agreement* is not to be read in clinical isolation from public international law'. Ibid. at 17.
21 P. J. Kuyper, 'The Law of the GATT As a Special Field of International Law', *Netherlands Yearbook of International Law* 25, 1994, 227.
22 See WTO General Council Document, *WTO Agreements and Electronic Commerce*, WT/GC/W/90, 14 July 1998, Introduction.
23 Which provides that, '[i]n the event of conflict between a provision of the General Agreement on Tariffs and Trade 1994 and a provision of another agreement in Annex 1A to the WTO Agreement, the provision of the other agreement shall prevail to the event of the conflict'.
24 Panel Report, *US – Gambling*, note 703.
25 Ibid. para. 6.281.
26 Ibid. para. 6.285.
27 Ibid. para. 6.286.
28 Ibid. para. 6.287.
29 Ibid. para. 7.2.
30 Panel Report, *China – Publications and Audiovisual Products*, para. 7.1248.
31 Ibid. paras 7.1249, 7.1250.
33 Ibid.
33 The 1993 Scheduling Guidelines indicate that where it is necessary to refine further a sectoral classification, this should be done on the basis of the CPC or other internationally recognized classification. See para.16 of the Guidelines.
34 Panel Report, *China – Publications and Audiovisual Products*, para. 7.1257.
35 Ibid. para. 7.1258.
36 Panel Report, *China – Publications and Audiovisual Products*, para. 7.4.

6 Renegotiate the WTO 'schedules of commitments'?

Technological development and treaty interpretation

Shin-yi Peng[1]

6.1 Introduction: technology evolution, the WTO and challenges in interpreting the 'schedules of commitments'

Digital convergence is an ongoing process.[2] The advent of digital technology has led to the emergence of a 'convergence' phenomenon. Computers, telecommunications and television, traditionally treated as separate media industries regulated under different regulatory regimes, are gradually emerging in the media industries, both at the global and the national levels.[3] This means that networks previously in distinct 'markets' can become 'direct competitors'.[4] In the ambits of international trade, unprecedented market changes have demonstrated that what used to work in the past to determine 'tariff concessions' for goods or 'market access commitments' for services may no longer be the right approach today. The fact is that the info-com sector has undergone significant changes, and the economic activities related to information technology products are far broader, more varied and much more global than was generally understood during the Uruguay Round and the ITA (Information Technology Agreement) negotiations.[5] Thus, a crucial question is whether these commitments (more than a decade old) are sufficient to handle today's commercial realities.[6]

It is evident that in the past decade the tension between 'technological development' and 'treaty interpretation' has been increasing, thereby posing new challenges for the trade negotiators and domestic regulators of information and communication technology ('ICT') industries worldwide.[7] It has also been empirically proved that the ICT-related 'schedule of commitments'[8] has been a subject of numerous disputes and continues to be a litigious area of law.[9] The examples of the problematic interpretation of schedules in WTO dispute settlement show how the question of classification, in terms of both tariff commitments and GATS market access commitments, under the trend of digital convergence, is increasingly raised in practice. It is therefore necessary to examine the issue of how to interpret 'schedules of commitments' in this rapidly changing digital era.

In goods, the specific commitments consist of maximum tariff levels. For agricultural goods, schedules also include tariff quotas, limits on export subsidies, and domestic support. In services, schedules contain market access commitments in sectors, and therefore the interpretation of service schedules defines the scope of the explicit commitments made. WTO members' schedules form 'integral parts' of the WTO covered agreements as provided by GATS Article XX:3, GATT Article II:7, the Agreement on Agriculture (AoA) Article 3:1, and GPA (Agreement on Government Procurement (WTO)) Article 24:12. As such they are treaty text and must therefore be interpreted according to the customary rules of interpretation of public international law, codified in Article 31 and, to the extent that it is appropriate, Article 32 of the Vienna Convention. In other words, since schedules are considered part of the WTO treaty language, the principles of treaty interpretation apply. This has been the approach taken by the Appellate Body, which has generally not differentiated the interpretation of schedules from other WTO treaty language.[10]

The question of whether tariff schedules should be interpreted like treaty language first arose in the *EC – Computer Equipment* dispute.[11] The Appellate Body sided with the EC and explained that '[t]ariff negotiations are a process of reciprocal demands and concessions, of "give and take"'.[12] In the Appellate Body's view, the schedule should be interpreted like any treaty language in accordance with the ordinary meaning to be given to the terms of the treaty in their context and in the light of its object and purpose. The WTO members' schedules are 'an integral part of the GATT 1994' and should thus be interpreted as the GATT 1994 in accordance with the Vienna Convention.[13] Since *EC – Computer Equipment*, panels and the Appellate Body have consistently interpreted schedules on goods and services as treaty language in accordance with Vienna Convention Articles 31 and 32. In *US – Gambling*, the Appellate Body confirmed its approach to the interpretation of goods schedules in *EC – Computer Equipment* and reasoned that service schedules should be interpreted in accordance with the customary principles of interpretation of public international law.[14]

Some commentators have stressed that the schedules are of a bilateral and contractual nature, and thus suggested that the 'hybrid feature' of the negotiation, drafting and conclusion of schedules may influence the weight given to certain means of interpretation in the Vienna Convention, as well as explain why other rules of international law are particularly instructive in determining the meaning of the treaty language in schedules.[15] Nevertheless, the concept of 'an integral part of the WTO covered Agreements' has been repeatedly emphasized by the Appellate Body. The idea of differential interpretative treatment of schedules was dismissed on the basis of the need to guarantee the security and predictability of the multilateral trading system set out in DSU Article 3.2.[16] The Appellate Body so far has not questioned the status of schedules of commitments as treaty language. Neither did the Appellate Body approach the interpretation of schedules differently from the interpretation of other WTO obligations.[17]

The interpretation of schedules has been the subject of several panel and Appellate Body reports in recent years, and it is anticipated that the ICT-related schedules will increasingly be challenged before the DSB. The assumption of the Appellate Body that schedules represent the common agreement among WTO members, and should be interpreted accordingly, becomes even more complex in the face of ever-changing technology. The first part of this chapter will discuss the implications of technological change for tariff and service schedules. In the main body of this chapter I will explore the issues of the approaches taken in *China – Publications and Audiovisual Products* and *EC – IT Products* and analyse the limits of the Vienna Convention in identifying the 'common intention' of members. In the final part of the chapter I will summarize my main points and further stress the importance of integrating the principle of 'technological neutrality' into the WTO law.

6.2 Technological development and tariff schedules

6.2.1 The EC – Computer Equipment *dispute: Legitimate expectations*

The *EC – Computer Equipment* dispute concerns the customs classification in the European Communities[18] of local area network ('LAN') equipment[19] and multimedia personal computers ('PCs'). As part of the Uruguay Round, the EC had bound its tariff rates for automatic data processing ('ADP') machines at 4.9 per cent. According to the United States, the complaining party of the dispute, during the Uruguay Round and for a short period after its conclusion, the EC classified LAN equipment and PCs as ADP machines. In May 1995, however, the EC adopted a new regulation classifying LAN adapter cards as telecommunications apparatus, a category subject to generally higher duties, in the range of 4.6 per cent to 7.5 per cent. With respect to multimedia PCs, in April 1996, a United Kingdom tribunal upheld a customs administration determination classifying PCs with multimedia capabilities as television receivers, thereby subjecting those machines to a 14 per cent tariff.[20]

The Panel in its report in *EC – Computer Equipment* discussed at length whether the 'legitimate expectation' of the United States was relevant for establishing a violation of GATT Article II. The Panel referred to the United States' legitimate expectations of access to the EC as a contextual source for interpreting the EC's tariff schedule. On appeal the Appellate Body reversed this reasoning, observing that '[t]he security and predictability of tariff concessions would be seriously undermined if the concessions in Members' Schedules were to be interpreted on the basis of the *subjective views* of certain exporting Members alone' (emphasis added). The Appellate Body emphasized that the security and predictability of 'the reciprocal and mutually advantageous arrangements directed to the substantial reduction of tariffs and other barriers to trade' is an object and purpose of the WTO Agreement. The Appellate Body was of the view that the 'legitimate expectations' of an exporting member are not relevant in determining whether the EC violated Article II:1 of the GATT1994.[21]

Rather, the Appellate Body chose to rest its interpretation on the methodology set out in Article 31 of the Vienna Convention, and explained its finding by clarifying that 'the purpose of treaty interpretation under Article 31 of the Vienna Convention is to ascertain the *common* intentions of the parties'. These common intentions, as stressed by the Appellate Body, cannot be ascertained on the basis of the subjective and unilaterally determined 'expectations' of one of the parties to a treaty. The Appellate Body mentioned a wide range of sources in arriving at a meaning of the EC's tariff concession, a meaning that went beyond the 'expectations' of any one country in the litigation and ultimately approximated the common intent of all parties to the treaty.[22]

To conclude, in *EC – Computer Equipment* – a leading case on how technological change may impact tariff schedules – when faced with the interpretation of 'automatic data processing equipment' in a tariff schedule, the Appellate Body did not question whether it would be useful to examine how concessions in schedules of goods and services were negotiated, drafted and concluded. It appears that the Appellate Body did contemplate the possibility that schedules may be of a different character than treaties and therefore may require more tailored interpretative means. However, it rejected the alternative to treaty interpretation, i.e. to interpret schedules in the light of 'legitimate expectations' of the exporting WTO members, on the ground that this would undermine the security and predictability of schedules. The Appellate Body upheld a rigid application of the DSU Article 3.2, and stressed that 'the *common intentions* [of the members] cannot be ascertained on the basis of the *subjective* and *unilaterally determined* expectations of one of the parties to the treaty' (emphasis added).[23] However, as discussed in the Section 6.3 of this chapter, the disputing parties in *China – Publications and Audiovisual Products* as well as in *EC – IT Products* again articulated their arguments on the basis of a similar approach – to rely on factual evidence that is of unilaterally subjective character.

6.2.2 The EC – IT Products *dispute: 'evolving' coverage*

Along these lines, the ongoing litigation brought by the United States, Japan and Taiwan[24] against the EC tariff regime on IT products is also a good example of how technological changes may impact tariff schedules.[25] The EC has classified flat panel computer monitors with digital video interface ('DVI') under tariff codes that are not covered by the ITA, and has subjected them to a 14 per cent duty. The question at core is whether or not the EC is entitled to exclude the 'flat panel display devices' from the scope of the concessions merely because they are capable of receiving and reproducing signals from both 'automatic data processing machines' and other sources. In addition, under the EC tariff regime, only a product with a telephony-based or cable-based modem qualifies for duty-free treatment – any product that communicates using a wireless, ISDN or Ethernet modem is reclassified out of the duty-free tariff line and is subject to a 14 per cent duty. Moreover, the EC issued a new regulation that classifies multifunction printers, having scanning, laser printing and laser copying capabilities, under the HS (Harmonized System) subheading 9009.12, as photocopying apparatus, carrying a 6 per cent duty.[26]

The EC is an original participant in the ITA, and modified its schedule in accordance with the procedures indicated in the previous section. The EC incorporated the tariff commitments set out in Attachment A and Attachment B into its schedule.[27] Attachment A defines products by tariff heading, and Attachment B provides a narrative description of specific products covered by the ITA. Those commitments thus became a part of the EC 'schedule', as stipulated in GATT 1994 Article II:1.[28] As a result, those tariff commitments became WTO obligations of the EC pursuant to Articles II:1(a)[29] and II:1(b)[30] of GATT 1994. This dispute is mainly about whether certain products are within the scope of the tariff concessions made by the EC pursuant to the ITA as the complainants have alleged, or if they are within the scope of other concessions included in the EC schedule, which do not provide for duty-free treatment.[31]

With respect to 'flat panel display devices', the EC pointed out that the multifunctional LCD monitor *did not exist at the time the concessions were being negotiated*.[32] This casts an important light on the circumstances under which the concessions were made in view of the extremely detailed technical language used in the narrative of the product definitions in Attachment B to the ITA. The EC stressed how the radical changes in monitor technology from the time the ITA was negotiated have made it exceptionally difficult to define a 'monitor' in order to place it in the relevant legal framework.[33] It argued that the multifunctional LCD monitor, which can usually display even television signals, fundamentally challenges the established legal categorizations.[34] The EC is of the opinion that WTO members should realize that the multifunctional LCD monitor is a 'new product', the result of the convergence of the IT and the multimedia consumer electronics industries.[35]

With respect to 'set top boxes that have a communication function', it seemed to the EC that all the three complainants agree that this dispute depends on the interpretation of the narrative description of certain set top boxes contained in the EC schedule and the ITA. In the EC's view, however, the complainants misinterpret the content of the description. If interpreted correctly, the narrative description does not support their claim. The EC classifies set top boxes that connect to the Internet via ISDN, W-LAN or Ethernet devices in Heading 8528 71 19 (i.e. outside the duty-free Heading 8528 71 13) because ISDN/W-LAN/Ethernet devices are not *'modems'* (emphasis added).[36] The set top boxes that are at issue are not entitled to the ITA treatment because they simply do not fulfil the narrative description.[37] In the view of the EC,[38] the complainants avoided addressing any difference between the product existing at the time of the conclusion of the ITA (e.g. telephony-based or cable modem) and the product of today (i.e. ISDN, W-LAN or Ethernet devices) that is under dispute.

With respect to the 'multifunctional machines', contrary to the complainants' assertions,[39]the EC is of the view that multifunctional machines are not a technologically advanced version of printers. In the EC's view, multifunctional machines are best described as different devices, each with a specific function (photocopiers, printers and/or facsimile machines), that have been merged into a single machine capable of performing various functions simultaneously. Major manufacturers, such as Ricoh and Canon, describe their range of multifunctional machines as being 'copier-based'.[40] It is the EC's view that the essential difference between analogue photocopying and digital photocopying is that the latter digitalizes the image, but this difference does not bring digital photocopiers outside the scope of HS 96 9009 12.[41] Thus, multifunctional machines cannot be classified directly under subheading 8471 60 unless they are used *'solely or principally'* with a computer (emphasis added).[42]

It is interesting to review how creative were the arguments and interpretations presented as to whether 'new product' can be assumed to be covered by the concessions just because it happens to also perform similar functions as a product that is covered by the concessions. Was the narrative description of Attachment B to the ITA written in a way to accommodate technical developments of the products? Are we really convinced that the members' commitments flowing from the ITA are 'open-ended' and 'accumulate any new product'?

6.2.3 Renegotiate the tariff commitments?

The *EC – Computer Equipment* dispute, which occurred at a relatively early stage of the development of information technology, raised the question of how to interpret tariff concessions considering technological changes. The ongoing litigation on *EC – IT Products* provides an opportunity to revisit the issue of tariff classification, and to offer a creative space for treaty interpretation under this digital convergence trend.

On the one hand, technology is organic; new features were being developed, and advances were made 'before the ink was dry' on the ITA.[43] As argued by the United States Trade Representative, 'if ITA participants only provided duty-free treatment to the products with technologies that existed at the time the ITA was concluded, very few ITA products would be eligible for duty-free treatment today'.[44] The IT sector is organic and technologically innovative, where evolution is the nature of the beast, and thus we must read the existing commitments accordingly. The intent of the ITA was to be much more inclusive and dynamic, because otherwise, eventually, nothing would be covered by the ITA, simply because technology by its very nature evolves.[45] Trade regimes, therefore, are urged to *'evolve* in a manner that enhances market access opportunities for information technology products' (emphasis added).[46]

On the other hand, information technology has been evolving rapidly and is converging with entertainment, communication and other technologies, thereby creating an ever-increasing potential for specific information technology products to fall in between the scope of the ITA. The EC argued that judicial interpretation may not be the most appropriate way to clarify the question of whether certain products are covered by the ITA. Members must revisit the product coverage in general by means of consensus, not only by litigation. What is covered and what is not covered is significant and will form a forever and rapidly changing landscape. In the view of the EC, the necessity to renegotiate the ITA in the face of ever-changing technology exists. More important, there is a need to further develop a mechanism that will allow us to deal with technological change.[47]

Indeed, a cursory analysis of relevant provisions of the ITA reveals that the treaty language is not entirely clear. The preamble and paragraph 1 of the ITA seem to support the complainants' interpretation of the EC schedule. In particular, they refer to provisions such as the aim of 'achieving maximum freedom of world trade in information technology products',[48] that the ITA 'endeavours to encourage the continued technological development of the information technology industry'[49] and that trade regimes 'should evolve in a manner that enhances market access opportunities for information technology products'.[50] Do these provisions reflect that the ITA participants contemplated a 'positive evolution in market access'?[51] It is arguable that if every advance in technology necessitated renegotiating, economic operators would be discouraged from innovating.[52] From this aspect, the objective embodied in the ITA provisions reflects an attempt to encourage technological development. However, if we take a closer look at the ITA provision, paragraph 3 of the ITA Annex,[53] on a mechanism for 'future negotiation' and for 'updating the product coverage', it seems to show that the ITA participants were well aware of the rapidly advancing nature of the IT industry, and they considered that the ITA's language was not expected to cover every 'new product' that may come along in the quickly converging IT sector.[54] How should the above provisions together be read and the scope of the existing concessions in the ITA be decided?

6.3 Technological development and GATS schedules

6.3.1 The China publications and audiovisual products dispute: The confusing fact-finding process and misleading evidence

Just as the interpretations of GATT provisions have dynamically evolved in response to the several hundred GATT dispute settlement procedures, so the interpretation of GATS provisions will evolve over time. In the context of services trade, the *China – Publications and Audiovisual Products* dispute,[55] which directly involves interaction with technological change, has practical significance for classification/scheduling issues.

China, in its GATS schedule, made both market access and national treatment commitments regarding sound recording distribution services. In particular, under market access for mode 3 in Sector 2D, China committed to permit foreign service suppliers to establish contractual joint ventures with Chinese partners to engage in sound recording distribution.[56] China scheduled no national treatment limitations under mode 3 for these Chinese foreign contractual joint ventures. Given these commitments, Chinese foreign contractual joint ventures, including majority foreign-owned joint ventures, likewise should enjoy national treatment regarding sound recording distribution. The Chinese domestic legal framework,[57] however, greatly limits the ability of foreign-invested enterprises to engage in the distribution of sound recordings by prohibiting these enterprises from engaging in their electronic distribution, e.g. through the Internet and mobile telecommunications networks.[58]

This prohibition does not extend to wholly Chinese-owned enterprises. In other words, China's measures, by creating a regime for sound recording distribution that treats foreign-invested sound recordings distributors much less favourably than wholly Chinese-owned sound recording distributors, impose more stringent requirements on those foreign-invested enterprises that their wholly Chinese-owned counterparts must face. The United States therefore claimed that China's measures are inconsistent with Article XVII of the GATS.[59] China argued, however, that at the time of the negotiation of China's GATS commitments, the legal framework governing the exploitation of music, and, more precisely, the distribution of sound recordings, addressed exclusively the distribution of sound recordings in their traditional, hard-copy format. China further argued that, when properly applied, the rules of treaty interpretation confirm that network music services are not covered by its GATS commitments and that those commitments are strictly limited to the distribution of sound recordings in physical form.[60]

Both parties submitted a significant amount of 'evidence' (i.e. exhibits) in support of their positions. China, in order to argue that network music services did not constitute an established business operating within a legal framework at the time of negotiations on China's accession to the WTO, submitted several pieces of evidence, including:[61]

- Network music services only emerged fully after China acceded to the WTO in 2001. Until the breakthrough of network music services around 2003, these services were largely illegal. No international consensus on the protection of IPR (intellectual property rights) had been reached allowing a worldwide legal exploitation of music over the Internet until the entry into force of the WCT in 2002. In China the first network music service platforms were launched around 2001.[62] Therefore, the electronic distribution of sound recordings was a new phenomenon that did not exist at the time of China's accession.[63]

The United States, on the other hand, argued that the circumstances surrounding the conclusion of China's WTO accession demonstrated that the electronic means of delivery for music were part of the landscape as China's commitments were being negotiated, and that China was *aware* that music was being distributed electronically at the time of China's accession. The United States provided even more 'exhibits' to 'prove' that the electronic distribution of sound recordings was a reality long before China's accession and that China itself was *aware* of this development, including:[64]

- According to the testimony of David Hughes of Sony Music, he 'first became involved in the digital distribution of music in September 1996', a time period well before China's WTO accession.
- According to the Federation of the Phonographic Industry ('IFPI'), developments in the online distribution of music 'build on a process that goes back to 1998 when eMusic.com began selling MP3 singles and albums on the web in the US'
- Steamwaves, another American service, was launched in 1999 and was one of the first to offer a streaming subscription service.
- China's own involvement in international for a dating back to the early 1990s demonstrates that China, like the WTO members with which it was negotiating, was aware of the electronic distribution of music prior to its WTO accession. For example, in October 1995 at the WIPO World Forum on the Protection of Intellectual Creations in the Information Society, Mr Shen Rengan, Deputy Director General of the National Copyright Administration of China in Beijing, participated in a working session.
- Within the WTO context, discussions regarding electronic delivery of services also took place prior to China's accession. For example, the Work Programme on Electronic Commerce's Progress Report to the General Council states that '[i]t was the general view that the electronic delivery of services falls within the scope of the GATS, since the Agreement applies to all services regardless of the means by which they are delivered, and that electronic delivery can take place under any of the four modes of supply.'[65]
- In early 2000, a Houston-based company and the government of China formed a joint venture to launch an MP3 website. This was a website permitting the electronic delivery of sound recordings from the Internet to a user's MP3 music listening device.
- Numerous websites, such as chinamp3.com and suflash.com, were distributing music electronically in China prior to 2000.

As can be seen, with respect to supplementary means of interpretation under Article 32 of the Vienna Convention, the circumstances of conclusion, the fact-finding process and the considerable 'evidence/exhibits' are rather confusing, if not misleading. Both parties seemed to focus principally on the questions of 'whether the electronic distribution of sound recordings was *unknown* at the time of China's December 2001 accession to the WTO', 'whether the electronic distribution of sound recordings was a phenomenon *known* to China and other WTO Members before China joined the WTO' and 'whether China was *unaware* of the existence of the joint venture between the Chinese government and a Houston-based company to supply music online and therefore was unaware of the electronic distribution at the time of its WTO accession'. The core questions here are: How well should a trade negotiator understand the development of technology, and to what extent can it be relevant in the context of Article 32 of the Vienna Convention? Why is it so critically important for the parties in dispute to demonstrate the negotiators' 'awareness' of the current status of technology? How can the fact, if proven true, that the electronic distribution of sound recordings was a phenomenon known to China at the time of China's accession affect the Panel's decision? And the further puzzle arises as to whether very similar or identically worded commitments (e.g. 'cellular mobile phone services') could be given different meanings (i.e. 2G v. 3G mobile services) depending on the date of a member's accession to the WTO (e.g. 1994 for Korea v. 2002 for Taiwan) because the meaning to be attributed to those terms can only be the meaning that they had at the time the schedule was concluded (i.e. 2G in 1994 v. 3G in 2002).[66]

6.3.2 Renegotiate the GATS specific commitments?

At the core of the issue is the 'temporal variation' in language.[67] Human language changes. It changes depending on the social context and technological environment. Language is under constant movement, bit by bit, and varies over time.[68] In the context of technology, 'old language' acquires partly or even completely new meanings. Changes such as these must also affect the language used in treaties.[69]

We cannot deny that the meaning of 'sound recording distribution services' at the time of China's accession to the WTO was substantially different from that of 'sound recording distribution services' at the time of interpretation by the Panel. To illustrate, the increasing adoption of broadband and mobile technologies and the widespread adoption of smartphones and portable music playing devices continue to drive the digital music market. Sales of recorded music in CD format have declined steadily since 2000, as consumers increasingly have moved towards digital downloading.[70] The majority of music is now sold in digital format, downloaded by consumers to laptops, MP3 players, or other devices. According to the IFPI report, in 2009, for the first time ever, more than a quarter of the recorded music industry's global revenues (27 per cent) came from digital channels. In the United States, the world's largest music market, online and mobile revenues now account for around 40 per cent of music sales.[71] Particularly noteworthy, mobile digital contents continued to perform favourably, achieving major growth of 39 per cent in sales of full single-track downloads service, which accounted for 60 per cent of all mobile digital contents, and 53 per cent of overall digital music delivery in terms of sales.[72] The music industry landscape, indeed, has been undergoing major structural changes as companies from other industries become integrated into music distribution, and business models transform to adapt to changing market demands. China thus repeatedly stressed in its written submissions that the only viable way to address this unresolved issue should be via requests–offers negotiation, and not via the 'fast track' of the WTO dispute settlement mechanism.[73]

China – Publications and Audiovisual Products may have a wider impact on the interpretation of GATS schedules of commitments, especially the sectors in which technology-enabled businesses are developing most rapidly. Shall we interpret a GATS market access commitment using the 'ordinary meaning' at the time of its conclusion (i.e. historical language) or the 'ordinary meaning' at the time of interpretation (i.e. contemporary language)?[74]

The following part explains how to tackle the problem caused by these social variations for the interpretation of treaties, and how a schedule of commitment is interpreted to include a new product/service not existing at the time of negotiation.

6.4 A critical review of the interpretative approaches taken in the disputes of EC IT products and China audiovisual services

6.4.1 *The 'object and purpose' of the treaty*[75]

6.4.1.1 *Goods schedules: enhance market access for IT products?*

The recent decisions of the Panel and the Appellate Body in *EC – IT Products* and *China – Audiovisual Services* touched upon a number of issues of ongoing significance to the treaty interpretation in this digital world. In *EC – IT Products*, the complainants argued that the ITA may be relevant in analysing the 'object and purpose' of GATT 1994 because the ITA is an instrument related to GATT 1994. As indicated in Section II-C of this article, the ITA arguably contains a number of mechanisms to encourage technological development, including broad product coverage and Attachment B. In the complainants' view, those provisions in the ITA that express desires such as 'to achieve maximum freedom of world trade in information technology products' contradict the EC's view that a digital product should no longer be entitled to duty-free treatment simply because technology advances.[76] To some degree, it is fair to say that the complainants seek to justify an extensive reading of the scope of ITA by arguing that it is necessary in order to further the 'object and purpose' of the ITA.[77] It is their position that the EC concession must cover 'all' devices that fit squarely within its terms regardless of how their other functionality may change or improve over time.

The Panel was facing several questions, including: Is there an interpretative principle whereby tariff concessions must be broadly construed in order to promote the expansion of trade between members? Was the complainants' interpretative approach overly broad and therefore might it compromise the legal certainty and predictability of tariff concessions, creating the risk that members will become reluctant to pursue the ITA liberalization process?

In the Panel Report, the Panel took a position that provisions of the ITA are not relevant in determining the object and purpose of the WTO Agreement. The Panel pointed out that the ITA constitutes a separate plurilateral arrangement made among a subset of WTO members. Owing to the application of the most favoured nation principle and Article II of GATT 1994, the duty bindings agreed to by the ITA participants were also extended to all WTO members. That does not mean, however, that the objectives of the ITA participants of having participants' tariff regimes 'evolve' in a manner that 'enhances market access for information technology products' and 'encourag[ing] the continued technological development of the information technology industry' can be considered a basis for determining the object and purpose of the WTO Agreement and GATT 1994.[78] Having said that, the Panel indicated that the relevant object and purpose in this dispute is the *general object and purpose* of the WTO Agreement as a whole, including GATT 1994, which is to provide security and predictability in the reciprocal and mutually advantageous concessions negotiated by parties for the reduction of tariffs and other barriers to trade (emphasis added).[79] The Panel then concluded that by interpreting the terms of the relevant EC concessions in light of 'the "general object and purpose" of the WTO Agreement as a whole' it saw nothing that would override or contradict its preliminary conclusion that the EC concessions require duty-free treatment for the products in dispute. In other words, the Panel reached the conclusion, based on the general object and purpose of the WTO Agreement as a whole, not the ITA, that the objectives of security and predictability require that concessions cover products even if those products did not exist in that form at the time the concessions were granted as long as they comply with the wording of the concessions concerned.[80]

6.4.1.2 Services schedules: 'sufficiently generic' terms?

In *China – Publications and Audiovisual Products*, the 'object and purpose' of the GATS plays a significant key role in determining China's commitments in dispute. The Chinese government in its first submission was of the view that unduly extending the scope of members' GATS commitments would be against the principle of *progressive liberalization* as reflected in the Preamble, which indicates that the Agreement is aimed at establishing 'a multilateral framework of principles and rules for trade in services with a view to the expansion of such trade under conditions of transparency and progressive liberalization'. The principle of progressive liberalization is reflected in the structure of the GATS, which contemplates that WTO members undertake specific commitments through successive rounds of multilateral negotiations with a view to liberalizing their service markets incrementally, rather than immediately and completely at the time of the acceptance of the GATS. In light of this *general object and purpose*, China also asserted that the principle of 'progressive liberalization' required the Panel to base its analysis of the relevant terms in China's GATS schedule on *their meaning at the time of China's accession to the WTO*.[81]

The United States responded that compliance with current commitments is essential to the credibility and success of 'progressive liberalization' in the future.[82] On appeal, China again claimed that the Panel interpreted the entry 'sound recording distribution services' according to the *contemporary meaning* of the words it contains, but that the principle of progressive liberalization does not allow for the expansion of the scope of the commitments of a WTO member by interpreting the terms used in the schedule based on *the meaning of those terms at the time of interpretation*.[83]

The Appellate Body found that the task of ascertaining the meaning of a concession in a schedule, like the task of interpreting any other treaty text, involves identifying the *common intention* of the members. Regarding the 'object and purpose' of the GATS, the decisive paragraph of the Appellate Body decision reads as follows:

> We consider that the terms used in China's GATS Schedule ('sound recording' and 'distribution') are *sufficiently generic* that what they apply to *may change over time*. In this respect, we note that GATS Schedules, like the GATS itself and all WTO agreements, constitute multilateral treaties with *continuing obligations* that WTO Members entered into *for an indefinite period of time*, regardless of whether they were original Members or acceded after 1995 (emphasis added).[84]

In other words, the Appellate Body throws in a wild card by stating that the commitments in dispute are generic terms. The Appellate Body appears here to be implying that the content of 'generic terms', such as 'sound recording' and 'distribution', is assumed by the members to change through time.[85] On that basis, the Appellate Body concluded that the analysis supports the interpretation of China's commitment on 'sound recording distribution services' as including the electronic distribution of sound recordings. Interestingly, the Appellate Body did not refer to any GATS provisions supporting this proposition in its reasoning. It did not say anything about how to determine if a term is 'generic' enough. Neither did it elaborate on the distinction between 'time-bound' and 'timeless' WTO obligations. This raised a critical question as to the definitions of members' GATS-specific commitments.[86] Are we really convinced that WTO members' commitments flowing from the GATS, when expressed in a 'sufficiently generic way', are 'open-ended' and 'accumulate any new services'? The key questions remain unanswered. It could be argued that the Appellate Body did not go far enough in its 'activism'.

6.4.2 The 'state of technology' that existed at the time of the negotiations[87]

6.4.2.1 Goods schedules: technological development and product evolution

The supplementary interpretation principle 'the circumstances of conclusion of the treaty', under the Article 32 of the Vienna Convention, was heavily used and replied upon by the parties in *EC – IT Products* and *China – Publications and Audiovisual Products*. Were the terms of the EC concession 'frozen' in time at the conclusion of the ITA? As indicated in Section 6.2.2 of this chapter, the complainants and third parties to this dispute strongly criticized that the EC's argument (that the ITA merely covers IT products existing in 1996) ignores the 'enhancement', 'development' and 'evolvement' aspects of the ITA.[88]

As discussed earlier, the core issue in *EC – IT Products* is whether in the particular technological development of a product should be excluded the possibility that a particular product would fall within the scope of an ITA concession, especially those based on Attachment B of the ITA. On this issue the Panel should, at least, have considered two questions. First, to what extent is the 'state of technology' that existed at the time of the negotiations relevant to determining the scope of the commitments?[89] Second, how should 'technological development' and 'product evolution' be dealt with in interpreting concessions?

Not surprisingly, however, the Panel avoided directly responding to the arguments regarding 'the circumstances of conclusion' made by the parties proposed as 'supplementary means' of interpretation. In the Panel's view, 'it is neither desirable nor possible to answer such questions in the abstract and without reference to the terms of the concessions that are being interpreted'.[90] In this context, the Panel explained that it had applied the customary rules of interpretation of public international law, as set out in Article 31 of the Vienna Convention, and had examined the ordinary meaning of the terms of the EC's commitment, in the context provided by the ITA, other relevant parts of the EC schedule, and the schedules of other WTO members. Having said that, the Panel decided that 'there is no need to consider further the particular status of technology at the time of negotiating the concession in assessing the scope of the concession before the Panel'.[91] Thus, for instance, the Panel did not consider the question of whether the fact that DVI was developed after the conclusion of the ITA should be operated to exclude flat panel display devices with DVIs from the scope of the concession.

While the Panel was prudent enough and did not allow itself to fall into the trap of the 'investigation' of the technological history of IT products, it somehow departed from its interpretative approach and to some degree responded to the parties' arguments regarding the state of technology at the time of ITA negotiations. For example, in response to the EC's argument that multifunctional monitors are 'new products' that did not exist at the time of the negotiations, the Panel indicated that 'multifunctionality was *not unknown* at the time of the negotiations'.[92] The Panel also in its footnote cited factual evidence supporting its viewpoint that negotiators were *at least aware* of a wide array of technology at the time of considering the 'panel display devices' concession.[93]

It is obvious that the Panel was *reluctant to draw a firm* conclusion on how 'technological development' should be dealt with in interpreting concessions. The reasoning was unsatisfying, and it left the question: In what situation would negotiators' awareness of new technology be relevant in determining the scope of the commitments' completely unanswered?

6.4.2.2 *Services schedules: technical possibility and commercial reality*

As indicated in the Section 6.3.1 of this chapter, both parties submitted a significant amount of 'evidence' in support of their positions regarding the 'circumstances of conclusion'. The Chinese allegation was based on the 'technical, legal and commercial impossibility', emphasizing that any interpretation of China's relevant commitments under Sector 2D must necessarily incorporate the circumstances surrounding the negotiations. China was of the view that, considering that at the time of the negotiations the sound recording distribution service only covered the distribution of sound recordings in physical form, the service in question could not form part of China's commitments.[94]

The Panel considered that, in seeking to confirm the 'common intention of members' with respect to a commitment in a GATS schedule, evidence on the technical feasibility or commercial reality of a service at the time of the service commitment may constitute circumstances relevant to the interpretation of its scope under Article 32 of the Vienna Convention. In this context, the Panel found that the evidence presented by the parties suggested that the electronic distribution of music had become a *technical possibility* and *commercial reality* before the entry into force of China's GATS schedule following its accession to the WTO on 11 December 2001.[95] In the view of the Panel, the record also indicated that China was *aware* of such fact. The Panel therefore was not persuaded that the meaning of the phrase 'sound recording distribution services' could not extend to the distribution of sound recordings in non-physical form, for the reason that negotiators of China's GATS schedule had at the time *no conception of the technical or commercial viability* of this form of distribution.[96]

Regarding the circumstances of the conclusion of the treaty, the Appellate Body could easily have decided this issue based on the Panel's reasoning, but the Appellate Body instead took a different position and utilized a different approach. The Appellate Body spent several paragraphs in the *China – Publications and Audiovisual Products* report to clarify certain important aspects of the Panel's reasoning and characterize the Panel as having 'simply found that this element did not establish that China could not have undertaken a commitment on the electronic distribution of sound recordings in 2001'. The

Appellate Body emphasized that the Panel 'did not itself draw interpretative conclusions on the basis of the evidence of the conclusion of the treaty'.[97]

As the reasoning of the Appellate Body shows, the Appellate Body on this issue distanced itself from the Panel Report and gently chided the Panel by modifying the Panel's reasoning.[98] To some degree, the Appellate Body's ambiguous stance on the (in)significance of 'technical possibility' and 'commercial reality' makes it seem that the issue has been slightly addressed: The Appellate Body rejected China's argument about the factual situation and about the significance of the circumstances of the conclusion of the treaty, implying that at least in this dispute the commercial or legal status of the business at the time of China's accession is not relevant.

6.4.3 Identifying the common intention of members?

The assumption of the Appellate Body that schedules represent the common agreement among WTO members and should be interpreted accordingly becomes even more complex in the face of ever-changing technology. In *EC – Computer Equipment*, a leading case on how technological change may impact tariff schedules, when faced with the interpretation of 'automatic data processing equipment' in a tariff schedule, the Appellate Body did not question whether it would be useful to examine how concessions in schedules of goods and services were negotiated, drafted and concluded. However, it rejected the alternative to treaty interpretation, i.e. to interpret schedules in the light of 'legitimate expectations' of the exporting WTO members, on the ground that this would undermine the security and predictability of schedules. The Appellate Body upheld a rigid application of DSU Article 3.2, and stressed that the common intentions of the members cannot be ascertained on the basis of the *subjective and unilaterally determined expectations* of one of the parties to the treaty.

Along these lines, as the reasoning of the Appellate Body in *China – Publications and Audiovisual Products* shows, the Appellate Body rejected China's argument about the factual situation, i.e. the technical or commercial viability of electronic distribution of sound recording, and about the significance of the 'circumstances of the conclusion of the treaty', i.e. the electronic distribution of sound recordings was *unknown* at the time of China's accession to the WTO, and China was *unaware* of the existence of such services.

In a more recent Panel Report in *EC – IT Products*, again, when determining the scope of the EC tariff commitments on certain IT products, the Panel examined the ordinary meaning of the terms of the EC concession, in the context provided by the ITA, other relevant parts of the EC schedule and the schedules of other WTO members. The Panel established that the products in dispute are covered by the EC concession based on the above approaches, implying that the fact that the EC was *unaware* of the state of technology that existed at the time of the negotiations is of limited relevance to the question at issue.

Both cases tackled the issue of whether the existence or otherwise of certain technologies at the time of the conclusion of the treaty negotiations is relevant to the interpretation of the tariff or service schedules, and both cases reached confusing and somehow self-contradictory conclusions: (1) Both panels were convinced by the evidence submitted by the complaining parties that the 'new' technologies were known at the time of the treaty negotiation, and that the responding parties to the disputes were aware of such technological development. (2) Both panels took the position that even if it were accepted that the responding parties' claims are factually accurate that the products/services were unknown at the time of the negotiations, such facts are of limited relevance to the question at issue. In other words, both panels did not themselves draw interpretative conclusions on the basis of the evidence of the conclusion of the treaty. (3) The 'state of technology' and the negotiators' subjective awareness might be relevant or even of significance in future cases – leaving open the possibility for another WTO member to argue in a subsequent dispute.

What is meant by the circumstances of conclusion is not indicated in the Vienna Convention. The circumstances that cause a treaty to be drawn up, affect its content and attach to its conclusion are all possible factors that are in practice taken into account.[99] In theory, evidence on the technical feasibility or commercial reality of a product/service at the time of the commitment indeed may constitute circumstances relevant to the interpretation of its scope under Article 32 of the Vienna Convention. We cannot ignore the fact that all the parties involved in *EC – IT Products* and *China – Publications and Audiovisual Products* submitted a significant amount of exhibits in support of their positions regarding the 'circumstances of conclusion'. It is understandable that the panels and/or the Appellate Body would not dare to radically take a position on this issue. However, given the potentially far-reaching consequences of the Panel's interpretation on how to interpret 'schedules of commitments' in this rapidly changing digital era, one would expect that it presented a well-reasoned legal analysis on Article 32 of the Vienna Convention.

6.4.4 Integrating the principle of 'technological neutrality' into WTO law

In addition, in *China – Publications and Audiovisual Products* the Appellate Body's reasoning on 'object and purpose' is of great practical significance and will have critically important implications for future disputes as to how to interpret 'schedules of commitments' in this rapidly changing digital era. Although different types of schedule vary in their structure, it remains interesting to see how the reports of the Appellate Body in *China – Publications and Audiovisual Products* will affect the possible appellate proceeding on *EC – IT Products*, in particular the interpretation of Attachment B of the ITA.[100] Is the term 'monitor' *sufficiently generic* and therefore the definition of the terms *may change over time*? Is the term 'modem' a generic term and therefore should not be interpreted in an overly narrow or technical sense? Do the tariff commitments set out in Attachment B of the ITA constitute multilateral treaties with continuing obligations so as to ensure that the tariff regimes will *evolve* over time?

In *China – Publications and Audiovisual Products* the Appellate Body seems to imply that the content of 'generic terms' in the schedules of commitments is assumed by the members to change through time. It did not, however, say anything about how to determine whether a term is 'generic' enough. Neither did it elaborate on the distinction between 'time-bound' and 'timeless' WTO obligations, leaving open the possibility for later WTO litigation to materialize the meaning.

Having said that, I am of the view that the notion of 'generic terms' and the principle of 'technological neutrality'[101] conceptually reinforce each other, and that the latter itself might well serve as the rationale for the former. In *US – Gambling*, the Panel stated that 'a market access commitment . . . implies the right of other Members' service suppliers to supply a service through *all* means of delivery, whether by mail, telephone, Internet etc., unless otherwise specified in a Member's Schedule'.[102] As the United States argued before the *China – Publications and Audiovisual Products* Panel, the GATS is *technologically neutral* in the sense that it does not contain any provisions that distinguish between the different technological means through which a service may be supplied.[103] The United States invoked the principle of 'technological neutrality' to argue that any practical differences that may exist between the supply of sound recordings in physical and digital form are simply differences with respect to the 'means of delivery'.[104] According to the principle of technological neutrality, the differences between the physical and digital distributions are not relevant to the interpretation of the scope of a GATS commitment, unless specified in a member's schedule.[105] The United States further stressed that China's position, if accepted, would suggest that the GATS and members' commitments must be *renegotiated* each time a new technology results in a new means of supplying a service. This would be an unworkable outcome, and would be inconsistent with the principle of technological neutrality.[106] The GATS is sufficiently dynamic to cover new technological innovations affecting the delivery of services.

'Technological neutrality' has been well established as a general regulatory principle under the International Telecommunication Union framework.[107] As far as possible a technologically neutral position – the idea that there should be *equivalent treatment of equivalent services*, regardless of the delivery means – should be adopted by the regulator.[108] In fact, in the past years many negotiating proposals have stressed the need to consider the coverage of ICT-related commitments.[109] Issues mentioned, among others, mainly concern digital convergence, the blurring distinction between telecom, computer and audiovisual services, and the integration of the ICT industry.[110]

The EU approach,[111] for example, is designed to impact neutrally on different business models and technologies and to provide a way forward that will be able to deal with future technologies, particularly those involving convergence,[112] especially to deal with ambiguities arising from convergence and rapid development of ICT market.

The Panel and the Appellate Body offered no response to those arguments regarding the principle of technological neutrality.[113] It is apparent, however, that the Appellate Body's reasoning in *China – Publications and Audiovisual Products* on the basis of the notion of the 'generic terms' is conceptually linked and theoretically relevant to the principle of technological neutrality. The United States and the Appellate Body have produced two closed-linked lines of legal arguments, but the Appellate Body just missed an opportunity to elaborate on the principle of technological neutrality. I am of the view that the Appellate Body's reasoning on the so-called 'sufficiently generic terms' and the US position on the principle of 'technological neutrality' can be mutually supportive and reinforcing. WTO members and the Appellate Body must seriously consider ways to integrate the principle of 'technological neutrality' into the WTO jurisprudence.

6.5 Conclusion

Information technology is eliminating historical differences between devices and network platforms,[114] as well as blurring the lines between physical networks and the service providers that use those networks.[115] *EC – Computer Equipment, EC – IT Products* and *China – Publications and Audiovisual Products* offer a creative space for treaty interpretation considering the digital convergence trend.

The interpretation of schedules has been the subject of several panel and Appellate Body reports in recent years, and it is anticipated that the ICT-related schedules will increasingly be challenged before the DSB. The recent decisions of the Panels and Appellate Body in *EC – IT Products* and *China – Publications and Audiovisual Products* may become significant leading cases – and it is highly likely that the WTO case law will be built incrementally upon them. Given the potentially far-reaching consequences of the Panels/Appellate Body's interpretation, one would expect that they presented a well-reasoned legal basis.

I conclude that the Panel appropriately recognized in *EC – IT Products* that the ITA is not relevant in determining the object and purpose of the WTO Agreement and therefore the complainants' overly broad interpretative approach may compromise the legal certainty and predictability of tariff concessions. The Panel's finding is remarkable in that it resolved an ongoing discussion on whether the objectives of the ITA participants of having participants' tariff regimes 'evolve' in a manner that 'enhances market access for information technology products' can be considered a basis for determining the object and purpose of GATT 1994. However, the Panel should have fully elaborated upon the question of in what situation and to what extent the 'state of technology' that existed at the time of the negotiations can be relevant to determining the scope of the commitments.

I also conclude that two aspects of the Appellate Body's decision in *China – Publications and Audiovisual Products* have significant implications for the question of how to interpret 'schedules of commitments' in this rapidly changing digital era. First, despite the lack of legal reasoning, the Appellate Body took a 'brave' but necessary position on the issue of whether the definition of 'sound recording distribution services' is alterable and evolutionary through time. Second, the Appellate Body clarified that the fact that a service was technically feasible and commercially viable at the time of a member's WTO accession does not necessarily mean that that member's GATS commitments include that service. As the Appellate Body's view alone is not a satisfactory basis for such an important holding, this chapter suggests that the conclusion ought to be supported in light of the principle of 'technological neutrality'.

Notes

1 This chapter was originally published as an article in *Cornell International Law Journal*, 45(2), 2012, 403–30. Professor of Law, National Tsing Hua University, Taiwan, Republic of China. Email: sypeng@mx.nthu.edu.tw. Website: www.sypeng.idv.tw. SSRN Author Page: http://ssrn.com/author=723329.

2 It is evident that products and services in the information and communication technologies sector have gone through a dramatic technological convergence. We all experience the trend towards converting different kinds of information into data on computer files and then delivering those files over the same wires or airwaves. Most of us likely will get our telephone calls, television shows, recorded music, website access, and email over a single line via a single device, and as such the distinctions between each medium/device stops making sense.

3 The emergence of the convergence phenomenon is largely attributed to the invention of digital technology in the 1990s, which makes possible the delivery of media content in different technological forms. R. Wu and G. Leung, 'Media Policy and Regulation in the Age of Convergence – the Hong Kong Experience', *Hong Kong Law Journal* 30, 2000, 454, at 458–60.

4 S. Wunsch-Vincent, *The WTO, The Internet and Trade in Digital Products*, Oxford: Hart Publishing, 2006, pp. 13–32.

5 Ministerial Declaration on Trade in Information Technology Products, 13 December 1996, WT/MIN(96)/16, submission paras 17–18.

6 See S. Peng, 'Trade in Telecommunications Services: Doha and Beyond', *Journal of World Trade* 41(2), 2007, 293–318. See also S. Peng, 'Liberalization of Trade in Television Services: The Negotiation Dilemma and Challenges for the Future', *Journal of World Trade* 43 (4), 2009, 657–82.

7 D. Roseman, 'Domestic Regulation and Trade in Telecommunications Services: Experience and Prospects under the GATS', in A. Mattoo and P. Sauve (eds) *Domestic Regulation and Service Trade Liberalization*, Oxford: Oxford University Press, 2003, pp. 83, 85. See also D. Luff, 'Telecommunications and Audio-visual Services: Considerations for a Convergence Policy at the World Trade Organization Level', *Journal of World Trade* 38(6), 2004, 1059–86.

8 WTO Secretariat, *A Handbook on Reading WTO Goods and Services Schedules*, 2009, 508.

9 That is, Appellate Body Report, *EC – Computer Equipment*, Panel Report, *Mexico – Telecoms*. Appellate Body Report, *US – Gambling*. Request for Consultations by the United States, *China – Measures Affecting Financial Information Services and Foreign Financial Information Suppliers*, WT/DS373/1, S/L/320. First Written Submission of

the United States of America, *EC – IT Products*, Appellate Body Report, *China – Publications and Audiovisual Products*.

10 I. Van Damme, 'The Interpretation of Schedules of Commitments', *Journal of World Trade* 41(1), 2007, 1–52. I. Van Damme, *Treaty Interpretation by the WTO Appellate Body*, Oxford: Oxford University Press, 2009, pp. 93–102.

11 Panel Report, *EC – Computer Equipment*. Appellate Body Report, *EC – Computer Equipment*.

12 Ibid. Appellate Body Report, para. 109.

13 Ibid.

14 See generally Damme, op. cit.

15 Ibid. Tariff concessions are often negotiated for a considerable period of time on a bilateral basis between WTO members without the possibility of the involvement of all WTO members. The process of negotiating, drafting and concluding schedules of commitments can in various degrees be unilateral.

16 Ibid.

17 Ibid.

18 For the purpose of this chapter, the terms of 'EC' and 'EU' are interchangeable. The European Union (until 30 November 2009 known officially in the WTO as the European Communities for legal reasons) has been a WTO member since 1 January 1995. Since 1 December 2009 'European Union' has been the official name in the WTO as well as in the outside world.

19 For example, network or adaptor cards, along with devices such as hubs, bridges, routers, repeaters, LAN switches, and various cables and modules.

20 Panel Report, *EC – Computer Equipment*, paras 2.1–7.17.

21 Appellate Body Report, *EC – Computer Equipment*, paras 80–99.

22 C. Carmody, 'WTO Obligations as Collective', *European Journal of International Law* 17, 2006, 419.

23 Appellate Body Report, *EC – Computer Equipment*, para. 84.

24 On 28 May 2008 the United States and Japan requested WTO consultations with the EC with respect to its tariff treatment of certain information technology products. They were joined by Taiwan on 12 June 2008. WTO, Trade Topics, Dispute Settlement, available at *www.wto.org/english/tratop_e/dispu_e/dispu_e.htm* (accessed 6 August 2013).

25 See generally Second Written Submission of the European Communities, *EC – IT Products*, paras 6–26, 16 June 2009.

26 First Written Submission of Japan, *EC – IT Products*, paras 15–20, 5 March 2009.

27 ITA, para. 2 states: 'Pursuant to the modalities set forth in the Annex to this Declaration, each party shall bind and eliminate customs duties and other duties and charges of any kind, within the meaning of Article II:1(b) of the General Agreement on Tariffs and Trade 1994, with respect to the following: (a) all products classified (or classifiable) with Harmonized System (1996) ('HS') headings listed in Attachment A to the Annex to this Declaration; and (b) all products specified in Attachment B to the Annex to this Declaration, whether or not they are included in Attachment A; through equal rate reductions of customs duties beginning in 1997 and concluding in 2000, recognizing that extended staging of reductions and, before implementation, expansion of product coverage may be necessary in limited circumstances.'

28 GATT, Article II, Schedules of Concessions.

29 GATT, Article II(a) states: 'Each contracting party shall accord to the commerce of the other contracting parties treatment no less favorable than that provided for in the appropriate Part of the appropriate Schedule annexed to this Agreement.'

30 GATT, Article II(b) states: 'The products described in Part I of the Schedule relating to any contracting party, which are the products of territories of other contracting parties, shall, on their importation into the territory to which the Schedule relates,

and subject to the terms, conditions or qualifications set forth in that Schedule, be exempt from ordinary customs duties in excess of those set forth and provided therein. Such products shall also be exempt from all other duties or charges of any kind imposed on or in connection with the importation in excess of those imposed on the date of this Agreement or those directly and mandatorily required to be imposed thereafter by legislation in force in the importing territory on that date.'

31 If 'Flat Panel Display Devices', 'Set Top Boxes which have a Communication Function', and 'Multifunctional Machines' are within the scope of the tariff concessions made by the EC pursuant to the ITA, then the tariff commitments at issue are contained in the EC Schedule. As such, the EC's actions to impose duties on the products in question are inconsistent with Article II:1(a) and (b) of GATT.

32 First Written Submission of the European Communities, *EC – IT Products*, paras 30–50, 2 April 2009.

33 Ibid.

34 Ibid.

35 Ibid.

36 Ibid., paras 265–80.

37 In response to the complainant's argument that 'any kind of digital-to-analog converter constitutes a modem', the EC argued that such a proposition, if accepted, would lead to the absurd situation where any device that converts signals would be a modem, e.g. a television or an MP3/MP4 player would be considered as a modem. Ibid. See also Second Written Submission of the European Communities, *EC – IT Products*, paras 19–31, 16 June 2009.

38 First Written Submission of the European Communities, *EC – IT Products*, paras 205–35, 2 April 2009.

39 Ibid. paras 330–8.

40 Furthermore, many manufacturers of multifunctional machines market some of their machines in a copy-only version, with the printing and fax functions being offered as options. Ibid. para. 333.

41 Ibid. paras 371–2.

42 Second Written Submission of the European Communities, *EC – IT Products*, paras 125–33, 16 June 2009.

43 Ambassador Susan C. Schwab, United States Trade Representative Remarks on EU, ITA, WTO Case, 22 April 2008, available at www.ustr.gov (accessed 6 August 2013).

44 Ibid.

45 Indeed, as the Preamble to the ITA suggests, the ITA was concluded in part for the purpose of encouraging innovation and the spread of technology throughout the world: '*Considering* the key role of trade in information technology products in the development of information industries and in the dynamic expansion of the world economy; *Recognizing* the goals of raising standards of living and expanding the production of and trade in goods; *Desiring* to achieve maximum freedom of world trade in information technology products; *Desiring* to encourage the continued technological development of the information technology industry on a world-wide basis; *Mindful* of the positive contribution information technology makes to global economic growth and welfare; *Having agreed* to put into effect the results of these negotiations which involve concessions additional to those included in the Schedules attached to the Marrakesh Protocol to the General Agreement on Tariffs and Trade 1994; and *Recognizing* that the results of these negotiations also involve some concessions offered in negotiations leading to the establishment of Schedules annexed to the Marrakesh Protocol.'

46 ITA, para. 1.

47 World Trade Online, European Commission to Seek ITA Renegotiation on Four Points, 25 July 2008.

48 ITA, Preamble.
49 Ibid.
50 ITA, para. 1.
51 Panel Report, *EC – IT Products*, para. 7.355, 16 August 2010.
52 First Written Submission of the United States of America, *EC – IT Products*, para. 61, 5 March 2009.
53 ITA, para. 3 states: 'Participants shall meet periodically under the auspices of the Council on Trade in Goods to review the product coverage specified in the Attachments, with a view to agreeing, by consensus, whether in the light of technological developments, experience in applying the tariff concessions, or changes to the HS nomenclature, the Attachments should be modified to incorporate additional products, and to consult on non-tariff barriers to trade in information technology products. Such consultations shall be without prejudice to rights and obligations under the WTO Agreement.'
54 First Written Submission of the European Communities, *EC – IT Products*, para. 15, 2 April 2009.
55 First Written Submission of the United States of America, *China – Publications and Audiovisual Products*. First Written Submission of the People's Republic of China, *China – Publications and Audiovisual Products*. First Oral Statement of the United States of America, *China – Publications and Audiovisual Products*. Second Written Submission of the United States of America, *China – Publications and Audiovisual Products*. Second Oral Statement of the United States of America, *China – Publications and Audiovisual Products*. Panel Report, *China – Publications and Audiovisual Products*. Appellee Submission of the United States of America, *China – Publications and Audiovisual Products*. Appellate Body Report, *China – Publications and Audiovisual Products*.
56 Panel Report, *China – Publications and Audiovisual Products*, paras 7.1300–7.1311.
57 First Written Submission of the United States of America, *China – Publications and Audiovisual Products*, para. 357.
58 China maintains these restrictions through three measures: (1) the Interim Rules on the Management of Internet Culture; (2) the Notice of the Ministry of Culture on Some Issues Relating to Implementation of the 'Interim Rules on the Management of Internet Culture'; and (3) the Several Opinions on the Development and Management of Network Music.
59 First Written Submission of the United States of America, *China – Publications and Audiovisual Products*, paras 140–55.
60 First Written Submission of the People's Republic of China, *China – Publications and Audiovisual Products*, paras 389–403.
61 Panel Report, *China – Publications and Audiovisual Products*, paras 7.1161–7.1167.
62 First Written Submission of the People's Republic of China, *China – Publications and Audiovisual Products*, paras 389–403.
63 Ibid. at paras 443–8.
64 Second Oral Statement of the United States of America, *China – Publications and Audiovisual Products*, paras 33–6. See e.g. First Written Submission of the United States of America, *China – Publications and Audiovisual Products*, para. 51. See e.g. First Oral Statement of the United States of America, *China – Publications and Audiovisual Products*, para. 68. First Oral Statement of the United States of America, *China – Publications and Audiovisual Products*, para. 63.58–66. Second Written Submission of the United States of America, *China – Publications and Audiovisual Products*, para. 154.
65 Work Programme on Electronic Commerce, Progress Report to the 45 General Council, adopted by the Council for the Trade in Services on 19 July 1999, S/L/74.
66 Section 6.4 of this chapter will further discuss these issues.
67 U. Linderfalk, *On the Interpretation of Treaties*, Berlin: Springer, 2007, pp. 73–95.

68 Ibid. at 73.
69 Ibid.
70 International Federation of the Phonographic Industry (IFPI) Report, *Digital Music Report*, 2010, available at www.ifpi.org/content/section_statistics/index.html (accessed 8 March 2010).
71 Ibid.
72 Ibid.
73 First Written Submission of the People's Republic of China, *China – Publications and Audiovisual Products*, para. 448.
74 U. Linderfalk, *On the Interpretation of Treaties*, Berlin: Springer, 2007, pp. 73–95.
75 Vienna Convention, Article 31: General rule of interpretation: '1. A treaty shall be interpreted in good faith in accordance with the ordinary meaning to be given to the terms of the treaty in their context and in the light of its object and purpose. 2. The context for the purpose of the interpretation of a treaty shall comprise, in addition to the text, including its preamble and annexes: (*a*) any agreement relating to the treaty which was made between all the parties in connection with the conclusion of the treaty; (*b*) any instrument which was made by one or more parties in connection with the conclusion of the treaty and accepted by the other parties as an instrument related to the treaty. 3. There shall be taken into account, together with the context: (*a*) any subsequent agreement between the parties regarding the interpretation of the treaty or the application of its provisions; (*b*) any subsequent practice in the application of the treaty which establishes the agreement of the parties regarding its interpretation; (*c*) any relevant rules of international law applicable in the relations between the parties. 4. A special meaning shall be given to a term if it is established that the parties so intended.'
76 Panel Report, *EC – IT Products*, para. 7.538, 16 August 2010.
77 Such an approach, however, has been strongly criticized by the EC as 'a short-sighted', 'simplistic way of reading the treaty' that may have negative systemic implication; see the executive summary of the oral statement by the EC at the first substantive meeting, para 8.
78 Panel Report, *EC – IT Products*, para. 7.548, 16 August 2010.
79 Panel Report, *EC – IT Products*, paras 7.549, 7.1329, 16 August 2010.
80 Panel Report, *EC – IT Products*, para. 7.927, 16 August 2010.
81 Panel Report, *China –Publications and Audiovisual Products*, para. 7.1219.
82 United States' Appellee's Submission, paras 106.
83 Ibid.
84 Appellate Body Report, *China –Publications and Audiovisual Products*, para. 396.
85 See generally R. Gardiner, *Treaty Interpretation*, Oxford: Oxford University Press, 2008, pp. 172–3.
86 Ibid.
87 Vienna Convention, Article 32: Supplementary means of interpretation: 'Recourse may be had to supplementary means of interpretation, including the preparatory work of the treaty and the circumstances of its conclusion, in order to confirm the meaning resulting from the application of Article 31, or to determine the meaning when the interpretation according to Article 31: (*a*) leaves the meaning ambiguous or obscure; or (*b*) leads to a result which is manifestly absurd or unreasonable.'
88 Oral statement by Hong Kong, China at the First Substantive Meeting, *EC – IT Products*, para. 6.
89 Panel Report, *EC – IT Products*, para. 7.596, 16 August 2010.
90 Panel Report, *EC – IT Products*, para. 7.596, 16 August 2010.
91 Ibid. para. 7.600.
92 Ibid. para. 7.601.
93 Ibid. at note 807.
94 First Written Submission of the People's Republic of China, *China – Publications and Audiovisual Products*, paras 476–82.

95 Panel Report, *China – Publications and Audiovisual Products*, paras 7.1235–7.1247.
96 Ibid.
97 Appellate Body Report, *China – Publications and Audiovisual Products*, paras 407–10.
98 T. Voon and A. Mitchell, 'Open for Business? China's Telecommunications Service Market and the WTO', *Journal of International Economic Law* 13, 2010, 321–78.
99 Gardiner, op. cit. at 343.
100 The EC pointed out that the multifunctional LCD monitor did not exist at the time the concessions were being negotiated. This casts an important light on the circumstances under which the concessions were made in view of the extremely detailed technical language used in the narrative of the product definitions in attachment B to the ITA. The EC stressed how the radical changes in monitor technology from the time the ITA was negotiated have made it exceptionally difficult to define a 'monitor' in order to place it in the relevant legal framework.
101 R. Weber, 'Digital Trade in WTO-Law – Taking Stock and Looking Ahead', *Asian Journal of WTO & International Health Law and Policy* 5, 2010, 11–24.
102 Appellate Body Report, *US – Gambling*. Panel Report on *US – Gambling*, para. 6.285
103 First Oral Statement of the United States of America, *China – Publications and Audiovisual Products*, para. 54.
104 Ibid.
105 Panel Report, *China – Publications and Audiovisual Products*, paras 7.1248 7.1264.
106 Second Oral Statement of the United States of America, *China – Publications and Audiovisual Products*, paras 46–53.
107 International Telecommunication Union (ITU), *Regulatory Implications of Broadband*, available at www.itu.int/osg/spu/ni/broadband/workshop/southafricafinal.pdf (accessed 20 June 2010).
108 ITU, World Telecommunication Policy Forum (WTPF 2001), Final Report, at 23, available at www.itu.int/osg/spu/wtpf/wtpf2001/sgreport/finalreport31Jan_files/finalreport31Jan.doc (accessed 25 September 2006). *See also* ITU, Telecommunication Development Bureau, Document 1/090-E (Rev.1), at 13, available at www.itu.int/ITU-D/study_groups/SGP_1998–2002/SG1/Documents/2000/090r1e.doc (accessed 24 July 2006).
109 Information Note by the Secretariat, Council for Trade in Services, Special Session: Telecommunications Services, JOB(05)/208, 26 September 2005.
110 Statement by Japan, Report of the Meeting held on 21, 22 and 25 February 2005, TN/S/M/14, para. 46.
111 Communication from the European Communities, Classification in the Telecom Sector under the WTO-GATS Framework (hereinafter 'EC Paper'), TN/S/W/27, S/CSC/W/44, 10 February 2005. See also Information Note by the Secretariat, Council for Trade in Services, Special Session: Telecommunications Services, JOB(05)/208, 26 September 2005.
112 S. Peng, 'Trade in Telecommunications Services: Doha and Beyond', *Journal of World Trade* 41(2), 2007, 293–318.
113 Panel Report, *China – Publications and Audiovisual Products*, para. 7.1258.
114 D. Geradin and M. Kerf, 'Levelling the Playing Field: Is the WTO Adequately Equipped to Prevent Anti-Competitive Practices in Telecommunications', in D. Geradin and D. Luff (eds), *The WTO and Global Convergence in Telecommunications and Audio-Visual Services*, Cambridge: Cambridge University Press, 2004, pp. 131, 146. See also D. Luff, 'Telecommunications and Audiovisual Services: Considerations for a Convergence Policy at the World Trade Organization Level', *Journal of World Trade* 38(6), 2004, 1059–86.
115 M. Hukill, R. Ono and C. Vallath (eds), *Electronic Communication Convergence*, Thousand Oaks, CA: Sage, 2000.

Part III

Cross-cutting issues in trade, investment, science and technology

7 Australia's plain packaging of tobacco products

Science and health measures in international economic law[1]

Andrew Higgins,[2] *Andrew Mitchell*[3] *and James Munro*[4]

7.1 Introduction

What constitutes sufficient evidence to justify the introduction of a public health measure that has never been tried before? Every effective public health measure started life as an experiment at some point.

Australia's introduction of plain packaging of cigarettes, which is a world's first, and the international legal challenges to Australia's plain packaging legislation put into the spotlight how public health experts, governments and lawyers respectively address this question. Those legal challenges have been brought by Ukraine,[5] Honduras,[6] the Dominican Republic,[7] and Cuba[8] in the WTO, and by Philip Morris Asia under the Agreement between the Government of Hong Kong and the Government of Australia for the Promotion and Protection of Investments ('Hong Kong–Australia BIT').[9] They raise questions as to the standard and onus of proof required to justify new and innovative public health measures, and how international tribunals should handle uncertainty in scientific evidence.

In this chapter, we evaluate these questions in light of the case study of Australia's plain packaging measures. In the next section, we set out the importance of being able to establish a rational, science-based connection between the plain packaging measures and their public health objectives. In Section 7.3, we consider how international economic law accounts for the difficulties associated with gathering accurate scientific data on the effectiveness of a measure that operates in a multifaceted social context. For instance, such a context may include the concurrent application of complementary measures or attempts to undermine the measure by external social actors. Section 7.4 then considers the relationship between a science-based measure and its objective in international economic law. Section 7.5 looks at the crucial question of how tribunals in international economic law have managed uncertainty in scientific evidence, such as scientific disagreements over findings or gaps in scientific data. Finally, Section 7.6 evaluates the standard of proof required of scientific evidence in international economic law. We find that tribunals and panels in trade and investment disputes have demonstrated a welcome degree of flexibility in approaching scientific evidence. However, uncertainty remains in a number of key areas of international economic law, and this makes it difficult to foresee exactly how a tribunal or panel will manage the role of science in a given dispute.

7.2 Australia's plain packaging of tobacco and the importance of science in its international legal challenges

It is generally accepted that the evidence needed to justify a measure partly depends on the gravity of harm that the measure is trying to prevent or reduce, and the risks of not acting. In the case of tobacco use, the gravity of the harm is beyond dispute. Tobacco use is the only legally available consumer product[10] that will kill a third to a half of all people who use it exactly in the way intended by the manufacturer.[11] It is a global pandemic that kills 6 million people each year, including an estimated 600,000 non-smokers who die from exposure to tobacco smoke.[12] Yet millions of young people start tobacco use each year,[13] and millions of long-term users continue to smoke because they cannot break their addiction to nicotine.[14] The international community recognizes that concerted action is needed to reduce this pandemic – a commitment that is reflected in the first treaty negotiated under the auspices of WHO, the WHO Framework Convention on Tobacco Control, which has 176 parties.[15] The Guidelines to the Framework Convention on Tobacco Control state that 'Parties should consider adopting measures to restrict or prohibit the use of logos, colours, brand images or promotional information on packaging other than brand names and product names displayed in a standard colour and font style (plain packaging).'[16] Further:[17]

> Packaging and product design are important elements of advertising and promotion. Parties should consider adopting plain packaging requirements to eliminate the effects of advertising or promotion on packaging. Packaging, individual cigarettes or other tobacco products should carry no advertising or promotion, including design features that make products attractive.

But that still leaves the question, will it work, or, more specifically, is there sufficient evidence available to suggest it is likely to achieve its objectives? This is a pivotal question because Australia will likely need to establish a rational causal relationship between its plain packaging measures and public health goals to mount a successful defence against the legal challenges mentioned above.

With respect to the WTO challenges, the need to establish a rational causal relationship will likely manifest itself in the so-called 'necessity' test.[18] This is because the complainants have alleged violations of GATT, the TBT

Agreement, and the TRIPS Agreement. While each of these instruments reserves policy space for public health measures to some degree, under some of these WTO Agreements such measures must be 'necessary' to protect human health.[19] The need for measures to be 'necessary' to achieve the objective at issue gives rise to an examination of the extent to which the measures contribute to the objective and whether there exist any alternative measures that contribute to the same degree and are less trade restrictive.[20] The Appellate Body has acknowledged that multiple measures may be needed to address a particular goal and also that it may not be possible to quantify the contribution. Particularly given that this is the first time that plain packaging has been implemented, it is likely that the Panel and Appellate Body would not require scientific evidence demonstrating a causal relationship – since that may not be possible for a measure that has only just come in.[21]

With respect to the challenge under the Hong Kong–Australia BIT, a rational causal relationship between the measures and their public policy goals could refute Philip Morris Asia's claims of indirect expropriation and breaches of the fair and equitable treatment and unreasonable impairment standards.[22] This is because it would assist in demonstrating that the measure is not arbitrary but reasonable, proportionate and a legitimate exercise of regulatory powers.[23] The Tribunal's views on whether these factors apply to plain packaging will likely be crucial to the outcome of the case.[24]

7.3 Gathering scientific data in a multifaceted social context

Predicting the impacts of any public health measure will always be a fraught exercise when the problem involves a complex web of chemical, psychological, social and commercial factors. One has to consider how tobacco users and potential users are likely to react to plain packaging and whether the scope and timing of its effects will be different for teenagers and young adults who might be at risk of taking up smoking, compared with the likely effects on regular adult smokers, of which the overwhelming majority are addicted. But this is only half of the picture. The reaction of manufacturers and suppliers of the products causing the harm is also a critical consideration. The tobacco industry is extremely profitable,[25] sells a highly addictive product and operates in an oligopolistic market.[26] This combination of forces means that the industry has considerable interest in, and capacity to influence, how the 'market' reacts to plain packaging at least in the short and medium term. For example the industry could try to use pricing strategies to ameliorate the effects of plain packaging on people's desire to use tobacco products. Some tobacco companies have already gone on record claiming that the industry will react to plain packaging by reducing prices and as a consequence tobacco use is likely to go up, not down.[27]

Recognizing that tobacco use is a complex social problem, the evidence as to whether any new tobacco control measure is likely to work will not be found in laboratory experiments. There are also significant difficulties in carrying out 'real world' or ecological experiments for several reasons. First, there are the obvious difficulties in measuring the impact of a single measure on a population that controls for all the other possible factors affecting smoking behaviour, and the possibility that multiple tobacco control policies may produce synergistic effects. Countries that have been successful in reducing smoking prevalence generally have a comprehensive range of tobacco control measures, which always leaves scope to argue that one or more of those measure are not making a material impact, because it is the other measures that are doing all the work. Sometimes the industry has been heard to argue that reductions in prevalence may not be owing to any measures but rather to a society's negative attitudes towards smoking, although how those negative attitudes were formed is not explained.[28] The most reliable way of measuring the incremental effects of a single measure would be a behavioural study involving two sufficiently similar and representative population groups whose environments are the same in every respect but for the measure being tested.[29] But finding such populations would be extremely difficult. Even if it were possible, the scale of the experiment might prompt the industry to complain that the measure was effectively being introduced without evidence.

WTO jurisprudence has shown a degree of flexibility in accounting for these kinds of difficulties. The Appellate Body has recognized that there will inevitably be gaps in scientific knowledge. However, such gaps do not necessarily render available knowledge insufficient:[30]

> The nature of scientific inquiry is such that it is always possible to conduct more research or obtain additional information. The possibility of conducting further research or of analyzing additional information, by itself, should not mean that the relevant scientific evidence is or becomes insufficient.

Perhaps in recognition of the difficulties in gathering conclusive scientific evidence in certain instances, the Appellate Body has permitted the use of quantitative projections or qualitative reasoning to demonstrate that a measure is 'apt to produce a material contribution to the achievement of its objective'.[31] This kind of evidence may be used in lieu of evidence of *actual* contribution to the objective.[32]

Relatedly, the Appellate Body has also held that a given measure need only *contribute* to the objective at issue, rather than comprehensively *achieve* the objective, in order to satisfy the 'necessity' test.[33] In this regard, WTO jurisprudence acknowledges the convoluted interplay between cause and effect where a suite of measures is pursued to address multifaceted problems:[34]

> [C]ertain complex public health or environmental problems may be tackled only with a comprehensive policy comprising a multiplicity of interacting measures. Substituting one element of this comprehensive

policy for another would weaken the policy by reducing the synergies between its components, as well as its total effect.

As such, difficulties in isolating the precise effects of plain packaging where it is implemented as part of a broader suite of measures are unlikely to have a significantly detrimental impact on Australia's defence of plain packaging's WTO compatibility.

7.4 The relationship between a science-based measure and its objectives

No single policy measure will affect all the factors that influence smoking behaviour, and there is universal consensus that effective tobacco control strategies require a comprehensive suite of measures affecting all aspects of supply and demand for tobacco use.[35] Not only does this ensure that all the factors influencing tobacco use are 'covered', but it is also intended to produce synergies between the various tobacco control policies that are being pursued. Hence, in order to assess the likely effects of plain packaging, or any tobacco control measure, one has to take into account the context in which they operate, how they interact with other tobacco control policies, as well as the countervailing factors that encourage tobacco use.[36]

To state that the objective of the plain packaging measure is to reduce tobacco use is to simplify what the measure is designed to do and, equally importantly, how it is designed to do it. This is not to confuse ends with means but rather to appreciate the complex nature of tobacco use and that there are many factors that both promote and discourage it. Factors that contribute to the decision to start or continue using tobacco products or not taking up smoking or trying to quit include peer and family influences, the influence of marketing by the industry, the financial costs of using, the social acceptability of smoking, the pharmacological and psychological effects of addiction, people's understanding of the health consequences of smoking both to them and to others around them, the restrictions on where and when people are allowed to smoke, the degree to which smoking is considered socially unacceptable, and professional and medical assistance in helping people overcome their addiction.[37]

For any young person contemplating smoking or beginning to experiment with cigarettes, or for any regular addicted smoker contemplating whether to quit, there is a range of factors pulling them in both directions.[38]

While the short definition of tobacco control, at least from a government's perspective, may be initiatives designed to reduce tobacco use,[39] the longer and more accurate definition is initiatives that strengthen the factors that discourage tobacco initiation and use, while at the same minimizing the influence of factors that promote and sustain tobacco use.

The framing, nature and gravity of the objectives are often key issues in both WTO disputes and investor-state arbitration. While provisions in the WTO Agreement often prescribe a list of permissible objectives that may justify prima facie violations of otherwise-protected norms (such as public health or public morals),[40] WTO jurisprudence has accorded member states a degree of deference in determining their own levels of protection or regulatory outcomes.[41]

By contrast, international investment treaties are often silent as to protected public policy objectives.[42] On one hand, this gives states greater latitude in the range of public policy objectives they can use to justify prima facie violations. On the other hand, however, this has led to some tribunals reviewing not only whether a measure is necessary and proportionate to achieve an objective, but also the efficacy of the objective itself.[43] Reviewing the legitimacy of a state's public policy objective and evaluating whether it is sufficiently important or grave to justify a violation of a protected investment norm could be viewed as an excessive intrusion into national sovereignty, and other tribunals have opted for a more deferential approach.[44]

That said, the objectives pursued through plain packaging are unlikely to raise significant controversies in either legal challenge. This is because the harm caused by tobacco to human health is well established, and it is beyond dispute that the protection of human health is the core public policy objective.

7.5 Accounting for uncertainty in scientific evidence

The behavioural effects of tobacco plain packaging are necessarily attended by a degree of uncertainty, at least at this point in time.

As mentioned above, WTO jurisprudence has demonstrated a degree of flexibility in relation to these kinds of limitation in collecting scientific evidence. However, given this complex context in which the effectiveness of plain packaging will be measured, one might be tempted to conclude that it is really impossible to know whether a tobacco control measure will work before it is adopted and therefore the only option is to trial the measure and assess its impacts, taking into account that it is designed to work in conjunction with other policies, after it is given sufficient time to work.

Even if this is the case – that it is impossible to know whether plain packaging will work prior to its adoption – it is noteworthy that WTO jurisprudence has been willing to accept that there may be a degree of uncertainty regarding scientific evidence. For instance, the Appellate Body has stated that, in justifying a measure as 'necessary to protect human health', a member may rely

> on scientific sources which . . . may represent a divergent, but qualified and respected, opinion. In SPS cases, the Appellate Body has recognised that a Member is not obliged, in setting health policy, automatically to follow what . . . may constitute a majority scientific opinion.[45]

This represents an acknowledgement that there need not necessarily be one conclusively 'correct' scientific answer, or that the scientific evidence may be attended by some uncertainty. Divergent pieces of scientific evidence may be valid if they meet a requisite level of quality. In a similar vein, the Appellate Body stated that:[46]

> WTO Members should be permitted to take a provisional measure where new evidence from a qualified and respected source puts into question the relationship between the pre-existing body of scientific evidence and the conclusions regarding the risks. We are referring to circumstances where new scientific evidence casts doubts as to whether the previously existing body of scientific evidence still permits of a sufficiently objective assessment of risk.

This passage similarly demonstrates a degree of comfort in WTO jurisprudence with uncertainty or doubt in relation to scientific evidence, and that it may change over time.

7.6 Plain packaging and the standard of proof in international economic law

The case of plain packaging is much stronger than just a 'suck it and see' approach to what is a major public health issue. This is because there is a significant amount of experimental evidence as to the effects of plain packaging on people's perceptions and beliefs about tobacco products and tobacco users, and a very large body of evidence, built up over decades, as to how those perceptions and beliefs about tobacco products, and the people who use them, influence tobacco use among both adolescents and addicted smokers.

One of the features of plain packaging is that it is designed to increase the effectiveness of factors that discourage tobacco use while also minimizing the impact of the countervailing influence of tobacco promotion by the industry to promote it. The objectives of plain packaging, as set out in Australia's Tobacco Plain Packaging Act, are to:

> (a) reduce the appeal of tobacco products to consumers; and
> (b) increase the effectiveness of health warnings on the retail packaging of tobacco products; and
> (c) reduce the ability of the retail packaging of tobacco products to mislead consumers about the harmful effects of smoking or using tobacco products.[47]

There is a growing body of evidence, and a strong consensus in the public health community, that plain packaging will achieve all of these objectives.

The 2012 US Surgeon General's Report concluded that:

> Plain packaging has several potential effects. First, it enhances the effectiveness of health warnings by increasing their noticeability, recall, and believability. . . . Second, plain packaging has the potential to reduce

> the level of false beliefs about the harmfulness of different brands. . . . Third, plain packaging makes smoking less appealing.[48]

A systematic review of the literature carried out for the UK Department of Health as part of its consultation on standardized packaging concluded that there was consistency in study findings regarding the potential impacts of plain packaging.[49] Almost every experimental study examining its effects found a statistically significant impact on one of the outcomes measured. The industry claims that many if not all of these studies are methodologically flawed, and, in any event, do not prove that plain packaging will reduce smoking prevalence.[50] In relation to the first claim, the fact that almost all of the studies, many of which are published in independent peer review journals, are finding positive results regardless of the population being studied, or the methodology used, represents a degree of convergence that is hard to ignore.

As for the second claim, it is true that no plain packaging study can prove that plain packaging will change behaviour because, as yet, there are no behavioural studies measuring its impact in the real world. Nonetheless there is considerable evidence that all of the likely proximal effects of plain packaging are themselves factors that influence smoking behaviour and prevalence.

The industry accepts that its retail packaging is a form of marketing (a 'bonsai billboard' as Counsel for Imperial Tobacco put it in the industry's unsuccessful constitutional challenge to Australia's plain packaging laws),[51] but it asserts that marketing only influences brand choice, and has no impact on people's decisions to smoke or to continue smoking or to quit.[52] Measuring the precise impact of tobacco marketing on smoking initiation and use is hampered by at least two things: first, it would be unethical to deliberately expose people, especially children, to tobacco marketing to measure how it affects their behaviour; and second, the sort of detailed sales data that may show the impact of advertising expenditure or marketing campaigns on consumption rates among different population groups is held by the industry, and it has refused to make this data available, even to its own experts.[53] Notwithstanding these difficulties, that the marketing of a consumer product does not have the potential to increase demand for the product is inconsistent with expert opinion on marketing and common sense.[54] For example, the idea that advertisements for Coca-Cola only influence people who have already decided that they want to buy a cola-flavoured carbonated beverage seems implausible.[55] A majority of studies that have examined the relationship between tobacco marketing and prevalence have found a causal link. The 2012 US Surgeon General's Report concluded that 'advertising and promotional activities by tobacco companies have been shown to cause the onset and continuation of smoking among adolescents and young adults'.[56] It also concluded that 'research conducted by the tobacco industry consistently demonstrates that the brand imagery portrayed on packages is particularly influential during youth and young adulthood – the period in which smoking behaviour and brand preferences develop'.[57]

Plain packaging will remove this very important influence on youth and young adults and do it in a way that gives greater prominence to the text and pictorial warnings conveying information about the harmful effects of smoking. Colourful and stylish pack designs make smoking more appealing, but they also distract and detract from government mandated health warnings. By contrast, plain packaging will present smokers and potential smokers with the unvarnished truth about the nature of the product and the deadly consequences of using it. This is why plain packaging, in conjunction with other measures, is also predicted to have an impact on addicted smokers' decision-making processes. The health consequences of smoking are known to be a major motivating factor for people contemplating quitting.[58] Moreover, some smokers who are concerned about their health choose brands with lighter colour packaging in the mistaken belief that they are less harmful than others. Plain packaging may help correct that belief.[59]

While the foregoing evidence suggests that plain packaging is likely to be an effective tool in achieving public health goals, it is almost certain to be disputed in the legal challenges mentioned above. This gives rise to a key question: what is the applicable standard of proof for demonstrating the effectiveness of plain packing in the legal challenges?

The term 'standard of proof' refers to the degree of persuasion that the adjudicator must reach in order to decide an issue.[60] The applicable standard of proof can be pivotal to the outcome of a case.[61] For instance, the 'beyond reasonable doubt' standard sets a particularly high threshold of proof, whereas the 'balance of probabilities' and 'preponderance of evidence' standards simply demand that a proposition be shown to be more probable than not, and the 'prima facie' standard seems to accept evidence sufficient to establish a fact or raise a presumption unless rebutted or disproved by the opposing party.

Importantly, both the WTO Agreement and most international investment treaties are silent as to the applicable standard of proof. This is reflective of public international law more generally, where few international instruments specify a standard of proof and where the question of which standard to apply has received scant attention from international courts and tribunals.[62]

In respect of WTO law, the Appellate Body has made no definitive statement on the applicable standard of proof in WTO disputes. While a number of commentators have sought to distil the legal standard from the existing practice of panels, they have split between those arguing that a 'prima facie' standard is applied,[63] and those arguing that a 'preponderance of evidence' standard is applied.[64] On one hand, panels make frequent references to whether a party has established a 'prima facie case' in respect of a particular issue, and at least one panel accepted prima facie evidence purely on the grounds that it had not been rebutted.[65] On the other hand, WTO disputes are often laden with elaborate and complicated factual evidence that is contested rigorously.

In this context, it is unsurprising that WTO jurisprudence offers only limited guidance. The Panel in *Canada – Dairy* explicitly rejected the application of a 'beyond reasonable doubt' standard,[66] and the Appellate Body stated in

US – Carbon Steel that the 'nature and extent of the evidence required to satisfy the burden of proof will vary from case to case'.[67] Similarly, in *US – Wool Shirts and Blouses* it stated that:[68]

> In the context of the GATT 1994 and the WTO Agreement, precisely how much and precisely what kind of evidence will be required to establish such a presumption will necessarily vary from measure to measure, provision to provision, and case to case.

These statements on the 'varying' nature of the standard of proof under WTO dispute settlement make it difficult for litigants to approximate the degree of evidence they are required to adduce to ground their claims of fact. Equally, they make it difficult to foresee whether the existing scientific evidence on the effectiveness of plain packaging will suffice. Significantly, however, the Conference of the Parties to the WHO Framework Convention on Tobacco Control has adopted the Article 11 and 13 guidelines,[69] and both the World Health Organization and the Convention Secretariat of the World Health Organization Framework Convention on Tobacco control have expressed support for Australia's initiative.[70] This is likely to provide a degree of objective legitimacy to Australia's position that plain packaging is a proportionate response to the adverse health effects of tobacco products.

In respect of international investment law, there is a concomitant dearth of guidance on the applicable standard of proof. As a general proposition, however, tribunals seem to apply the 'balance of probabilities' standard, which may be adjusted higher or lower depending on the particular factual question before it.[71] For instance, the Tribunal in *Rompetrol v. Romania* decided to apply the 'balance of probabilities' standard for ordinary questions of fact, yet decided to apply a higher standard in relation to allegations of bad faith, and decided to apply a lower standard in relation to facts asserted by one party and accepted by the other.[72]

The Tribunal in *Tokios Tokelés v. Ukraine*, in an acknowledgment of the limited guidance on standard of proof in investor-state arbitration, canvassed three possibilities:[73]

> As regards the standard, three possibilities have attracted support. First, the usual standard, which requires the party making an assertion to persuade the decision-maker that it is more likely than not to be true. Second, that where the dispute concerns an allegation against a person or body in high authority the burden may be lower, simply because direct proof is likely to be hard to find. Third [where the dispute concerns an allegation against a person or body in high authority], the standard is higher than the balance of probabilities.

In a slightly different approach to the Tribunal in *Rompetrol v. Romania*, the Tribunal in *Tokios Tokelés v. Ukraine* questioned the underlying logic of the second and third possibilities, and opted for a general 'balance of probabilities' standard.

The award in *Methanex v. United States of America* provides an indication of how investor-state tribunals manage disputed scientific evidence in investment claims. Although the impugned measure in that case had been based on a scientific report, there were scientific disagreements about its findings. Despite these disagreements, the Tribunal was willing to accept the report because it was peer reviewed, its findings were transparent, and it reflected a 'serious, objective and scientific approach'.[74] On that basis, the Tribunal found that the measure was 'motivated by the honest belief, held in good faith and on reasonable scientific grounds'.[75] This approach seems to focus less on proof being established on a standard of 'balance of probabilities' or 'beyond reasonable doubt', and more on the bona fides of the process that led to the scientific conclusion. Certainly, a perception that there existed a conflict of interest in the production of scientific evidence will likely dilute its probative value.

Since the question of whether plain packaging is effective in meeting its goals does not involve any grave allegations impugning the reputations of individuals and will very likely be contested, it seems appropriate that the so-called 'normal standard for claims of breach of the protection under a bilateral investment treaty' should apply – the 'balance of probabilities'.[76] While the ultimate outcome will depend on the factual evidence presented by the disputing parties, it seems likely at this stage that there exists sufficient scientific evidence for Australia to satisfy that standard of proof.

7.7 Conclusion

A tobacco control measure that targets both ends of the rope in 'the tug of war' for adolescents and addicted smokers is likely to make a material contribution to a nation's tobacco control strategy. Most of the evidence to date indicates that plain packaging will make a contribution to reducing prevalence. On the one hand plain packaging ensures that only accurate information about the health consequences of smoking is communicated via the pack and communicated in a way that increases the salience of the information; on the other hand, it denies the industry an important medium to promote its products to smokers and young people who are susceptible to taking up smoking. Estimating the size of the impact from plain packaging in advance of its introduction is probably impossible, and even after its introduction there will be scope for debate about its impact, given that there are a multitude of confounding factors. The tobacco industry may drop prices to counteract the effects of plain packaging too, but the primary policy tool for regulating price related marketing is excise taxes. Australia increased the rate of excise by 25 per cent in 2010 as part of its new suite of measures, which includes plain packaging, to further reduce tobacco prevalence[77] and the government recently announced that it plans to introduce further increases in 2014.[78] No single measure can do all the work of a successful tobacco control strategy. However, most of the available evidence suggests that plain packaging will make a material contribution to the goal of reducing tobacco use over time.

It is in this context that dispute settlement bodies convened under both the WTO Agreement and the Hong Kong–Australia BIT will be called upon to assess the plain packaging laws. Despite the difficulties in measuring with precision the magnitude of their contribution to public health objectives in the *real* world, investor-state tribunals and WTO panels and the Appellate Body should be somewhat flexible in considering the scientific evidence justifying their adoption. Past cases demonstrate that there is usually an acceptable margin of scientific uncertainty or divergences in scientific opinion, provided that the scientific evidence relied upon meets a given threshold of quality. For instance, if scientific evidence is produced through transparent and arm's-length processes by recognized experts and is subject to peer review or other quality controls, it is more likely to meet the applicable standard of proof. That said, the exact quantity and quality of evidence required to establish a causal connection, and whether a dispute settlement body will focus more on the processes involved in the generation of scientific evidence or on the merits of the evidence itself, remain key outstanding questions. The international legal challenges to Australia's plain packaging laws could play an important role in bringing clarity to those areas of international economic law.

Notes

1 We would like to thank Jonathan Liberman and Tania Voon for their helpful comments. Andrew Higgins was principally responsible for the discussion of public health measures and the evidence on the potential effects of plain packaging. Andrew Mitchell and James Munro were principally responsible for the discussion of the treatment of this evidence in international trade and investment law.

2 Departmental Lecturer in Law, Faculty of Law, University of Oxford and Victorian Barrister. Email: andrew.higgins@law.ox.ac.uk. Since 2011 Andrew Higgins has advised the Australian government in relation to the legal challenges to its plain packaging laws. The views expressed in the chapter are the author's own and are not necessarily shared by the Australian government.

3 Professor, University of Melbourne Law School; Director, Global Economic Law Network; Barrister and Solicitor of the Supreme Court of Victoria and the High Court of Australia. Email: a.mitchell@unimelb.edu.au. Andrew Mitchell has provided formal and informal advice to governments, intergovernmental organizations and NGOs in relation to plain tobacco packaging and related issues. I have also received research grants from the Australian National Preventive Health Agency and the Australian Research Council to conduct independent research in conjunction with Cancer Council Victoria on the relationship between international trade and investment law and common risk factors for non-communicable diseases. The views expressed in this chapter are the author's own are not necessarily shared by the Australian government.

4 LLB (Hons) (Melb), BA (Melb); PhD (Law) Candidate, Melbourne Law School. Email munroj@unimelb.edu.au. James is currently engaged as a Research Assistant at the

University of Melbourne under a grant from the Australian National Preventive Health Agency. He is on leave from a position in the Attorney-General's Department, Australian government. The views expressed in the chapter are the author's own and are not necessarily shared by any employer.

5 Request for the Establishment of a Panel by Ukraine, Australia – Tobacco Plain Packaging.

6 Request for the Establishment of a Panel by Honduras, Australia – Certain Measures Concerning Trademarks, Geographical Indications and Other Plain Packaging Requirements Applicable to Tobacco Products and Packaging; WT/ DS435/16 (17 October 2012).

7 Request for the Establishment of a Panel by Dominican Republic, Australia – Certain Measures Concerning Trademarks, Geographical Indications and Other Plain Packaging Requirements Applicable to Tobacco Products and Packaging, WT/DS441/15 (9 November 2012).

8 Request for Consultations by Cuba, Australia – Certain Measures Concerning Trademarks, Geographical Indications and Other Plain Packaging Requirements Applicable to Tobacco Products and Packaging,WT/DS458/1 (7 May 2013).

9 Agreement between the Government of Hong Kong and the Government of Australia for the Promotion and Protection of Investments, signed 15 September 1993, 1748 UNTS 385 (entered into force 15 October 1993) ('Hong Kong–Australia BIT'); Philip Morris Limited, 'Philip Morris Asia Initiates Legal Action Against the Australian Government Over Plain Packaging', Press Release, 27 June 2011, available at www.pmi.com/eng/media_center/press_releases/pages/PM_Asia_plain_packaging.aspx (accessed 6 August 2013). See also e.g. C. Kenny, 'Big Tobacco Ignites Legal War', *The Australian*, 27 June 2011; International Centre for Trade and Sustainable Development, 'Philip Morris Launches Legal Battle Over Australian Cigarette Packaging', *Bridges Weekly Trade News Digest* 15(24), 29 June 2011.

10 J. Walton, J. Barondess and S. Lock (eds), *The Oxford Medical Companion*, Oxford: Oxford University Press, USA, 1994.

11 World Health Organization, 'WHO Report on the Global Tobacco Epidemic', 2008, at 14, available at www.who.int/tobacco/mpower/2008/en/index.html (accessed 6 August 2013).

12 World Health Organization, 'WHO Report on the Global Tobacco Epidemic', 2011, at 7, available at www.who.int/tobacco/global_report/2011/en/ (accessed 6 August 2013).

13 In 2008 it was estimated that there were approximately 1 billion smokers: World Health Organization, WHO Report on the Global Tobacco Pandemic, 2008, at 15, available at www.who.int/tobacco/mpower/2008/en/index.html (accessed 6 August 2013).

14 The 2000 Royal College of Physicians Report on nicotine addiction states that 'nicotine is highly addictive, to a degree similar or in some respects exceeding addiction to "hard" drugs such as heroin or cocaine'. It further observed that 95 per cent of smokers were addicted to nicotine: Royal College of Physicians of London, *Nicotine Addiction in Britain*, February 2000, at xiv.

15 WHO, 'Parties to the WHO Framework Convention on Tobacco Control', available at www.who.int/fctc/signatories_parties/en/index.html (accessed 6 August 2013).

16 WHO, Guidelines for Implementation of Article 11 of the Framework Convention on Tobacco Control (Packaging and Labelling of Tobacco Products), November 2008, available at www.who.int/fctc/guidelines/article_11.pdf (accessed 6 August 2013).

17 WHO, Guidelines for Implementation of Article 13 of the Framework Convention on Tobacco Control (Tobacco Advertising, Promotion and Sponsorship), November 2008, available at www.who.int/fctc/guidelines/article_13.pdf (accessed 6 August 2013).

18 See A. Mitchell and C. Henckels, 'Variations on a Theme: Comparing the Concept of "Necessity" in International Investment Law and WTO Law', *Chicago Journal of International Law*, forthcoming 2013.

19 GATT Article 21(b); TRIPS Article 8; TBT Agreement preambular recital 6.

20 Appellate Body Report, *Brazil –Retreaded Tyres* at [150], [151]; Appellate Body Report, *China –Publications and Audiovisual Products* at [319]; Appellate Body Report, *US – Gambling* at [309]–[311]. See also Mitchell and Henckels, op. cit.

21 Appellate Body Report, *Brazil –Retreaded Tyres*.

22 See T. Voon and A. Mitchell, 'Time to Quit? Assessing International Investment Claims Against Plain Tobacco Packaging in Australia', *Journal of International Economic Law* 14(3), 2011, 515, 533, 536, 539.

23 *Saluka Investments v. Czech Republic (Partial Award)* (Permanent Court of Arbitration, 17 March 2006) [305]–[308]; Andrew Newcombe and Lluís Paradell, *Law and Practice of Investment Treaties: Standards of Treatment*, The Hague: Kluwer Law International, 2009 at 267, 281, 288, 356–8, 362–5.

24 Voon and Mitchell, op. cit. at 533, 536, 539.

25 The three tobacco companies that dominate the Australian market have combined revenues of over $2.8 million dollars per year: *Tobacco in Australia Facts and Issues*, 4th edn, Cancer Council of Victoria, [10.4], available at www.tobaccoinaustralia.org.au/chapter-10-tobacco-industry/10–4-the-tobacco-companies-operating-in-australia (accessed 6 August 2013).

26 Philip Morris, British American Tobacco and Imperial combined have over 98 per cent of the market: ibid.

27 See e.g. British American Tobacco Australia, *Submission on the Tobacco Plain Packaging Bill 2011*, 6 June 2011, at 18; Philip Morris International's submission to the UK Department of Health consultation on standardised packaging of tobacco products, 9 August 2012, at 10.

28 See e.g. *United States v. Philip Morris et al.* CV-99–2496 (D.D.C.) (GK) Professor J. Heckman, Defendant Economics Expert, Written Direct Testimony, at 45.

29 To control for other factors that affect smoking prevalence and ensure that the findings can be extrapolated to the general population.

30 Appellate Body Report, *Canada – Continued Suspension* at [702].

31 Appellate Body Report, *Brazil –Retreaded Tyres* at [151].

32 Mitchell and Henckels, op. cit.

33 Appellate Body Report, *Brazil –Retreaded Tyres* at [150], [151]; T. Voon and A. Mitchell, 'Implications of WTO Law for Plain Packaging of Tobacco Products' in T. Voon, A. Mitchell and J. Liberman (eds), *Public Health and Plain Packaging of Cigarettes: Legal Issues*, Cheltenham, UK and Northampton, MA: Edward Elgar, 2012 at 126–7. Of course the contribution is balanced with other factors. If a measure is extremely trade-restrictive, a greater level of contribution would be needed. See G. Ayres and A. Mitchell, 'General and Security Exceptions Under the GATT 1994 and the GATS' in I. Carr, S. Alam and Md J. H. Bhuiyan (eds), *International Trade Law and the WTO*, Annandale, NSW: Federation Press, 2013, Chapter 9.

34 Appellate Body Report, *Brazil –Retreaded Tyres* at [151].

35 World Bank (Washington), *Curbing the Epidemic: Governments and the Economics of Tobacco Control*, 1999, available at www.worldbank.org/tobacco/ (accessed 6 August 2013); US Surgeon General's Report, *Reducing Tobacco Use*, 2000, available at www.cdc.gov/tobacco/data_statistics/sgr/2000/complete_report/index.htm (accessed 6 August 2013); Article 5(4) of the Framework Convention on Tobacco Control states: 'Comprehensive multisectoral measures and responses to reduce consumption of all tobacco products at the national, regional and international levels are essential so as to prevent, in accordance with public health principles, the incidence of diseases,

premature disability and mortality due to tobacco consumption and exposure to tobacco smoke.'

36 US Surgeon General's Report, *Reducing Tobacco Use*, 2000, available at www.cdc.gov/tobacco/data_statistics/sgr/2000/complete_report/index.htm (accessed 6 August 2013).

37 A helpful overview of the factors influencing tobacco use can be found in the US Surgeon General's Report, *Reducing Tobacco Use*, 2000, Ch. 1, available at www.cdc.gov/tobacco/data_statistics/sgr/2000/complete_report/index.htm (accessed 6 August 2013).

38 Ibid.

39 For example the Council of Australian Governments has committed itself to reduce smoking prevalence to 10 per cent or less by 2018, which was cited in the Explanatory Memorandum to the Tobacco Plain Packaging Act 2011. Similarly, the long title of the same Act is 'An Act to discourage the use of *tobacco* products, and for related purposes'.

40 See e.g. GATT Article XX; *Marrakesh Agreement Establishing the World Trade Organization*, opened for signature 15 April 1994, 1867 UNTS 3 (entered into force 1 January 1995) annex 1B ('General Agreement on Trade in Services') Article XIV.

41 But see generally M. M. Du, 'Autonomy in Setting Appropriate Level of Protection under the WTO Law: Rhetoric or Reality?', *Journal of International Economic Law* 13, 2010, 1077.

42 Mitchell and Henckels, op. cit.

43 See e.g. *Continental Casualty v. Argentine Republic (Award)* (ICSID Arbitral Tribunal, Case No. ARB/03/09, 5 September 2008) [226]; *Metalclad v. Mexico (Award)* (ad hoc Arbitral Tribunal, ICSID Additional Facility Rules, Case No. ARB(AF)/97/1, 25 August 2000) [90]–[98]; *Tecmed v. Mexico (Award)* (ICSID Arbitral Tribunal, Case No. ARB(AF)/00/2, 29 May 2003) [133], [135], [137], [139], [145]–[147], [154], [157]–[158], [164], [166], [172]–[173]; *Ronald Lauder v. Czech Republic* (Award) (UNCITRAL Arbitration Rules, 3 September 2001) [263]–[264], [297]; *Lauder v. Czech Republic (Final Award)* (Ad Hoc Arbitral Tribunal, UNCITRAL Rules, 3 September 2001) [263]–[264], [297]. See also C. Henckels, 'Indirect Expropriation and the Right to Regulate: Revisiting Proportionality Analysis and the Standard of Review in Investor-State Arbitration', *Journal of International Economic Law* 15, 2012, 223 at 232–3.

44 See e.g. *SD Myers v. Canada (First Partial Award)* (ad hoc Arbitral Tribunal, UNCITRAL Rules, 13 November 2000) [195], [255], [281], [285]; *Glamis Gold v. United States (Award)* (ad hoc Arbitral Tribunal, UNCITRAL Rules, 14 May 2009) [624]–[625].

45 Appellate Body Report, *Canada – Continued Suspension* at [529].

46 Appellate Body Report, *Canada – Continued Suspension* at [703].

47 Tobacco Plain Packaging Act 2011 (Cth), section 3(2).

48 US Surgeon General's Report, *Preventing Tobacco Use Among Youth and Young Adults*, 2012, at 532, available at www.surgeongeneral.gov/library/reports/preventing-youth-tobacco-use/ (accessed 6 August 2013).

49 C. Moodie, M. Stead, L. Bauld, A. McNeill, K. Angus, K. Hinds, I. Kwan, J. Thomas, G. Hastings and A. O'Mara-Eves, *Plain Packaging: A Systematic Review* 2012, available at http://eprints.ioe.ac.uk/16381/1/Moodie_et_al._2012._Plain_Tobacco_Packaging._A_Systematic_Review.pdf (accessed 6 August 2013).

50 See Philip Morris International's submission to the UK Department of Health consultation on standardised packaging of tobacco products, 9 August 2012, at 3.

51 *JT International SA v. Commonwealth of Australia; British American Tobacco Australasia Limited & Ors v. The Commonwealth of Australia [2012] HCATrans 91 (17 April 2012).*

52 See e.g. Written Submissions of Philip Morris Limited (as intervener) in *British American Tobacco Australasia Limited & Ors v. The Commonwealth of Australia* S389/2011 [8].

53 *United States v. Philip Morris et al. CV-99–2496 (D.D.C.) (GK) Professor James Heckman, Defendant Economics Expert, Trial Testimony, 13 April 2005*, pp. 18945–6 (where Professor Heckman confirmed that he had asked Philip Morris for their sales data but was not provided with it).

54 Indeed, it is hard to find a marketing expert not paid by the tobacco industry who does not accept that marketing of consumer products both can be, and is, designed to turn people who are unaware of the product into loyal customers: see e.g. *United States v. Philip Morris et al. CV-99–2496 (D.D.C.) (GK)* Professor Robert Dolan, Claimant Marketing Expert, Written Direct Testimony, at 43–4.

55 While it is possible that Coke marketing may influence people who are already thirsty, there is no similar pre-existing demand for using tobacco products.

56 US Surgeon General's Report, *Preventing Tobacco Use Among Youth and Young Adults 2012*, available at www.surgeongeneral.gov/library/reports/preventing-youth-tobacco-use/ (accessed 6 August 2013) at 8.

57 Ibid. 530.

58 Australian Institute of Health and Welfare, *National Household Drug Strategy Survey 2010*, available at www.aihw.gov.au/publication-detail/?id=32212254712 (accessed 6 August 2013) at 46. The industry is fully aware of the importance of health as a motivating factor in quitting behaviour. For example, Philip Morris conducted a major study on quitting in 1988 involving 506 smokers. A memorandum entitled 'Critical issues–1988 Progress Report', which was sent to PM's Director of Market Research, stated under the heading 'Smoker Dynamics' that '[t]he research results indicated that the number one reason for people quitting smoking was health concerns' (Bates No. 2080009523).

59 See e.g. D. Hammond and C. Parkinson, 'The impact of cigarette design on perceptions of risk', *Journal of Public Health* 31(3), 2009, 345. See also National Cancer Institute, Monograph 13, 'Risks Associated with Smoking Cigarettes with Low Machine Measured Yields of Tar and Nicotine', 2001 at Chapter 6.

60 J. Waincymer, *Procedure and Evidence in International Arbitration*, The Hague: Kluwer Law International, 2012 at [10.4.3]; M. Grando, *Evidence, Proof and Fact-Finding in WTO Dispute Settlement*, Oxford: Oxford University Press, 2009 at 137.

61 M. Grando, op.cit. at 137–8.

62 M. Grando, op.cit. at 90–2.

63 P. Mavroidis, 'Development of WTO Dispute Settlement Procedures Through Case-Law (We Will Fix It)' in F. Ortino and E. U. Petersmann (eds), *The WTO Dispute Settlement System 1995–2003*, The Hague: Kluwer Law International, 2004 at 153, 172.

64 E. McGovern, *International Trade Regulation*, 3rd edn, Exeter: Globefield Press, 1995 at 2.23–63; J. Waincymer, *WTO Litigation: Procedural Aspects of Formal Dispute Settlement*, Nottingham: Cameron May, 2002 at 568.

65 Panel Report, *Canada – Aircraft* at [9.225]; also M. Grando, *Evidence, Proof and Fact-Finding in WTO Dispute Settlement*, Oxford: Oxford University Press, 2009 at 148–9.

66 Panel Report, *Canada – Dairy* (Article 21.5 – New Zealand and US) at [5.67].

67 Appellate Body Report, *US – Carbon Steel* at [157].

68 Appellate Body Report, *US – Wool Shirts and Blouses* at 14.

69 At its third session in November 2008, the Conference of the Parties ('COP') adopted guidelines for implementation of Article 11 of the WHO FCTC on 'Packaging and labelling of Tobacco Products' (decision FCTC/COP3(10)) and guidelines for implementation of Article 13 of the WHO FCTC on 'Tobacco advertising, promotion and sponsorship' (decision FCTC/COP3(12)).

70 WHO, Submission re Australia Plain Packaging Legislation (June 2011); Convention Secretariat WHO FCTC, Submission in respect of Australia's draft Tobacco Plain Packaging Bill 2011 (6 June 2011).

71 *RomPetrol v. Romania (Award)* (ICSID Arbitral Tribunal, Case No. ARB/06/03, 6 May 2013) [178]–[183]; *Tokios Tokelés v. Ukraine (Award)* (ICSID Arbitral Tribunal, Case No. ARB/02/18, 26 July 2007) [124]; *Asian Agricultural Products Ltd v. Sri Lanka (Final Award)* (ICSID Arbitral Tribunal, Case No. ARB/87/3, 27 June 1990) [56].

72 *RomPetrol v. Romania (Award)* (ICSID Arbitral Tribunal, Case No. ARB/06/03, 6 May 2013) [178], [183].

73 *Tokios Tokelés v. Ukraine (Award)* (ICSID Arbitral Tribunal, Case No. ARB/02/18, 26 July 2007) [124].

74 *Methanex v. United States (Partial Award)* (ad hoc Arbitral Tribunal, UNCITRAL Rules, 7 August 2002) [101].

75 *Methanex v. United States (Partial Award)* (ad hoc Arbitral Tribunal, UNCITRAL Rules, 7 August 2002) [102].

76 *RomPetrol v. Romania (Award)* (ICSID Arbitral Tribunal, Case No. ARB/06/03, 6 May 2013) [178].

77 For an assessment on its impacts including reductions in prevalence see the post-implementation review carried out by the Australian government, available at http://ris.finance.gov.au/2013/05/20/25-per-cent-tobacco-excise-increase-post-implementation-review-treasury/(accessed 6 August 2013).

78 S. Parnell, 'Excise Designed to Increase Quit Campaign', *The Australian*, 15 May 2013, available at www.theaustralian.com.au/national-affairs/treasury/excise-designed-to-speed-quit-campaign/story-fndbwnla-1226642545616 (accessed 6 August 2013).

8 Science as a common proxy for rational regulation across international trade and investment law

Jürgen Kurtz[1]

8.1 Introduction

There is deep controversy over the contemporary scope and operation of the obligation to extend fair and equitable treatment in the field of international investment law, and as with much of that field, the causes of that controversy can be traced – with some precision – to the investor-state arbitral case law. Early tribunals, for instance, failed to give fair and equitable treatment independent operation by conflating its operation with other treaty standards,[2] or even ignored the precise textual structure of particular treaty clauses under adjudication.[3] Later awards push the juridical envelope in even more problematic and troubling directions. In *Metalclad v. Mexico* for instance, the Tribunal used the NAFTA's articulation of 'transparency' as a general treaty objective to build a highly stringent standard of application for NAFTA Article 1105.[4] The Tribunal ruled that this requires a NAFTA state to ensure that all relevant legal requirements must be capable of being readily known to foreign investors and that '[t]here should be no room for doubt or uncertainty on such matters'.[5] This interpretative approach was rightly criticized by a judge of the Supreme Court of British Columbia (within the seat of arbitration) as a misstatement of the applicable law given the failure to follow NAFTA Article 1105's express textual connection to treatment at international law.[6] *Metalclad* can be critiqued on deeper grounds than pure hermeneutics. Substantively, that award sets an extraordinarily high standard of public regulation to which all states might aspire, but very few (especially developing countries) would realistically attain.[7] The crude approach taken in the *Metalclad* award is neither exceptional nor aberrant. It is echoed across the later *Tecmed v. Mexico* award, especially in the strict formula that a state must 'act in a consistent manner, free from ambiguity and totally transparently in its relations with the foreign investor'.[8] Here, too, poor hermeneutics tell part of the story. The *Tecmed* Tribunal elected to orientate its expansive approach by repeatedly invoking the 'basic expectations' of foreign investors[9] looking to invest in a host state rather than assessing the precise bargain set down by the states parties as signatories to the applicable treaty, as is required by the customary rules of treaty interpretation.[10]

This problematic line of jurisprudence has prompted a distinct reaction by state parties, which is to narrow and confine the operation of fair and equitable treatment in their newer treaties. The classic strategy so far has been to tie the treaty standard to parts of customary international law.[11] In some respects, this treaty move is deeply puzzling. The historiography of international investment law is characterized by an original and deep-seated desire by capital-exporting states to use treaties to displace particular customary rules. Moreover, if the broader goal of investment law is to deliver certainty (to both foreign investors and states), then custom – with the notorious difficulty of locating its constituent elements, especially *opinio juris* – seems poorly equipped as a robust and tractable standard.

While the method chosen by states parties is questionable, the overall objective is sound. Underpinning contemporary recalibration of investment treaties is a strategy that seeks to match particular treaty standards against objective risks faced by foreign investors operating in host states. This is fundamentally desirable as it aims to develop a rigorous (even theoretical) foundation for the operation of the treaty system rather than merely relying on broad and undefined assertions of its role as 'protecting' foreign investment.[12] Increasingly, states parties are sensibly asking themselves: what key risks are we protecting foreign investors from and why?

Across this debate on the contours of fair and equitable treatment, one possible basis for exploring the legitimate application of that legal standard has been ignored. That is, whether fair and equitable treatment has some role to play in testing the underlying rationality of host state regulatory choice, specifically by examining a state's invocation of scientific justification in its defence of a given measure against breach. This proffered role reveals a potential, albeit loose, commonality with the law of the WTO. Since the completion of the Uruguay Round, a degree of scientific justification has been required of WTO members when promulgating certain measures under the SPS Agreement. Under Article 2(2) of the SPS Agreement:

> Members shall ensure that any sanitary or phytosanitary measure is applied only to the extent necessary to protect human, animal or plant life or health, is based on scientific principles and is not maintained without sufficient scientific evidence, except as provided for in paragraph 7 of Article 5.

This part of the SPS Agreement represents a dramatic shift in legal coverage and philosophy. Classically, the GATT 1947 only disciplined discriminatory domestic taxes or regulations that sought to protect domestic production from foreign competition under a conservative negative integration ethos.[13] Put simply, GATT members were free to regulate domestically as they saw fit to do so. Trade law would only strike down such interventions if they were poisoned by protectionist animus. Yet under the SPS Agreement, even non-discriminatory measures in an importing state can be challenged because, for example, they impose greater compliance burdens on producers in the exporting state. Those burdens may not be strictly protectionist but reflect instead heterogeneity in regulatory preferences and methodologies between different countries. If the importing state cannot now show that its non-discriminatory measures are truly required for safety and health purposes, as informed by scientific inquiry, those measures may not stand under the SPS Agreement. The SPS Agreement thus ushers in a harder positive integration edge to a member state's commitments in the WTO.

Paradoxically, perhaps, stronger legal coverage of this type may appear less controversial to the traditional proponents of international investment law than the community of scholars and practitioners schooled in the nuances of the shift from the GATT 1947 to the WTO. Compared with trade law, the idiom of international investment law has always prioritized the establishment of absolute rather than relative standards of protection (such as the continuing requirement to pay compensation where the state directly expropriates foreign investment even when acting for a public purpose and in a non-discriminatory manner). To that extent, the usage of scientific justification as a possible proxy for rational regulation – which, if properly formulated, would still allow for legitimate variances in individual state choice on risk regulation – is a more modest legal strategy than the overblown and intrusive demands made of host states by the vast majority of the fair and equitable case law. Nonetheless, this approach clearly represents a relatively new and untested reading of fair and equitable treatment that, at least in a certain part of the treaty network, may be rendered difficult by a given treaty formula. Nor is this approach necessarily suitable for all types of regulation that might come up for adjudication under the fair and equitable standard.

For these reasons, the next section begins conservatively by sketching an idealized method of using science to review risk regulation at international law. It does so specifically by drawing on both the text and adjudication of the SPS Agreement to discern lessons that might productively be used as a model in the investment treaty context. Section 8.3 then offers a scoping of the iterations of the fair and equitable clause in the diffuse network of bilateral and regional investment treaties in order to explore the varying possibilities by which scientific assessment might be used across that doctrinal spectrum. Section 8.4 then turns to the relatively few arbitral cases that have directly used scientific evidence as part of a fair and equitable treatment analysis and compares those methodologies and findings against the idealized approach put forward earlier.

8.2 What role should science play in international adjudication of risk regulation? Lessons from the WTO SPS Agreement

State laws or regulations that are passed to address risks to public health or the environment often impact on market operators within a state, or indeed beyond the state. Those impacts can, on first principles, be either positive or negative. Regulatory interventions that mandate use of a product for public purposes by definition create new market opportunities that are favourable to economic actors. Consider in this respect the core factual matrix in *Methanex v. US*.[14] Methanex, a Canadian corporation, produced methanol in the US that when converted into methyl tertiary butyl ether ('MTBE') could be used as an octane enhancer in unleaded gasoline. The very market for such oxygenates was originally created by Californian environmental regulation designed to limit gasoline-related air pollution:

> Methanex entered a political economy in which it was widely known, if not notorious, that governmental environmental and health protection institutions at the federal and state level, operating under the vigilant eyes of the media, interested corporations, non-governmental organizations and a politically active electorate, continuously monitored the use and impact of chemical compounds and commonly prohibited or restricted the use of some of those compounds for environmental and/or health reasons. *Indeed, the very market for MTBE in the United States was the result of precisely this regulatory process* (emphasis added).[15]

At the other end of the spectrum, regulation can render current activities more costly or even ban access of the relevant product or service to consumers in the regulating state by prohibiting production (including by foreign investors) or import from another state.[16] In the latter scenario, a state may be forced to defend that measure when it comprises the subject of complaint before a WTO panel and/or investor-state arbitral tribunal. This, in turn, raises the question of what role scientific evidence should play in the process of examining the consistency of that measure with both of these key international law commitments.

We encounter at this point a fundamental disjuncture between the separate strands of international trade and investment law. The WTO sets out an elaborate and detailed taxonomy within the SPS Agreement whereby member states are required to ensure that certain classes of domestic regulation are based on particular international standards.[17] Annex A of the SPS Agreement defines international standards by reference to the work of various standard-setting organizations such as, in the case of food safety, the Codex Alimentarius Commission.[18] Where regulations 'conform to' a given international standard, they are presumed to be consistent with the SPS Agreement and the GATT.[19] There is then significant legal incentive built into this structure for WTO members to defer their regulatory choice to the work of external standard-setting bodies as a means of acquiring legal cover from WTO compliance. In this way, the SPS Agreements offers the possibility of a certain level of harmonization of risk regulation across the membership of the WTO. But, crucially, regulatory pluralism is still permitted in this taxonomy. In the event that no such international standard exists (which is often very common) or that the state wishes to regulate at a *higher* level of protection than that delineated in a given standard, its measure is required to be based on a formal process of risk assessment that must take into account, *inter alia*, available scientific evidence.[20] This is only a thumbnail sketch that fails to capture the full complexity (and, arguably, contradictions) of the SPS Agreement. It is nonetheless already sufficient to highlight an obvious but fundamental distinction with international investment law. There is no equivalent to this thick and sequential architecture within the usual framing of bilateral and regional investment treaties. At most, there are the sparse formulae of fair and equitable treatment across the network of investment treaties. We might then begin by examining what general principles might be distilled in a legal approach that potentially uses science and/or international standards when assessing state liability for breach of fair and equitable treatment.

The first issue goes to the type of measure that might be properly examined in light of a science-based approach to fair and equitable treatment. It would certainly be imprudent to extend this reading to *all* state laws or regulations regardless of their subject matter. Instead, such an approach would really only be justifiable where scientific examination is central and critical to the inherent rationality of the measure. WTO law offers a useful comparator in this respect. Under the SPS Agreement, a measure *only* falls within the scope of that treaty (as a 'sanitary or phytosanitary measure') if its purposes fall within a delineated list including those applied 'to protect human or animal plant life or health within the territory of the Member from risks arising from additives, contaminants, toxins or disease-causing organisms in foods, beverages or feedstuff'.[21] As we will see later, the subset of fair and equitable cases that has mirrored some of the inquiries in the SPS Agreement has generally engaged purposes of this sort.

There is a second, more fundamental issue implicated in a science-based approach to fair and equitable treatment when reviewing risk regulation by states. There may well be distinct textual limits to the framing of a given fair and equitable clause, which could constrain an adjudicator's ability to examine scientific evidence as part of its assessment of the legality of a given measure. This scoping issue is addressed separately below. But even assuming no such textual constraint, there is a delicate question of the nature and purpose of the legal obligation whose implications can again be revealed via comparison with WTO law. In the latter, there is a positive obligation on all WTO members either to use international standards as a basis for SPS measures or to ensure that science informs a process of risk assessment. There is no textual equivalent of this hard and automatic obligation in investment law and we should not easily imply one. For one thing, this would dramatically increase the types of commitment of (especially developing) states under investment law, without the recognition of the budgetary and capacity constraints that are finessed (albeit imperfectly) through mechanisms such as qualified mutual recognition,[22] offers of technical assistance[23] and conferral of special and differential treatment[24] in the SPS Agreement. More generally, the SPS Agreement comprises but one part of a large and complex bargain negotiated at the end of the Uruguay Round, with any given WTO member potentially able to identify benefits in other parts of the large set of WTO commitments that might offset the costs imposed on them by the SPS Agreement. Neither of these considerations is at play in the context of adjudication of the fair and equitable treatment in a dedicated investment construct such as a BIT. Thus, an alternative course of action would be to proceed cautiously so that an investment adjudicator would only examine the issue of scientific justification where a state itself has explicitly and publicly relied on scientific evidence in the promulgation of a measure under review and/or it clearly pleads science as part of its investment treaty defence. In these settings, the state itself has bought the question of scientific support into the juridical mix, making it arguably appropriate for both claimants and adjudicator to engage with that topic.

Yet when faced with this particular category of risk regulation, an adjudicator will still need to come to a principled view on what role science should play in an assessment of consistency with the treaty obligation to accord fair and equitable treatment. Science can be used by states parties in one or both of two parts of a regulatory approach designed to reduce risk. First, a state may use science in the evaluation of the optimal level of risk that that state chooses to enforce in its territory. Scientific inquiry can be used, for instance, to determine the probability that a certain risk will materialize. This, though, is only one part of a complicated matrix that shapes the ultimate manner in which states choose to manage their risk profile. One would expect, for instance, that the level of acceptable risk would legitimately differ between various countries. Variances in local conditions will play a part to the extent that there are different exposures to a given risk depending on climatic and geographical factors.[25] Most importantly, however, the choice of the optimal level of risk will normally be tied to deep and complex societal preferences in the degree of risk aversion acceptable to the populace of a given state. Nonetheless, by providing citizens (or at least their representative agents) with accurate information about risks, scientific evidence can play an important role in improving the quality of democratic deliberation surrounding value-laden issues of risk regulation.[26] Aside from setting a state's optimal level of risk, science can also properly inform a second and equally vital question of *how* a state responds to achieve its optimal level of risk exposure. For instance, science might offer objective support that a given measure is especially effective in achieving a state's level of risk tolerance. It might be the case, for instance, that scientific assessment has explored the costs and benefits associated with alternative strategies for control of risk. That assessment could in turn offer clear and objective support that the state's chosen measure, as endorsed or contemplated in that scientific report, achieves its desired level of protection. Here, too, there are appropriate and obvious limits to the role that science can play, not least the fact that states face very different resource constraints that will shape their willingness to pay for particular risk-reducing measures.

When it comes to the law of the WTO, the most important starting point is that member states retain full autonomy in setting their own level of acceptable risk (being the first option referred to above). This deference to state choice on the optimal level of risk can be observed both on a careful reading of the text of the SPS Agreement and in most of the jurisprudence of the Appellate Body interpreting that treaty. For instance, Article 4(1) of the SPS Agreement is clearly premised on this understanding:

> Members shall accept the sanitary and phytosanitary measures of other Members as equivalent, even if these measures differ from their own or from those used by other Members trading in the same product, if the exporting Member objectively demonstrates to the importing Member that its measures achieve the Member's appropriate level of sanitary or phytosanitary protection (emphasis added).[27]

There are various affirmations of the freedom of WTO members to set their optimal levels of protection peppered throughout the rest of the SPS Agreement. Article 5(4) for instance requires WTO members to 'take into account the objective of minimizing negative trade effects' when *they* are 'determining the appropriate level of sanitary or phytosanitary protection'.[28] The Appellate Body too has clearly affirmed this key start point in a number of cases, including *Australia – Salmon*:

> We do not believe that Article 11 of the DSU, or any other provision of the DSU or of the *SPS Agreement*, entitles the Panel or the Appellate Body, for the purpose of applying Article 5.6 in the present case, to substitute its own reasoning about the implied level of protection for that expressed consistently by Australia. The determination of the appropriate level of protection, a notion defined in paragraph 5 of Annex A, as 'the level of protection deemed appropriate by the Member establishing a sanitary . . . measure', is a *prerogative* of the Member concerned and not of a panel or of the Appellate Body (italics in the original).[29]

By comparison, a WTO panel has a mandate to question the SPS consistency of the means chosen by the state to achieve its freely determined optimal level of risk (the second possibility referred to earlier). In *Australia – Salmon*, the Appellate Body clearly noted the separation between a state's regulatory goal and the means chosen to achieve that goal within the SPS Agreement: 'The "appropriate level of protection" established by a Member and the "SPS measure" have to be clearly distinguished. They are not one and the same thing. The first is an *objective*, the second is an *instrument* chosen to attain or implement that objective.'[30] Having separated these items and now understanding that it is only the latter that is justiciable, we are left with the question of the actual legal test(s) applied to determine the use of science and consistency of a state's elected measure with the SPS Agreement.

Assuming that there is no relevant international standard or that the member wants to implement a measure at a higher level of protection than that set out in the international standard, the first and primary test is that a state's measure must be 'based on' risk assessment,[31] which requires a state to take into account, inter alia, 'available scientific evidence'.[32] In *EC – Hormones*, the Appellate Body sensibly understood this obligation – in line with what the text naturally suggests – as requiring a 'rational relationship' between the chosen measure and a state's risk assessment.[33] Under this approach, all that is required of the WTO member is evidentiary support within the risk assessment for a rational connection between the chosen measure and the achievement of the state's optimal level of risk. Rationality review of this sort boils down to a fairly minimal requirement that there must be *some* contribution by the SPS measure to the reduction or elimination of the identified risks. The Appellate Body even went on to confirm that a measure could still be 'based on' risk assessment if underlying scientific opinion were divided:

> We do not believe that a risk assessment has to come to a monolithic conclusion that coincides with the scientific conclusion or view implicit in the SPS measure. The risk assessment could set out both the prevailing view representing the 'mainstream' of scientific opinion, as well as the opinions of scientists taking a divergent view. Article 5.1 does not require that the risk must necessarily embody only a view of a majority of the relevant scientific community. In some cases, the very existence of divergent views presented by qualified scientists who have investigated the particular issue at hand may indicate a state of scientific uncertainty. Sometimes the divergence may indicate a roughly equal balance of scientific opinion, which may itself be a form of scientific uncertainty. In most cases, responsible and representative governments may act in good faith on the basis of what, at a given time, may be a divergent opinion from qualified and respected sources. By itself, this does not necessarily signal the absence of a reasonable relationship between the SPS measure and the risk assessment, especially where the risk involved is life-threatening in character and is perceived to constitute a clear and imminent threat to public health and safety. Determination of the presence or absence of that relationship can only be done on a case-to-case basis, after account is taken of all considerations rationally bearing upon the issue of potential adverse health effects.[34]

This part of the *EC – Hormones* report is of considerable importance both substantively and as a question of optics. It affords enormous (while entirely appropriate) latitude for states in the use of science across risk regulation endeavours. Science is by no means a simple trump card that is automatically and conclusively determinative of regulatory integrity (and thus dispositive of whether or not there is breach of the SPS Agreement). Instead, it operates (including through state reliance on minority scientific opinion) as one key input to improve the overall rationality of democratic deliberation of risk regulation.

The picture thus painted is one of a highly sensitive and democratic approach under WTO law to the role of science in contribution to a rational regulatory process. To be sure, there are a few other provisions within the SPS Agreement that cannot be easily reconciled with this reading.[35] Leaving those outlying components aside, however, the major part of WTO law described above, it is submitted, offers a constructive benchmark for considering how investor-state arbitral tribunals should approach the usage of science in a particular fair and equitable treatment inquiry. I now turn to the question of whether and how the textual construction of the fair and equitable standard might control the use of such a model in investment treaty arbitration.

8.3 Three key iterations of the fair and equitable standard

One of the key features of the field of international investment law is its diffuse and heterogeneous structure. As a result, there are very different forms and categories of the fair and equitable standard. These textual differences are not simply accidental but are often the result of deliberate state choice tied to their specific experience as respondents to investor-state arbitration. Adjudicators must give effect to those differences and not simply conflate or ignore them as has been the occasional practice of past arbitral tribunals. As a result, the authority of arbitral tribunals to examine the scientific justification of a given measure as part of a fair and equitable assessment may, as a threshold matter, depend significantly on the precise form of the treaty construct under adjudication.

There are three principal categories of the fair and equitable standard, which can be sorted from the most recent (and restrictive) to the oldest (and broadest) iterations. First, we have what might be described as the 'post-NAFTA Chapter 11 model'. This is a revision of the fair and equitable treatment standard by some of the NAFTA states based on their experience as repeat litigants in Chapter 11 arbitration. For instance, Article 5(1) of the 2004 US Model BIT provides: 'Each Party shall accord to covered investments treatment in accordance with customary international law, including fair and equitable treatment and full protection and security.'[36]

In this first category, the negotiators have clearly opted to use custom as the applicable standard of protection rather than allow fair and equitable treatment to operate independently of those rules. Put more formally, fair and equitable treatment is a subset of those customary protections. This, however, only begs the question of which part of the broad universe of customary rules should apply. The negotiators offer further guidance in Article 5(2) of the 2004 US Model BIT:

> For greater certainty, paragraph 1 prescribes the customary international law minimum standard of treatment of aliens as the minimum standard of treatment to be afforded to covered investments. The concepts of 'fair and equitable treatment' and 'full protection and security' do not require treatment in addition to or beyond that which is required by that standard, and do not create additional substantive rights.[37]

From one view, this restrictive formula might preclude an adjudicator entirely from using science when assessing possible breaches of the fair and equitable standard. Those tribunals that have taken the search for the objective evidence of custom seriously have affirmed its classic foundations as an exceptional remedy for individual aliens harmed through very particular executive or judicial misconduct in the host state. Thus, the *Glamis Gold* Tribunal ruled that

> to violate the customary international law minimum standard of treatment codified in Article 1105 of the NAFTA, an act must be sufficiently egregious and shocking – a gross denial of justice, manifest arbitrariness, blatant unfairness, a complete lack of due process, evident discrimination, or a manifest lack of reasons – so as to fall below accepted international standards and constitute a breach of Article 1105(1).[38]

This formula may, however, be less prohibitive than it appears on first reading. One could potentially still plead a state's simple refusal to consider scientific evidence in the final promulgation of a measure as a form of 'manifest arbitrariness' or displaying a 'manifest lack of reasons'.[39] Take, for instance, a scenario where a state specifically commissions scientific inquiry into harm associated with exposure to a given product, and then fails entirely to consider that scientific evidence in its choice of responding to a given level of risk whether in the form of an outright ban on use or restrictive regulation.

It is also important to bear in mind that customary international law is inherently evolutionary. The Tribunal in *Glamis Gold* required the claimant to provide evidence that custom had moved in the direction pleaded by it, a burden that the claimant failed to discharge.[40] One can question the appropriateness of this allocation of the burden of proof but, for present purposes, it evidences the fundamental point that custom can evolve in such a way to contemplate or address scientific justification of a given measure. Relatedly and in that vein, scholars have long argued that the precautionary principle has emerged as a norm of customary international law. That principle reinforces the ability of a state to act cautiously when setting health standards in the face of insufficient scientific information, a flexibility that is available as a matter of right for WTO members under Article 5.7 of the SPS Agreement.[41] One could imagine a state invoking that principle as part of its investment treaty defence, which in turn would enable a claimant to adduce competing evidence on the question of the sufficiency of scientific evidence addressing the particular risk at issue. This, though, remains something of a remote possibility. Other international courts – including the WTO Appellate Body and the International Court of Justice – have refused to firmly conclude that the precautionary principle has fully crystallized into a binding norm of customary international law.[42]

By contrast, the remaining two variants of fair and equitable treatment provide a much clearer opening for the potential use of science and international standards. The fair and equitable treatment clause of the 1994 US Model BIT for instance provides: 'Each Party shall at all times accord to covered investments fair and equitable treatment and full protection and security, and shall in no case accord treatment less favourable than that required by international law.'[43] The treaty structure here plainly positions 'international law' (presumably comprising custom) as a baseline but also contemplates fair and equitable protection rising to provide separate protection above that watermark. In the words of the *Azurix* Tribunal, which examined a BIT with this exact treaty language, the purpose of the reference to international law 'is to set a floor, not a ceiling' in contradistinction to the first drafting variant considered above.[44] Relatedly and lastly, there are many formulations of fair and equitable treatment, especially in treaties concluded by European states, that make no reference to custom or general international law whatsoever.[45] Here the discretion of the adjudicator is obviously the greatest, given that she is tasked with giving some content to a completely independent treaty standard. The usage by the respondent state of scientific evidence and/or international standards might well serve as a useful proxy for rational regulation and thus the provision of fair and equitable treatment to the foreign investor.

But, to recap, that type of inquiry would generally only be reasonable where the state itself has invoked science/international standards in its promulgation of the measure under review and/or pleads the same as part of its treaty defence. Where that is the case, we are still left with the delicate question of how arbitral tribunals should use that evidence in assessing the exact degree and form of regulatory rationality. Section 8.2 sought to draw out an idealized structure from parts of WTO law and jurisprudence. I now turn to an evaluation of how well arbitral tribunals have performed in their use of scientific evidence to date, as measured against this robust benchmark discerned from the law of the WTO.

8.4 Science, risk assessment and international investment law

There are two key arbitral awards that have grappled with the thorny nexus between scientific evidence and the fair and equitable standard. Even within this limited grouping, one can discern an evolving sophistication in the use of science when adjudging risk regulation as a matter of investment treaty breach. *Methanex v. USA* is the first award of this sort. As noted earlier, the facts of *Methanex* involved a phased Californian ban on the use of MTBE, an octane enhancer in unleaded gasoline. The use of oxygenates in refined petroleum was required by Californian and federal law in order to reduce gasoline-related air pollution.[46] California had chosen to phase out the use of MTBE on the basis that the additive was contaminating drinking water supplies owing to leaking underground storage tanks and therefore posed a risk to human health.[47] While MTBE was banned, other oxygenates, particularly ethanol, could continue to be used in the Californian market.[48] Methanex, a Canadian-based corporation, was a major producer of methanol, a key component of MTBE.[49]

Methanex claimed that the Californian ban breached, *inter alia*, national treatment under NAFTA Article 1102 as well as the obligation to accord it fair and equitable treatment under NAFTA Article 1105. In macro terms, there is a curious disjuncture between the legal reasoning adopted by the Tribunal compared to its treatment and assessment of the factual record. The former, at least when it comes to national treatment, is inherently contradictory, superficial and relies on mistaken comparisons with WTO law. The criticism here is not one of outcome, given that the Tribunal correctly found the Californian ban to be non-discriminatory, but it is certainly directed at both methodology and hermeneutics.[50] A similar puzzling superficiality infuses into the Tribunal's fair and equitable analysis, although, to be fair, this may have been influenced by the claimant's pleadings. The Tribunal devotes an enormous amount of time to assessing whether or not NAFTA Article 1105 includes an entirely distinct constraint on discrimination (in addition to that of national treatment)[51] without assessing any potential role it might play in separately testing for arbitrariness – understood as an absence of legitimate cause for the measure under review – even in the absence of discrimination. Of course, the latter prospect offers a logical legal avenue through which science might be considered as part of an assessment of the fair and equitable standard.

Despite the opportunity forgone in its legal rulings, the careful factual analysis adopted by the *Methanex* Tribunal reflects a deeply sensitive approach to international adjudication of risk regulation that channels part of the idealized method distilled earlier from the law of the WTO. In the early components of the award, the Tribunal exhaustively records the factual chronology of the election of the Californian legislature to ban the use of MTBE. The origins of the ban lay in the decision of the Californian legislature to commission and fund an independent agent – the University of California – to scientifically assess various risks associated with the use of MTBE.[52] These included the risk to human health and the environment through MTBE leaking from underground storage tanks into groundwater supplies.[53] In November 1998, the University of California released its 600 page report, which concluded that there were 'significant risks and costs associated with water contamination due to the use of MTBE'.[54] The report recommended a phase-out of the use of MTBE on the condition that assessment is undertaken 'of the environmental impact of using other oxygenates such as ethanol'.[55]

Measured against the WTO-based taxonomy introduced earlier, California has at this stage clearly employed scientific evidence as part of identifying the level of risk it is willing to tolerate from exposure to MTBE. Yet this was only, as is usually the case, one of a range of inputs in assessing a given risk preference. The findings of the University of California report were the subject of three days of public hearings and testimony,[56] at which 'government officials and members of the public (including MTBE and methanol producers) had an opportunity to ask questions and present oral testimony'.[57] This testimony 'indicated broad-based support for the finding by the University of California that MTBE usage in gasoline constituted a serious threat to California's drinking water and that a ban on the use of MTBE in California RFG was warranted'.[58] Note, however, that at this stage there is still no determinative scientific justification for one proposed measure to achieve the state's preferred level of risk, being the phase-out of the use of MTBE. The researchers at the University of California had explicitly raised the need for California to *also* examine the general environmental impact associated with the use of ethanol. This is, of course, perfectly rational and vividly illustrates the manner in which scientific inquiry can appropriately bolster and discipline domestic regulation. It would be plainly insensible for California to ban the use of MTBE in the event that a substitute like ethanol causes the exact same risk to human health and water contamination.

Notably, California did specifically commission the Californian Environmental Protection Agency ('EPA') to undertake a second inquiry that focused on this precise question of the environmental and health effects of ethanol. In December 1999, the Californian EPA released its report, which found that 'impacts [on water contamination] associated with the use of ethanol would be significantly less and more manageable than those associated with continued use of MTBE'.[59] At this stage then, there is hard scientific justification for the rationality of choosing one measure (that singles out MTBE) over another (which would deal with both forms of gasoline enhancer). Indeed, it was only *after* the release of this second report that the Californian legislature elected to phase out the use of MTBE while continuing to allow ethanol to be used as an oxygenate in the Californian marketplace.[60]

On a more general basis, the Tribunal devotes significant attention to extensive witness testimony on the rigour and sufficiency of the scientific justification offered in these reports.[61] This, too, feeds into the principled conclusion that the ban on MTBE was 'not the product of a political sham engineered by California' but 'a serious, objective and scientific approach to a complex problem'.[62] Regrettably, however, this careful and extensive assessment of the environmental justifications for the MTBE ban receives no attention whatsoever in the Tribunal's legal analysis of fair and equitable treatment. It is instead quarantined in the factual findings of the award. Yet this review of the legislative record provides clear and compelling evidence, as the Tribunal itself determines, of a clearly rational and science-based approach to risk regulation.

Chemtura v. Canada is the second and most recent case to directly assess scientific evidence as part of a fair and equitable challenge.[63] The *Chemtura* award matches the sensitivity of the *Methanex* approach in its treatment of scientific evidence but also explicitly (and largely thoughtfully) incorporates those factual findings in its legal evaluation of the fair and equitable standard. At issue was the legality of Canada's ban on lindane, a pesticide used in the production of canola. Lindane was first registered for sale in the Canadian market in 1938.[64] But owing to concerns associated with its health and environmental effects, lindane's use as a pesticide was progressively restricted across a broad range of countries from the 1970s, including the US.[65] Restriction on the use of lindane was not simply a question of unilateral state action. In 1998, the Aarhus Protocol on Persistent Organic Pollutants to the UNECE Convention on Long-Range Transboundary Air Pollution of 1979 ('Aarhus Protocol') was adopted by a range of states (including Canada).[66] This Protocol limits usage of lindane to six specific uses and required a general reassessment of its safety.[67] In May 2009, lindane was also included on the list of chemicals designated for elimination under the Stockholm Convention on Persistent Organic Pollutants.[68]

The genesis of this dispute lies in the opposition by the US to the importation of lindane-treated canola seeds from Canada. In early 1998, the US Environmental Protection Agency announced that it would only allow US farmers to use Canadian lindane-treated canola seeds until 1 June 1998.[69] This in turn triggered concern amid the Canadian canola industry that failure to comply with this prescription might eventually cause a general imposition of US import restrictions on canola (whether treated with lindane or not).[70] In late 1998, those industry groups sought and achieved a pledge by the claimant (Chemtura) as well as other lindane producers to voluntarily remove canola from the registered uses of lindane-containing products.[71] This commitment was communicated to the Canadian regulator – the Pest Management Regulatory Agency ('PMRA') – but was conditioned by the claimant on, inter alia, a requirement that PMRA approve the use of substitutes for lindane in the treatment of canola. While PMRA pledged to work with registrants to facilitate access to alternatives, it explicitly denied a commitment to register such substitutes.[72]

Within the next few months, the PMRA announced the commencement of a special review on the use of lindane.[73] By late 2001, the PMRA had concluded that there were significant health concerns surrounding the margin of lindane exposure for workers during the treatment of canola seeds and announced a phase-out of lindane products by suspension of registrations or voluntary discontinuation.[74] The claimant sought departmental review of this decision, which was granted by the relevant Minister. By 2005, the Board of Review recommended that PMRA 'reconsider potential opportunities for mitigating its concern for health related issues associated with the use of lindane' and that it 'seek and consider input from the Claimant and other interested parties'.[75] The PMRA then launched its second review by seeking data and other information by registrants of lindane products.[76] The claimant submitted information in three instalments including a dedicated report on lindane risk mitigation.[77] PMRA then prepared a second draft report, which reached similar conclusions as did the first special review on the risks presented by lindane.[78] A full understanding of this detailed factual matrix is required in order to assess the Tribunal's principal rulings. These in turn revolve around three major allegations by Chemtura of breach of the fair and equitable standard.

First, the claimant submitted that Canada had acted without a bona fide purpose when initiating its review of lindane. Specifically, the claimant argued that

> PMRA undertook the special review as a result of a trade irritant and not as part of its mandate as a regulatory agency or as apart of an international commitment undertaken by Canada under the Aarhus Protocol to the LRTAP Convention.[79]

On one view, this first line of attack by the claimant is puzzling. Doctrinally at least, past arbitral tribunals have ruled that constraints imposed on foreign investors in Canada and implemented as a result of a negotiated agreement to settle a trade dispute between the US and Canada are in fact 'rational' measures for the purposes of parts of NAFTA Chapter 11.[80] Even assuming somehow that this should be characterized as a problematic motivation, it does not necessarily follow that the Canadian measure should be tainted. In the real word of democratic regulatory politics, a regulation is rarely enacted to serve only one purpose. Arguably, what should matter is the true cause of the underlying regulation. The *Chemtura* Tribunal engages this more nuanced question only elliptically. It fails to take into account seriously the clear temporal connection between the start of the lindane review and the suggested trade dispute with the US, which plausibly suggests that the latter might well be a possible motivating factor. Instead, the Tribunal jumps straight to what it ascertains as the true cause of the risk assessment (rather than the measure itself), which it locates rather bluntly in 'Canada's international obligations', specifically the Aarhus Protocol.[81]

There is a hidden dimension to this unquestioning deferral to an external international law commitment that could well be of importance in future cases in ways that go beyond the specifics of this case. Suppose that a state simply pleads that its measure is justified by virtue of an external standard or treaty commitment addressing particular environmental challenges, and makes no attempt to undertake any form of independent risk assessment whatsoever. When it comes to the SPS Agreement, member states can shield themselves from further scrutiny provided that their measures 'conform to' select international standards, guidelines or recommendations.[82] The wording here is relatively strict, insofar as it logically requires a direct correspondence between the measure and the international standard. For the most part, the adjudicator should be mainly concerned with reviewing an end outcome rather than the regulatory process leading up to the measure. This would also seem a reasonable starting point when considering how to deal with this first hypothetical in the investment treaty context. Alternatively, however, a state may more commonly elect – as Canada seems to have done in *Chemtura* – to supplement its treaty commitments with dedicated scientific review of the product concerned. In this second hypothetical, it would be a mistake to use the same strict standard (of 'conform to') in testing the state's use of the external norm. Indeed, that qualitative difference is enshrined in WTO law. Separately to the strict option in Article 3(2), Article 3(1) generally requires WTO members to 'base their' SPS measures on international standards as part of a general project of harmonization.[83] Somewhat ironically given Canada's position as a respondent in this case, the Appellate Body in *EC – Hormones* explicitly rejected Canada's argument (as a complainant in the WTO dispute) that the use of these different terms was just accidental.[84] Instead, it rightly noted that a measure can be based on an external standard where some but not all of the elements of the standard are incorporated.[85] The adjudicator now would be much more concerned with the process leading up to a particular outcome, and the role played by the external standard in shaping regulatory deliberation and preferences. In this second hypothetical scenario then, a state should have much greater latitude to pick and choose from the external norm while supplementing its inquiry through dedicated risk assessment. The adjudicator's task is in turn to consider the totality of that evidence rather than to crudely isolate whether there is just strict conformity with the external standard only. In *EC – Hormones*, the Appellate Body properly understood the fundamental difference between these two hypotheticals. It rejected the Panel's interpretation that 'based on' in Article 3.1 means the same thing as 'conform to' in Article 3.2, noting that this interpretation would 'transform those standards, guidelines and recommendations into binding norms' that 'the SPS Agreement itself set out no indication of any intent on the part of the Members to do so'.[86] The *Chemtura* Tribunal's tendency to defer to external legal standards raises, at least as a possibility, that future tribunals will insist (perhaps as a counterpoint to a finding of legality) that the underlying measure comply strictly with that standard in a way that is not required under the law of the WTO.

The second of the claimant's primary allegations is clearly problematic given that it questions the Canadian regulator's use of science in the review process. Although not without doubt, the overall framing of this claim appears to be directed at the sensitive question of how science is employed to set a state's optimal level of risk.[87] Importantly, the Tribunal is quick to reject that implicit invitation. Echoing the Appellate Body in *EC – Hormones*, it ruled that 'it is not for the Tribunal to judge the correctness or adequacy of the scientific results of the Special Review, not even those questioned by the Board of Review'.[88] Indeed, it endorsed expert witness evidence that the Canadian agency had responsibly chosen a conservative safety tolerance, implying that this choice is the state's alone.[89] This is not the only sensible parallel at play with WTO law. As in *EC – Hormones*, albeit more summarily, the *Chemtura* Tribunal explicitly recognizes that 'scientific divergence . . . cannot in and of itself serve as a basis for a finding of breach of Article 1105 of NAFTA'.[90]

Lastly, the third key claim echoes the SPS taxonomy by explicitly focusing on the appropriateness of Canada's chosen measure – presented by the claimant as termination of lindane registration – in achieving its optimal level of risk.[91] In particular, the claimant argued that it was unreasonably deprived of a progressive phase-out of its lindane registration. Fundamentally then, this part of the claim questions whether there is dedicated support within the risk assessment undertaken by the Canadian regulator for the measure eventually implemented. On a superficial view, the claimant's argument here has some merit. The initial risk review concluded that termination of lindane 'could be effected through phase-out by suspension of registrations or voluntary discontinuation'.[92] While the former ('suspension') would prevent sale immediately, the latter ('voluntary discontinuation') would progressively allow a market operator such as Chemtura to at least sell existing inventory. The problem, though, for the claimant was that the evidence showed that PMRA had in fact extended an offer of voluntary discontinuation to it.[93] This was, however, conditioned on the claimant submitting information regarding existing inventory and historical sales, an obvious regulatory precaution to ensure that this flexibility is not abused by a market participant. While the claimant provided *some* information in response to this request, it did so under the warning that it 'in no way concurs with PMRA's proposal for voluntary discontinuance'.[94] This in turn led the PMRA to decide that the claimant had not chosen to accept the voluntary option of discontinuance leading it to suspend registration. For the Tribunal, the 'elusive behaviour of the Claimant' was understandably the reason to rule that there was no breach of NAFTA Article 1105.[95] This last component of the ruling reflects a welcome appreciation of the often messy, real-word context of regulation in certain settings. While in abstract, Canada's risk assessment offers support for the claimant's plea of less restrictive regulation, the broader record of the claimant's behaviour provides a perfectly rational justification for the employment of the more stringent option.

8.5 Conclusion

The *Methanex* and *Chemtura* awards represent welcome green shoots in the opaque and unconvincing jurisprudence surrounding the fair and equitable standard. They, first and foremost, offer a clearly principled orientation for the operation of that standard in a defined category of cases. Yet future arbitral tribunals can and should do more in modelling robust legal structures and analysis on the usage of science and/or international standards in the law of the WTO. This is not to suggest that all parts of the complex architecture and jurisprudence of the SPS Agreement should be unthinkingly transported into investment treaty arbitration. There are key legal and strategic reasons for proceeding more cautiously when adjudicating the fair and equitable standard. But where a state itself brings scientific inquiry and/or international standards into the juridical mix, then an adjudicator should offer a structured and rigorous methodology for determining how these elements are to be used when assessing breach. A careful baseline that draws on the law of the WTO provides precisely that sort of taxonomy. Lastly, this is an area where the complex intersection between self-interest (of various actors) and the legitimacy of the broader system may well productively coincide. Properly formulated and employed, a structured use of science and international standards as a condition of regulatory rationality in a fair and equitable inquiry could, at the margins, bolster clearly lagging state confidence in the activation and operation of investment treaty protections.

Notes

1 Associate Professor, University of Melbourne Law School, Australia. I wish to thank Rob Howse and Ernst-Ulrich Petersmann for their comments on an earlier version of this chapter. All errors and omissions remain mine alone. Email: j.kurtz@unimelb.edu.au.

2 *SD Myers v. Canada*, Partial Award (UNCITRAL, 3 November 2000), paras 259–69.

3 *Compare Pope & Talbot v. Canada*, Award on the Merits of Phase 2 (UNCITRAL, 2 April 2011), paras 110–11 (ruling that NAFTA Article 1105 adopts an additive component that extends beyond the scope of protection at customary international law) with *Mexico v. Metalclad Corporation*, 2001 BCSC 664, Supreme Court of British Columbia (Tysoe, J.), at paras 64–6 (criticizing the *Pope & Talbot* award as ignoring the plain text of that treaty provision).

4 North American Free Trade Agreement, signed Dec. 17, 1992, 32 ILM 289, 605 (1993) (entry into force 1 January 1994), at Article 102(1) ('The objectives of this Agreement, as elaborated more specifically through its principles and rules, including national treatment, most-favored-nation treatment and transparency, are to . . .').

5 *Metalclad Corporation v. Mexico*, Award (ICSID Case No. ARB(AF)/97/1, 30 August 2000), para. 76.

6 *Mexico v. Metalclad Corporation*, 2001 BCSC 664, Supreme Court of British Columbia (Tysoe J.), paras 68–70.

7 See J. E. Alvarez, 'Contemporary Foreign Investment Law: An 'Empire of the Law' or the 'Law of Empire'?', *Alabama Law Review* 60, 2008), 964–5, (describing the *Metalclad* award as leading to 'particularized standards of good governance requiring a level of transparency that even US municipalities would find difficult to satisfy').

8 *Tecnicas Medioambientales Tecmed S.A. v. Mexico*, Award (ICSID Case no. ARB(AF)/00/2, 29 May 2003), at para. 154.

9 Ibid.

10 'A treaty shall be interpreted in good faith in accordance with the *ordinary meaning* to be given to the *terms of the treaty* in their context and in the light of its object and purpose' (emphasis added). Vienna Convention on the Law of Treaties, signed on 23 May 1969, 1155 UNTS 331, Article 31(1).

11 2004 US Model BIT, Article 5(1) and (2) extracted in C. McLachlan, L. Shore and M. Weiniger, *International Investment Arbitration: Substantive Principles*, Oxford: Oxford University Press, 2007, 397.

12 For an example of the latter, consider this formulation by the Tribunal in *SGS v. Philippines*: 'The BIT is a treaty for the promotion and reciprocal protection of

investments . . . [i]t is legitimate to resolve uncertainties in its interpretation so as to favour the protection of covered investments.' *SGS Société Générale de Siurveillance v. Republic of the Philippines*, Decision on Jurisdiction (ICSID Case No. ARB/01/13, 29 January 2004), at para. 116.

13 GATT 1947, Article III(1).

14 *Methanex Corporation v. United States of America*, Final Award of the Tribunal on Jurisdiction and Merits (UNITRAL, 3 August 2008).

15 Ibid. Pt IV, Chp. D, para. 9.

16 'Governments, in their exercise of regulatory power, frequently change their laws and regulations in response to changing economic circumstances or changing political, economic or social considerations. Those changes may well make certain activities less profitable or even uneconomic to continue.' *Feldman v. Mexico*, Award (ICSID Case No. ARB(AF)/99/1, 16 December, 2002), at para. 112.

17 The SPS Agreement Article 3(1) states: 'To harmonize sanitary and phytosanitary measures on as wide a basis as possible, Members shall base their sanitary and phytosanitary measures on international standards, guidelines or recommendations, where they exist, except as otherwise provided for in this Agreement, and in particular in paragraph 3.'

18 Ibid. Annex A(3) (International standards, guidelines and recommendations).

19 Ibid. Article 3(2).

20 Ibid. Article 3(3).

21 Ibid. Annex A(1) (Sanitary or phytosanitary measure).

22 Ibid. Article 4 (Equivalence).

23 Ibid. Article 9 (Technical Assistance).

24 Ibid. Article 10 (Special and Differential Treatment).

25 Indeed, this is enshrined to some degree in the very text of the SPS Agreement. See Ibid. Article 6 (Adaptation to Regional Conditions, Including Pest or Disease-Free Areas and Areas of Low Pest or Disease Prevalence). See also D. Neven and J. Weiler, 'Japan – Measures Affecting the Importation of Apples (AB-2003–4): One Bad Apple? (DS245/AB/R): A Comment' in Henrik Horn and Petros Mavroidis (eds), *The WTO Case Law of 2003*, American Law Institute, 2005, 288.

26 For an extended analysis of this point, see R. Howse, 'Democracy, Science and Free Trade: Risk Regulation on Trial at the World Trade Organization', *Michigan Law Review*, 98, 2000, 98, 2333–8.

27 SPS Agreement, Article 4(1).

28 Ibid. Article 5(4).

29 Appellate Body Report, *Australia – Salmon*, para. 199.

30 Ibid. para. 200.

31 SPS Agreement Article5(1).

32 Ibid. Article 5(2).

33 Appellate Body Report, *EC – Hormones*, at para. 193.

34 Ibid. para. 194.

35 Howse, op. cit., pp. 2353–7 (exploring how Articles 2(2) and 5(6) of the SPS Agreement 'seem to require certain substantive regulatory trade-offs and thereby constrain the outcomes of democratic regulation').

36 2004 US Model BIT Article 5(1).

37 Ibid. Article 5(2).

38 *Glamis Gold, Ltd. v. USA*, Award (UNCITRAL, 8 June 2009), para. 616.

39 For an exploration of this line of inquiry but with a focus on an applicable standard of arbitrariness, see M. Orellana, 'The Role of Science in Investment Arbitrations Concerning Public Health and the Environment', *Yearbook of International Environmental Law* 17, 2006, 63–6.

40 *Glamis Gold v. US*, para. 601 states: 'If, as Claimant argues, the customary international law minimum standard of treatment has indeed moved to require something less than the 'egregious', 'outrageous', or 'shocking' standard as elucidated in *Neer*, then the burden of establishing what the standard now requires is upon Claimant.'

41 The SPS Agreement, Article 5(7) states: 'In cases where relevant scientific evidence is insufficient, a Member may provisionally adopt sanitary or phytosanitary measures on the basis of available pertinent information, including that from the relevant international organizations as well as from sanitary or phytosanitary measures applied by other Members. In such circumstances, Members shall seek to obtain the additional information necessary for a more objective assessment of risk and review the sanitary or phytosanitary measure accordingly within a reasonable period of time.'

42 In Appellate Body Report, *EC – Hormones* para. 123, the Appellate Body ruled: 'The status of the precautionary principle in international law continues to be the subject of debate among academics, law practitioners, regulators and judges. The precautionary principle is regarded by some as having crystallized into a general principle of customary international environmental law. Whether it has been widely accepted by Members as a principle of general or customary international law appears less than clear. We consider, however, that it is unnecessary, and probably imprudent, for the Appellate Body in this appeal to take a position on this important, but abstract, question. We note that the Panel itself did not make any definitive finding with regard to the status of the precautionary principle in international law and that the precautionary principle, at least outside the field of international environmental law, still awaits authoritative formulation (footnotes omitted)'.

43 1994 US Model BIT, Article II(3)(a) extracted in McLachlan, op. cit.

44 *Azurix Corp v. The Argentine Republic*, Award (ICSID Case No. ARB/01/12, 14 July 2006), para. 361.

45 For example, the 2005 German Model Treaty simply provides: 'Each Contrasting State shall in its territory in any case accord investments by investors of the other Contracting State fair and equitable treatment as well as full protection under the Treaty.' German Model BIT, Article 2(2) extracted in McLachlan, op. cit. p. 418.

46 *Methanex v. US*, Pt. III, Chp. A, paras 4–6.

47 Ibid. Pt. III, Chp. A, paras 32–4.

48 Ibid.

49 'It is Methanex's case that approximately one third of its methanol production is utilized in the fuel sector, principally for use in methanol-based MTBE.' Ibid. Pt. II, Chp. D, para. 3.

50 J. Kurtz, 'The Use and Abuse of WTO Law in Investor-State Arbitration: Competition and its Discontents' 20(3) *European Journal of International Law*, 2009, 749.

51 Ibid. Pt. IV, Chp. C, paras 9–27.

52 Ibid. Pt. III, Chp. A, para. 1.

53 Ibid. Pt. III, Chp. A, para. 2 (Topic Three).

54 Ibid. Pt. III, Chp. A, para. 9.

55 Ibid. Pt. III, Chp. A, paras 14 and 16.

56 There were three days of public hearings on the University of California Report. At these hearings, 'government officials and members of the public (including MTBE and methanol producers) had an opportunity to ask questions and present oral testimony'. This testimony 'indicated broad-based support for the finding by the University of California that MTBE usage in gasoline constituted a serious threat to California's drinking water and that a ban on the use of MTBE in California RFG was warranted'. Ibid. Pt. III, Chp. A, paras 17–9.

57 Ibid.

58 Ibid.
59 Ibid. Pt. III, Chp. A, paras 30–1.
60 Ibid. Pt. III, Chp. A, para. 32.
61 Ibid. Pt. III, Chp. A, paras 37–100.
62 Ibid. Pt. III, Chp. A, para. 101.
63 *Chemtura Corporation v. Government of Canada*, Award (UNCITRAL, 2 August 2010),
64 Ibid. para. 6.
65 Ibid. paras 7 and 135.
66 Ibid. para. 135.
67 Ibid.
68 Ibid. para. 136.
69 Ibid. para. 13.
70 Ibid. para. 15.
71 Ibid. para. 18.
72 Ibid. para. 19.
73 Ibid. para. 21.
74 Ibid. para. 30.
75 Ibid. para. 40.
76 Ibid. para. 41.
77 Ibid. para. 43.
78 Ibid. para. 44.
79 Ibid. para. 137.
80 In *Pope & Talbot v. Canada*, the Canadian measure – allocation of quotas for softwood lumber exports from 'covered provinces' in Canada to the US – was one of Canada's specific obligations under the 1996 Softwood Lumber Agreement, which had been negotiated to settle a trade dispute with the US. The Tribunal in that case read national treatment in such a way as to excuse a measure 'if it bears a reasonable relationship to rational policies not motivated by preference of domestic over foreign owned investments'. The Tribunal went on to dismiss the foreign investor's claim because, inter alia, the quota system was connected to the SLA and thus 'reasonably related to the rational policy of removing the threat of [countervailing duty] actions'. *Pope & Talbot v. Canada*, paras 18, 79 and 87.
81 *Chemtura v. Canada*, paras 138–43.
82 SPS Agreement, Article 3(2).
83 Ibid. Article 3(1).
84 *EC – Beef Hormones*, para. 164.
85 *Chemtura v. Canada*, para. 163.
86 Ibid. para. 165.
87 '[T]he Claimant further argues that the scientific basis for the outcome of the Special Review was insufficient.' Ibid. para. 153.
88 Ibid.
89 Ibid. para. 154.
90 Ibid.
91 'As the third and fourth measures in breach of Article 1105(1) of NAFTA, the Claimant identified the termination of Chemtura's lindane registrations, despite the availability of less prejudicial avenues, and the prohibition imposed on Claimant to sell any lindane products thereafter.' Ibid. Para. 181.
92 Ibid. para. 186.
93 Ibid. para. 187.
94 Ibid. para. 188.
95 Ibid. para. 192.

9 Climate change

Trading, investing and the interaction of law, science and technology

Kate Miles

9.1 Introduction

It is, perhaps, difficult to think of a more interdisciplinary field in which so many areas and issues converge than climate change. It engages in various ways the expertise and concern of scientists, regulators, planning specialists, entrepreneurs, financiers, lawyers, policymakers, local communities, indigenous peoples, architects, engineers, industrial designers and so many more. Multiple sectors are deeply affected by climate-related issues, including energy, water, insurance, agriculture, horticulture, fishing, forestry, tourism and transport, and it is this inherent merging of interests that requires significant interaction between those fields. On the international plane, these considerations are part of the backdrop to, and sit within, a legal framework designed to regulate state interaction on climate change.[1] Interestingly, however, it is both this marrying of interests and the very nature of the subject of climate change itself that may lead to an even greater emphasis on 'science-influenced' principles within international law than has been the case to date.

The ever-increasing complexity of the issues with which international law is required to grapple has recently seen, among other effects, a notable visibility of science and technology in international law. This is not simply because of the advent of new products that require accommodation within existing legal frameworks,[2] although this is certainly an important factor for consideration. Nor is it restricted to its evidentiary role in providing key factual and expert evidence in disputes before international courts and tribunals,[3] although, again, this is a noteworthy aspect upon which this chapter also reflects. It is, however, also visible in the development of new principles of law, in the propulsion of existing rules in new directions and, ultimately, through challenging the application of accepted norms, in the progression of the law. These amorphous processes are, of course, very much intertwined with the treatment of new products and technology and with the use of scientific expertise as evidence in disputes. It is the sum of these incidences, however, that has wider implications and that is the underlying enquiry for this chapter – in particular, the proposition that science and technology are influencing the development of international law in fundamental ways, that they play an increasingly pivotal role in trade and investment regulation and dispute settlement and, more specifically, that they will also be central to the treatment of climate-related issues within international economic law.

9.2 Science and technology in international law

It is clear that science and technology perform multiple roles within international law. It is in this section of the chapter that I explore several of those functions in a more general sense, including the way in which science is central to shifts in global risk regulation, its use in international litigation and the response of international law to new technologies.

9.2.1 Science and global risk regulation

International law and policy regarding health and environmental matters, by their very nature, require a certain degree of science-based decision-making. Among many elements, this involves assessing substantive scientific material, employing technical risk analysis, applying different methods of risk management and gauging appropriate levels of precaution, this last element of which has given rise to the discourse on the competing methodologies of the 'sound science' regulatory paradigm and the emergence of the precautionary principle.[4] However, such complex matters of global significance also implicate a range of other values beyond purely those derived from science.[5] And it is the treatment of non-scientific values within a global risk regulation context that has caused some consternation. In particular, there are concerns as to the way in which the values and perspectives from other disciplines regarding risk have been subject to subtle processes of minimization and the prioritizing of a technical, purist view of science over and above more blended approaches to risk regulation.[6] Indeed, there has been a palpable shift in the role and authority occupied by science within international law and this is, in part, down to what Jacqueline Peel has described as the 'scientization of risk', in which society increasingly perceives risk in scientific terms and regards it as being explicable only through the input of scientific expertise; hence, the pervasive turning to positivist science-based risk assessment techniques in both decision-making and the design of international regulatory mechanisms in the field of health and the environment.[7] This authoritative position within international legal regimes and dispute settlement fora is also influenced by perceptions of science and scientific expertise as providing objective and neutral information, as the purveyor of irrefutable truths, if you like, and that this can provide impartial answers in the face of the seemingly variable nature of international law and policy.[8]

This traditional narrative, however, does not sit comfortably with alternative conceptualizations of the nature of scientific research. In particular, with theories in which the uncertainties, value judgements, understandings and implicit assumptions that operate on the processes of scientific research are acknowledged and explored.[9] Or those that frame and explore scientific knowledge as a form of social construct, as an organic process of evolving understandings and continuous interactive exchanges of hypothesis and refutation, or that perceptions of environmental and health risk are, in fact, variable and embedded within a cultural framework, reflecting the socio-cultural world view of the community from which an individual scientist originates.[10]

It is, of course, evident that scientific disputes have recently arisen around a broad spectrum of subjects, the essence of which is a divergence of scientific opinion among experts as to the future impacts, effects or outcomes of contested activities or substances.[11] In other words, science is not always able to provide exact, conclusive answers, particularly where there is uncertainty, imperfect knowledge or conflicting scientific opinion.[12] In such circumstances, it is the individual expert's beliefs on risk that are engaged, their interpretation of data, their conjectures on projected consequences and their own view on appropriate responses in any given case, not a definitive answer.[13] Appreciating the inevitability of such professionally based and legitimate variation is of particular significance for issues that inherently involve uncertainty and incomplete knowledge, such as climate change.

Managing risk at the international level has produced a variety of regulatory mechanisms. It is to be expected that treaty regimes for which science is central to their subject matter would engage extensively with issues of risk, uncertainty and future impacts. Certainly, multilateral environmental agreements and, interestingly, international soft law instruments and voluntary codes for private sector conduct have developed sophisticated mechanisms to contend with scientific uncertainty and to minimize future adverse environmental impacts from current activities.[14] For example, procedural obligations such as environmental impact assessment or prior informed consent seek to identify and minimize potential risk factors in planned activity. These have found form in treaties such as the United Nations Convention on Biological Diversity[15] and the Convention on the Control of Transboundary Movement of Hazardous Wastes;[16] in the private equity lending criteria of voluntary codes such as the Equator Principles;[17] and in soft law instruments such as the Rio Declaration.[18] It is also in this context that important legal concepts have emerged. The development and use of substantive principles such as the precautionary principle, sustainable development, the principle of preventative action, and common but differentiated responsibility are ways in which the need to address notions of risk, scientific uncertainty, responsibility, international cooperation and equity have been translated into international legal frameworks.[19]

What is interesting is the extent to which science is now also forming a core component of regulatory structures for subject areas beyond those for which science is obviously relevant, such as the environmental sphere. It now reaches extensively into, for example, international economic law, specifically, the treaty framework of the WTO. In this context, it is the SPS Agreement that has, as its very subject matter and approach to regulation, one inherently grounded in science. Indeed, the 'language of risk' is increasingly employed in attempts to structure appropriate regulatory frameworks to manage global issues, to take adequate account of uncertainty and to assess competing risk perspectives.[20] Certainly, as evidenced by the express wording of the SPS Agreement, trade law is engaging in a very direct manner with the language of risk regulation and provides a central role for science in the operation of the SPS regime.[21] Article 2.2 exemplifies this approach:

> Members shall ensure that any sanitary or phytosanitary measure is applied only to the extent necessary to protect human, animal or plant life or health, is based on scientific principles and is not maintained without sufficient scientific evidence. . . .

Taking this path has generated controversy. In fact, it has been argued that the emphasis on scientific evidence exemplified by the SPS Agreement, and implicitly also present in other contexts, can, in fact, perpetuate an inflexible, homogenous and ultimately unrealistic concept of risk.[22] And that this 'one-dimensional', as Peel describes it, or unduly narrow approach does not reflect or encompass the complexities of risk, particularly in circumstances where there is uncertainty, ambiguity, lack of consensus or incomplete knowledge.[23]

Although obviously dealing with a more general subject area than the SPS Agreement, it is clear that investment treaties are yet to acknowledge a role for science in quite such an explicit fashion. This lack of express reliance within the treaties themselves has not, however, precluded a significant role in the practical conduct of proceedings. In the course of examining the way in which scientific evidence is used in international disputes, the treatment given to such expertise in the contentious setting of investor-state arbitration is also considered below. First, however, this chapter continues with a discussion on its function in the non-contentious context for climate regulation. Climate-related disputes are discussed below in Section 9.3 of this chapter.

Against the backdrop of an increasingly pronounced role for science in risk regulation, it is not surprising, therefore, to see the prominence of science within the regulatory regimes established to address climate change. At the international level, the governance model for managing climate-related risks embodies a composite of science, policy and law. Certainly, it hardly needs mentioning that it was the scientific community that identified the issue and the need for a global management programme, but science also features prominently within the provisions of the United Nations Framework Convention on Climate Change ('UNFCCC'), the text of which refers throughout the treaty in multiple forms to the role of science in responding to climate change.[24] A discrete scientific body, the Intergovernmental Panel on Climate Change ('IPCC') was established specifically to evaluate the current state of scientific, technical and socio-economic knowledge on climate change and its impacts,[25] and it continues to provide assessments of information on climate change and interacts closely with the Secretariat and state parties to the UNFCCC.[26] An additional scientific advisory body was also created by the UNFCCC, the Subsidiary Body for Scientific and Technical Advice, to assist the Secretariat and party states in addressing issues of a scientific, technological or methodological nature that may arise under the UNFCCC.[27]

The regulatory structures set up under the UNFCCC's Kyoto Protocol also point to the significance of scientific expertise and technological innovation within the global climate change governance model.[28] In particular, the novel approach embodied in the Protocol's flexible 'Kyoto Mechanisms', as they are known, reflects a desire to foster a constructive blending of science, technology, investment and law. In this regard, the carbon emissions reduction regimes are complemented by the Clean Development Mechanism ('CDM'), joint implementation projects and carbon trading schemes, which employ different techniques, but all share the objective of achieving carbon emissions reductions through innovative mechanisms.[29] It is the CDM and the joint implementation projects, in particular, that are designed to encourage investment flows into low-carbon projects and renewable energy technology,[30] and it is in this non-contentious framework that the environmental objectives of the climate treaties and the financial objectives of investors are mutually supportive.[31] Indeed, the Kyoto Mechanisms have created new markets and provided a regulatory structure to encourage investment in climate-related technology and renewable energy sources.[32] This is again indicative of the interdisciplinary nature of the response that is required for an issue such as climate change. The arrangements implemented under the UNFCCC and the Kyoto Protocol represent an approach to managing global risk that has science as its impetus and embedded throughout the regulatory structures, but it is also very much integrated with law, policy and finance. It is clear that while science and technological innovation are central to the climate change regime, they are also insufficient without input from other sectors and disciplines to manage the risks associated with climate-related issues.

This approach is also reflected in domestic climate change regulatory regimes in which science is at the heart of interdisciplinary operations, such as that recently implemented in Australia.[33] In this particular instance, scientific expertise has been specifically integrated into the governance model through the establishment of an expert advisory body, the Climate Change Authority, which comprises specialists in climate science, climate change mitigation, economics, environmental and land-resource management, carbon trading, and investment.[34] Its role is to review the working of Australia's carbon pricing mechanism, to advise the government on national emissions targets and annual caps, and to evaluate the integrity of emissions reduction units generated from international sources.[35]

In a non-contentious context, scientific expertise is fulfilling a central function in international and domestic climate-related regulatory regimes, and doing so in an integrated fashion, operating in conjunction with input from other disciplines. Peel has argued that the appropriate role for science in global risk governance is as one of several influential factors contributing to health and environmental outcomes, rather than as the sole determining element, and that the operation of the IPCC reflects just such an integrated approach.[36] Interestingly, this increasing reliance on science in global risk management and its fusion with law and policy has implications for both regulatory approaches and dispute resolution, and not only in a general sense, but for the climate sector as well. As science-based decision-making and regulation are increasingly challenged within the trade and investment context and new climate-related technologies are beginning to appear as the subject of international disputes, the question of the role for scientific expertise, variable risk perceptions and values drawn from multiple disciplines becomes all the more pertinent.[37] However, before examining specifically how these issues may be played out in the context of disputes involving climate change, the role of science in international litigation more generally needs to be considered.

9.2.2 Scientific expert evidence

Distinct from its regulatory function and cultural influence, science also performs a significant role in both national and international disputes. Much as in the non-contentious setting, this function has also led to an interesting mode of interaction between science and international economic law. In the context of international litigation, it is the use of scientific expert evidence to support the legal arguments presented that can be particularly influential on decision-makers and, indeed, determine the outcome of a dispute. There are, however, structural distinctions as between domestic and international courts and tribunals that do have relevance for current trends in the approach to scientific expertise in international litigation.

Philippe Sands points out that international courts are increasingly required to function in a manner that is substantially different from the way in which they were originally conceived.[38] Unlike domestic systems with their combined tasks of ascertaining the facts and addressing legal questions, international courts were largely established with a view to determining matters of law, not as first instance 'fact-finders', and, although each forum has its own discrete rules, their procedural structures do tend to reflect that primary purpose.[39] Such courts are now, however, often obliged to contend with complex and sophisticated scientific material and evaluate conflicting scientific reports without necessarily possessing specialist knowledge themselves or availing themselves of the opportunity to access assistance from specialists.[40] Inevitably, therefore, in health or environment-related cases, there is a heavy reliance on the input of experts as witnesses or as advocates themselves. When this is, at times, coupled with a reluctance to engage in in-depth questioning of the scientific evidence, there is, perhaps, then a risk that courts can be overly deferential to scientific expertise or that the weight given to individual written reports could be misplaced. The shift in culture, discussed at the beginning of this chapter, that has brought about the 'scientization of risk' not only affects approaches to regulation; it also impacts upon the perceptions of scientific expert evidence in international litigation, raising the value of that evidence above that of 'opinion' to 'irrefutable truth'. A core concern is that the deference shown to scientific reports in international dispute resolution fora can effectively operate so as to absolve the courts from determining themselves key matters of fact and their implications.[41] Or, perhaps, the risk is that the evidence is not given sufficient consideration at all.[42] The exact effect of specific scientific evidence on judicial panels in international cases is not often ascertainable from the judgments issued by courts. Although what Sands makes clear is that, in matters in which scientific expertise is crucial to the issues in dispute, then strong legal submissions will not suffice on their own to succeed in the case; science-based evidence, its presentation and the authority of the individual experts will be central to a court's decision.[43] Furthermore, with an appreciation of this reliance on scientific evidence, it becomes all the more important to consider matters of procedure. In particular, consideration needs to be given to the way in which individual courts and tribunals adopt different procedural approaches towards evidentiary issues, and scientific expertise can influence the impact that such evidence may, or may not, have on the adjudicators in any given case.

In discussing these issues, it is useful to look to the practice of key international dispute settlement fora such as the International Court of Justice ('ICJ'). The ICJ, for example, takes a particularly conservative approach to the presentation of oral evidence and it is clear that the problematic aspects Sands has identified were evident in the procedural treatment of scientific expertise in the *Gabčikovo-Nagymaros*[44] and *Pulp Mills*[45] proceedings. In both cases, the parties incorporated scientific experts as part of the legal team, rather than as witnesses.[46] Despite the paucity of specific rules of evidence guiding the practice of the ICJ, there is scope for the court to hear oral evidence and the cross-examination of witnesses;[47] the court is not, however, in the habit of availing itself of this opportunity.[48] Without the benefit of extensive cross-examination, this can leave the court with the difficult task of evaluating several equally credible, but conflicting, scientific reports. Indicating a desire to change these practices, the court's disapproval was discernible in *Pulp Mills*, in which the court stated expressly that in future cases scientific evidence should be presented by witnesses so that questioning can occur.[49] It is, indeed, a move of note. However, the immediate impact of this change on decision-making is, perhaps, not immense as the court still rarely engages in questioning of either the evidence or counsels' submissions during the hearing. As such, the evidence remains, on the whole, untested at the oral phase of the merits proceedings, the result being not dissimilar to scientific experts appearing as counsel.

The use of scientific expertise within international law has been particularly visible in disputes containing trade or investment and health or environmental aspects – never more so, perhaps, than when ascertaining the appropriate response for international legal regimes to the development of new technologies. I have in mind, in this regard, the protracted *EC – Hormones*[50] trade dispute over the use of growth hormones in cattle and the importation of beef products containing meat from such animals, the *GMOs* case,[51] and investment disputes such as *Methanex*.[52] Furthermore, for our purposes, this discussion takes place against a backdrop of climate-related considerations. In particular, what does the approach adopted in these trade and investment disputes to the advent of new technologies and to the use of scientific expertise indicate for future treatment of such issues in a climate-related context? Before embarking on that enquiry, however, this next section briefly considers yet another significant factor in the interaction between science, international economic law and climate change – the influence of science in the shaping of the legal principles themselves.

9.2.3 The science behind new principles

The development and validation of new principles in international environmental law has historically been a sporadic process, largely responsive to particular incidents, advances in scientific knowledge, or the need to manage new technology.[53] The importance of science and technology in this process should not be underestimated. Indeed, Sands describes them as having 'played a significant catalytic role: without the availability of scientific evidence, new rules of law are unlikely to be put in place'.[54] Evidently, owing to the nature of the subject matter of international environmental law, scientific knowledge is central to the design of appropriate legal frameworks and responses to specific issues. The emergence of particular rules and principles, however, is a complex, interactive process involving multiple state and non-state actors and the expertise from many disciplines.[55] What is of particular interest is the way in which these principles have then begun to appear in more diverse contexts, and, specifically, in an interplay with other fields of international law. In this way, the consideration of science-driven principles has found a subtle expansion beyond the realm of their original application. And in being given effect within novel settings, principles, such as sustainable development or the precautionary principle, have been given additional layers of meaning, have continued to evolve, or have even possibly been restricted or, at least, shaped to fit the frameworks of other areas of international law.

This type of development can be seen in the treatment of the principles of sustainable development and the precautionary principle within cases such as *Gabčikovo-Nagymaros*[56] and *EC – Hormones*[57] – not strictly speaking environmental disputes, but matters involving treaty interpretation and international trade rules respectively, and which also contain environmental elements. For example, among many issues in *Gabčikovo-Nagymaros*, the ICJ needed to consider the effect of new scientific knowledge and norms of international environmental law on the implementation of obligations contained in a treaty negotiated and concluded in the 1970s for the construction and operation of a system of dams. In particular, as the science improved and new monitoring techniques developed, so did the understanding of the ecological processes involved in the water flows of the Danube and the impact of lock and barrage systems on water ways. This led to Hungary's desire to modify its conduct under its treaty obligations to reflect that new scientific understanding. On this point, the Court stated that the new norms did, indeed, have to be considered:[58]

> Such new norms have to be taken into consideration, and such new standards given proper weight, not only when States consider new activities, but also when continuing with activities begun in the past. This need to reconcile economic development with protection of the environment is aptly expressed in the concept of sustainable development. For the purposes of the present case, this means that the Parties should together look afresh at the effects on the environment of the operation of the Gabčikovo power plant.

These references to applying new norms in *Gabčikovo-Nagymaros* were later picked up on by the Appellate Body in the *EC – Hormones* dispute in its consideration of the precautionary principle.[59] As discussed above, it is the concept of precaution that has become so significant to risk assessment in the trade context, taking on the opposing conceptual mantle to that of the 'sound science' approach. In *EC – Hormones*, the central question was whether or not the measures put in place by the EC as regards hormone-treated meat products complied with the risk assessment requirements of the SPS Agreement and, among many issues, key scientific disagreement surrounded the data gathered, its sufficiency, the manner in which it was produced, its interpretation and its implications.[60] The EC sought to rely on the precautionary principle and the scientific uncertainties surrounding the long-term effects on humans of the use of hormones in beef products to justify its prohibitions on importation of such products.

On these issues, the Appellate Body noted that the 'precautionary principle has been incorporated and given a specific meaning within Article 5.7 of the SPS Agreement'.[61] It was held, however, that it did not override the operation of Articles 5.1 and 5.2 of the SPS Agreement. The concern, of course, is that the fundamentals of the principle will be subsumed within the WTO understanding of risk assessment as embodied within the SPS Agreement and that the core element of precaution will be watered down. The Appellate Body also noted the existence of opinion that precaution had 'crystallised into a general principle of customary international environmental law', although it stopped short of adopting that approach itself.[62] One of the difficulties surrounding the precautionary principle, of course, is its various shades of meaning; its definition, meaning and scope remain unsettled with possible applications ranging across a wide spectrum of interpretation.[63] In one sense, the principle requires nothing more than states to take care in decision-making; in another, it permits the taking of action to prevent harm to the environment even where there is scientific uncertainty; and, at a more exacting level, the Rio Declaration requires that scientific uncertainty shall not be used to prevent action.[64] Although this unresolved aspect of the principle is a source of contention, it does also allow for the moulding of the principle to fit different circumstances and, as such, the way in which principles from international environmental law are shaped in other contexts will continue to need to be observed. Certainly, the precautionary principle is an attempt to reflect in law the realities of incomplete or inconclusive scientific knowledge and evidence about impacts on the environment and the need to address risk. For this reason, particularly with respect to disputes containing environmental components, such as those impacting on climate-related matters, it is to be expected that principles from the environmental field will continue to appear in an international economic law context and evolve further over time.

9.3 Science in investment disputes

The inherent nature of international disputes inevitably means they are multi-layered, one consequence of which is that trade and investment disputes are not solely about trade and investment, but encompass many issues. Sands makes this point about environmental disputes not being able to be classified as solely 'environmental',[65] and the same can be said of trade and investment – there are intersecting issues involved in these cases and, with that intersection, come competing value systems. That contest stretches into the use of science by both parties to such disputes and it is certainly the case that the differing scientific approaches advocated by each side, generally a positivist 'sound science' model as opposed to one grounded in precaution, also reflect the overall positions adopted in the wider dispute.

Although the subject of science within trade disputes was touched on above, it is dealt with extensively in other chapters in this volume. As such, the analysis in this section focuses on the treatment of science in the investment context, and the way in which investment tribunals should approach questions of science and scientific evidence before them is, without doubt, a complex and controversial issue. It is also important to reflect on this aspect in the context of this chapter's consideration of climate change, as the issues that arise more generally in the investment–environmental law and policy nexus apply equally in the more specific subset embodied in the investment–climate change nexus.

Bilateral investment treaties do not engage with the language of risk in the direct manner of trade agreements such as the SPS Agreement, but the disputes that arise out of investor protections often require a sophisticated understanding of new technologies and scientific evidence. This can manifest in the context of either an investor challenge to government regulation enacted for health or environmental protection purposes, or objections to governmental decisions on the grounds that they are allegedly arbitrary or have allegedly been made without due process because they were not consistent with forms of risk analysis advocated by the investor claimant as being required. In these circumstances, a tribunal in an investor-state dispute will usually need to engage with scientific material to some extent. While the exact nature of that engagement will depend upon the specific elements of the case and the arguments that are put forward by the parties, the focus will almost certainly be on the quality of the science relied upon by the host state in support of its actions and decision-making.[66]

Bilateral investment treaties and investment provisions within certain free trade agreements[67] contain a series of investor protections, including prohibitions on uncompensated expropriation, guarantees of national treatment and requirements to treat foreign investors and their investments in accordance with the fair and equitable treatment standard.[68] In a dispute revolving around the introduction of new regulation or governmental measures for purposes of health or environmental protection, foreign investors tend to allege that the action taken constitutes a breach of these particular protection guarantees. In the case of an alleged expropriation, the complaint will involve a claim that state action resulted in a substantial deprivation of the use or enjoyment of the investment by the investor. With respect to national treatment claims, the issues will centre on whether or not foreign investors have been discriminated against in any relevant way; specifically, whether foreign investors have received less favourable treatment from the host state than it accorded its own domestic investors in 'like circumstances'. In order to meet the requirements of the fair and equitable treatment standard, a host state must have acted in accordance with the legitimate expectations of the investor, complied with due process obligations, and have maintained a stable legal and business environment for investor operations. In the health and environmental protection context, allegations of a breach of the fair and equitable treatment standard tend to involve challenges to administrative decision-making, prohibitions on certain activities, or the introduction of new regulation.[69] Examples include cases where the host state introduced a product ban to prevent contamination of groundwater with chemicals,[70] where public announcements were made warning residents not to drink water contaminated with toxic bacteria,[71] following the introduction of plain packaging legislation on cigarette packets,[72] where prohibitions on the use of certain pesticides had been enacted,[73] and following the institution of a ban on a fuel additive to protect human health and the environment.[74]

The use of scientific evidence has been crucial for the parties to such disputes, ultimately either in justifying the state's decisions or in supporting investor complaints. In this regard, when dealing with science-based governmental decision-making, affected investors analyse the quality and nature of the scientific evidence relied upon to ascertain whether there was any ulterior motive that would constitute a breach of an international investment agreement. The rationale for this approach is that where 'junk science' or 'unsound science' has been utilized rather than 'sound science', this would indicate a protectionist, rather than a legitimate scientific, purpose in taking the governmental measures.[75] As explored in the first part of this chapter, this particular discourse also, of course, involves issues of differing societal approaches to risk and perceptions of precaution, not solely matters of scientific data. The 'sound science' model has been used to argue that concerns about, for example, GMOs in the food chain are simply down to irrational fear on the part of the community and should not, therefore, be permitted to prevail over 'sound' scientific evidence in governmental decision-making.[76] In this way, such disputes are also about asserting the state's right to set its own domestic regulation so as to reflect its individual comfort levels apropos of a particular risk, and investment disputes such as *Methanex v. US*[77] illustrate these tensions.

Methanex entailed a challenge by a Canadian investor to health and environmental regulation enacted in California in response to concerns at contaminated groundwater.[78] The claim, filed under the investment protection provisions of the North American Free Trade Agreement ('NAFTA'), alleged that California's actions constituted expropriation, breach of the fair and equitable standard, and discrimination amounting to a breach of the treaty's national treatment requirements.[79] It was the scientific studies conducted by California that triggered the introduction of new regulations that were so central to the case. Methyl tertiary butyl ether ('MTBE') is a fuel additive, a key component of which is methanol, and Methanex Corporation was the principal supplier of methanol to California.[80] On the discovery of MTBE in Californian drinking water, it became apparent that the chemical was seeping out from storage tanks into the state's groundwater and the state commissioned studies to be conducted by the University of California into the impacts of MTBE on human health and the environment.[81] Following the completion of the University's report, California took the view that MTBE-contaminated water posed a significant risk to human health and to the quality of the environment, and the Governor of California issued an Executive Order in 1999 declaring that use of the chemical would be phased out by 2002.[82]

In support of its allegations of discrimination and that the environmental protection purpose of the Executive Order was a 'sham' designed to favour the domestic ethanol sector, the investor focused on scientific data available for the risks and benefits of MTBE, data relating to its use, storage and options for managing leakage and, in particular, on the scientific data that formed the basis for the report issued by the University of California. Methanex Corporation produced several expert witnesses to challenge the University report, contesting its methodology, the data upon which it relied, the risk assessments conducted and the conclusions drawn from the raw material. Methanex experts also highlighted the very different way in which MTBE leakage is managed in the European Union, namely that the efforts are concentrated on ensuring appropriate storage tank systems rather than a prohibition on the use of the substance.[83] The Tribunal took a somewhat problematic approach to the assessment of the conflicting scientific material. It found that, in principle, the scientific evidence relied upon by the state to justify its actions must merely have been 'reasonable' and implied that the tribunal would not itself have to determine the 'correctness' of the science, but then did, in fact, go on to comment on the accuracy of the science, stating that:[84]

> [I]n all material respects, the Tribunal is not persuaded that the UC Report was scientifically incorrect: the Tribunal was much impressed by the scientific witnesses presented by the USA and tested under cross-examination by Methanex; and the Tribunal accepts without reservation these experts' conclusions.

Despite re-emphasizing its accord with the substantive findings of the University of California's scientists, the Tribunal also went on to make statements that, if applied in the future, should provide plenty of scope for governmental regulation: '[T]he question is whether the scientific conclusions which were presented to the Governor were so faulty that the Tribunal may reasonably infer that the science merely provided a convenient excuse for the hidden regulation of methanol producers.'[85]

A '*so faulty* that the science has to be a front' standard[86] seems a relatively high threshold for an investor to have to meet. However, in practice, it is unlikely to operate in such a straightforward fashion as even in the *Methanex* decision itself, the Tribunal felt compelled to refer to its own conviction as to the accuracy and persuasive nature of the science presented by the state. It may well be that in the course of deciding such disputes, the arbitrators will sense a need to go beyond a 'so faulty' assessment and, as the *Methanex* arbitrators did, also seek to determine the 'correctness' of the science behind the state's decision to impose the contested regulation.[87] In the process of preferring one party's view of the overall applicable circumstances, including the science, facts and the application of the law, over the case of the other, an arbitral tribunal is effectively replacing the state's judgment with its own. It is, of course, questionable whether such second-guessing of a state's decisions, its reliance on particular scientific data and its responses to perceived risk is desirable, which, in turn, gives rise to notions of greater deference to national autonomy. However, review systems of state conduct to assess whether violations of investor protections have occurred are obviously necessary. Accordingly, an alternative approach is advocated by Céline Lévesque, who argues that an assessment of procedure rather than substance is a more appropriate method of gauging the reasonableness of the state's reliance on a particular set of scientific data.[88]

Lévesque proposes that where certain objective criteria have been met regarding both the process of the formation of the scientific conclusions and the process involved in the resultant governmental decision-making, then this would point to compliance with investor protection obligations. She argues that fulfilling the requirements of a form of 'scientific due process' would indicate that the contested regulation was not, in fact, arbitrary and discusses a range of possible criteria.[89] In particular, she suggests a series of indicators and scientific norms that should be considered in reviewing science-based governmental decision-making, including:[90]

(a) whether or not the state's decision was informed by international standards;
(b) whether the decision-making procedures followed transparency and participatory requirements;
(c) whether the scientific material and conclusions were subject to peer review; and
(d) whether the 'norms of science' were met in the production of the scientific data and its analysis, those being, universalism, communalism, disinterestedness, and organised scepticism.

Lévesque argues that if a process-oriented enquiry according to criteria such as those set out above were adopted by arbitral tribunals when confronted with issues of science-based decision-making, then the undesirable effect of deciding on the actual 'correctness' of the scientific material could be avoided.[91] This is a particularly important consideration where the science is uncertain or the appropriate regulatory response to scientific information is contested. It will be interesting to see whether the suggestions of Lévesque are taken up in future investment disputes containing environmental components. Certainly, as climate-related issues begin to emerge in contentious contexts, the way in which scientific expertise and new technologies are treated will become increasingly important. Building on this discussion of the role of science and expert evidence within investor-state arbitration, the next section examines these issues as they pertain to climate change.

9.4 Climate change, trade and investment

As we have seen, science has been central to several high profile trade and investment disputes in which governments have sought to take measures for reasons of public health or environmental protection. With respect to climate change, the role of science and technology within international law is also a complex one. The science of climate change has undoubtedly driven the development of regulatory frameworks at the international level,[92] the implementation of domestic climate-related measures,[93] and even the framing of climate-related disputes taking shape in international fora, courts and tribunals,[94] and it is certainly playing a role in responses to climate issues within international economic law. In another sense, the science and technology needs at the heart of climate issues have also created immeasurable investment opportunities – inspiring innovation in low-carbon technology, generating private sector investment flows into renewable energy projects, and building markets for new products and services.[95] Ranging from the development of the seemingly simplest of low-carbon technologies such as energy efficient light bulbs,[96] to large-scale renewable energy facilities, to the invention and design of new carbon management technologies such as carbon capture and storage,[97] to the 6,755 individual registered projects at the CDM,[98] the capital in-flows from private sector investment in the transition to a low-carbon economy are enabling and promoting initiatives such as these.[99] Despite this activity, however, investment levels in renewable energy and low-carbon technology are still insufficient to meet current and future energy needs and additional funding could be encouraged through domestic and international policies, the measures in regulatory regimes, market mechanisms and financial incentive programmes, such as feed-in tariffs, mandatory renewable energy quotas, technology development grants and tax exemptions.[100] The way in which such initiatives sit within the framework of international economic law and interact with its rules is complex and can potentially be both supportive of and constraining on climate policy depending on the context.[101]

With this in mind, it is interesting to reflect on the emerging responses within international economic law to the new technologies or regulatory measures that are being developed to mitigate climate change. In many ways, however, the climate-related nature of the products or technology is purely incidental to the dispute and the application of the trade or investment rules. These are not 'climate change' issues as such. Rather, these are matters of alleged inconsistencies with trade and investment rules that happen to involve climate-related regulation or the treatment of climate-related products. And, as I have discussed elsewhere, it is likely that this is the way in which we will continue to see the international economic law and climate change intersect played out in dispute settlement fora.[102]

Investor protections have been invoked regarding both the instigation and the withdrawal of climate-related measures. Separate sets of investors have declared the potential for harm in proposed governmental action on climate and in the revocation of climate-related measures. In one example, in 2009, foreign investors in Australian coal-fired power generators threatened to invoke the Hong Kong–Australia bilateral investment treaty if the national emissions trading scheme was enacted as initially proposed under the Carbon Pollution Reduction Scheme.[103] CLP Holdings Ltd stated that the effect of the draft scheme and planned levels of compensation conflicted with Australia's treaty obligations and that 'if laws to cut carbon emissions led to a fall in value of its Australian assets, it would seek to recover losses'.[104] As it transpired, the scheme was not enacted as proposed, the compensation provision was adjusted and the threat of arbitration dissipated.

Climate-related issues are also emerging indirectly in investor-state arbitration, just as they have in ordinary contract matters[105] or domestic planning and development disputes, in which the contested matters relate to planning conditions imposed as a result of the changing climate, such as permits for carbon emissions, water use restrictions, or coastal development prohibitions.[106] Contractual issues and administrative decision-making were involved in the dispute over the non-transference of carbon emissions reduction units ('ERU's) in *Naftrac Limited v. National Environmental Investment Agency*

(Ukraine).[107] The Cyprus-based investor Naftrac alleged that it was forced out of a joint implementation gas efficiency project in which the ERUs generated by the methane leak-prevention programme could have been sold by Naftrac on carbon markets. Ukraine asserted that Naftrac did not meet the requisite licensing requirements.[108] The Arbitral Tribunal dismissed the claim in December 2012. Planning permission issues were at the centre of the 2009 dispute in *Vattenfall AB v. Federal Republic of Germany* over the manner in which local authorities in Hamburg granted emissions and water use permits for the operation of a coal-fired power plant and the conditions that were attached to their use.[109] Furthermore, in this case, consideration of climate change was, in fact, expressly referred to by the claimant as a factor in the authority's decision to review the issuing of the permits.[110] During this process, the Hamburg authorities sought to place requirements relating to the amount and condition of water to be extracted and returned to the River Elbe and to require Vattenfall to install a carbon capture and storage plant. Final authorization for the project was eventually granted but with restrictions that Vattenfall considered to be commercially untenable; hence, the initiation of proceedings.[111] Ultimately, the dispute was settled in 2011 following the renegotiation of the environmental conditions of the permits. However, in many ways, the claim filed was indicative of a core energy sector response to new restrictive environmental measures, being to turn to court action in one form or another, also illustrated by the recent Request for Arbitration again filed by Vattenfall against Germany. On this later occasion, the claim was triggered by the state's planned phase-out of nuclear energy plants by 2022.[112] This particular dispute is ongoing and, along with other cases,[113] gives an indication of investor response to regulation that detrimentally affects foreign investors. As with this nuclear energy phase-out, it is likely that, should a similar financial need arise with respect to carbon-intensive interests, there would also be no hesitation in pursuing compensation through investor-state arbitral mechanisms.

This assertion is also borne out in the approach that has been adopted by other energy sector investors, albeit in a different category of the industry – those investing in low-carbon energy projects. Matters have moved beyond the stage of threatened action, proceedings having recently been initiated in a dispute involving an obstructed wind power project in Canada. In January 2013, Windstream Energy LLC filed a claim alleging that an Ontario moratorium on offshore wind developments subsequent to the awarding of a contract to develop just such a project is a breach of the investor protections guaranteed in NAFTA.[114] According to the claimant, Ontario implemented policies to encourage investment in renewable energy sources and enacted legislation in 2009, the Green Energy Act, creating a feed-in tariff programme that guaranteed preferential prices for electricity generated from approved renewable sources. In 2010, Windstream Energy was awarded a contract under the preferentially priced feed-in tariff programme to establish and operate an offshore wind power project.[115] However, in 2011 – an election year and in the context of increasing public concerns at regional energy costs – Ontario announced a moratorium on the development of further offshore wind power projects, the stated basis being that additional scientific research had to be conducted.[116] Accordingly, following this effective shelving of its project despite its contract to develop a new offshore wind power project, Windstream Energy is seeking to recover its losses through investor-state arbitration.

Even in such circumstances, it is, perhaps, still overstating the case to declare that international investment law is a 'force for good' and 'can reinforce the credibility of climate change mitigation policies', as Anatole Boute has asserted.[117] Rather, it is, I would suggest, more accurate to claim that investment law protects investors and, accordingly, it is simply a tool available to protect investors in low-carbon and carbon-intensive projects should they be harmed by governmental action in such a way as to breach an applicable investment treaty.[118] Either way, however, it remains an encroachment on host state domestic policy space. The impact of investor claims may well encourage governments to consider closely whether to roll back existing incentives for investment in low-carbon projects as Boute suggests and provide investors in the renewable energy sector with greater certainty in assessing non-commercial risk, but it could also just as credibly discourage the introduction of new such incentives in the first place. If states consider that they may be unduly constrained in their regulatory flexibility on their renewable energy policies, they may be hesitant to make more proactive provision in the future.

Ontario's renewable energy policies have also featured at the WTO. The *Renewable Energy Generation Sector* dispute between Canada and Japan/the EU, on which the WTO Appellate Body recently released its report, implicates both regulatory aspects and the way in which new climate-related technologies are surfacing in international courts and tribunals.[119] The complaint centres on a range of domestic content requirements adopted by the government of the Province of Ontario with respect to the supply of equipment to renewable energy generation facilities. Domestic measures enacted by Ontario in 2009 required that in order to qualify for, and benefit from, the financially advantageous Ontario feed-in tariff programme, electricity generators using solar photovoltaic and wind power technology had to source a defined percentage of their equipment from within Ontario – depending on when the project was operational, 50 to 60 per cent if solar and 25 to 50 per cent if wind power. Japan argued that such requirements breached several WTO Agreements, including Article III of the GATT and Article 2.1 of the TRIMS Agreement,[120] on the basis that they accorded less favourable treatment to imported equipment than that afforded to like products manufactured within Ontario. The Panel largely agreed with Japan and the EU, determining that there had been a breach of these particular treaty provisions. On appeal, the Appellate Body essentially upheld these findings of the Panel.[121]

Rather than dissipating, however, these types of issue appear to be gathering momentum as further complaints emerge. For example, in February of this year, the United States requested consultations with India concerning the local content requirements that are a prerequisite for participation in its national solar energy programme, the Jawaharlal Nehru National Solar Mission ('NSM').[122] Similar to the complaint in the Canada–Japan/EU dispute, the United States alleges that these conditions in the Indian programme discriminate against foreign solar cell and module manufacturers by requiring solar power developers to purchase domestic equipment in order to qualify for the financially advantageous NSM. In April 2013, India filed a set of formal questions at the WTO for the United States to answer regarding access to its incentive programmes in the renewable energy sector, such participation being contingent on compliance with local content requirements.[123]

Additional action has also been taken on a number of fronts. For example, in November 2012, China filed a Request for Consultations at the WTO with the EU regarding the restrictions on access to the guaranteed pricing structures of the feed-in tariff programmes implemented by Italy and Greece, which are, again, dependent on meeting local content requirements.[124] In December 2011, the United States requested formal consultations at the WTO with China regarding state funding for the manufacturing of wind power equipment.[125] In a separate course of action, the United States launched additional investigations into the alleged subsidizing of wind towers from both Vietnam and China, which concluded in 2013 with the United States International Trade Commission finding evidence of subsidies and that material injury had occurred to the United States wind tower industry.[126] Following the commencement in September 2012 of investigations by the EU into alleged dumping of Chinese solar panels on to the European market, the European Commission has recently recommended the imposition of anti-dumping levies on imported Chinese solar panels of up to 68 per cent, although final decisions on this will not be forthcoming before December 2013.[127] However, in November 2012, both China and India initiated their own anti-dumping and subsidy investigations into the production processes of solar cells from several of countries, including the United States and the EU.[128]

The development of new technologies, such as solar and wind power equipment, is a core component in the collective response to global climate change. As illustrated by the actions discussed above, however, the practices that individual states are employing in the manufacture and use of climate-related technology are increasingly bringing them into the domain of international economic law. It will be interesting to see the way in which this mode of interaction continues to play out in the future and its long-term effects on the renewable energy sector.

A further layer to these issues is to consider the way in which international economic law is being used to respond to new regulatory climate-related measures that increase costs for those operating within the regulatory sphere. The science behind our understanding of the global and pervasive nature of climate change has certainly driven the development of more intrusive measures by certain states seeking to extend the reach and effectiveness of their climate change mitigation strategies. A particularly controversial manifestation of this intersection between climate and international economic law has been the purported application of an aviation carbon tax on flights to and from European and non-European states. In 2008, the European Union Emissions Trading Scheme ('EU ETS') was extended to include commercial aviation, effectively applying a levy for carbon emissions resulting from flights.[129] The European Directive controversially also provided that, from January 2012, the scheme would include international aviation, with the levy applying to all flights landing in or departing from an EU state.[130]

Several states, including China, India, the United States and Russia, have objected strongly to the initiative, threatening a range of retaliatory responses. The Air Transport Association of America and several airlines pursued a case in the European Court of Justice challenging the regulatory measure on the grounds that it contravened customary international law. They argued that it violated the sovereignty of third states in purporting to regulate emissions levels beyond EU jurisdiction and was contrary to the United States–European Union Air Transport Agreement (known as the 'Open Skies Agreement').[131] In December 2011, however, the Court determined that the application of the levy to non-European flights was compatible with international law. Despite this finding, the scope of the EU ETS coverage remained controversial. China threatened to stall the Hong Kong Airlines purchase of planes from the European-based Airbus.[132] India threatened to retaliate with sanctions barring EU carriers from entering Indian airspace.[133] China and India prohibited their airlines from complying with the EU ETS carbon disclosure data and charging requirements,[134] the United States enacted legislation designed to exempts its airlines from any future application of the EU tax,[135] and over 20 states continued to apply diplomatic pressure through the making of a formal declaration, known as the Moscow Declaration, objecting to the inclusion of non-EU flights in the EU ETS.[136] In November 2012, however, the EU announced that it would suspend the application of the aviation tax to flights to and from non-European states for a year with a view to continuing negotiations at the International Civil Aviation Organization for an agreement on the international regulation of carbon emissions from aviation. The levy continues to apply to flights within and between EU countries.[137]

Concerns have also been expressed as to the compatibility more generally of the EU ETS with WTO Agreements;[138] the potential has been noted for future disputes over border tax adjustments imposed to take account of carbon price differences;[139] and litigation relating to the wider operation of the EU ETS was pursued in the European Court of Justice on its enactment.[140] On that occasion, a series of claims was brought by the steel manufacturer Arcelor. The company argued that the steel sector was discriminated against within the EU ETS as comparable sectors, such as the aluminium industry, were not subject to the carbon emissions-constrained programme. The ECJ held that the sectors were, indeed, comparable on the grounds that they all produced significant levels of emissions and, therefore, all contributed to the causes of dangerous climate change. However, the differential treatment was justified as the scheme was both novel and complex and the various industries produced different levels of emissions.[141] Just as the Court focused on the operational aspects of the programme, it is also likely that any investor-state arbitral panel faced with similar issues will consider the way in which new schemes have been implemented, how they have been applied to particular facilities and the effect of the measures on the investor.[142]

9.5 Conclusion

The role of science and technology within international economic law encompasses a multi-layered set of issues in itself. The complexities of then considering these matters as they pertain to climate change ensure that the issues become even more involved. Without doubt, the climate–trade–investment interface has many facets to it. Some arise out of the innate synergies, such as the need for funding flows and cross-border trading in the renewable energy sector, where the objectives of trade rules, investor protection principles, and climate law and policy can all be met. Such alignments are particularly important for innovation in the design of new low-carbon technology, the continued development of carbon markets and the thriving of the renewable energy industry in general. As we have seen, however, almost paradoxically, the relationship between international economic law and climate-related measures and technology has both a mutually supportive and conflicting character dependent on the circumstances. This seemingly contradictory state of affairs arises out of the fact that international investment law and trade rules are not designed to promote social 'goods' other than free trade and the protection of investors. Accordingly, at times the rules will protect investors and industries in environmentally friendly products and activities; and, at other times, they will protect those that do not further environmental protection. Any promotion of environmental policies, such as the mitigation of climate change, is currently purely incidental and if there is to be more direct engagement then deliberate provision within international economic rules will need to be considered. In any case, it is inevitable that climate-related disputes of the kind that are emerging will continue and we will see more investor and trade complaints involving feed-in tariff rollbacks, local content requirements and government subsidies in the renewable energy sector, challenges to inclusion in carbon-constraining programmes, opposition to phase-outs and objections to climate-related conditions placed on operating permits.

The role of science and technology will, of course, remain central to these issues. Not only does the science drive the regulatory frameworks governing climate policy, but the state measures adopted and innovative technologies developed to fulfil the objectives of climate mitigation will continue to be the subject of dispute. With this in mind, it is important to recognize that the approach to scientific expertise within both a regulatory and contentious context is significant for outcomes, to understand that the variable nature of risk perceptions is an important factor in science-based decision-making, and to appreciate that science-related principles of international law are likely to continue to develop substantively and in their mode of application in the future. Climate change is, however, a global interdisciplinary challenge that affects multiple sectors, demands interaction between fields and requires the input from a raft of different types of expert. In the course of navigating this complex area, therefore, it is important not to lose sight of the need for space in climate law and policy for a full range of expertise, perspectives, values and interests – and, particularly so, in its ongoing relationship with international economic law.

Notes

1 *United Nations Framework Convention on Climate Change*, opened for signature 9 May 1992, 31 ILM 849 (entered into force 24 March 1994) ('UNFCCC').

2 See, for example, Appellate Report, *EC – Hormones*; see also Panel Report, *EC Report – 1 Marketing of Biotech Products.*

3 See, for example, the use of scientific evidence in Case Concerning the Gabčikovo-Nagymaros Project (Hungary/Slovakia) (1997) ICJ Rep 7.

4 J. Peel, *Science and Risk Regulation in International Law*, Cambridge: Cambridge University Press, 2010 at 115–32. For a general discussion on the precautionary principle, see P. Sands and J. Peel, *Principles of International Environmental Law*, 3rd edn, Cambridge: Cambridge University Press, 2012.

5 Peel, op. cit. at 4–11, 332–3.

6 Peel, op. cit. at 4–11, 58–66, 85–8, 108–9.

7 Ibid. at 59, 71–82.

8 Ibid. at 79–81, 88–94, 108–10.

9 J. Peel, 'Of Apples and Oranges (and Hormones in Beef): Science and the Standard of Review in WTO Disputes under the SPS Agreement', *International and Comparative Law Quarterly* 61, 2012, 427 at 440. In particular, Peel discusses the work of S. Funtowicz and J. Ravetz as seminal to this field of study; see, for example, S. O. Functowicz and J. R. Ravetz, 'Science for the Post-Normal Age', *Futures* 25, 1993, 740.

10 Peel, op. cit. at 103–7; see, for example, the work of T. S. Kuhn, *The Structure of Scientific Revolutions*, 4th edn, Chicago: University of Chicago Press, 2012; see also S. Jasanoff, 'What Judges Should Know about the Sociology of Science', *Jurimetrics Journal* 32, 1992, 345 at 346–8; see also M. Douglas and A. Wildavsky, *Risk and Culture: An Essay on the Selection of Technical and Environmental Dangers*, Berkeley, CA: University of California Press, 1982.

11 C. E. Foster, *Science and the Precautionary Principle in International Courts and Tribunals: Expert Evidence, Burden of Proof and Finality*, Cambridge: Cambridge University Press, 2011 at xiii–xiv. Foster refers to the divergence of scientific opinion surrounding the use of growth hormones in cattle, the appropriate level of risk with respect to potential impacts of genetically modified organisms, sustainable fishing practices, nuclear waste and others.

12 Ibid. at xiii.

13 Ibid. at xv, 10–11.

14 Ibid. at 7–8.

15 United Nations Convention on Biological Diversity, opened for signature 5 June 1992, (1992) 31 ILM 822, Arts. 7 and 14 (entered into force 29 December 1993).

16 Convention on the Control of Transboundary Movement of Hazardous Wastes and their Disposal, opened for signature 22 March 1989, (1989) 28 ILM 657 (entered into force 1992).

17 *Equator Principles*, Washington, DC, 4 June 2003 available at www.equator-principles.com (accessed 12 March 2013).

18 Rio Declaration on Environment and Development, Report of the UNCED, UN Doc. A/CONF.151/6/Rev.1 (1992), (1992) 31 ILM 874, Principle 17.

19 For a detailed discussion on these principles, see Sands and Peel, op. cit.; for examples of the use of these principles in treaty regimes, see UNFCCC; Kyoto Protocol to the United Nations Framework Convention on Climate Change, opened for signature 11 December 1997, (1998) 37 ILM 22 (entered into force 16 February 2005); United Nations Convention on Biological Diversity, opened for signature 5 June 1992, (1992) 31 ILM 822, arts. 7 and 14, (entered into force 29 December 1993); United Nations Convention on the Law of the Sea, opened for signature 10 December 1982, (1982) 21 ILM 1261 (entered into force 16 November 1994).

20 Peel, op. cit. at 1–11.

21 See the discussion in Markus Wagner, 'Law Talk vs. Science Talk: The Languages of Law and Science in WTO Proceedings', *Fordham International Law Journal* 35, 2011, 151 at 154.

22 Peel, op. cit. at 440.

23 Ibid. at 440–42.

24 UNFCCC.

25 Intergovernmental Panel on Climate Change, *Organization*, *History*, available at www.ipcc.ch (accessed 18 April 2013).

26 Ibid.

27 UNFCCC Article 9.

28 Kyoto Protocol to the United Nations Framework Convention on Climate Change, opened for signature 11 December 1997 (1998) 37 ILM 22 (entered into force 16 February 2005).

29 Ibid. Articles 2, 6, 17 and 17.

30 J. Werksman and C. Santoro, 'Investing in Sustainable Development: The Potential Interaction between the Kyoto Protocol and the Multilateral Agreement on Investment', in W. Bradnee Chambers, *Inter-Linkages: The Kyoto Protocol and the International Trade and Investment Regimes*, New York: United Nations University Press, 2001, at 191, 193; K. Kulovesi, 'The Private Sector and the Implementation of the Kyoto Protocol: Experiences, Challenges and Prospects', *Review of European Community and International Environmental Law* 16(2), 2007, 145 at 147.

31 See further the discussion in K. Miles, 'Arbitrating Climate Change: Regulatory Regimes and Investor-State Disputes', *Climate Law* 1, 2010, 63.

32 Kulovesi, op. cit.; B. J. Richardson, *Socially Responsible Investment Law: Regulating the Unseen Polluters*, Oxford: Oxford University Press, 2008 at 39; see for example the discussion in UNEP, Investors Flock to Renewable Energy and Efficiency Technologies: Climate Change Worries, High Oil Prices and Government Help Top Factors Fuelling Hot Renewable Energy Investment Climate, Press Release, 20 June 2007 available at www.unep.org/Documents.Multilingual/Default.asp?DocumentID=512&ArticleID=5616&l=en (accessed 17 May 2013).

33 Clean Energy Act 2011 (No. 131 of 2011, Cth, Australia).

34 Climate Change Authority Act 2011 (2011, Cth, Australia); see also the discussion in R. J. Keenan, L. Caripis, A. Foerster, L. Godden and J. Peel, 'Science and the Governance of Australia's Climate Regime', *Nature Climate Change* 2, 2012, 477.

35 Keenan *et al.*, op. cit.

36 Peel, op. cit. at 334–6.

37 For a discussion on the potential interaction between investment rules and climate mitigation, see J. Werksman, K. A. Baumert and N. K. Dubash, 'Will International Investment Rules Obstruct Climate Protection Policies? An Examination of the Clean Development Mechanism', *International Environmental Agreements: Politics, Law and Economics* 3, 2003, 59; see also K. Miles, *International Investment Law and Climate Change: Issues in the Transition to a Low Carbon World*, Society of International Economic Law, Inaugural Conference, July 2008, available at http://papers.ssrn.com/sol3/papers.cfm?abstract id=1154588 (accessed 16 March 2013).

38 P. Sands, 'Water and International Law: Science and Evidence in International Litigation', *Environmental Law and Management* 22, 2010, 151 at 153.

39 Ibid.

40 Foster, op. cit. at 77; P. Sands, *Litigating Environmental Disputes: Courts, Tribunals and the Progressive Development of International Environmental Law*, 2007, 4, OECD Global Forum on International Investment, available at https://www1.oecd.org/investment/globalforum/40311090.pdf (accessed 12 January 2013).

41 See the discussion in Foster, op. cit. at 137; see also C. E. Foster, 'Adjudication, Arbitration and the Turn to Public Law "Standards of Review": Putting the Precautionary Principle in the Crucible', *Journal of International Dispute Settlement*, 2012, 1.

42 Sands, op. cit. at 155.

43 Ibid.

44 Case Concerning the Gabčikovo-Nagymaros Project (Hungary/Slovakia) (1997) ICJ Rep 7.

45 Case Concerning Pulp Mills on the River Uruguay (*Argentina v. Uruguay*), Judgment 20 April 2010, (2010) ICJ Rep.

46 Sands, op. cit. at 155; see also A. Riddell, 'Scientific Evidence in the International Court of Justice – Problems and Possibilities', *Finnish Yearbook of International Law* 20, 2009, 229.

47 *Statute of the International Court of Justice*, Articles 48 and 49; Rules of the International Court of Justice, Article 62.

48 Riddell, op. cit. at 231–2; Foster, op. cit. at 87.

49 Case Concerning Pulp Mills on the River Uruguay (*Argentina v. Uruguay*), Judgment 20 April 2010, (2010) ICJ Rep., para. 167.

50 Appellate Body Report, *EC – Hormones*.

51 Panel Report, EC el Report, 29 Marketing of Biotech Products.

52 *Methanex Corporation v. United States of America*, 44 International Legal Materials 1345 (2005).

53 Sands and Peel, 22–3.

54 Ibid. at 23.

55 Ibid.

56 Case Concerning the Gabčikovo-Nagymaros Project (Hungary/Slovakia) (1997) ICJ Rep 7.

57 Appellate Body Report, *EC – Hormones*.

58 Case Concerning the Gabčikovo-Nagymaros Project (Hungary/Slovakia) (1997) ICJ Rep 7, para. 140.

59 Appellate Body Report, *EC – Hormones*, para. 124; see also the discussion in Foster, op. cit. at 242–3.

60 Foster, op. cit. at 63–6.

61 Appellate Body Report, *EC – Hormones*, para. 120.

62 Ibid. at para. 123.

63 Sands, op. cit. at 222.

64 Ibid. at 222; *Rio Declaration on Environment and Development, Report of the UNCED*, UN Doc. A/CONF.151/6/Rev.1 (1992), (1992) 31 ILM 874.

65 Sands, op. cit.
66 C. Lévesque, 'Science in the Hands of International Investment Tribunals: A Case for "Scientific Due Process"', *Finnish Yearbook of International Law* 20, 2009, 259 at 263–4.
67 See, for example, *North American Free Trade Agreement* (NAFTA), adopted 17 December 1992, (1992) 32 ILM 612, Chapter 11 (entered into force 1 January 1994).
68 See generally C. McLachlan, L. Shore, and M. Weiniger, *International Investment Arbitration: Substantive Principles*, Oxford: Oxford University Press, 2007; see also R. Dolzer and C. Schreuer, *Principles of International Investment Law*, 2nd edn, Oxford: Oxford University Press, 2012.
69 See generally Dolzer and Schreuer, op. cit.; see also McLachlan *et al.*, op. cit.; see also A. Newcombe and L. Paradell, *Law and Practice of Investment Treaties: Standards of Treatment*, The Hague: Kluwer Law International, 2009.
70 *Methanex Corporation v. United States of America*, 44 International Legal Materials 1345 (2005).
71 *Azurix Corp. v. Republic of Argentina* (Award), ICSID Case No. ARB/01/12 (2006).
72 *Philip Morris Asia Limited v. The Commonwealth of Australia*, In the Matter of Arbitration under the Arbitration Rules of the United Nations Commission on International Trade Law 2010, *Notice of Arbitration*, 21 November 2011.
73 *Dow Agro Sciences LLC v. Government of Canada*, Notice of Arbitration Under the UNCITRAL Rules and the North American Free Trade Agreement, 31 March 2009.
74 *Ethyl Corporation v. Canada*, Jurisdiction Phase, 38 International Legal Materials 708 (1999).
75 See the discussion in Lévesque, op. cit. at 267–8.
76 Peel, above note 4, 86–8; see, for an example of a proponent of such views, C. R. Sunstein, *Laws of Fear: Beyond the Precautionary Principle*, Cambridge: Cambridge University Press, 2005; C. R. Sunstein, 'Misfearing: A Reply' *Harvard Law Review* 119, 2006, 1110.
77 *Methanex Corporation v. United States of America*, 44 International Legal Materials 1345 (2005).
78 Ibid.
79 Ibid. 1371–2; NAFTA, adopted 17 December 1992, 1992 32 ILM 612 (entered into force 1 January 1994).
80 *Methanex Corporation v. United States of America*, 44 International Legal Materials 1345 (2005), 1368; see also the discussion in H. Mann, 'The Final Decision in Methanex v. United States: Some New Wine in Some New Bottles', 2005, available at www.iisd.org/pdf/2005/commentary_methanex.pdf (accessed 11 February 2013).
81 S. E. Gaines, 'Methanex Corp. v. United States', *The American Journal of International Law* 100, 2006, 683.
82 *Methanex Corporation v. United States of America*, 44 International Legal Materials 1345 (2005), 1370; Governor of California, Executive Order D-5–99, 25 March 1999.
83 *Methanex Corporation v. United States of America*, 44 International Legal Materials 1345 (2005), Rejoinder of the Respondent United States of America (2004); see the discussion in Lévesque, op. cit. at 271–4.
84 *Methanex Corporation v. United States of America*, 44 International Legal Materials 1345 (2005) – find page (para. 101 Chapter A Part III)
85 Ibid. at Part IV, Chapter E, para.19.
86 See the discussion in Lévesque, op. cit. at 273–4.
87 Ibid. op. cit. at 260.
88 Ibid.
89 Ibid.; see also M. A. Orellana, 'The Role of Science in Investment Arbitrations Concerning Public Health and the Environment', *Yearbook of International Environmental Law* 17, 2006, 48.

90 Lévesque, op. cit. at 260–1; Lévesque refers to the work of R. K. Merton in determining the relevant scientific principles for consideration, particularly to R. K. Merton, 'The Normative Structure of Science –1942' in R. K. Merton, *The Sociology of Science: Theoretical and Empirical Investigations*, University of Chicago Press, 1973.

91 Lévesque, op. cit. at 287–8.

92 See, for example, United Nations Framework Convention on Climate Change, opened for signature 9 May 1992, 31 ILM 849 (entered into force 24 March 1994); Kyoto Protocol to the United Nations Framework Convention on Climate Change, opened for signature 11 December 1997 (1998) 37 ILM 22 (entered into force 16 February 2005).

93 See, for example, *Clean Energy Act 2011* (No. 131 of 2011, Cth, Australia).

94 See, for example, Panel Report, *Canada – Renewable Energy*; *Arcelor S.A. v. European Parliament and Council* (2004) Case T-16/04; Belgian Arbitration Court, Arrest No. 92/2006, 7 June 2007; French Council of State, Arrest No. 287110, 8 February 2007; *Société Arcelor Atlantique et Lorraine and others v. Premier Ministre, Ministre de l'Économie, des Finances et de l'Industrie, Ministre de l'Écologie et du Développement Durable*, Case C-127/07, *Official Journal of the European Union*, 26/5/2007, C117/8; Judgment of the European Court of Justice (ECJ), 16 December 2008; *Windstream Energy LLC v. Government of Canada*, Notice of Arbitration under the Arbitration Rules of the United Nations Commission on International Trade Law and the North American Free Trade Agreement, 28 January 2013.

95 B. S. Gentry and J. Ronk, 'International Investment Agreements and Investments in Renewable Energy' in L. Parker, J. Ronk, B. Gentry, M. Wilder and J. Cameron (eds), *From Barriers to Opportunities: Renewable Energy Issues in Law and Policy*, 2007, 25 at 59–64.

96 R. Beschizza, 'Ed Hammer, Creator of Energy-Saving Light Bulb Remembers', *Wired*, 20 August 2007, available at www.wired.com/gadgetlab/2007/08/ed-hammer-creat/ (accessed 17 May 2013).

97 See the discussion on carbon capture and storage in Catherine Redgwell, 'International Legal Responses to the Challenges of a Lower-Carbon Future: Climate Change, Carbon Capture and Storage, and Biofuels' in D. L. Zillman, C. Redgwell, Y. Omorogbe and L. Barrera-Hernández (eds), *Beyond the Carbon Economy: Energy Law in Transition*, Oxford: Oxford University Press, 2008, 85.

98 UNFCCC Secretariat, Clean Development Mechanism, *CDM Statistics*, April 2013, available at http://cdm.unfccc.int/Statistics/Public/CDMinsights/index.html (accessed 17 May 2013).

99 UNEP, Renewable Energy and Efficiency Technologies: Climate Change Worries, High Oil Prices and Government Help Top Factors Fuelling Hot Renewable Energy Investment Climate, Press Release, 20 June 2007, available at www.unep.org/Documents.Multilingual/Default.asp?DocumentID=512&ArticleID=5616&l=en (accessed 17 May 2013); UNEP, Renewable Energy Accelerates Meteoric Rise: 2007 Global Status Report Shows Perceptions Lag Reality, Press Release, 28 February 2008, available at www.unep.org/Documents.Multilingual/Default.asp?DocumentID=528&ArticleID=5754&l=en (accessed 17 May 2013); UNEP, Environment Ministers Meet to Accelerate Transition to a Low Carbon Society: Huge Investment Opportunities in Energy Savings to Renewables and Reduced Deforestation to Climate Proofing if Markets can be Mobilized, Press Release, February 2008, available at www.unep.org/Documents.Multilingual/Default.asp?DocumentID=528&ArticleID=5745&l=en (accessed 17 May 2013).

100 Gentry and Ronk, op. cit.; see also D. L. Zillman *et al.*, 'Introduction' in D. L. Zillman, C. Redgwell, Y. Omorogbe and L. Barrera-Hernández (eds), *Beyond the Carbon Economy: Energy Law in Transition*, Oxford: Oxford University Press, 2008, 1.

101 K. Miles, 'Arbitrating Climate Change: Regulatory Regimes and Investor-State Disputes' *Climate Law* 1, 2010, 63.

102 Ibid.

103 P. Smith, 'Canberra Faces Legal Challenge Over Carbon Scheme', *Financial Times*, 24 November 2009, available at www.ft.com/cms/s/0/00cced94-d898–11de-b63a-00144feabdc0.html?catid=24 (accessed 24 March 2013); Agreement between the Government of Hong Kong and the Government of Australia for the Promotion and Protection of Investments, signed on 15 September 1993, available at www.unctad.org/ sections/dite/iia/docs/bits/hongkong_australia.pdf (accessed 4 February 2013).

104 Smith, op. cit.

105 See the discussion in C. Brown, 'The Settlement of Disputes Arising in Flexibility Mechanism Transactions under the Kyoto Protocol', *Arbitration International* 21(3), 2005, 361; D. Ratcliff, 'Arbitration in "Flexible-Mechanism" Contracts', in D. Freestone and C. Streck (eds), *Legal Aspects of Implementing the Kyoto Protocol: Making Kyoto Work*, Oxford: Oxford University Press, 2005, 377.

106 See, for example, the following Australian cases: *Northcape Properties Pty Ltd v. District Council of Yorke Peninsula* [2008] SASC 57; *Gippsland Coastal Board v. South Gippsland Shire Council* (No 2) [2008] VCAT 1545; *Gray v. Minister for Planning* (2006) 152 LGERA 258 regarding a coal mine proposal.

107 *Naftrac Limited v. National Environmental Investment Agency (Ukraine)*, Permanent Court of Arbitration, Final Award, 4 December 2012, as reported in Russian Legal Information Agency, $185 Million Environmental Lawsuit against Ukraine Dismissed, 12 December 2012, available at http://rapsinews.com/judicial_news/20121212/265749721.html (accessed 17 May 2013).

108 See the discussion in J. E. Viñuales, *Foreign Investment and the Environment in International Law*, Cambridge: Cambridge University Press, 2012, 265.

109 *Vattenfall AB v. Federal Republic of Germany*, Request for Arbitration, 30 March 2009 (ICSID Case No. ARB/09/6)

110 Ibid. at para. 16.

111 Ibid. at paras 20, 36.

112 *Vattenfall AB and others v. Federal Republic of Germany*, Request for Arbitration, 31 May 2012 (ICSID Case No. ARB/12/12); *Atomic Energy Act, 13th Amendment 2011* (Germany, 2011).

113 See, for example, *Dow Agro Sciences LLC v. Government of Canada*, Notice of Arbitration Under the UNCITRAL Rules and the North American Free Trade Agreement, 31 March 2009; *Methanex Corporation v. United States of America*, 44 International Legal Materials 1345 (2005); *S. D. Myers, Inc. v. Canada*, Partial Award (Decision on the Merits), November 2000, 40 International Legal Materials 1408 (2001); *Ethyl Corporation v. Canada*, Jurisdiction Phase, 38 International Legal Materials 708 (1999).

114 *Windstream Energy LLC v. Government of Canada*, Notice of Arbitration under the Arbitration Rules of the United Nations Commission on International Trade Law and the North American Free Trade Agreement, 28 January 2013.

115 Ibid. at paras 12, 29–31.

116 Ibid. at paras 29–31.

117 A. Boute, 'Combating Climate Change through Investment Arbitration', *Fordham International Law Journal* 35, 2012, 613 at 616, 619.

118 Miles, op. cit.

119 Appellate Body Report, *Canada – Renewable Energy*.

120 *Agreement on Trade-Related Investment Measures*, Annex 1A, *Agreement Establishing the World Trade Organization*, opened for signature 15 April 1994, (1994) 33 ILM 28 (entered into force 1 January 1995).

121 Appellate Body Report, *Canada – Renewable Energy*.

122 *India – Certain Measures Relating to Solar Cells and Solar Modules*, Request for Consultations by United States, WT/DS456/1, 11 February 2013.

123 Certain Local Content Requirements in Some of the Renewable Energy Sector Programs, Questions by India to the United States, G/TRIMS/W/117, 17 April 2013.

124 European Union and Certain Member States – Certain Measures Affecting the Renewable Energy Generation Sector, WT/DS452/1, 7 November 2012.

125 *China – Measures Concerning Wind Power Equipment*, Request for Consultations by United States, WT/DS419/1, 6 January 2011.

126 United States International Trade Commission, Utility Scale Wind Towers from China and Vietnam, Investigation Nos. 701-TA-486 and 731-TA-1195–1196 (Final), February 2013.

127 European Commission, *EU Initiates Anti-Dumping Investigation on Solar Panel Imports from China*, Memo, Press Release, 6 September 2012, available at http://europa.eu/rapid/press-release_MEMO-12–647_en.htm (accessed 17 May 2013); S. Enkhart, 'EU: Big Discrepancy Expected between Provisional and Final AD Solar Duties', *PV Magazine*, 17 May 2013, available at www.pv-magazine.com/news/details/beitrag/eu–big-discrepancy-expected-between-provisional-and-final-ad-solar-duties-_100011340/#axzz2TYrRQwiG (accessed 17 May 2013).

128 D. J. Levine and P. D. Walther, 'Wave of Trade Disputes Complicates Global Market for Renewable Energy Firms, Particularly Solar Sector', *Bloomberg Law*, 2013, available at http://about.bloomberglaw.com/practitioner-contributions/wave-of-trade-disputes-complicates-global-market-for-renewable-energy-firms-particularly-solar-sector/ (accessed 17 May 2013).

129 Directive 2008/101/EC of the European Parliament and of the Council of 19 November 2008 amending Directive 2003/87/EC so as to include aviation activities in the scheme for greenhouse gas emission allowance trading within the Community.

130 Ibid. at para.16.

131 *Air Transport Association of America and Others v. Secretary of State for Energy and Climate Change*, Case C-366/10, Judgment, 21 December 2011; *Air Transport Agreement*, United States and European Union, 25 and 30 April 2007, E.U. Series 005/2011: Cm 8137, [2007] O.J. (L 134/4).

132 BBC News, Europe, *China 'Blocks Airbus Deals' in EU Carbon Levy Spat*, 8 March 2012, available at www.bbc.co.uk/news/world-europe-17298117 (accessed 17 May 2013).

133 J. Fontanella-Kahn, A. Parker and J. Chaffin, 'India Warns EU Over Airline Carbon Tax', *Financial Times*, 24 May 2012, available at www.ft.com/cms/s/0/aceffc00-a58d-11e1-a77b-00144feabdc0.html#axzz2Terxj54U (accessed 17 May 2013).

134 See reports such as D. Kayha, 'Air Wars: Fears of Trade War Over EU Airline Carbon Cap', *BBC News*, 21 December 2011, available at www.bbc.co.uk/news/business-14325571 (accessed 17 May 2013); see also 'EU Suspends Extension of Plane Emissions Trading Rules', *BBC News, Business*, 12 November 2012, available at www.bbc.co.uk/news/business-20299388 (accessed 17 May 2013).

135 *The European Union Emissions Trading Scheme Prohibition Act of 2011* (Pub. L. No. 112–200, Fed., United States of America, 27 November 2012).

136 *Joint Declaration of the Moscow Meeting on Inclusion of International Civil Aviation in the EU-ETS* (22 February 2012) available at www.greenaironline.com/photos/Moscow_Declaration.pdf (accessed 17 May 2013).

137 European Commission, Proposal for a Decision of the European Parliament and of the Council derogating temporarily from Directive 2003/87/EC of the European Parliament and of the Council establishing a scheme for greenhouse gas emission allowance trading within the Community, COM (2012) 697, November 2012.

138 See, for example, the discussion in M. Martin, 'Trade Law Implications of Restricting Participation in the European Union Emissions Trading Scheme', *Georgetown*

International Environmental Law Review 19, 2007, 437; W. Bradnee Chambers, 'International Trade Law and the Kyoto Protocol: Potential Incompatibilities' in W. B. Chambers (ed.), *Inter-Linkages: The Kyoto Protocol and the International Trade and Investment Regimes*, Tokyo: United Nations University Press, 2001, 87.

139 D. Helm, C. Hepburn and G. Ruta, 'Trade, Climate Change and the Political Game Theory of Border Carbon Adjustments', *Centre for Climate Change Economics and Policy Working Paper*, No. 92, May 2012; Centre for International Sustainable Development Law, *Legal Analysis on the Inclusion of Civil Aviation in the European Union Emissions Trading Scheme*, May 2012, available at http://cisdl.org/public/docs/news/CISDL_EU_ETS_Expansion_Legal_Brief.pdf (accessed 17 May 2013).

140 *Arcelor S.A. v. European Parliament and Council* (2004) Case T-16/04; Belgian Arbitration Court, Arrest No. 92/2006, 7 June 2007; French Council of State, Arrest No. 287110, 8 February 2007.

141 *Société Arcelor Atlantique et Lorraine et al. v. Premier Ministre, Ministre de l'Économie, des Finances et de l'Industrie, Ministre de l'Écologie et du Développement Durable*, Case C-127/07, Official Journal of the European Union, 26/5/2007, C117/8; Judgment of the Court of Justice, 16 December 2008.

142 Miles, op. cit.

Part IV

Trade, intellectual property, science and technology

10 Trade agreement cats and the digital technology mouse

Peter K. Yu[1]

10.1 Introduction

In the legal field, especially in cyber law, voluminous literature has discussed how the law has a tough time responding to challenges posed by new technology. As if they are playing a cat-and-mouse game, lawmakers try hard to introduce changes only to find a new set of disruptive technologies already obsolescing those earlier changes. As some literature suggested, if regulation is to keep pace with technological change, it needs to be supplemented by customary norms, private contracts, technological self-help or other extra-legal measures.[2] Although policymakers and commentators continue to struggle to develop forward-looking solutions to stay ahead of technological change, they now have a better and deeper understanding of the interplay between law and technology.

In international economic law, a similar cat-and-mouse game is being played when trade agreements encounter digital technology. While policymakers and commentators have devoted a considerable amount of time, effort, energy and resources to developing treaties to promote technological developments and scientific innovations, they rarely focus on the interplay between trade agreements and digital technology. In fact, such a topic remains one of the least understood areas in international trade law. It was not until recently that trade scholars began to pay greater attention to this area.[3] To some extent, countries are now only 'at the beginning in finding and defining an appropriate transnational and international regulatory framework governing digital technologies, the associated opportunities and risks'.[4]

Although computing technology already existed when the GATT contracting parties negotiated the TRIPS Agreement in the late 1980s and early 1990s, the World Wide Web had yet to enter the mainstream. In fact, many of today's latest technologies, such as peer-to-peer file-sharing services, online distribution platforms, social networks, smartphone applications and cloud computing, had not yet appeared. Thanks to the high speed and low costs of reproduction and distribution, the anonymous architecture, the many-to-many communication capabilities and the borderless environment, the Internet and the digital revolution have created massive, unprecedented global intellectual property challenges for industries, policymakers and commentators.

In the past three decades, the copyright industries and their supportive governments have aggressively pushed for introducing high intellectual property standards into trade agreements. This chapter examines the uneasy case of using trade agreements to provide copyright protection in the digital environment. It begins by discussing two widely discussed multilateral solutions: the TRIPS Agreement and the 1996 WIPO Internet Treaties. The chapter then explores the industries' increasing push for solutions outside multilateral fora. Non-multilateral solutions that have been advanced thus far range from the establishment of bilateral or regional trade agreements to the recent negotiation of plurilateral 'country club' agreements, including the ACTA and the TPP (Trans Pacific Partnership) Agreement. This chapter concludes by identifying eight issues that domestic policymakers and international negotiators should seriously consider.

This chapter was written to complement Kimberlee Weatherall's chapter in this volume. Both chapters examine ACTA, TPP and other bilateral, plurilateral and regional efforts to strengthen the protection and enforcement of intellectual property rights. Whereas the present chapter focuses on copyright protection in the digital environment, Weatherall's chapter emphasizes intellectual property issues relating to patents, science, and research and development. Both chapters should be read together to acquire a full understanding of the goals, negotiation and impacts of ACTA, TPP and other recent non-multilateral trade and intellectual property agreements.

10.2 TRIPS Agreement

The negotiation of the TRIPS Agreement began with the GATT Ministerial Conference in Punta del Este, Uruguay. Held in September 1986, this conference took place at a critical point in time when the negotiations over the revision of the Paris Convention for the Protection of Industrial Property, a cornerstone international intellectual property agreement, broke down between developed and developing countries.[5] Through this Ministerial Conference, the GATT contracting parties set out their negotiating objectives for the Uruguay Round. As the Ministerial Declaration of 20 September 1986 stated in a section titled 'Trade-related aspects of intellectual property rights, including trade in counterfeit goods':

> In order to reduce the distortions and impediments to international trade, and taking into account the need to promote effective and adequate protection of intellectual property rights, and to ensure that measures and procedures to enforce intellectual property rights do not themselves become barriers to legitimate trade, the negotiations shall aim to clarify GATT provisions and elaborate as appropriate new rules and disciplines.
>
> Negotiations shall aim to develop a multilateral framework of principles, rules and disciplines dealing with international trade in counterfeit goods, taking into account work already undertaken in the GATT.

> These negotiations shall be without prejudice to other complementary initiatives that may be taken in the World Intellectual Property Organization and elsewhere to deal with these matters.

Commencing in the late 1980s, the Uruguay Round negotiations concluded in 1994 with the formation of the WTO and the adoption of the Marrakesh Agreement Establishing the World Trade Organization. Included in Annex 1C of this founding document was the TRIPS Agreement, which contains 73 articles on the protection and enforcement of intellectual property rights. Part I, section II of the Agreement specifically addresses the availability, scope and use of copyright and related rights. Article 9.1 incorporates by reference the Paris Act of the Berne Convention for the Protection of Literary and Artistic Works ('Berne Convention'), the key international copyright treaty. Articles 10 to 14 cover issues related to computer programs, compilations of data, rental rights, the term of protection, limitations and exceptions (including the now-famous three-step test), and the protection of performers, phonogram producers and broadcasting organizations.

Although the TRIPS Agreement was adopted in 1994, shortly before Internet surfing and electronic commerce became part of our daily life, the agreement actually incorporated standards that were set much earlier. As Daniel Gervais, who was working at the Secretariat at the time of the Uruguay Round negotiations, recounted: 'TRIPS adjusted the level of intellectual property protection to what was the highest common denominator among major industrialized countries as of 1991.'[6] At that time, many *demandeur* countries did not anticipate the technological change that the information revolution was about to unleash. Even if they had had the foresight to anticipate such a change, it is unlikely that they would have succeeded in introducing new norms in this area. For example, the biotechnology revolution had already raised many difficult policy and ethical questions by the mid-1980s. Yet, Article 27 provides very limited coverage of biotechnology-related issues.[7]

In retrospect, the arrival of the World Wide Web rendered the TRIPS Agreement obsolete even before it entered into effect. To be certain, Articles 10, 11 and 14 cover protection for computer programs. However, they do not speak to or anticipate challenges posed by the Internet and the new digital environment. As Marci Hamilton aptly observed:

> Despite its broad sweep and its unstated aspirations, TRIPS arrives on the scene already outdated. TRIPS reached fruition at the same time that the on-line era became irrevocable. Yet it makes no concession, not even a nod, to the fact that a significant portion of the international intellectual property market will soon be conducted on-line.[8]

Likewise, Jerome Reichman wrote:

> [The principal weakness of the TRIPS Agreement] stems from the drafters' technical inability and political reluctance to address the problems facing

> innovators and investors at work on important new technologies in an Age of Information. The drafters' decision to stuff these new technologies into the overworked and increasingly obsolete patent and copyright paradigms simply ignores the systemic contradictions and economic disutilities this same approach was already generating in the domestic intellectual property systems.[9]

In sum, because of the time lag in the adoption of the TRIPS standards, the lack of foresight on the part of negotiators from *demandeur* countries and the inevitable challenges in negotiating a comprehensive intellectual property agreement in the trade forum, the TRIPS Agreement has been rather ill-equipped to respond to challenges posed by the Internet, new communications technologies and peer-to-peer file-sharing networks. Today, these technologies have caused serious and widespread problems of unauthorized copying throughout the world. Since 2003, the US recording industry alone has filed lawsuits against more than 35,000 individuals for illegal distribution of copyrighted works via peer-to-peer networks.[10] Courts in the developed world, such as Australia, Canada and the United States, have also been inundated with cases addressing secondary copyright liability.[11]

10.3 WIPO Internet Treaties

Shortly after the TRIPS Agreement entered into effect, countries returned to WIPO to update international copyright standards. Although the United States, members of the European Union, Japan and other developed countries pushed aggressively for the use of the GATT/WTO to discuss trade-related intellectual property issues, they had not abandoned WIPO as a policymaking forum. In fact, WIPO continues to provide attractive conditions for making intellectual property policies, especially when those policies are highly technical or when disagreements over those policies could not be easily resolved by the WTO's mandatory dispute settlement process.[12]

In December 1996, WIPO hosted a Diplomatic Conference in Geneva to consider proposals to update international intellectual property norms in light of new challenges posed by digital technology. The origins of this Diplomatic Conference can be traced back to 1989, when WIPO established a Committee of Experts to explore the need for a supplementary agreement to the Berne Convention to clarify existing or establish new international copyright norms.[13] This request was routine and understandable. Although the Berne Convention was previously revised roughly every 10 to 20 years, the 1971 Paris conference marked the last time the convention was revised.

Initially, the United States was not actively involved in the Diplomatic Conference. While the European Commission surveyed many challenging questions concerning copyright law in the digital context in its 1988 Green Paper,[14] the United States was primarily interested in the narrow issue of copyright protection for computer programs. As Pamela Samuelson recounted, 'insofar as the United States had a digital agenda at WIPO in the early period of Berne Protocol negotiations, it was to persuade the international community to use copyright law to protect computer programs'.[15] Such a limited focus, to some extent, explained why most of the TRIPS copyright provisions were devoted to protecting computer programs.

As the Internet grew in size and scope, however, intellectual property problems in the digital environment began to attract the attention of major US businesses and their supportive law- and policymakers. In 1995, the Clinton administration released its Information Infrastructure Task Force White Paper.[16] This White Paper turned out to be fairly controversial in the United States, and many legislative proposals seeking to implement that document failed to report out of congressional committees.[17] Nevertheless, the administration persisted in promoting its digital agenda in both Geneva and Washington, and it pressed aggressively for the adoption of its proposals in the 1996 WIPO Diplomatic Conference. As Professor Samuelson recounted:

> Clinton administration officials sought approval in Geneva for international norms that would have (1) granted copyright owners an exclusive right to control virtually all temporary reproductions of protected works in the random access memory of computers; (2) treated digital transmissions of protected works as distributions of copies to the public; (3) curtailed the power of states to adopt exceptions and limitations on the exclusive rights of copyright owners, including fair use and first sale privileges; (4) enabled copyright owners to challenge the manufacture and sale of technologies or services capable of circumventing technological protection for copyrighted works; (5) protected the integrity of rights management information attached to protected works in digital form; and (6) created a sui generis form of legal protection for the contents of databases.[18]

Except for the final item concerning database protection, the Geneva agenda was identical to the digital copyright agenda the administration had pushed in Washington based on its controversial White Paper.

As Professor Samuelson recalled:

> [F]or a time, it appeared that administration officials might be able to get in Geneva what they could not get from the US Congress, . . . [and the Diplomatic Conference might have provided] the potential for an end run around Congress.[19]

Had the Clinton administration officials succeeded in Geneva, they, in her view,

> would almost certainly have then argued to Congress that ratification of the treaties was necessary to confirm US leadership in the world intellectual property community and to promote the interests of US copyright industries in the world market for information products and services.[20]

Fortunately for the Internet-surfing public, the disagreement within WIPO, in particular the opposition from developing countries, and the active participation of non-governmental organizations made it difficult for the United States to advance its proposals.[21] In the end, 'none of the original US-sponsored digital agenda proposals emerged unscathed from the negotiation process, and at least one—the proposed database treaty—did not emerge at all'.[22]

Despite this setback, the United States managed to update the multilateral intellectual property regime in areas that are of major interest to the copyright industries. First, based on the agreed statement the United States pushed forward in the Diplomatic Conference's eleventh hour, 'it is now clear that copyright law applies in the digital environment, and that storage of protected works is a reproduction that can be controlled by copyright owners'.[23] Second, the WIPO Copyright Treaty ('WCT') and the WIPO Performances and Phonograms Treaty ('WPPT') – the two new treaties emerging out of the Diplomatic Conference – protect rightholders from digital transmissions that constitute communications to the public.[24] The treaties also reaffirmed the three-step test enunciated in the TRIPS Agreement, which limits a contracting party's ability to adopt exceptions or limitations in 'certain special cases which do not conflict with a normal exploitation of the work and do not unreasonably prejudice the legitimate interests of the right holder'.[25] Finally, the WIPO Internet Treaties require each party to adopt adequate protection and effective remedies against circumvention technologies and services.[26] The treaties further protect rights management information from alteration or removal in situations where such alteration or removal has been used to conceal or facilitate infringement.[27]

In 2002, six years after the Geneva Diplomatic Conference, the WIPO Internet treaties finally attained the 30 requisite accessions or ratifications needed for the treaties to enter into force.[28] Had the European Union been less ambitious in implementing these treaties through a new harmonization directive, the treaties might have entered into force even earlier.[29] With both the WCT and the WPPT now ratified, the multilateral intellectual property regime has finally been updated to reflect changes brought about by the Internet and the new digital environment – a feat that the TRIPS Agreement failed to accomplish in the international trade forum.

10.4 Industry push for non-multilateral solutions

Notwithstanding the adoption of the WIPO Internet Treaties and the earlier TRIPS Agreement, the copyright industries and their supportive governments remained dissatisfied with the protection offered in the existing multilateral intellectual property regime. Such dissatisfaction reflected at least five different sets of frustrations and concerns.

First, standards provided in the TRIPS Agreement and the WIPO Internet Treaties are international minimum standards.[30] Article 1.1 of the TRIPS

Agreement explicitly states that 'Members may . . . implement in their law more extensive protection than is required by this Agreement, provided that such protection does not contravene the provisions of this Agreement.' In fact, because the TRIPS and WIPO standards were achieved through political compromises between developed and developing countries, they understandably failed to provide adequate protection against the new challenges posed by digital technology. It is therefore no surprise that the copyright industries found it necessary to push for new and higher standards based on their needs, interests, goals and priorities.

Second, although more than 100 countries *negotiated* the WIPO Internet Treaties, most of these countries, including signatory countries, did not quickly ratify the instruments. As a result, the protections offered *on paper* in these Treaties did not quickly translate to protections *in action* at the domestic level. A notable example is Canada. Despite signing the WIPO Internet Treaties on 22 December 1997, it has not until recently reformed its copyright system to provide the implementation legislation needed to ratify the Treaties. From Bill C-60 to Bill C-61 to Bill C-32 to finally Bill C-11, it took Canadian legislators close to a decade to agree on reforms to overhaul its domestic copyright system.[31] Owing in part to this delay, the US Trade Representative ('USTR') repeatedly put Canada on either the Watch List or the Priority Watch List in its Section 301 Report. As the 2012 report noted:

> Canada remains on the Priority Watch List in 2012, subject to review if Canada enacts long-awaited copyright legislation. The Government of Canada has given priority to that legislation. The United States welcomes that prioritization and looks forward to studying the legislation once it is finalized, and will consider, among other things, whether it fully implements the WIPO Internet Treaties, and whether it fully addresses the challenges of piracy over the Internet.[32]

Following Canada's adoption of the Copyright Modernization Act, which includes legislation to implement the WIPO Internet Treaties, the USTR immediately downgraded the country back to the Watch List in 2013.[33]

Third, even with the updated standards provided by the WIPO Internet Treaties, digital technology has been developing much faster than the protections international negotiators could achieve through multilateral trade agreements. For example, peer-to-peer file-sharing technologies were not even contemplated when the WIPO Internet Treaties were being negotiated in the 1996 Diplomatic Conference. As the US Court of Appeals for the District of Columbia Circuit memorably wrote in a case involving the Digital Millennium Copyright Act (DMCA) – the law that the United States adopted to implement the WIPO Internet Treaties – 'P2P software was "not even a glimmer in anyone's eye when the DMCA was enacted"'.[34]

Fourth, similar to the growth of the Internet and new communications technologies, the sophistication of piracy and counterfeiting networks has greatly increased in recent years. According to Moisés Naím, the former editor-in-chief of *Foreign Policy*, today's illicit trade is no longer limited to rigid, top-down organizations; it has been extended to 'unchartable networks of intermediaries that operate across many borders and provide different services', including both legitimate and illicit services.[35] Some of these intermediaries 'are permanently linked and others vary in their composition, activities, and geographical scope depending on markets and circumstances'.[36]

Finally, as I noted in a recent article, the challenges confronting the enforcement of intellectual property rights are no longer limited to cross-border and digital enforcement challenges.[37] Instead, a new form of 'transborder enforcement challenges' emerge to exploit the global platform provided by the Internet and new communications technologies. Combining both cross-border and digital enforcement challenges, these new hybrid challenges benefit pirates and counterfeiters in two ways. First, they exploit the jurisdictional loopholes that become available when goods no longer have to go through traditional checkpoints at the border. Second, the availability of electronic commerce has provided the support needed to hide illicit activities and ill-gotten gains. As Naím explained:

> [The Internet's] value to traffickers is immense, and its specific uses too many to enumerate. Those involved in illicit transactions communicate with one another from the privacy and anonymity of Web-based e-mail accounts, frequently changed and accessed from cybercafes and unobtrusive venues. They monitor shipments using the tracing services that FedEx and its peers provide. They offer goods for sale via online display cases. . . . The Internet recruits mercenaries, advertises unscrupulous transport companies, hosts professional-looking Web sites that are electronic fronts for bogus businesses. . . . The Internet allows traffickers to communicate privately and efficiently, to operate as many transactions as possible in virtual rather than geographic space, and creates new ways to move and conceal funds. All this without concern for physical location, freeing the traffickers to play across borders and cover their tracks without impeding the actual flow of goods.[38]

In January 2011, MarkMonitor, a brand protection and management firm, published a report showing that traffic to sites suspected of offering pirated digital content or counterfeit goods amounted to more than 146 million visits per day and 53 billion visits per year. According to the report, 'the top-three websites classified as "digital piracy"– rapidshare.com, megavideo.com, and megaupload.com – collectively generate more than 21 billion visits per year'.[39] Along with these sites, downloading services, cyberlockers, online auction sites, trading platforms, bulletin boards, warez groups and underground networks have created significant challenges for copyright holders. As the USTR reported, massive piracy threats have been posed by such notorious Internet sites as Baidu in China, VKontakte in Russia, allofmp3.com clones in Russia and Ukraine, isoHunt in Canada and The Pirate Bay in Sweden.[40] The problems created by the Internet are so severe that the US National Intellectual Property Rights Coordination Center has recently begun to seize Internet domain names that are tied to piratical and counterfeiting activities. Thus far, seizure orders have 'targeted online retailers of a diverse array of counterfeit goods, including sports equipment, shoes, handbags, athletic apparel and sunglasses as well as illegal copies of copyrighted DVD boxed sets, music and software'.[41]

In sum, the emergence of transborder enforcement challenges has underscored the impossibility of tackling domestic problems alone without considering their foreign counterparts. The existence of these challenges further calls for the establishment of higher benchmarks for global intellectual property enforcement. Given the wide divergence between developed and developing countries and the latter's still ongoing struggle to comply with the WTO and WIPO standards, it would be rather hard for the copyright industries and their supportive governments to push for new and higher benchmarks through multilateral negotiations. As a result, these industries and their governments have begun to look for alternative fora to develop these benchmarks.

10.5 Free trade and economic partnership agreements

Since the early 2000s, the European Union and the United States actively established bilateral, plurilateral and regional trade agreements – free trade agreements ('FTAs') for the United States and FTAs and economic partnership agreements ('EPAs') for the European Union. The United States, for example, has used FTAs widely to transplant US laws on to the soil of its less powerful trading partners. As the US Trade Act of 2002 explicitly stated:

> The principal negotiating objectives of the United States regarding trade-related intellectual property are . . . to further promote adequate and effective protection of intellectual property rights, including through . . . ensuring that the provisions of any multilateral or bilateral trade agreement governing intellectual property rights that is entered into by the United States reflect a standard of protection similar to that found in United States law. . . .

From the standpoint of the United States' trading partners, however, the transplant of US intellectual property laws has been rather controversial and at times unpopular. Because these laws often provide protections in excess of the levels required by the TRIPS Agreement, and to some extent also the WIPO Internet Treaties, the intellectual property provisions in US FTAs threaten to ignore the local needs, national interests, technological capabilities, institutional capacities and public health conditions of many developing country trading partners.

To illustrate the high TRIPS-plus standards found in US FTAs, consider the Australia–United States Free Trade Agreement ('AUSFTA'), one of the earlier US FTAs. Adopted on 18 May 2004, this bilateral agreement includes in Chapter 17 distinct provisions on copyrights, trademarks, patents and other forms of intellectual property rights. Article 17.1.4 states that '[e]ach Party shall ratify or accede to the WIPO Copyright Treaty (1996) and the WIPO Performances and Phonograms Treaty (1996) by the date of entry into force of this Agreement, subject to the fulfilment of their necessary internal requirements'. Article 17.4.2 further states that

> [e]ach Party shall provide to authors, performers, and producers of phonograms the right to authorize or prohibit the making available to the public of the original and copies of their works, performances, and phonograms through sale or other transfer of ownership.

In addition, Article 17.4.7 requires each party to

> provide adequate legal protection and effective legal remedies against the circumvention of effective technological measures that authors, performers, and producers of phonograms use in connection with the exercise of their rights and that restrict unauthorized acts in respect of their works, performances, and phonograms.

Drawing on the language of both the WIPO Internet Treaties and the DMCA, that provision includes more than 900 words of detailed stipulations and qualifications. In relation to criminal procedure and penalties, Article 17.4.7(a) specifically requires each party to 'provide for criminal procedures and penalties to be applied where any person is found to have engaged wilfully and for the purposes of commercial advantage or financial gain in any of the above activities'. Also building on the WIPO Internet Treaties and the DMCA, Article 17.4.8 requires each party to 'provide adequate and effective legal remedies to protect rights management information'.

Finally, Article 17.5 requires each Party to

> provide to authors the exclusive right to authorise or prohibit the communication to the public of their works, by wire or wireless means, including the making available to the public of their works in such a way that Members of the public may access these works from a place and at a time individually chosen by them.

Article 17.6 also provides detailed provisions concerning the transmission, communication and making available to the public of performances or phonograms.

Providing another excellent illustration is the United States–Korea Free Trade Agreement ('KORUSFTA'), a much more recent FTA. Signed originally on

30 June 2007, a few years after the completion of AUSFTA, KORUSFTA did not enter into force until the United States and South Korea concluded new agreements on 3 December 2010. Strongly resembling their counterparts in AUSFTA, the copyright provisions in KORUSFTA provide an excellent case study on how US negotiators strategically use past FTAs – in this case, AUSFTA – to develop later FTAs.

Apart from provisions concerning the WIPO Internet Treaties, such as the rights to transmission, communication and making available to the public, anti-circumvention protection and the protection of rights management information, the intellectual property chapter (Chapter 18) of KORUSFTA includes new provisions that have not appeared in AUSFTA. For instance, in the provision addressing the enforcement of intellectual property rights, Article 18.10.30 provides specific provisions on Internet service provider liability. As the provision states:

> For the purpose of providing enforcement procedures that permit effective action against any act of copyright infringement covered by this Chapter, including expeditious remedies to prevent infringements and criminal and civil remedies that constitute a deterrent to further infringements, each Party shall provide, consistent with the framework set out in this Article:
>
> (a) legal incentives for service providers to cooperate with copyright owners in deterring the unauthorized storage and transmission of copyrighted materials; and
>
> (b) limitations in its law regarding the scope of remedies available against service providers for copyright infringements that they do not control, initiate, or direct, and that take place through systems or networks controlled or operated by them or on their behalf. . . .

In addition, KORUSFTA includes two side confirmation letters. Focusing on limitations on Internet service provider liability, the first letter provides clarification on Article 18.10.30. The second one, which is titled 'Online Piracy Prevention', lays out the specific actions South Korea needs to undertake following the entry of the FTA. As the letter states in amazing breadth and detail:

> The Parties agree on the objective of shutting down Internet sites that permit the unauthorized reproduction, distribution, or transmission of copyright works, of regularly assessing and actively seeking to reduce the impact of new technological means for committing online copyright piracy, and of providing generally for more effective enforcement of intellectual property rights on the Internet. Korea agrees that internet piracy of works and other subject matter protected by copyright (including unauthorized reproduction and distribution of such works and other subject matter on the Internet) is a matter of priority for law enforcement

> of intellectual property rights. Korea also agrees on the objective of shutting down Internet sites that permit the unauthorized downloading (and other forms of piracy) of copyright works, including so-called webhard services, and providing for more effective enforcement of intellectual property rights on the Internet, including in particular with regard to peer-to-peer (P2P) services. To this end, Korea will strengthen enforcement of intellectual property rights in Korea, and work to prevent, investigate, and prosecute Internet piracy. As part of this effort, Korea will work with the private sector and with the United States and other foreign authorities.
>
> In furtherance thereof, Korea agrees to issue as soon as possible, but no later than six months after the date the Agreement enters into force, a policy directive establishing clear jurisdiction for a division or joint investigation team to engage in effective enforcement against online piracy. This team will investigate and initiate criminal actions to address online piracy, including with respect to US and other foreign works, whether ex officio or at the request of a right holder. The team will take these actions in a manner that is transparent to right holders. In addition to prosecuting direct infringers, Korea agrees to prosecute individuals and companies that profit from developing and maintaining services that effectively induce infringement.

To a large extent, the copyright provisions in both AUSFTA and KORUSFTA illustrate well the United States' use of templates and standardized terms in FTA negotiations to maximize effectiveness and efficiency. As Peter Drahos observed:

> For the United States, there are very strong incentives for a standardization of bilateral treaty standards. So, for example, the [bilateral investment treaty] which the United States signed with Nicaragua in 1995 was based on the prototype that the United States had developed for such treaties in 1994. Similarly, the Free Trade Agreement . . . that the United States has negotiated with Jordan will serve as a model for the other FTAs being negotiated with Chile and Singapore.[42]

In an earlier article concerning ACTA, I also identified at least three reasons behind the United States' use of FTA templates.[43] First, the US Trade Act of 2002, based on which these bilateral or plurilateral agreements were negotiated, called on negotiators to develop provisions that 'reflect a standard of protection similar to that found in United States law'. Although FTA provisions are similar, they were not based on their predecessors, but rather the ultimate template – namely, US laws. Second, such an approach would encourage standardization of protections. In doing so, FTAs would help foster an environment where countries can consolidate negotiation gains through FTAs at the multilateral level. Third, as Andrew Christie, Sophie Waller and Kimberlee Weatherall noted:

> An FTA will have a more realistic chance of obtaining the necessary approval if it follows an already established model. This is because part of the Congressional approval process involves the review of the text by certain Industry Advisory Committees. At least in relation to IP, the relevant committee has a history of drawing very explicit comparisons with prior FTAs. Provisions that are seen to be less IP-protective than provisions in past FTAs attract negative comment.[44]

The use of templates therefore has practical significance: it enhances the possibility for congressional approval of these bilateral or plurilateral trade agreements.

10.6 Anti-Counterfeiting Trade Agreement

While the United States and the European Union have been actively negotiating FTAs or EPAs, they also work closely with other developed and like-minded countries to develop a new anti-counterfeiting trade agreement. The intent to negotiate this agreement was announced in October 2007, two weeks after WIPO adopted its recommendations for the Development Agenda.[45] As the USTR formally declared in the press release:

> The goal [of the new agreement] is to set a new, higher benchmark for enforcement that countries can join on a voluntary basis. . . . The envisioned ACTA will include commitments in three areas: (1) strengthening international cooperation, (2) improving enforcement practices, and (3) providing a strong legal framework for [intellectual property rights] enforcement.[46]

Following the announcement, 11 rounds of negotiations were held over a span of close to 3 years, and 37 countries participated in the full negotiations.[47] While countries were initially worried about ACTA's inconsistencies with their existing laws and international treaty obligations, the Agreement was finally adopted on 15 April 2011. A few months later, eight countries – Australia, Canada, Japan, Morocco, New Zealand, Singapore, South Korea and the United States – signed the Agreement at a ceremony in Japan. In preparation to join the TPP negotiations, Mexico also signed the Agreement in July 2012. As of this writing, Switzerland and five members of the European Union (Cyprus, Estonia, Germany, the Netherlands and Slovakia) have refrained from signing the Agreement. Because Article 40.1 states that ACTA will not enter into force until six parties have deposited their instruments of ratification, it remains unclear if and when this Agreement will enter into force. Thus far, Japan is the only country that has ever ratified ACTA.

Out of the six chapters in the Agreement, Chapter II, which lays out the legal framework for the enforcement of intellectual property rights, is both the longest and the most controversial. This chapter is further divided into five different sections: (a) general obligations; (b) civil enforcement; (c) border measures; (d) criminal enforcement; and (e) enforcement of intellectual property rights in the digital environment. Section (e) is the most relevant for our purposes; it contains only a single provision (Article 27) laying out the framework for enforcing intellectual property rights in the digital environment.

In that provision, Articles 27.1 and 27.2 extend to the digital environment those civil and criminal enforcement provisions laid out in other sections of Chapter II. These sub-provisions further require each ACTA party to

> ensure that enforcement procedures . . . are available under its law so as to permit effective action against an act of infringement of intellectual property rights . . . in the digital environment [and over digital networks], including expeditious remedies to prevent infringement and remedies which constitute a deterrent to further infringements.[48]

Article 27.3 requires each party to 'endeavour to promote cooperative efforts within the business community to effectively address trademark and copyright or related rights infringement'. Article 27.4 states further that the party

> may provide . . . its competent authorities with the authority to order an online service provider to disclose expeditiously to a right holder information sufficient to identify a subscriber whose account was allegedly used for infringement, where that right holder has filed a legally sufficient claim of trademark or copyright or related rights infringement, and where such information is being sought for the purpose of protecting or enforcing those rights.

In addition, Articles 27.5 and 27.6 require each party to adopt adequate protection and effective remedies against circumvention technologies and services. Article 27.7 further requires the parties to prohibit the removal of rights management information. Finally, through the incorporation of Chapter II, section 4 of ACTA (including Article 23.4) by reference, Article 27.1 calls for countries to introduce 'criminal liability for aiding and abetting' of intellectual property infringement in the digital environment – penalties that do not yet exist in the United States.[49]

Based on these provisions, ACTA has clearly gone beyond what the US, the EU and other negotiating governments initially intended, or at least what they claimed they had initially intended. Instead of setting enforcement norms for a narrow category of intellectual property violations – namely, counterfeiting – the copyright industries have now seemingly captured ACTA to target profit-minimizing Internet-related activities undertaken by ordinary citizens.[50] In the view of Eddan Katz, the former International Affairs Director of the Electronic Frontier Foundation, ACTA is as much 'a regime for global Internet regulation' as it is an international intellectual property agreement.[51]

At the early stages of the ACTA negotiations – that is, before the official release of a joint consolidated draft in April 2010 – the scope of the Agreement was even more ambitious than what these final provisions reveal. Based on leaked documents, proposals that had been advanced at those stages included provisions introducing the graduated response system,[52] the DMCA-style notice-and-take-down mechanism[53] and criminal liability for all forms of intellectual property infringement.[54] While the United States backed the first two proposals, the European Union supported the last one.

At the end of the ACTA negotiations, however, the final text contains more moderate provisions, leading some commentators to refer to the final text as 'ACTA Lite'.[55] Instead of elevating the intellectual property standards of both the European Union and the United States, ACTA merely provides the lowest common denominator of standards found in these two trading powers. To alleviate intrusion on fundamental rights and to provide flexibility, the Agreement also includes three safeguard clauses.[56] In identical language, Articles 27.2, 27.3 and 27.4 emphasize the need to 'preserv[e] fundamental principles such as freedom of expression, fair process, and privacy'. Article 27.3 further demands the 'preserv[ation of] legitimate competition', while Articles 27.2 and 27.4 call for 'implement[ation] in a manner that avoids the creation of barriers to legitimate activity, including electronic commerce'. Throughout the agreement, ACTA also includes a wide variety of optional provisions. The most revealing and encompassing example is footnote 2 of the Agreement, which stipulates that '[a] Party may exclude patents and protection of undisclosed information from the scope of [the entire section on civil enforcement]'.

10.7 Trans-Pacific Partnership Agreement

While the United States was actively completing the ACTA negotiations, it also began negotiating the TPP with other countries in the Asia-Pacific region. This Agreement began as a quadrilateral agreement known as the Trans-Pacific Strategic Economic Partnership Agreement, or more commonly as 'P4'. As Meredith Lewis recounted:

> [The negotiations were initially] launched by Chile, New Zealand and Singapore at the APEC leaders' summit in 2002. These original negotiations contemplated an agreement amongst the three participating countries, to be known as the Pacific Three Closer Economic Partnership (P3 CEP). However, Brunei attended a number of rounds as an observer, and ultimately joined the Agreement as a 'founding member'. The Agreement was signed by New Zealand, Chile and Singapore on July 18, 2005 and by Brunei on August 2, 2005, following the conclusion of negotiations in June 2005.[57]

In March 2010, shortly before the eighth round of the ACTA negotiations in Wellington, New Zealand, the TPP negotiations began among the United

States, Australia, Peru and Vietnam for an expanded agreement. Since then, Malaysia, Mexico, Canada and Japan have joined the negotiations.

It is anticipated that TPP will include an intellectual property chapter, similar to those intellectual property chapters found in existing US FTAs. As the USTR stated in its update on the TPP negotiations in November 2011:

> TPP countries have agreed to reinforce and develop existing [TRIPS] rights and obligations to ensure an effective and balanced approach to intellectual property rights among the TPP countries. Proposals are under discussion on many forms of intellectual property, including trademarks, geographical indications, copyright and related rights, patents, trade secrets, data required for the approval of certain regulated products, as well as intellectual property enforcement and genetic resources and traditional knowledge. TPP countries have agreed to reflect in the text a shared commitment to the Doha Declaration on TRIPS and Public Health.[58]

Although it remains unclear what Internet-related intellectual property provisions will ultimately be included in the TPP intellectual property chapter, the provisions in this new plurilateral agreement are likely to be more restrictive than those found in ACTA, for several reasons.

First, in the TPP negotiations, the United States has more political and economic leverage over its negotiating partners than in the ACTA negotiations. Although ACTA brought together two major intellectual property powers – the European Union and the United States – the continuous disagreements between these two powers resulted in the adoption of a more moderate agreement.[59] As Weatherall rightly pointed out in a recent article, ACTA tells us as much about the disagreement between the negotiating parties as it does about what higher standards these countries wanted to adopt.[60] While the United States wanted to have stronger mandates concerning digital enforcement, the European Union was not ready to agree to provisions that it had not yet harmonized, such as those concerning the introduction of a graduated response system or safe harbours for online service providers.

Compared with the ACTA negotiations, the dynamics of the TPP negotiations have been rather different. Without the European Union at the negotiation table, the United States is able to rely more on its sheer economic and geopolitical strengths to push for provisions that are in the interest of its copyright industries. Thus, as far as online copyright protection and enforcement are concerned, TPP is likely to track more closely the high US standards than the compromised standards developed in ACTA. In fact, if the United States needs to make compromises in the TPP negotiations, those compromises are likely to be found in other trade-related areas, not in the intellectual property area.

Second, the United States has more and better items to offer to trading partners in the TPP negotiations. Unlike ACTA, which focuses narrowly on intellectual property protection and enforcement, the TPP is trade-based and has a much broader scope. Because the negotiations involve more cross-cutting issues, the US negotiators will be able to offer 'carrots' that they otherwise could not provide during the ACTA negotiations.[61] For instance, New Zealand may find it beneficial to make greater concessions in the intellectual property area if the United States is willing to allow for more exports in dairy, lamb, wool and other sheep products. Because negotiating parties place differing values on trade and trade-related items, some parties may be willing to concede more on copyright protection and enforcement in the digital environment in exchange for greater benefits in other trade or trade-related areas. TPP therefore could provide a greater threat to the protection of due process, free speech and other civil liberties in the digital environment.

Third, although the ACTA negotiations already concluded, the TPP negotiations are still in progress. Being later in time, the latter negotiations may incorporate matters that did not have much traction during the ACTA negotiations. Should new issues arise, the TPP negotiators will also be able to include those new items in the negotiations. In fact, the TPP negotiators could even revive proposals that had already been rejected by the ACTA negotiators, especially those from the European Union. Among these rejected proposals were those calling for the introduction of the graduated response system and the DMCA-style notice-and-take-down mechanism.

Fourth, although both ACTA and TPP have raised similar concerns about transparency and accountability,[62] these concerns are somewhat different. While it is hard to justify the categorical non-disclosure of draft treaty texts, especially with respect to proposals advanced solely by US negotiators, it is more acceptable to refrain from disclosing sensitive information, such as tariffs, quotas or financial data.[63] Thus, as problematic and disturbing as the USTR's secretive approach in handling draft ACTA texts was, this agency may have a much stronger justification for refusing to disclose draft TPP texts this time.

Finally, the highly technical and trade-oriented nature of the TPP negotiations may greatly reduce the interest of the public at large in the negotiations. In fact, without the controversial issues surrounding the Internet and new communications technologies, one has to wonder whether the TPP negotiations could find their way to the mainstream media. The public at large is simply not interested in trade tariffs or trade remedies. Even when the ACTA negotiations were mostly about intellectual property protection and enforcement, they did not receive much coverage in the mainstream media.[64] With even less public scrutiny than ACTA, and arguably a significantly reduced watchdog effect, the TPP intellectual property chapter could favour the copyright industries more than it otherwise would have.

10.8 Eight issues for consideration

From the TRIPS Agreement's marriage of intellectual property and trade to the recent negotiation of FTAs, EPAs, ACTA and TPP, there is a tendency to rely on trade agreements to provide protection and enforcement of intellectual property rights. Such reliance, however, does not always take sufficient consideration of the challenges brought about by the Internet and new communications technologies. To help us identify these challenges, this section focuses on eight issues that policymakers and commentators should seriously consider.

First, from initial negotiation to final ratification to full implementation, it takes a considerable amount of time, effort, energy and resources to complete a trade agreement. The rate at which such an agreement is developed can hardly keep pace with the rate of technological change. As Colin Picker cautioned us, '[D]elay is the rule in the formation of international law. Usually, international law is created over long periods, by the gradual acceptance of customary state practice or after long treaty negotiations.'[65] Although the TRIPS negotiators were reluctant to introduce provisions to address new technology, it is unclear how much more they could have done in relation to the Internet and new communications technologies. Likewise, peer-to-peer file-sharing technologies had not even entered the mainstream at that time, even though the negotiators of the WIPO Internet Treaties sought to update the multilateral intellectual property regime in light of new online developments.

To a large extent, trade agreements have always played a cat-and-mouse game with new technology. Although such a challenge is not that much different from challenges found in the realm of domestic law – cyber law in particular – trade agreements seem to have a harder time catching up with technological change. As Jack Goldsmith and Tim Wu observed in their book, *Who Controls the Internet?*:

> With the unintended exception of international trade laws . . ., the predicted rise of international treaties to govern contested Internet issues simply has not happened. The paucity of Internet treaties is remarkable. After a decade of legal conflict, aside from the stalled cybercrime treaty, not a single treaty has been drafted and ratified related to issues like defamation, gambling, speech, privacy, and the like. For the Internet, unilateral action, conflict, and ad hoc accommodation are often the best the nations of the world can do.[66]

Second, as much of a challenge technology has posed to trade agreements and their implementation, trade agreements could also affect the development of future technology. As Robert Keohane and Joseph Nye rightly noted:

> [T]he information revolution has not transformed world politics to a new politics of complex interdependence. One reason is that information does not flow in a vacuum, but in political space that is already occupied. States have for the last four centuries established the political structure within which information flows across borders and other transactions take place.[67]

By dictating technological formats and interoperability, standards set by trade agreements and their implementing legislation could determine which type of technology will thrive, or even survive, under the international regulatory environment.

To complicate matters even further, treaties can either '[enter] too late to be relevant or too early to accurately manage the relevant technology'.[68] The latter was a primary concern of cyber law scholars in the early days of the World Wide Web. As Mike Godwin wrote at that time, '[T]he best thing to do, when technology opens up a new frontier for freedom of expression, is to sit and wait awhile and see how existing laws and institutions cope with the problems.'[69] Over the years, commentators have called for caution, restraint and flexibility in regulating technologies that are nascent or inchoate.[70] Many of them have also expressed concern about the stifling impact that legislation such as the DMCA and international agreements such as ACTA and TPP could have on future technological development.[71]

Third, it is worth noting that developed countries continue to disagree with each other over what they consider appropriate intrusion on national sovereignty in providing international standards of intellectual property protection and enforcement. It is no coincidence that the European Union and the United States could not agree during the ACTA negotiations on whether to introduce provisions concerning the graduated response system or the DMCA-style notice-and-take-down mechanism. It is also no surprise that industries within both trading powers continue to be divided over what and how international intellectual property standards should be developed.

Fourth, if developed countries find it difficult to agree on common standards concerning the protection and enforcement of intellectual property rights in the digital environment, it is logical that a greater divide exists between developed and developing countries in this contentious area. After all, at least in the short term, high intellectual property standards tend to favour developed countries at the expense of developing countries. Many developing countries are already deeply concerned about the high standards brought about by the TRIPS Agreement, the WIPO Internet Treaties and other multilateral intellectual property agreements. Many of these poorer countries also continue to struggle with problems brought about by the global digital divide – the proverbial gap between those who have access to information technology and digital content and those who do not.[72] It is therefore understandable why developing countries would find it inappropriate for developed countries to use bilateral, plurilateral and regional trade agreements to further strengthen standards of intellectual property protection and enforcement.

Fifth, the protection of intellectual property rights in the digital environment is a global challenge – similar to responses to illicit drug trafficking, refugees, illegal immigration, environmental degradation, illegal arms sales, nuclear proliferation, terrorism and corruption.[73] If such protection is to be robust and effective, countries need to work together to address challenges brought about by the Internet and new communications technologies. The development of the TRIPS Agreement was indeed an attempt to provide a multilateral solution to a global problem – in this case, piracy and counterfeiting. If multilateral solutions are still badly needed, efforts to push for non-multilateral solutions could undermine the stability of the existing multilateral system.[74] Such efforts could also alienate trading partners to the point that future multilateral discussions will become even more difficult.

This is particularly true in the context of both ACTA and TPP, where only developed and like-minded countries are invited to the negotiations. As Francis Gurry, the WIPO Director General, lamented, countries negotiating ACTA have 'tak[en] matters into their own hands to seek solutions outside of the multilateral system to the detriment of inclusiveness of the present system'.[75] In previous works, I also pointed out repeatedly that, by embracing an ill-advised 'country club' approach to international norm-setting, these plurilateral negotiations were doomed from the beginning.[76] After all, it is hard to imagine how a treaty solution could be effective if it was negotiated without the participation of the so-called 'BRICS' countries (Brazil, Russia, India, China and South Africa). At the time of writing, many of these countries remain the major sources of piracy and counterfeiting.

Sixth, greater harmonization of national standards may not be needed to respond to the challenges brought about by the Internet and new communications technologies. This point seemingly contradicts the fifth point, but it makes a lot of sense. Policymakers tend to believe that new solutions need to be developed when problems emerge. This tendency exists regardless of whether the problems are domestic or international. While having a good solution would be ideal, a solution that does not satisfactorily address the problem could make the problem worse.

At the moment, many countries, including developed country *demandeurs*, continue to push for solutions that address copyright challenges brought about by the Internet and new communications technologies. At this critical juncture, policymakers should seriously consider whether it is premature to harmonize national standards, especially those that are only newly introduced and incompletely tested. As Jerome Reichman and Keith Maskus observed in the patent context:

> The drive to further harmonize the international minimum standards of patent protection . . . has occurred at the very time when the domestic standards of the United States and the operations of its patent system are under critical assault. . . . How, under such circumstances, could it be timely to harmonize and elevate international standards of patent protection – even if that were demonstrably beneficial – when there is so little agreement in the US itself on how to rectify a dysfunctional apparatus that often seems out of control? . . . Further harmonization efforts in this climate thus amount to a gamble from which bad decisions and bad laws are far more likely to emerge than good laws that appropriately balance public and private interests.[77]

It is therefore no surprise that these two prominent scholars called for '[a] moratorium on stronger international intellectual property standards' after carefully examining the reform needs of the US patent system.[78]

Given Professors Reichman and Maskus' thought-provoking recommendation, one cannot help but wonder whether a similar moratorium should be imposed on new standards concerning the protection and enforcement of intellectual property rights in the digital environment. After all, countries may need more experimentation with new regulatory and economic policies at a time when the Internet and new communications technologies have created many new opportunities. Such regulatory experiments could benefit countries by helping them develop solutions that are more effectively tailored to their own social, economic, cultural and technological conditions.[79]

Seventh, trade agreements have become increasingly intrusive on people's daily lives. In the digital copyright area, for example, the provisions included in these agreements could have a serious impact on what and how one reads, communicates or creates; what and how one shares with friends and family members; and whether one could access needed but unavailable information. While critics of ACTA, TPP and the recent SOPA/PIPA legislation in the United States[80] might have exaggerated their claim that these treaties or legislative bills would 'break the Internet',[81] it is not hard to see their sincere concern about the adverse impacts that new and higher intellectual property standards would have on the online environment. It is also understandable why the service blackout launched by Wikipedia, Reddit, WordPress and other Internet companies on 18 January 2012 in protest of SOPA has earned considerable support from both the public at large and members of the policymaking circle.[82]

Finally, digital technology has changed the polity. As Milton Mueller recently observed, '[b]y converging different media forms and facilitating fully interactive communication, the Internet dramatically alters the cost and capabilities of group action'.[83] His observation dovetails the burgeoning literature on cyber protests, online activism and the growing impact of the Internet, social media and new communications technologies on domestic and global politics.[84] As a result, policymakers need to think more about how and how frequently they consult the public at large about technology-related standards in trade agreements.

From FTAs/EPAs to ACTA to TPP, virtually all of the recent non-multilateral trade agreements have been negotiated without a transparent and democratic process. It is indeed ironic – if not hypocritical – that these agreements include transparency provisions even when their negotiations were not transparent at all. Also worrying are the negative impacts these negotiations will have on the developed countries' ongoing effort to promote democracy and rule of law in other parts of the world. If policymakers find it challenging to negotiate non-multilateral trade agreements in the open, owing in part to the need to protect classified or highly sensitive information, at the very least they should frequently and adequately communicate to the public the contents of those agreements. They should also include ample opportunities for the public to provide feedback on these agreements, as opposed to only limited opportunities after the conclusion of the agreements.

10.9 Conclusion

Since the protection and enforcement of intellectual property rights have been incorporated into the TRIPS Agreement, the copyright industries and their supportive governments have actively pushed for both multilateral and non-multilateral solutions to address challenges brought about by the Internet and new communications technologies. Although many of these efforts make good sense in light of the serious economic injury inflicted by massive online intellectual property infringements, they have had very limited success thus far.

If policymakers are to become more successful in using trade agreements to foster protection and enforcement of intellectual property rights in the digital environment, they need to better understand the cat-and-mouse game involving trade agreements and digital technology. They also need to understand more deeply the complications created by non-multilateral agreements for the existing multilateral regime. In addition, they should seriously explore whether local standards need to be sufficiently developed before they seek international harmonization.

The literature on the interplay between law and technology has been developing for close to two decades now. It is about time we apply insights from this literature to the field of international economic law, the field of international trade in particular. Until policymakers can develop a better and deeper appreciation of the challenges that digital technology has posed to trade agreements, a considerable amount of their effort – at both the multilateral and non-multilateral levels – could go sorely wasted. In the end, the adopted trade agreements would just become a herd of old cats chasing an ever-evolving mouse.

Acknowledgements

This chapter draws on research from the author's earlier articles in the *Drake Law Review Discourse*, *IDEA: The Intellectual Property Law Review* and the *Loyola of Los Angeles Law Review*. The author is grateful to Erin Cassidy and Lindsey Purdy for excellent research and editorial assistance.

Notes

2 E.g. A. M. Froomkin, 'The Internet as a Source of Regulatory Arbitrage', in B. Kahin and C. Nesson (eds), *Borders in Cyberspace: Information Policy and the Global Information Infrastructure*, Cambridge, MA: MIT Press, 1997; D. R. Johnson and D. Post, 'Law and Borders – The Rise of Law in Cyberspace', *Stanford Law Review* 48, 1996, 1367 at 1367–402; I. T. Hardy, 'The Proper Legal Regime for "Cyberspace"', *University of Pittsburgh Law Review* 55, 1994, 993 at 993–1055.

3 Some of the rare exceptions are M. Burri and T. Cottier (eds), *Trade Governance in the Digital Age*, Cambridge: Cambridge University Press, 2012; J. P. Singh, *Negotiation and the Global Information Economy*, Cambridge: Cambridge University Press, 2008; J. P. Trachtman, *The Future of International Law: Global Government*, Cambridge: Cambridge University Press, 2013, pp. 85–117; T. Cottier, 'The Impact of New Technologies on Multilateral Trade Regulation and Governance', *Chicago-Kent Law Review* 72, 1996, 415 at 415–36; C. B. Picker, 'A View from 40,000 Feet: International Law and the Invisible Hand of Technology', *Cardozo Law Review* 23, 2001, 149 at 149–218.

4 M. Burri and T. Cottier, 'Introduction: Digital Technologies and International Trade Regulation', in Burri and Cottier (eds), op. cit. p. 3.

5 S. K. Sell, *Power and Ideas: North-South Politics of Intellectual Property and Antitrust*, Albany: State University of New York Press, 1998, pp. 123–30.

6 D. J. Gervais, 'The TRIPS Agreement and the Doha Round: History and Impact on Economic Development', in P. K. Yu (ed.), *Intellectual Property and Information Wealth: Issues and Practices in the Digital Age*, Westport, CT: Praeger Publishers, 2007, p. 43.

7 P. K. Yu, 'Teaching International Intellectual Property Law', *St. Louis University Law Journal* 52, 2008, 923 at 933.

8 M. A. Hamilton, 'The TRIPS Agreement: Imperialistic, Outdated, and Overprotective', *Vanderbilt Journal of Transnational Law* 29, 1996, 613 at 614–15.

9 J. H. Reichman, 'The Know-How Gap in the TRIPS Agreement: Why Software Fared Badly, and What Are the Solutions', *Hastings Communications and Entertainment Law Journal* 17, 1995, 763 at 766.

10 F. von Lohmann, 'RIAA v. The People Turns from Lawsuits to 3 Strikes', available at www.eff.org/deeplinks/2008/12/riaa-v.-people-turns-lawsuits-3-strikes (accessed 14 January 2013). On the industry's early lawsuits against file-sharing individuals, its 'battle strategies', and some of its rather unconvincing rhetoric, see P. K. Yu, 'Digital Copyright and Confuzzling Rhetoric', *Vanderbilt Journal of Entertainment and Technology Law* 13, 2011, 881 at 887–901; P. K. Yu, 'P2P and the Future of Private Copying', *University of Colorado Law Review* 76, 2005, 653 at 658–76; P. K. Yu, 'The Escalating Copyright Wars', *Hofstra Law Review* 32, 2004, 907 at 910–23.

11 E.g. *Metro-Goldwyn-Mayer Studios Inc. v. Grokster, Ltd.*, 545 US 913 (2005) (United States); *BMG Canada Inc. v. John Doe*, [2005] FCA 193 (Canada); *Universal Music Australia Pty Ltd v. Sharman License Holdings Ltd.* (2005) 65 IPR 289 (Australia).

12 P. K. Yu, 'A Tale of Two Development Agendas', *Ohio Northern University Law Review* 35, 2009, 465 at 521–2.

13 'Basic Proposal for the Substantive Provisions of the Treaty on Certain Questions Concerning the Protection of Literary and Artistic Works to Be Considered by the Diplomatic Conference on Certain Copyright and Neighboring Rights Questions', CRNR/DC/4, 30 August 1996, p. 2.

14 Commission of the European Communities, 'Green Paper on Copyright and the Challenge of Technology – Copyright Issues Requiring Immediate Action', COM (88) 172 final.

15 P. Samuelson, 'The US Digital Agenda at WIPO', *Virginia Journal of International Law* 37, 1997, 369 at 377.

16 Information Infrastructure Task Force, Intellectual Property and the National Information Infrastructure: The Report of the Working Group on Intellectual Property Rights, Washington, 1995.

17 Samuelson, op. cit. p. 373.

18 Samuelson, op. cit. pp. 372–3.

19 Samuelson, op. cit. pp. 373–4.

20 Samuelson, op. cit. pp. 374–5. On what commentators have described as 'policy laundering' and 'backdoor lawmaking', see P. K. Yu, 'The Political Economy of

Data Protection', *Chicago-Kent Law Review* 84, 2010, 777 at 786–9; P. K. Yu, 'Six Secret (and Now Open) Fears of ACTA', *SMU Law Review* 64, 2011, 975 at 1024–8.

21 P. K. Yu, 'Currents and Crosscurrents in the International Intellectual Property Regime', *Loyola of Los Angeles Law Review* 38, 2004, 323 at 372–3.

22 Samuelson, op. cit. pp. 374–5.

23 Samuelson, op. cit. pp. 390–2, 435.

24 WCT Article 8; WPPT Article 15.

25 WCT Article 10(1); WPPT Article 16(2).

26 WCT Article 11; WPPT Article 18.

27 WCT Article 12; WPPT Article 19.

28 The WCT and the WPPT entered into force on 6 March 2002 and 20 May 2002, respectively.

29 That directive eventually came in the form of the EU Directive on the Harmonisation of Certain Aspects of Copyright and Related Rights in the Information Society, 2001 O.J. (L 167) 10.

30 J. H. Reichman, 'Universal Minimum Standards of Intellectual Property Protection under the TRIPS Component of the WTO Agreement', *International Lawyer*, 29, 1995, 345–88.

31 On copyright reform in Canada, see M. A. Geist (ed.), *From 'Radical Extremism' to 'Balanced Copyright': Canadian Copyright and the Digital Agenda*, Toronto: Irwin Law, 2010.

32 Office of the US Trade Representative, *2012 Special 301 Report*, Washington, 2012, p. 25.

33 Office of the US Trade Representative, *2013 Special 301 Report*, Washington, 2013, p. 46.

34 *Recording Industry Association of America v. Verizon Internet Services Inc.*, 351 F.3d 1229, 1238 (D.C. Cir. 2003).

35 M. Naím, *Illicit: How Smugglers, Traffickers, and Copycats Are Hijacking the Global Economy*, New York: Doubleday, 2005, p. 219.

36 Naím, op. cit. pp. 219–20.

37 P. K. Yu, 'Enforcement, Enforcement, What Enforcement?', *IDEA* 52, 2012, 239 at 241–52.

38 Naím, op. cit. pp. 23–4.

39 MarkMonitor, Traffic Report: Online Piracy and Counterfeiting, Boise, 2011, p. 4.

40 Office of the US Trade Representative, *Out-of-Cycle Review of Notorious Markets*, Washington, 2011.

41 US Department of Justice, 'Federal Courts Order Seizure of 82 Website Domains Involved in Selling Counterfeit Goods as Part of DOJ and ICE Cyber Monday Crackdown', available at www.justice.gov/opa/pr/2010/November/10-ag-1355 (accessed 14 January 2013).

42 P. Drahos, 'BITs and BIPs: Bilateralism in Intellectual Property', *Journal of World Intellectual Property* 4, 2001, 791 at 794.

43 P. K. Yu, 'Sinic Trade Agreements', *U.C. Davis Law Review* 44, 2011, 953 at 1012–13.

44 A. Christie, S. Waller and K. Weatherall, 'Exporting the DMCA Through Free Trade Agreements', in C. Heath and A. Kamperman Sanders (eds), *Intellectual Property and Free Trade Agreements*, Oxford: Hart Publishing, 2007, p. 220.

45 On the WIPO Development Agenda, see Yu, 'A Tale of Two Development Agendas', op. cit.

46 Office of the US Trade Representative, 'Ambassador Schwab Announces US Will Seek New Trade Agreement to Fight Fakes', available at www.ustr.gov/ambassador-schwab-announces-us-will-seek-new-trade-agreement-fight-fakes (accessed 14 January 2013).

47 In addition to Japan, the United States and the European Union – the usual trilateral alliance for heightened intellectual property protection – the negotiating parties included Australia, Canada, Mexico, Morocco, New Zealand, Singapore, South Korea and Switzerland. Although Jordan and the United Arab Emirates also participated in the first round of the negotiations, they did not continue afterwards. 'EU ACTA Negotiator Confirms EU Wants Patent Provisions in ACTA', *Inside US Trade*, 8 May 2009, p. 11.

48 ACTA Article 27.1.

49 G. Hinze, 'Preliminary Analysis of the Officially Released ACTA Text', available at www.eff.org/deeplinks/2010/04/eff-analysis-officially-released-acta-text (accessed 14 January 2013).

50 Yu, 'Six Secret Fears', op. cit. p. 1086.

51 E. Katz, 'Stopping the ACTA Juggernaut', available at www.eff.org/deeplinks/2009/11/stopping-acta-juggernaut (accessed 14 January 2013).

52 Yu, 'Six Secret Fears', op. cit. pp. 1055–7. The graduated response system enables Internet service providers to take a wide variety of actions after giving users warnings about their potentially illegal online activities. These actions include suspension or termination of service, capping of bandwidth, and blocking of sites, portals and protocols. P. K. Yu, 'The Graduated Response', *Florida Law Review* 62, 2010, 1373 at 1373–430.

53 Yu, 'Six Secret Fears', op. cit. p. 1029.

54 Yu, 'Six Secret Fears', op. cit. p. 1086.

55 M. Ermert, 'Treaty Negotiators Turn to "ACTA Lite" in Hopes of Closure', *Intellectual Property Watch*, 8 September 2010.

56 On the language used in these safeguard clauses, see M. Blakeney, *Intellectual Property Enforcement: A Commentary on the Anti-Counterfeiting Trade Agreement (ACTA)*, Cheltenham, UK and Northampton, MA: Edward Elgar, 2012, pp. 279–87.

57 M. K. Lewis, 'Expanding the P-4 Trade Agreement into a Broader Trans-Pacific Partnership: Implications, Risks and Opportunities', *Asian Journal of WTO and International Health Law and Policy*, 4, 2009, 401 at 403–4.

58 Office of the US Trade Representative, 'Outlines of the Trans-Pacific Partnership Agreement', available at www.ustr.gov/about-us/press-office/fact-sheets/2011/november/outlines-trans-pacific-partnership-agreement (accessed 14 January 2013).

59 P. K. Yu, 'ACTA and Its Complex Politics', *WIPO Journal* 3, 2011, 1 at 11.

60 K. Weatherall, 'ACTA as a New Kind of International IP Lawmaking', *American University International Law Review* 26, 2011, 839 at 841–2.

61 Yu, 'ACTA and Its Complex Politics', op. cit. pp. 8–9.

62 D. S. Levine, 'Bring in the Nerds: Secrecy, National Security and the Creation of International Intellectual Property Law', *Cardozo Arts and Entertainment Law Journal* 30, 2012, 105 at 105–51; D. S. Levine, 'Transparency Soup: The ACTA Negotiating Process and "Black Box" Lawmaking', *American University International Law Review* 26, 2011, 811 at 811–37; Yu, 'Six Secret Fears', op. cit. pp. 998–1019.

63 Yu, 'Six Secret Fears', op. cit. p. 1007.

64 Yu, 'ACTA and Its Complex Politics', op. cit. p. 13.

65 Picker, op. cit. p. 183.

66 J. Goldsmith and T. Wu, *Who Controls the Internet? Illusions of a Borderless World*, Oxford: Oxford University Press, 2006, p. 167.

67 R. O. Keohane and J. S. Nye, *Power and Interdependence*, 3rd edn, New York: Addison Wesley Longman, 2001, p. 217.

68 Picker, op. cit. p. 151.

69 M. Godwin, *Cyber Rights: Defending Free Speech in the Digital Age*, New York: Times Books, 1998, pp. 299–300.

70 E.g. D. Gervais, 'The Regulation of Inchoate Technologies', *Houston Law Review* 47, 2010, 665 at 665–705; L. Lessig, 'The Path of Cyberlaw', *Yale Law Journal* 104, 1995, 1743 at 1752.

71 On the DMCA's undesirable lock-in effects, see D. L. Burk, 'Legal and Technical Standards in Digital Rights Management Technology', *Fordham Law Review* 74, 2005, 537 at 568; R. P. Wagner, 'Reconsidering the DMCA', *Houston Law Review* 42, 2005, 1107 at 1118; P. K. Yu, 'Anticircumvention and Anti-anticircumvention', *Denver University Law Review* 84, 2006, 13 at 57–9.

72 P. Norris, *Digital Divide: Civic Engagement, Information Poverty, and the Internet Worldwide*, Cambridge: Cambridge University Press, 2001; P. K. Yu, 'Bridging the Digital Divide: Equality in the Information Age', *Cardozo Arts and Entertainment Law Journal* 20, 2002, 1 at 1–52.

73 P. K. Yu, 'From Pirates to Partners: Protecting Intellectual Property in China in the Twenty-first Century', *American University Law Review* 50, 2000, 131 at 199 note 364.

74 Yu, 'Enforcement, Enforcement, What Enforcement?', op. cit. p. 259.

75 C. Saez, 'ACTA a Sign of Weakness in Multilateral System, WIPO Head Says', *Intellectual Property Watch*, 30 June 2010.

76 Yu, 'Six Secret Fears', op. cit. pp. 1074–83; Yu, 'ACTA and Its Complex Politics', op. cit. pp. 5–9.

77 K. E. Maskus and J. H. Reichman, 'The Globalization of Private Knowledge Goods and the Privatization of Global Public Goods', in *International Public Goods and Transfer of Technology under a Globalized Intellectual Property Regime*, K. E. Maskus and J. H. Reichman (eds), Cambridge: Cambridge University Press, 2005, pp. 24–6.

78 Maskus and Reichman, op. cit. pp. 36–9.

79 Yu, 'Anticircumvention and Anti-anticircumvention', op. cit. pp. 44–5; P. K. Yu, 'Digital Copyright Reform and Legal Transplants in Hong Kong', *University of Louisville Law Review* 48, 2010, 693 at 756–60.

80 Stop Online Piracy Act (SOPA), H.R. 3261, 112th Cong. (2011); Preventing Real Online Threats to Economic Creativity and Theft of Intellectual Property Act of 2011 (PIPA), S. 968, 112th Cong. (2011).

81 For example, the comedian Jon Stewart said SOPA would 'break the Internet', drawing on the catchy slogan widely used by the technology community. In the academic literature, Mark Lemley, David Levine and David Post also called on policymakers not to 'break the Internet'. M. Lemley, D. S. Levine and D. G. Post, 'Don't Break the Internet', *Stanford Law Review Online* 64, 2011, 34 at 34. There is no doubt that legislation such as SOPA and PIPA will change the way the Internet operates. However, as we learn from the Chinese experience, the Internet does not break easily; it can accommodate different types of regulation. Whether one finds the outcome appealing is, of course, a very different question.

82 P. K. Yu, 'The Alphabet Soup of Transborder Intellectual Property Enforcement', *Drake Law Review Discourse* 60, 2012, 16 at 29, 32–3.

83 M. L. Mueller, *Networks and States: The Global Politics of Internet Governance*, Cambridge, MA: MIT Press, 2010, p. 5.

84 E.g. R. MacKinnon, *Consent of the Networked: The Worldwide Struggle for Internet Freedom*, New York: Basic Books, 2012; M. McCaughey and M. D. Ayers (eds), *Cyberactivism: Online Activism in Theory and Practice*, New York: Routledge, 2003; W. van de Donk, B. D. Loader, P. G. Nixon and D. Rucht (eds), *Cyberprotest: New Media, Citizens and Social Movements*, New York: Routledge, 2004.

11 Ignoring the science

What we know about patents suggests dire consequences from ACTA and the TPPA

Kimberlee Weatherall[1]

11.1 Introduction

If your goal is a trade policy aimed at promoting creativity, innovation, scientific research and development, then intellectual property ('IP') is probably not the most important topic to address. Action in other areas could have more impact: cross-border movement of skilled workers, deepening cooperation on the regulation or assessment of new technologies, liberalizing higher education in advance of the disruptive impact of online courses,[2] or harnessing the innovation-engendering potential of government procurement policies without succumbing to protectionism. Nevertheless, there are some good arguments why harmonization of IP could benefit firms that depend on IP across a range of industries. Pragmatically speaking, too, IP is considered a necessary part of 'twenty-first-century trade agreements' (whatever such things might be).

Assuming then that IP is to be a topic of trade negotiations, the rational approach in formulating such a chapter would be to consider carefully the circumstances of countries involved in any negotiation, work out the problems that challenge IP-dependent firms involved in international trade between those countries, and consider how – and whether – those problems can be addressed through a treaty.

In the real world, international IP negotiations do not start from this point. As Yu's chapter in this collection usefully illustrates, no IP negotiation starts from a blank slate. On the contrary, the slate is very crowded these days with multilateral and bilateral agreements and some regional arrangements, all building on each other, accreted over the course of the twentieth century and occupying every policy space with increasing frequency and complexity in the first decade of the twenty-first. In addition, as Yu notes in his contribution to this volume, very real political constraints govern negotiators' approaches to trade negotiations. Nevertheless, it can be useful to review what we know about patent systems worldwide and what this tells us about what an IP agreement should, and should not do. This consideration can provide benchmarks against which we can assess and critique agreements reached in the politically constrained real world.

This chapter looks at what research into the operation of the IP system, and particularly IP enforcement, tells us about the issues that research-based firms face. As a complement to Yu's chapter, I focus on the 'science' side of IP, particularly patents, using research and information about domestic developments to critique the approach taken in the most recent IP negotiations affecting the Asia-Pacific region – namely, the Anti-Counterfeiting Trade Agreement ('ACTA')[3] concluded in late 2010, and the Trans-Pacific Partnership Agreement ('TPPA'), which at the time of writing is under negotiation. While much of the literature on patents in ACTA and the TPPA has focused on the (very important) impact on access to medicines, this chapter is concerned with the likely impact on the patent system more generally.

The next section describes both ACTA and the TPPA for those not familiar with these recent and prospective additions to the international IP landscape. Section 11.3 summarizes current research, particularly into IP enforcement, to identify what we know about the problems encountered by research-based firms, and considers the relevance of this research for international IP lawmaking efforts, seeking to show how ACTA and the US TPPA IP proposal not only fail to address the issues, but may even be harmful to domestic efforts to promote innovation through the IP system. Section 11.4 concludes.

11.2 Recent developments in international IP: introducing ACTA and the TPPA

11.2.1 Introduction to ACTA

ACTA is a plurilateral agreement addressing a range of matters relating to the enforcement of all forms of IP, both civil and criminal. The stated goal is to provide 'a high-level international framework that strengthens the global enforcement of intellectual property rights'.[4] The parties to the negotiation were Australia, the United States, Japan, the 27 nations of the European Union ('EU'), Mexico, Switzerland, Canada, Singapore, South Korea, New Zealand and Morocco. ACTA was concluded in December 2010 following several years of discussions, and 8 of the 11 negotiating countries officially signed the agreement on 1 October 2011.[5] The Agreement has six chapters, but the core obligations are found in Chapter 2, which deals with general principles (fairness, proportionality, etc.), civil enforcement (procedures and remedies), border measures, criminal enforcement, and enforcement in the digital environment. Subsequent chapters deal with enforcement practices, international cooperation and the administration of the agreement through an ACTA Committee.

ACTA fills a gap in the international IP framework by providing highly elaborated provisions on IP enforcement[6] not seen in existing multilateral agreements such as the Agreement on Trade-Related Aspects of Intellectual Property Rights ('TRIPS'). Examples of 'TRIPS-plus' provisions in ACTA include the obligations to provide for an account of profits as a remedy for IP infringement,[7] to provide statutory or at least additional damages[8] and legal costs,[9] obligations on an (alleged) infringer to provide information about the origin and distribution network of the infringing goods,[10] and powers for customs authorities to provide right holders with information on goods seized at the border.[11] Criminal provisions include secondary criminal liability for aiding and abetting activities[12] and liability of corporate persons,[13] an optional 'camcording' offence,[14] and provisions on enforcement in the digital environment more detailed than those found in the relevant multilateral treaties.[15] In sum, ACTA is 'significantly more stringent and rightholder friendly than the TRIPS Agreement'.[16]

Even so, the final text of ACTA was very different from the initial ambitions of countries such as the US, as reflected in earlier leaked texts;[17] although the negotiating parties were a 'coalition of the willing', all had their own IP systems with very different features that they were unwilling to change. Unsurprisingly, Europe was unwilling to adopt wholesale provisions based closely on US law over its own, painstakingly negotiated *acquis communautaire.* The final text of ACTA thus retreated from proposals to criminalize private infringements not undertaken for commercial purposes (a US proposal that would have required new EU law), digital enforcement provisions including more detailed anticircumvention provisions and secondary liability for intermediaries (another US proposal), compulsory inclusion of patents and geographical indications in border measures (an EU proposal controversial for the US) and compulsory statutory damages (a US proposal), among other changes.[18] ACTA is particularly weak on patents: they are explicitly excluded from the border measures, were never included in the criminal enforcement provisions, and even the basic section on civil enforcement allows a party to exclude patents.[19]

Notwithstanding, ACTA has been controversial, particularly owing to its provisions on digital enforcement.[20] The negotiations were seen as lacking in transparency, bypassing existing multilateral fora such as the WIPO and the WTO,[21] and unbalanced in that they sought to establish an international standard without the participation of the developing world. Although ACTA is a plurilateral agreement, there have been fears that the ACTA standards would later be imposed on other countries, perhaps as a precondition to trade negotiations.[22] Through 2012 ACTA struggled to gain acceptance even among the negotiating parties. Mass protests[23] and a petition with 2 million signatures[24] led the European Parliament to reject it.[25] The Australian Parliamentary Joint Standing Committee on Treaties expressed considerable reservations.[26] Twelve months after its conclusion only Japan had ratified ACTA.

11.2.2 Introduction to the TPPA

The TPPA is a very different kind of agreement from ACTA. Where ACTA relates only to IP, the TPPA is a proposed comprehensive regional FTA that at the time of writing is being negotiated among Australia, Brunei Darussalam,

Canada, Chile, Malaysia, Mexico, New Zealand, Peru, Singapore, the United States and Vietnam. As proposed, it will include chapters dealing with a full range of trade issues including market access for both goods and services, rules of origin, government procurement, investment and financial services, telecommunications, and sanitary and phytosanitary rules. The TPPA has been presented as an opportunity to tie together existing trade agreements and hence 'tame the tangle' of existing agreements.[27] But it is also being touted as an opportunity to create a platform for broader regional trade integration. In other words, the ambition is that other countries will, in the future, also accede to the Agreement, which can in time extend its membership throughout the Asia-Pacific region.[28]

With ACTA troubled, significant attention in IP circles has moved to negotiations for the TPPA,[29] both for IP enthusiasts (who hope that the TPPA IP chapter may achieve what ACTA failed to achieve) and civil society opponents (who fear that the outcome will revive proposals rejected in ACTA, particularly since Europe is not involved in the TPPA). Parties may be more willing to make changes to their own law through the TPPA than they were in ACTA, since the presence of other issues leads to the potential for trade-offs – stronger IP laws in Vietnam for better access for agricultural goods into the US market, for example.

At the time of writing, no negotiating text was officially available for the TPPA chapter. However, public statements from the USTR and an early leaked text attributed to the US and dated February 2011,[30] if genuine, suggest that the US sought a chapter in the style of its existing FTAs, with some new additions. Thus the US proposed,[31] as it generally does, limits on parallel importation,[32] extension of the copyright term for films and sound recordings to 95 years[33] and detailed regulations governing the management of geographical indications and their relationship with trademarks.[34] It had new ideas, too, such as a presumption of validity for patents and trademarks.[35] The proposal also revived some proposals that did not find acceptance in ACTA:

- statutory damages in copyright and (in a new innovation) for breaches of the anticircumvention provisions;[36]
- mandatory provision for customs authorities to seize allegedly infringing in-transit goods;[37]
- expansion of criminal liability in copyright to include private, non-commercial activities;[38]
- a level of detail on anticircumvention law based on past models of US FTAs – details not included in the ACTA;[39]
- a camcording offence;[40] and
- detailed online safe harbour provisions requiring online service providers to have a policy for the termination of repeat infringers.[41]

Further, the US proposal included none of the safeguards found in ACTA, such as reference to TRIPS Articles 7 and 8,[42] the protection of privacy,[43] a requirement that procedures be fair, equitable and proportionate,[44] and that measures not create barriers to legitimate trade.[45] The proposal even included a provision stating that domestic decisions on the distribution of enforcement resources 'shall not excuse that Party from complying with this Chapter' – the exact opposite of the position in ACTA.[46]

On patents, the US proposal for the TPPA was particularly aggressive. It included a broad concept of patentability (including controversial 'new form' and 'new use' patents that assist in the evergreening of pharmaceutical patents[47] and medical method patents[48]), a prohibition on pre-grant opposition,[49] and limits on the bases on which a patent application can be rejected to those standard in the US and similar countries: i.e. lack of inventive step, novelty, industrial application and *ordre public* or morality.[50] The US also proposed new and controversial provisions on the relationship between patents and pharmaceuticals, in a White Paper entitled 'Trans-Pacific Partnership Trade Goals to Enhance Access to Medicines'.[51] This proposal abandoned the US's previous differentiated approach, which imposed strong requirements only on developed nations, such as patent term adjustments to compensate for unreasonable delays that occur in granting a patent,[52] or in obtaining marketing approval for pharmaceutical patents,[53] data exclusivity protecting clinical test data submitted for marketing approval for five years,[54] and an obligation to refuse marketing approval to a company seeking to rely on clinical test data submitted by another without the consent of the previous patent owner during the patent term (known as 'patent linkage').[55] Developing countries, pursuant to an agreement known as the 'May 10, 2007 Bipartisan Trade Agreement',[56] were entitled to apply exceptions to protection for clinical test data, protect test data only as long as it was protected in the US, only optionally provide for patent term extensions to compensate for delays in the patent or marketing approval process, and were not required to 'link' drug regulatory agencies approval processes and patent issues. Under the US's 'new strategic initiative' proposed for the TPPA, Trade Enhancing Access to Medicines ('TEAM'), these 'pharmaceutical-specific IP protections' – patent term extensions, data exclusivity and patent linkage – would be available in all TPPA countries, but conditional on the pharmaceutical patent holder bringing medicine to TPPA markets within an agreed period (the 'access window').[57]

The US has experienced considerable resistance to its IP proposals in the TPPA negotiations,[58] particularly the patents provisions, and any finalized chapter would be unlikely to include all these strengthened rules. For the purposes of this chapter, however, the point is that both ACTA and the US proposals for the TPPA follow a similar and familiar model, based closely on US law and on IP chapters from past trade agreements, focusing on the details of IP legislation and regulations, mostly those governing rights and court-based enforcement procedures.

11.3 The state of play in IP enforcement and its relevance to IP negotiations

11.3.1 What are we missing?

As Yu notes in his contribution to this collection, the US model for IP negotiations, embodied in its proposals for both ACTA and the TPPA IP chapter, is to use text developed in earlier agreements or negotiations, and based closely on the US domestic law, with additions based on the complaints and suggestions of industry peak bodies. This starting text is then the subject of negotiation based on what other parties can accept and political trade-offs on both (or all) sides. Hence we see in US FTAs slight variations in the text between countries and additions and elaborations over time. In ACTA, which involved multiple parties including developed countries with their own highly developed systems such as Europe and Japan, we see more significant changes based on the need to accommodate these different systems.[59] The TPPA will no doubt be similar if successfully concluded.

This is inevitably a political process, where the text of past agreements strongly impacts future negotiations, and trade officials have strong incentives to adhere to previous drafts that have found political acceptance. To the extent that there is room to feed new information and ideas into the process information, such possibility may be limited to hearing the new demands from the loudest and most powerful lobby groups. There seems to be little room for assessing whether past agreements have achieved their stated goals in terms of actually raising IP standards, addressing challenges that IP-dependent industries may face in a global context, or providing incentives for innovation and creativity, which in theory should be the ultimate goal. In the past, I have argued that a close assessment of the actual impact of the IP chapters of US FTAs on the ground, in trading partners, raises real questions as to the benefits of demanding and achieving detailed and substantive obligations in the US style, without consideration of the particular circumstances that might pertain in a negotiating partner.[60] The IP chapter of the Australia–United States FTA had less pro-IP impact than touted, and led to anti-IP sentiment and some moves to weaken IP rights.

But it is not just the experience of FTAs on the ground that seems to be making little impact. Governments around the world, international institutions, academics and the private sector have all in recent years poured considerable resources into research on the operation and use of IP and IP enforcement systems.[61] As I will argue below, paying attention to this research raises further questions about the wisdom of the approach embodied in ACTA and the US TPPA IP proposal.

11.3.2 The state of knowledge regarding patents and enforcement

In research on patents, three broad questions have arisen: (1) how is the system being used; (2) how much infringement occurs; and (3) how successfully are firms able to enforce their patents? Overlaying all three questions are the big issues: how well is the system working and can it be made to work better?

One thing we do *not* know is how much IP infringement occurs – notwithstanding the billions in lost profits, taxes and jobs alleged by lobby groups such as the International Intellectual Property Alliance ('IIPA') or the Pharmaceutical Research and Manufacturers of America ('PhRMA'). Such claims are tainted by self-interest, some are based on anecdote while many have been criticized for their inflationary assumptions and omissions.[62] In any event, such reports do not tell us whether changes to the IP system proposed in ACTA or the TPPA would actually reduce infringement or, if so, whether IP-dependent industries would make more money.

But there is also a less publicized, but growing, body of independent academic research into patents. Most focuses on the US and the EU, but is relevant to an assessment of IP chapters. These countries have an impact through global litigation.[63] In addition, if patents have benefits anywhere it should be in the US and the EU where IP systems are supported by the rule of law, a bureaucracy not riddled with corruption, and an expert and independent court system.

Contrary to the blithe assumption that more IP means more innovation, the message from this independent academic evidence is very mixed indeed. Patent applications have been rising globally for some time.[64] This has strained patent office resources and squeezed the time that examiners have to consider applications, leading to delays in grant[65] and concerns about patent quality.[66] Nor are rising applications necessarily indicative of more innovation. Engagement with the IP system is highly skewed towards large firms and a small subset of small to medium enterprises ('SMEs'). For example, a 2007 survey of UK SMEs by Rogers, Helmers and Greenhalgh[67] found that only around 2.3 per cent of UK SMEs are IP active, and just under 5 per cent used one or more of the kinds of IP in the four-year period studied between 2001 and 2005. Many patents are also either unused, or used in ways that retard innovation. The PatVal-EU project[68] found that a sizeable proportion of patents (17 per cent) are not used at all, and a further 19 per cent are used only to block competitors.[69] Innovating firms also consistently rate formal IP protection lower than confidentiality agreements and other informal methods in capturing gains from innovation.[70]

There is little reliable information on infringement and enforcement. Because infringement is illegal, it is difficult to get reliable data. Such independent studies as exist, based on surveys of firms and/or inventors, suggest that somewhere between 25 and 40 per cent of IP owners may experience something they consider infringement (whether or not a court would agree).[71] However, many of these issues are successfully resolved or not pursued at all.[72] In jurisdictions that have been studied, between 0.5 and 2 per cent of patents are litigated.[73] One reason for this disparity is that even where apparent infringement occurs, it may simply be not important enough to pursue, or has been settled. Another obvious reason is cost, a problem in patent litigation that, despite years of studies and reforms on both sides of the Atlantic, has not been satisfactorily addressed.

There is evidence that where smaller firms have patents, those patents are important to them. The PatVal-EU study found that 80 per cent of patents owned by smaller firms were used, compared to 60 per cent of patents owned by large firms.[74] This, of course, makes sense – smaller firms are far less likely to register patents routinely. The fact that a small firm is using their patented technology does not necessarily mean that the patent *itself* is improving their position. There is some research to suggest that there is a 'patent premium' (i.e. patents increase the return on innovation);[75] other studies, however, suggest that the impact of IP rights on success of SMEs is minor. UK research suggests that IP-active SMEs are slightly more likely to grow to become large firms, and slightly less likely to have ceased operations.[76] Other US research suggests that smaller inventors realize substantially less value from patents than do large firms.[77] Smaller firms are also more likely to be involved in patent litigation.[78] This is likely owing to a combination of factors: their patents are more important to them, they may be less objective about their chances of success, making settlement more difficult, and they are unable to use large patent portfolios as leverage. In recent times, some of this activity by small firms may be by non-practising entities, or 'trolls' – litigation that may involve attacks on innovative firms by opportunistic actors.[79]

US academic economists, building on these piecemeal studies, made a case that there were serious problems with the US patent system. Jaffee and Lerner (2004)[80] charted evidence that since the mid-1980s patents in the US have become easier to obtain, more likely to be held valid, and more likely to be held infringed. This caused a massive growth in both patents and patent litigation, with the result that valuable technologies and innovative firms became ensnared in a web of patents, licensing negotiations and litigation. They proposed helping the Patent Office issue better quality patents by increasing the information available and making it easier for third parties to challenge patent grants both in the office and in court.[81] Bessen and Meurer (2008)[82] produced figures to suggest that by the late 1990s, owing in part to an explosion of litigation,[83] patents imposed more costs outside chemistry and pharmaceuticals on public firms than benefits. Bessen and Meurer proposed reforms aimed at reducing the patent flood – again by making patents harder to get – and improving patent quality, ensuring that the boundaries of patent rights are easily ascertained.[84] These books along with other reviews of the patent system in the early 2000s were influential: the resulting public concern may have been a reason that the US Supreme Court started taking patent cases again; there have been reforms within the US Patent Office;[85] and the America Invents Act of 2011 was introduced.[86]

This body of research raises important warnings as to what can happen when patents simultaneously become both easier to obtain and stronger. The result is more patents, with many negative effects. The fact that the Chinese Patent Office now receives more applications than any other in the world[87] may be as much cause for concern as it is for celebration.[88]

A different set of questions is raised by the cross-border aspects of patents. Cross-jurisdictional problems or inefficiencies would be of particular interest from a trade perspective, but there is only limited research on patents as they operate across multiple jurisdictions.[89] We know that a significant proportion of applications for trademarks and patents in national offices come from foreign applicants.[90] We know that there is IP infringement that crosses borders (as seizures at the border attest), and that at least some businesses consider IP in other countries to be a significant source of friction (although the proportion of businesses for whom this is a major issue may be less than the public discussion would suggest[91]). Another point of interest is the extent to which patents are litigated in multiple jurisdictions. Anecdotally, we know that some patent disputes resemble a war across multiple theatres. This has been documented in the pharmaceutical industry, but the most spectacular example in 2011–12 was the dispute between Apple and Samsung over patents and other IP rights in tablet computing, which generated litigation in at least ten different countries.

Such duplication is undesirable. It wastes money – re-litigating the same issues sucks up the time of the courts, lawyers and key business personnel. Different outcomes impose inefficiencies on global supply chains if firms are not able to sell the same products across all markets. This applies to both IP-owning firms and alleged infringers. If a patent is invalidated in only some jurisdictions, an alleged infringer may be able to sell in only some markets. Invalidation in multiple jurisdictions creates an additional cost for firms that already face disincentives, because they cannot capture all the benefits of invalidating a patent.[92] There are also costs imposed on societies where patents have not been invalidated although deemed invalid in other jurisdictions.

The extent of duplication of patent litigation is not known.[93] The best (or rather only) estimate we have is Dietmar Harhoff's study estimate of 2008, that between 146 and 311 infringement cases were being duplicated annually in the EU member states. By 2013, this number was likely to increase to between 202 and 431 duplicated cases. On this basis, total private savings would fall between EUR 148 and 289 million in 2013 resulting from access to a unified Patent Court.[94] Although Harhoff's study was focused on Europe, it seems reasonable to assume that similarly wasteful duplication of patent litigation occurs in the Asia-Pacific region.

11.3.3 What does this research imply for (ideal) IP negotiations?

So we know that IP applications are rising, imposing significant burdens on IP offices and leading to delays as well as questions about patent quality; that litigation is increasing; that outcomes of administrative (grant) and court processes are inconsistent; that there is gaming of both systems that in some cases perverts the purposes of IP law; and that infringement is occurring at a not insignificant rate, reducing the incentive effects of the system. There have been arguments that patents in the developed world have been too easy to get and too strong, leading to an explosion of patents and more litigation, and that outside chemistry and pharmaceuticals, patents cost firms more than they benefit. Many procedural reforms have been proposed in developed countries and some have been adopted.

The question is what all this implies for trade negotiations in IP.

The easy answer is nothing – the conclusions are too uncertain. But knowledge of the IP system will always be partial. It is not possible to measure the incentive effect of IP, for example. Economics and the other social sciences are not exact sciences. Policy must be made on the basis of our current knowledge.

A second simplistic conclusion would be that because we have duplicate applications and litigation, the best thing treaties can do is harmonize patentability standards. This could in theory provide efficiencies as patent offices could use each other's examination work and even decisions, and parties could use the outcome of (at least validity) litigation in one country to predict results elsewhere, promoting settlement. Moreover, perhaps patent offices in one country could use invalidity determinations by courts in other countries to invalidate local patents.

This conclusion does not, however, bear close examination. It assumes that efficiencies arising from common standards outweigh any cost. As Jaffe and Lerner, and Bessen and Meurer suggest, however, making patents easier to get (which common standards would do) means more patents – an outcome with significant costs – or would require more resources for more rigorous examination. Harmonizing standards without addressing this potential increase in demand may cause real problems. Nor is it clear that all countries *should* reach the same results on patentability. Some countries may wish to promote other policy objectives by imposing additional patentability requirements – such as disclosure of genetic resources or traditional knowledge used in making an invention.[95] Finally, it is not clear that a treaty can bring about these theoretical efficiencies. Common standards are already found, for example, across trilateral offices, and yet these offices reach different conclusions on patentability.[96] They are also found across Europe owing to the European Patent Convention and yet courts reach different conclusions on validity.[97] Disharmony in outcomes is more a matter of interpretation and application of the standards. It is unlikely that a trade agreement in itself can ever be written in the kind of detail that would harmonize standards; nor is it likely that countries will ever agree, for example, to actually require their offices or courts to reach the same results.[98] Harmonization of standards is more likely to occur through existing informal contacts between patent offices worldwide.[99] Such contacts are not really dealt with by ACTA (which has many provisions on cooperation but is not focused on grant procedures) or by the US TPPA proposal (which does not focus on cooperation at all).

What about harmonization of enforcement, ACTA or TPPA style? ACTA (if a country applies its civil enforcement standards to patents) attempts to harmonize procedures and remedies, and the US TPPA proposal contains many similar provisions without excluding patents. Again, closer examination suggests that this will not assist. First, as noted, the proportion of rights that ever reaches courts is very small, suggesting that alterations to remedies assist only a small proportion of rightholders. Moreover, there is nothing in ACTA or the US TPPA proposal that would address duplication of proceedings or forum shopping. Nor is there anything addressing more basic issues, such as the independence of the judiciary.

A second issue is that ACTA-style, detailed enforcement provisions uncritically adopt US or EU domestic arrangements. This could have some unintended side effects. One, as I have noted elsewhere, is the foreseeable impact of empowering officials (for example customs officers) with significant powers of seizure, determination of infringement and destruction of imported goods in countries still battling significant levels of official corruption.[100] A second, more subtle side effect is that ACTA (and equivalent text in the US TPPA proposal) embodies an 'all services platinum standard' model of courtroom enforcement proceedings, where IP owners can seek preliminary measures (such as injunctions and measures to preserve evidence such as *Anton Piller* orders), obtain information from an alleged infringer regarding the channels of distribution of the alleged infringing goods and a full suite of remedies including injunctions (including against third parties), damages, accounts of profits, costs orders, and orders for the destruction of goods and implements. Such a 'full service' standard is expensive and may not be appropriate for all IP cases or all jurisdictions. More importantly, it could have the side effect of forestalling countries' attempts to address the cost barrier, for example by experimenting with low-cost alternatives for small claims (including low-cost administrative alternatives[101]).

Third, the body of research into patents, and in particular the work of Jaffee and Lerner, and Bessen and Meurer, clearly warns against strengthening patents without first preparing for increased demand for patents and ensuring that quality will be maintained in the face of that increase. ACTA would lead to issues because it is designed to ensure that rightholders can get a full range of remedies in enforcement including provisional measures, increasing incentives to litigate. The US's original TPPA IP proposal would go even further in courting disaster of the kind identified. It would limit the grounds for rejecting patent applications (Articles 8.1, 8.10–8.12); extend the term of a patent if examination is delayed, thus increasing the incentives for hasty examination (Article 8.6); presume patents valid if challenged in court (Article 10.2); allow for treble damages for infringement, giving patent holders a further threat to convince challengers to settle (Article 12.4); and prevent countries wishing to use pre-grant third party challenge procedures to improve the quality of patents (Article 8.7). In short, the US proposes that countries should make it harder to ensure quality patents, make it harder to later challenge those patents and yet at the same time heighten the consequences of infringement. This would create perfect conditions for patent trolling, and the consequences that have so plagued the US system would seem practically inevitable.

Sharp-eyed readers may have noticed something of a gap in this analysis. I have had a great deal to say on what the research tells us an IP chapter should *not* do in addressing patent systems and enforcement. I have spent much less time talking about what a chapter *should* do. This gap, however, reflects not only the fact that criticism is easier than coming up with new proposals – it also reflects the state of our knowledge. As I noted at the outset of this chapter and elsewhere, a truly rational IP negotiation would *start* by ascertaining what real IP-related issues are faced by IP firms trading across borders within the area proposed to be covered by the TPPA or ACTA, and on these points, we simply do not have that research – at least not in unbiased or representative form. Although trade negotiators often consult with industry in the lead-up to and during trade negotiations, they do not conduct objective research that puts any complaints raised in the context of the broader economy. Perhaps another starting point would be to look at what the real barriers to the operation of patents have been in more integrated regions, such as the EU. Recent work there suggests that addressing issues of translation of patents would be one area where work could be done that might actually reduce costs for firms in real and useful ways. But, of course, all that is much harder than going with the laws, and the text, that trade negotiators know.

11.4 Conclusions

We have grown used to hearing that the latest efforts at international IP standard-setting, ACTA and proposals for IP in the TPPA will have a deleterious impact on digital copyright law and on access to essential medicines. We have heard much less about the potential impact on the patent system as a whole – a much less sexy topic, no doubt, but in the long term equally important. As WIPO's statistics suggest, Asian patent offices now account for the largest filing concentration for trademarks, patents, industrial designs and utility models, covering half of all patent applications.[102] In 2011, although the US still received the largest share of patent applications globally (at nearly 25 per cent), the three countries with the next highest proportions were all in Asia: China (nearly 20 per cent), Japan (17 per cent) and South Korea (8.6 per cent); the European Union received 7.6 per cent.[103]

It is perhaps not particularly surprising that the extensive work of academic economists and lawyers into the patent system has made little or no impact on the negotiation of IP in trade agreements. This academic work has faced serious headwinds from vested interests even in the domestic context, with patent reform efforts that started in the early 2000s only bearing (limited) fruit in 2012. As is noted by many, including Yu in his chapter in this collection, and by me in writing elsewhere, there are bureaucratic and institutional pressures that tend to lead trade agreement texts to follow their own trajectory and logic, which are quite divorced from the actual problems that the majority of firms may face in international trade.[104]

Nevertheless, the patent research explored in this chapter suggests that both ACTA and the US TPPA proposal are not likely, overall, to be helpful in addressing the most pressing issues in patent law today; they risk being positively counterproductive, and exporting to the world the US's own 'patent crisis'. The thought of a flood of low quality patents issuing from patent offices throughout the Asia-Pacific region (to the extent that this is not already a problem[105]) should give everyone – including the negotiators of these and future agreements – serious pause.

Notes

1 Associate Professor, University of Sydney.

2 S. Lester, 'Liberalizing Cross-Border Trade in Higher Education: The Coming Revolution of Online Universities', Policy Analysis No. 720, Cato Institute, 5 February 2013.

3 ACTA was concluded in December 2010. At the time of writing, only Japan had ratified the agreement. The agreement will enter into force once six countries ratify it. See Anti-Counterfeiting Trade Agreement, signed 1 October 2011 (not yet in force).

4 This statement is drawn from one of the many ACTA fact sheets published by the negotiating parties in the course of the negotiations. The wording of these fact sheets was agreed between the parties so that consistent documents were issued by all the negotiating governments. For this phrase, see European Union, 'The Anti-Counterfeiting Trade Agreement', 5 June 2008, available at http://trade.ec.europa.eu/doclib/docs/2008/june/tradoc_139085.pdf (accessed 6 August 2013).

5 The Agreement was signed on 1 October 2011 by the United States, Australia, Canada, Japan, Morocco, New Zealand, Singapore and South Korea. Mexico signed the agreement in July 2012. The European Parliament rejected the Agreement in 2012: Inside US Trade, 'Commission Takes Formal Step Signaling No "Realistic Chance" for ACTA', *Inside US Trade* 31(1), 2013. Switzerland deferred signing ACTA in May 2012 pending any further developments in Europe: ibid. ACTA will enter into force when (or if) six instruments of ratification, acceptance or approval have been deposited: Article 40.

6 Enforcement has been described as the 'Achilles heel' of the TRIPS: J. Reichman and D. Lange, 'Bargaining Around the TRIPS Agreement: The Case for Ongoing Public–Private Initiatives to Facilitate Worldwide Intellectual Property Transactions', *Duke Journal of Comparative & International Law* 9, 1998, 11, 34.

7 ACTA Article 9(2).

8 ACTA Article 9(3).

9 ACTA Article 9(5). Legal costs including attorneys' fees are optional under TRIPS Article 45.

10 ACTA Article 11. Under TRIPS Article 47, some more limited information is required.

11 ACTA Article 22. Under TRIPS, members *may* give competent authorities the authority to provide information to right holders.

12 ACTA Article 23(4).

13 ACTA Article 23(5).

14 ACTA Article 23(3).

15 ACTA Article 27; cf. WCT and WIPO Performances and Phonograms Treaty, adopted by Diplomatic Conference 20 December 1996, 36 ILM 76 (entered into force 20 May 2002).

16 A. K. Sanders, D. B. Shabalala, A. Moerland, M. Pugatch, P. Vergano, *The Anti-Counterfeiting Trade Agreement (ACTA): An Assessment*, Report for the Directorate-General for External Policies of the Union, Directorate B, June 2011, 6.

17 Earlier negotiating texts of ACTA, both 'official' and leaked, are collected at https://sites.google.com/site/iipenforcement/acta (accessed 6 August 2013).

18 For more detailed analysis, see K. Weatherall, 'Politics, Compromise, Text, and the Failures of the Anti-Counterfeiting Trade Agreement', *Sydney Law Review* 33, 2011, 229 (hereafter Weatherall, 'Politics, Compromise, Text'); also K. Weatherall, 'ACTA as a New Kind of International IP Lawmaking', *American University International Law Review* 26(3), 2011, 839 (hereafter Weatherall, 'New Kind').

19 ACTA, note 2.

20 For a discussion, see Weatherall, 'Politics, Compromise, Text'; see also P. Yu, 'Six Secret (and Now Open) Fears of *ACTA*', *Southern Methodist University Law Review* 64, 2011.

21 Weatherall, *Politics, Compromise, Text*, above note 18, 237; also Yu, ibid.

22 Weatherall, ibid. at 236; see also Kamperman Sanders *et al.*, op. cit. p. 9.

23 D. Lee, *ACTA: Europe Braced for Protests Over Anti-Piracy Treaty* (6 February 2012) BBC News, www.bbc.co.uk/news/technology-16906086 (accessed 6 August 2013).

24 D. Melvin, 'European Parliament Overwhelmingly Rejects ACTA Anti-Piracy Pact', *Associated Press Newswire*, 5 July 2012.

25 The parliamentary vote on ACTA saw 478 against and 39 in favour, with 165 abstentions: ibid.

26 Joint Standing Committee on Treaties, Parliament of Australia, Report 126: Treaty Tabled 21 November 2011: Anti-Counterfeiting Trade Agreement (Tokyo on 1 October 2011) (2012).

27 A. Capling and J. Ravenhill, 'Multilateralising Regionalism: What Role for the Trans-Pacific Partnership?', paper presented at the Australian Political Science Association Conference 2011, Australian National University, 26 September 2011, 5; see also J. Ravenhill, 'Extending the TPP: The Political Economy of Multilateralization in Asia', paper presented at the Asia-Pacific Trade Economists' Conference, Trade-Led Growth in Times of Crisis, Bangkok, 2–3 November 2009, 24–5.

28 See e.g. Department of Prime Minister and Cabinet, Commonwealth of Australia, *Australia in the Asian Century White Paper*, October 2012, 187; M. Solis, 'Last train for Asia-Pacific Integration? US Objectives in the TPP Negotiations',Working Paper No. 201102, Organization for Japan–US Studies, Waseda University, July 2011, 7; see also I. Fergusson and B. Vaughn, 'The Trans-Pacific Partnership Agreement', Congressional Research Service Paper R40502, 25 June 2010; Meredith Kolsky-Lewis, 'The Trans-Pacific Partnership: New Paradigm or Wolf in Sheep's Clothing?', *Boston College International and Comparative Law Review* 34, 2011, 27.

29 Inside US Trade, 'USTR Seeks to enact ACTA this year, but TPP seen as key new venue', *Inside US Trade* 30(28), 2012.

30 See the leaked US Proposal, *Trans-Pacific Partnership Agreement Intellectual Property Rights Chapter* (10 February 2011), Knowledge Ecology International, (hereafter 'US TPPA IP Proposal'), available at http://keionline.org/sites/default/files/tpp-10-feb2011-us-text-ipr-chapter.pdf (accessed 6 August 2013).

31 For a full analysis of the implications of the US proposal for Australian law, in the area of copyright and enforcement mechanisms, see K. Weatherall, 'An Australian Analysis of the February 2011 Leaked US TPPA IP Chapter Text – copyright and enforcement',Working Paper, Selected Works of K. Weatherall, July 2011.

32 US TPPA IP Proposal, above note 30, Article 4.2. No similar limitation presently exists in the Australia-US Free Trade Agreement: *Australia–US Free Trade Agreement*, signed 18 May 2004, [2005] ATS 1 (entered into force 1 January 2005) ('AUSFTA')

33 US TPPA IP Proposal, above note 30, Article 4.5. In AUSFTA, the copyright term for these items was extended to 75 years (from a previous 50 years).
34 US TPPA IP Proposal, above note 30, Article 2, especially Articles 2.14–2.22.
35 US TPPA IP Proposal, above note 30, Article 10.2.
36 US TPPA IP Proposal, above note 30, Articles 12.4, 12.2.
37 US TPPA IP Proposal, above note 30, Article 14.4.
38 US TPPA IP Proposal, above note 30, Article 15.1.
39 US TPPA IP Proposal, above note 30, Article 4.9.
40 US TPPA IP Proposal, above note 30, Article 15.3.
41 US TPPA IP Proposal, above note 30, Article 16.3.
42 ACTA, above note 3, Article 2.3.
43 ACTA Article 4.
44 ACTA Articles 6.2–3.
45 ACTA Article 6.1.
46 US TPPA IP Proposal, above note 30, Article 10.1. Article 2.2 of ACTA provides that '[n]othing in this Agreement creates any obligation with respect to the distribution of resources as between enforcement of intellectual property rights and enforcement of law in general'.
47 US TPPA IP Proposal, above note 30, Article 8.1.
48 US TPPA IP Proposal, above note 30, Article 8.2.
49 US TPPA IP Proposal, above note 30, Article 8.7.
50 US TPPA IP Proposal, above note 30, Articles 8.10–12.
51 United States Trade Representative, Trans-Pacific Partnership Trade Goals to Enhance Access to Medicines (2011).
52 Ibid. Article 18.8.6(a).
53 Ibid. Article 18.8.6(b).
54 Ibid. Article 18.9.1(a). In addition the Korean Agreement provides for three years' data exclusivity for data relating to a chemical entity previously approved for marketing in another pharmaceutical product.
55 Ibid. Article 18.9.5.
56 The genesis of these provisions is discussed in detail in I. M. Destler, 'American Trade Politics in 2007: Building Bipartisan Compromise', *Peterson Institute for International Economics Policy Brief* Number PB07–5, May 2007. The details of the Agreement may be found in a document entitled 'Peru & Panama FTA Changes', published by the House Ways and Means Committee, available at http://waysandmeans.house.gov/Media/pdf/110/05%2014%2007/05%2014%2007.pdf (accessed 6 August 2013). A more general introduction may be found in a document issued by the USTR, titled 'Bipartisan Trade Deal', May 2007, available at www.ustr.gov/sites/default/files/uploads/factsheets/2007/asset_upload_file127_11319.pdf (accessed 6 August 2013).
57 This is coupled too with a series of other proposals relating to medicines such as the elimination of tariffs on medicines, reducing customs obstacles, taking steps to curb trade in counterfeits, reducing internal barriers to distribution of medicines, and promoting 'transparency and procedural fairness' in the operation of government health care reimbursement programmes: White Paper, above note 51.
58 Inside US Trade, 'US Mulls Strategy on TPP Medicines Proposal in light of Stiff Resistance', *Inside US Trade* 30(17),2012; Inside US Trade, 'US TPP Access to Medicines Proposal Faces Stiff Opposition', *Inside US Trade* 30(11), 2012.
59 For a detailed discussion, see Weatherall, *Politics, Compromise, Text*, above note 18; see also Weatherall, 'New Kind', above note 18.
60 R. Burrell and K. Weatherall, 'Exporting Controversy? Reactions to the Copyright Provisions of the US–Australia Free Trade Agreement: Lessons for US Trade Policy', *University of Illinois Journal of Law, Technology and Policy* 2, 2008, 259

61 This section relies on a survey of patent enforcement research published in K. Weatherall and E. Webster, 'Patent Enforcement: A Review of the Literature', *Journal of Economic Surveys*, forthcoming, 2013.

62 For a slightly old review in the copyright area but indicative of the issues, see Australian Institute of Criminology, *Intellectual Property Crime and Enforcement in Australia*, Commonwealth of Australia, Canberra, 2008.

63 J. Bessen and M. Meurer, *Patent Failure: How Judges, Bureaucrats and Lawyers put Innovators at Risk*, Princeton, NJ: Princeton University Press, 2003, pp. 5–6.

64 World Intellectual Property Organization, *WIPO IP Facts and Figures*, 2012, 12 (noting that in the most recent year for which figures were available, 2010, patent applications worldwide rose 7.2 per cent to 2 million, and trademark applications rose 7.8 per cent to 3.6 million. There was nearly 11 per cent growth in [Patent Cooperation Treaty] applications in 2011: ibid. at note 19.

65 The average time to obtain a patent in the US was 32.4 months in 2012: US Patent and Trademark Office, *Performance and Accountability Report, Fiscal Year 2012*, 3. The European Patent Office website at the time of writing states that the patenting process takes three to five years.

66 According to the OECD, patent quality declined over the decade to 2011: Organisation for Economic Co-operation and Development, *OECD Science, Technology and Industry Scoreboard 2011*, 190.

67 M. Rogers, C. Helmers and C. Greenhalgh, *An Analysis of the Characteristics of Small and Medium Enterprises that Use Intellectual Property* (October 2007), available at www.ipo.gov.uk/ipresearch-characteristics-200710.pdf (accessed 6 August 2013).

68 PatVal EU is a large-scale survey of inventors in the EU.

69 P. Giuri and M. Mariani, 'Inventors and Invention Processes in Europe: Results from the PatVal-EU Survey', *Research Policy* 36, 2007, 1107.

70 R. Levin, A. Klevorick, R. Nelson and S. Winter, 'Appropriating the Returns from Industrial Research and Development', *Brookings Papers on Economic Activity* 3, 1987, 783; W. Cohen, R. Nelson and J. Walsh, 'Protecting their Intellectual Assets: Appropriability Conditions and Why US Manufacturing Firms Patent (Or Not)', NBER Working Paper No. W7552, 2000; A. Arundel, 'The Relative Effectiveness of Patents and Secrecy for Appropriation', *Research Policy* 30, 2001, 611; N. Harabi, 'Appropriability of Technical Innovations: An Empirical Analysis' *Research Policy* 24, 1995, 981; P. Jensen and E. Webster, 'Knowledge Management: Does Capture Impede Creation?', *Industrial and Corporate Change* 18, 2009, 701; Department for Business Enterprise and Regulatory Reform, United Kingdom, *Persistence and Change in UK Innovation, 2002–2006 – Report of the UK Innovation Survey (2007) and Statistical Annex* (2008), available at www.berr.gov.uk/dius/innovation/innovation-statistics/cis/page10957.html (accessed 6 August 2013).

71 For a summary of relevant studies and comments on methodology justifying this figure see Weatherall and Webster, above note 61, Table 1 and surrounding text.

72 K. Weatherall and E. Webster, 'Patent Infringement in Australia: Results from a Survey', *Federal Law Review* 38, 2010, 21.

73 A series of studies of the issue are summarized and discussed in Weatherall and Webster, above note 61, Table 2, and surrounding text.

74 Ibid.

75 P. Jensen, R. Thomson and J. Yong, 'Estimating the Patent Premium: Evidence from the Australian Inventor Survey', *Strategic Management Journal* 32, 2011, 1128.

76 Rogers *et al.*, above note 67. See also P. Jensen, E. Webster and H. Buddelmeyer, 'Innovation, Technological Conditions and New Firm Survival', *Economic Record* 84, 2008, 434; H. Buddelmeyer, P. Jensen and E. Webster, 'Innovation and the Determinants of Company Survival', *Oxford Economic Papers* 62, 2010, 261.

77 Bessen and Meurer, above note 63, Chapter 8.

78 J. Lanjouw and M. Schankerman, 'Protecting Intellectual Property Rights: Are Small Firms Handicapped?', *Journal of Law and Economics* XLVII, 2004, 45; Joshua Lerner, 'Patenting in the Shadow of Competitors', *Journal of Law and Economics* 38, 1995, 463; Deepak Somaya, 'Strategic Determinants of Decisions Not To Settle Patent Litigation', *Strategic Management Journal* 24, 2003, 17; J. Bessen and M. Meurer, 'Patent Litigation with Endogenous Disputes', *American Economic Review* 96, 2006, 77; J. Bessen and M. Meurer, 'Lessons for Patent Policy from Empirical Research on Patent Litigation', *Lewis & Clark Law Review* 9, 2005, 1; G. Ball and J. Kesan, 'Transaction Costs and Trolls: Strategic Behavior by Individual Inventors, Small Firms and Entrepreneurs in Patent Litigation', *Illinois Law and Economics Research Paper Series*, Research Paper No. *LE09–005*, 2009, available at http://papers.ssrn.com/pape.tar?abstract_id=1337166 (accessed 6 August 2013); K. Cremers, 'Determinants of Patent Litigation in Germany', ZEW Discussion Paper No. 04–72, 2004; Weatherall and Webster, above note 72.

79 Ball, op. cit.; J. Allison, M. Lemley and J. Walker, 'Extreme value or Trolls on Top – The Characteristics of the Most-Litigated Patents', *University of Pennsylvania Law Review* 158, 2009, 1; J. Allison, M. Lemley and J. Walker, 'Patent Quality and Settlement among Repeat Patent Litigants', *Georgetown Law Journal* 99, 2011, 677; C. Chien, 'Of Trolls, Davids, Goliaths, and Kings: Narrative Sand Evidence in the Litigation of High Tech Patents', *North Carolina Law Review* 87, 2009, 1571; D. Harhoff, 'Challenges Affecting the Use and Enforcement of Intellectual Property Rights', Research Paper, Strategic Advisory Board for Intellectual Property Policy, May 2009.

80 A. Jaffe and J. Lerner, *Innovation and its Discontents: How Our Broken Patent System is endangering Innovation and Progress, and What to Do About It*, Princeton, NJ: Princeton University Press, 2004.

81 Ibid. Chapter 7.

82 Bessen and Meurer above note 63.

83 The number of patent cases has increased, particularly in the US, although the rate of litigation per patent has not, because there are far more patents now than there were previously: ibid.

84 Ibid. Chapter 10.

85 For example, between 2000 and 2010, the [US Patent and Trademark Office ('PTO')]'s allowance rate plummeted from 70 per cent to 45 per cent, which was viewed by observers as a response to criticisms about the thoroughness of the PTO's review process: M. Liang, 'Chinese Patent Quality: Running the Numbers and Possible Remedies', *John Marshall Review of Intellectual Property Law* 11, 2012, 478, 511.

86 Among other things, the Act introduces post-grant administrative reviews similar to the opposition system in Europe, aimed at providing methods for improving patent quality.

87 World Intellectual Property Organization, *2012 World Intellectual Property Indicators*, 2012, 47–9.

88 Liang, op. cit. Questions are being asked about the quality of Chinese patents.

89 For a review of literature concerning IP in China and its importance to businesses from other countries, see A. Leahy, D. MacLaren, D. Morgan, K. Weatherall, E. Webster and J. Yong, 'In the Shadow of the China-Australia FTA Negotiations: What Australian Business Thinks about IP', *Economic Papers* 27(1), 2008, 2–4.

90 World Intellectual Property Organization, above note 64, 13 (29 per cent of trademark applications and 38 per cent of patent applications worldwide came from foreign applicants in 2010).

91 See Leahy, op. cit., finding that, despite lobby group claims regarding the importance of IP in China to Australian businesses, less than 0.4 per cent of businesses considered the issue 'very important' and 8 per cent considered it 'somewhat important'.

92 J. Farrell and R. Merges, 'Incentives to Challenge and Defendant Patents: Why Litigation Won't Reliably Fix Patent Office Errors and Why Administrative Patent Review Might Help', *Berkeley Technology Law Journal* 19, 2004, 943.

93 Dietmar Harhoff, *Economic Cost-Benefit Analysis of a Unified and Integrated Patent Litigation System, Final Report*, 26 February 2009, 15 (footnotes omitted, but in a footnote Harhoff lists a series of high profile patent cases where courts reached different conclusions on the same basic questions).

94 Ibid. Harhoff's calculations were supported by reference also to a European Commission report on the pharmaceutical sector that found a high degree of duplicated litigation in this space: European Directorate-General of Competition, *Pharmaceutical Sector Inquiry – Preliminary Report*, 2008, available at http://ec.europa.eu/competition/sectors/pharmaceuticals/inquiry/preliminary_report.pdf (accessed 6 August 2013).

95 Inside US Trade, 'US Mulls Strategy on TPP Medicines Proposal in Light of Stiff Resistance', *Inside US Trade* 30(17), 2012; Inside US Trade, 'Peru, N.Z. Still Pushing Traditional Knowledge, Genetic Resources in TPP' *Inside US Trade* 30(10), 2012. China has such a requirement: Liang, op. cit.

96 P. Jensen, A. Palangkaraya and E. Webster, 'Disharmony in International Patent Office Decisions', *Federal Circuit Bar Journal* 15, 2005–06,679.

97 Harhoff, op. cit.

98 The Australia–US Free Trade Agreement IP chapter perhaps comes as close as is possible to this, by requiring that '[e]ach Party shall endeavour to reduce differences in law and practice between the Parties' respective systems for the protection of marks, including differences that affect the cost to users' (Article 17.2.11) and (in Article 17.9.14) that '[e]ach Party shall endeavour to reduce differences in law and practice between their respective systems, including in respect of differences in determining the rights to an invention, the prior art effect of applications for patents, and the division of an application containing multiple inventions'. Even here, however, the obligations are fairly high level.

99 See generally P. Drahos, 'Trust Me: Patent Offices in Developing Countries', Working Paper, Centre for Governance of Knowledge and Development, Australian National University, November 2007.

100 See Weatherall 'New Kind' above note 18, pp. 854–5.

101 Note that if administrative procedures are adopted rather than court, then ACTA Article 7.2 requires that those administrative procedures conform in substance to the procedural provisions of Section 2 (civil enforcement). This could preclude, say, an administrative procedure in which only some pre-fixed amount of damages was available, since compensatory damages must be provided (Article 9.1) and pre-fixed damages must be at the election of the rightholder (Article 9.4).

102 WIPO, above at 14.

103 Ibid. at 17.

104 Burrell and Weatherall, op. cit.

105 Liang, op. cit.

Part V

Science and technology issues and the developing world

12 Discretionary injunctive relief for patent infringement

Partial remuneration after eBay and its implications for the developing world

Richard Li-dar Wang[1]

12.1 Introduction: automatic injunctive relief and the eBay decision

The right to exclude unauthorized use has been characterized as a key component of the owner's rights on property.[2] In the same vein, with regard to remedies for property encroachment, injunctive relief is commonly considered an extension of the owner's right to exclude and is granted almost automatically by the courts when the infringement of the property is vindicated.[3] Intellectual property, including patents, is not an exception in this respect. In the United States, the Court of Appeals for the Federal Circuit – the court that possesses the exclusive jurisdiction to hear patent law cases at the appellate level since 1982 – explicitly held in 1985 that injunctive relief shall be granted as a rule if the disputed patents were infringed, valid and enforceable.[4] Even before the establishment of the court, it was not uncommon for the district courts to grant injunctions in summary judgments when the infringement and validity of the patents at suit were founded.[5]

The rule of automatic injunctive relief for patent infringement was consistently maintained for a couple of decades. Somewhat surprisingly, the Supreme Court of the United States overturned that rule in its eBay decision of 2006.[6] In that case, the Court held that rather than invariably granted, injunctive relief shall be determined at the court's sound discretion and adjudicated on the basis of the four traditional factors in equity. The invention at suit was a business method for operating electronic marketplaces, which is a system for creating or receiving digital images and textual description of a product, and incorporating the two into a data record for presenting the product on the electronic marketplace, and generating an identification code to track that product.[7] EBay Inc and its subsidiary Half.com, Inc operated popular Internet marketplaces, allowing individual sellers to post products and sell them online through auction or at fixed prices. The patentee, MerExchange,

LLC, failed to reach licence agreements with the two Internet operators and initiated an infringement lawsuit against them.[8]

The Federal Circuit ruled for MerExchange, following its general rule and granting permanent injunctions as a relief for patent infringement.[9] The Supreme Court overruled that holding, stating that even though the Patent Act proclaims that 'patents shall have the attributes of personal property',[10] including 'the right to exclude others from making, using, offering for sale, or selling the invention',[11] in the meantime the Act still indicates that '[t]he several courts having jurisdiction . . . may grant injunctions in accordance with the principles of equity to prevent the violation of any right secured by patent, on such terms as the court deems reasonable'.[12] Under well-established principles of equity, the Supreme Court ruled, a plaintiff-patentee has to satisfy a four-factor test for permanent injunctions. The plaintiff must reveal: (1) that it has suffered an irreparable injury; (2) that monetary damages are inadequate to compensate for that injury; (3) that, considering the balance of hardships between the plaintiff and defendant, an injunction is warranted; and (4) that the public interest would not be adversely affected by injunctive relief. The district court has the right to evaluate those four factors and exercises its equitable discretion to determine granting or denying of permanent injunctions, which is reviewable on appeal only for abuse of discretion.[13]

The eBay decision abandoned the automatic injunction rule for patent infringement, and opened the door for reflecting the nature and magnitude of patents' right to exclude and injunctive relief for their infringement. Following this introductory section, Section 12.2 of this essay reviews the case law development in the United States after the eBay decision. Section 12.3 continues to explore relevant patent theories and finds that the eBay case exemplifies the feature of partial remuneration that has been hidden in the patent system. Section 12.4 tries to articulate a better way to adjudicate injunctive relief. Six indicators and the notion of the layered remedy system are put forward. Section 12.5 turns to look at the implications that discretionary injunctions may bring for developing countries. A short remark in Section 12.6 concludes this work.

12.2 The development of injunctive relief in the post-eBay era

In the aftermath of the milestone judgment, lower courts have interpreted the eBay case in divergent ways, yet some general tendencies in applying the four-factor test have emerged so far.[14] In the concurring opinion joined by three other liberal justices, Justice Kennedy candidly indicated that for those patentees that do not exploit the claimed invention by themselves but simply license others to practise the technology (so-called non-practising entities, 'NPE'), monetary damages may be sufficient to compensate the royalty loss of the patentees. Injunctive relief could otherwise provide undue leverage in licensing negotiation, empowering the patentees to squeeze out extravagant fees from companies that seek to practise the claimed technologies.[15] Taking Justice Kennedy's concurrence as a guide, trial courts normally construe the eBay decision as directing them to reject injunctive relief when the plaintiff-patentee is an NPE.[16]

On the contrary, in cases of head-to-head competition, courts usually find that patent infringement causes irreparable harm to the plaintiff, and sustain its request for permanent injunctions.[17] As explained in the *Smith & Nephew* case,[18] the directly competing product of infringers erodes the sales volume and market share of the patentees, and in turn interferes with their ability to establish relationships with new customers. The resulting loss of profits, market share and brand name recognition constitutes injuries that tend to last in the relevant market and are difficult to calculate.[19] The competitive harm is therefore irreparable, and monetary damages may not be enough to compensate for the loss in lieu of a permanent injunction.[20] In fact, a survey on district court decisions from 2006 to 2008 reveals that since eBay, 'with two exceptions, permanent injunctions were issued in all twenty-six cases where courts found direct competition between a plaintiff and the infringer'.[21]

12.3 Liability rule and the strength of patent protection reconsidered: arguing for partial remuneration to inventors

Monetary remedies without injunctive relief in patent infringement cases are frequently associated with the theory of liability rule. In their groundbreaking article in 1972, Calabresi and Melamed put forward their theory of property and liability rules.[22] They divided the modality of protecting economic entitlement into three types. The liability rule means that the state protects the entitlement by way of adjudicating the price for its usage *ex post* after the entitlement is exploited. The opposite modality of protection is the property rule, which demands the user to strike a deal beforehand. Exploitation of the entitlement is forbidden if no prior consent from the owner is secured.[23] Injunctive relief inhibits continued use by the infringers and *ex ante* negotiation are therefore necessary. It plays a crucial role in the enforcement mechanism in support of the property rule.[24]

Since the rise of economic analysis in the field of intellectual property, commentators have been using the framework of property and liability rules to analyse various aspects of patent law.[25] Traditionally, scholarly discussion of the liability rule has centred on the issue of transaction cost.[26] The eBay decision channels the focus of concern instead to the benefit that patents may generate to the public. Some scholars emphasize the patent grant as a quid pro quo in exchange for the inventor's contribution to the public. Based on this rationale, the scope of patent protection and the strength of remedies (including monetary and injunctive relief) upon finding infringement should be proportionate to the magnitude of technological progress and research and development ('R&D') investment that the inventor contributes to the relevant state of the art. In other words, the patent system should refrain from rewarding inventors beyond the extent that he or she benefits the public.[27]

Additionally, Ted Sichelman points out that patents should not be considered as a set of private rights that are created to reward the labour of the inventor or the social value she brings about through the invention. The patent system would be better conceived as a public regulatory scheme.[28] Every aspect of the system should closely track the magnitude of incentive necessary for inducing the specific invention, which could be approximately measured by the R&D cost.[29] Remuneration beyond such a level, even just restoring the patentee to the status quo before the infringement, will be excessive and inadequate. Such supra-optimal remedies would generate redundant patent racing, which may bring about unnecessary deadweight loss and R&D duplication, which therefore is not preferable.[30]

In light of the theoretical reflection in the post-eBay era, the function of the liability rule is no longer limited to alleviating transaction costs. The rule is now instrumental in adjusting the strength of patent protection, so as to avoid over-incentivizing specific types of innovation. Particularly, the denial of injunctive relief could be used to eliminate excessive protection towards certain inventions and bring it back on track with the original goal of the patent system.

The primary goal of the patent system is to incentivize innovation, not to recognize natural rights as we usually do as to real and personal properties. The public needs to provide a substantial amount of benefits to induce and encourage the R&D endeavours of the inventors, but such incentive need not be up to the extent that equates to the value of the invention. Positive externalities are common and pervasive, even in real and personal properties, but the property law has never intended to internalize completely those benefits to the owners.[31] In a competitive market, as a matter of fact, we only reimburse suppliers the marginal costs they spend in producing the goods or services. If that condition has been met, namely the market price set at the point where $MR = MC$, then there would be no undersupply of goods or services, and allocative efficiency could be achieved.[32]

In the patent field, the law just provides exclusive rights for a limited period of time. When the patent term expires, the claimed invention falls back to the public domain and is eternally open to everyone. The protection that the patent system affords to the claimed invention simply covers a portion of its utility value to the public. In essence, unlike real or personal properties, full reimbursement to inventors has never been established as a goal or a reality in the patent world.

Unpatentable subject matters could serve as a good example to illustrate the relationship between patent protection and the R&D cost of the claimed invention. The patent law does not protect certain types of major discovery, such as abstract ideas, algorithms, other laws of nature and physical phenomena,[33] no matter how valuable they are to the human being or how many endeavours it takes to achieve those accomplishments. The reason behind their non-patentability lies either in that the patent protection for such discoveries costs the public too much,[34] or in that no considerable incentive seems necessary for sustaining supply of this type of innovation.[35] This case is a salient instance of partial remuneration in the patent system.

12.4 Proper use of discretionary injunctive relief: from partial remuneration to layered remedies

Injunctive relief is a prominent feature of the property rule that constructs the basic framework of property law. Property rights are typical private rights. According to John Locke, property is a natural right of human beings, which should be kept whole in facing possible harms.[36] If a property right is unfortunately infringed, the right to exclude and the injunctive remedy play a critical role in preventing further encroachment and securing full remuneration for the owner.

As for patents, injunctive relief could cut off the sales of alleged infringing products on the market, and is hence a powerful threat to alleged infringers in negotiation for licensing or infringement settlement. For multi-component products where the cost of switching infringing components to non-infringing ones is very high, injunctive relief could furnish patentees with the ability to demand and attain remarkably higher royalties than they would get through reasonable compensation as the courts may adjudicate in infringement litigations. In this situation, injunctions that are automatically granted would lend the component patentee unwarranted leverage over the whole product, creating an opportunity to hijack the product from the market. Consequently, if the infringing component is insignificant to the consumer's demand and its switching cost is high, granting injunctions on multi-component products is not an advisable remedy in infringement litigation.[37]

Further, we can use denial of injunctive relief as a tool to adjust the incentive that patent law affords to inventors, in order to tailor this incentive more closely to the contribution the inventors bring to society through the patented inventions and the cost actually incurred in the R&D process. Four indicators are suitable for evaluating the inventor's contribution and R&D endeavours:[38] (1) the need for the invention in the normal course of business; (2) the prospect of profits even without patent protection; (3) great upfront investment; and (4) competitors that are trying to develop the invention. In addition, there are two situations under which compensation of actual damages is insufficient to mobilize an adequate amount of innovation activities, and injunctive relief may therefore be necessary;[39] (5) infringement is hard to detect; and (6) the net social welfare of the invention is exceptionally high in relation to the benefits the inventors may retain. Employing those indicators as a guide, we could have a better standard for judging on the granting or denial of injunctive reliefs.

There may be counterarguments that stress the importance of injunctions in preventing possible infringement. The patent law scholarship has nevertheless shown that efficient patent infringement exists under certain circumstances. This is especially true when the infringement eliminates the last few units of monopolistic profits the inventor might obtain through patent protection. The reason is that the last few units of monopoly profits engender the most marginal deadweight loss of social welfare.[40] In contrast, the marginal R&D productivity decreases rapidly when the R&D investment increases.[41] Thus small curtailment of the expected monopoly rent of the inventors may not substantially dampen their incentive to innovate, disclose or commercialize. Even if the incentive were affected, generally it might be offset by the relative gain of social welfare.

Premised on the thought that patent protection should be commensurate with the R&D investment of the claimed inventions, the remedy for infringement should actually be layered to reflect different levels of R&D cost. The layered remedy system may be structured with three levels of relief. Level 1 comprises only monetary compensation for actual damages, and is suitable for ordinary inventions that do not require significant investment in R&D. On the contrary, Level 3 consists of monetary damages and injunctive relief, and is set for inventions in demand of high R&D inputs. The Level 2 remedy is heightened monetary compensation consisting of actual and enhanced damages, which is aimed at redressing inventions of significant R&D cost but not high enough or unsuitable for injunctive relief. The six indicators as put forth above would work here as well, helping to evaluate which level of remedies a valid and infringed patent should enjoy.

12.5 Developing countries and the TRIPS Agreement

Scholarly discussion after eBay brings the public back to the discourse of injunctive relief in the patent law. It serves as a bridge, enabling more public policy concerns to be taken into account under the patent system. Developing countries frequently have more conflicting policy concerns with regard to patent protection. The development after eBay, particularly the change from automatic injunctions to discretionary ones, allowing courts to consider the inventor's actual public contribution and R&D investment in presiding on injunctive relief, could greatly assist developing countries in resolving their problems.

With regard to new innovations, developing countries are typically faced with two kinds of public policy concern. On one hand, developing countries are calling for employing new technologies to meet their societal needs, including igniting economic growth and tackling social problems, such as public health concerns and essential medicine deficiencies. On the other hand, situated in a globalized economic environment, the governments of developing countries have to provide substantial incentive by way of patents to encourage technology transfer, foreign direct investment and domestic technical innovation. As a result, a patent system with at least a moderate strength of protection has to be in place in those countries. In order to accommodate divergent public concerns surrounding individual inventions, discretionary injunctive relief could play a positive role in fine-tuning the strength of patent protection on a case-by-case basis, and make the patent system more tailored to the diverging social contexts presented in various developing countries.

For instance, developing countries could use indicators (1) to (4) and (6) as put forward in the last section to evaluate the benefit that the invention at issue may bring to their domestic society, and gauge accordingly the appropriate strength of patent remedies through discretionary injunctions. In the course of that evaluation, in addition to the technological and industrial development at the international level, the courts of developing countries should keep an eye on their domestic settings. In using indicators (1), (2) and (4) to estimate the possibility that the invention would still come along if not conceived by the inventor, the courts should not only examine the incentive already existing in relevant industries, but also put emphasis on the possibility that the invention might be introduced into their countries. Indicator (6) is a double-edged sword for the developing world. On one hand, extra incentives should be provided for those inventions of which positive externalities are exceptionally high. On the other hand, injunctive relief may not meet the social needs in making use of the same inventions. More focused discussion and nuanced standards thus have to be developed and articulated as to this point.[42]

The TRIPS Agreement has been the most important international convention in the patent field. It establishes the minimum standard of patent protection for all WTO members. In paragraph 4 of the preamble, the Agreement recognizes that intellectual property rights are private rights.[43] Fortunately, the same Agreement still leaves room for discretionary injunctive relief. Paragraph 2 of Article 44 authorizes WTO members to provide only declaratory judgments and adequate compensation as remedies for infringement of intellectual property. Developing countries should leverage the leeway as stipulated in the TRIPS Agreement and make good use of the discretion allowed for injunctive relief. Hopefully that flexibility can help develop better practices of patent enforcement that are more compatible with the social and economic contexts of individual WTO members.

12.6 Concluding reflections

The right to exclude and injunctive relief have been deemed as the most prominent features of patent rights. It was not until the eBay decision of the US Supreme Court in 2006 that the door was opened for discretionary injunctions in patent infringement cases. This chapter has examined the development of case law and scholarly discussion on injunctions in the post-eBay era. Pure monetary relief without accompanying injunctions in infringement cases is normally associated with the theory of liability rule. Since Calabresi and Melamed's seminal article in 1972, scholarly discussion of the liability rules has centred on the issue of transaction costs. The eBay decision channels the focus instead to another important aspect of the patent system, namely the contribution that the patent and its claimed invention may create to the public.

The author finds that the eBay decision illustrates the fact that patents are not private rights that demand full remuneration when being infringed, but rather a tool of incentivizing sufficient innovations to the public. The strength of patent protection towards individual inventions should be closely tailored to the extent that is necessary for maintaining adequate supply of the specific invention. Along this line of thought, the remedies for patent infringement need not redress all the losses that the patentee suffers. They should be capable of recovering for the patentee the R&D cost, but not the whole value that the claimed invention generates to the public. Positive externalities do not need to be internalized and efficient infringement actually does occur in the patent field. By restraining from over-incentivizing, the patent system could ameliorate the deadweight loss resulting from excessive protection.

Discretionary injunctive relief affords excellent flexibility for courts to adjust the strength of patents according to the R&D cost of the claimed inventions. Six indicators were further put forward to assess the necessary magnitude of the incentive to promote specific inventions, which can serve as a useful guide for courts to exert discretion and determine granting or denying of injunctive relief in infringement lawsuits. Those indicators could also help the patent law develop a layered remedy system in proportion to different levels of R&D cost for the claimed inventions.

Typically, developing countries face conflicting policy concerns towards innovations. Discretionary injunctive relief enables those countries to adjust the strength of patent protection on a case-by-case basis, which in turn could help the developing world overcome its dilemma. Such relief for patent infringement is in compliance with the TRIPS Agreement. The same six indicators could further assist courts in developing countries to adjudicate on injunctive relief more wisely and consistently.

Notes

1 Associate Professor and Deputy Director, Institute of Technology Law, National Chiao Tung University (Hsinchu, Taiwan). SJD. 2007, Indiana University Maurer School of Law (US). Email: rcdwie@gmail.com. Many thanks to Miss Tien-hsin Wang for her valuable contribution in preparing this chapter. An earlier draft of this work with the title of 'Liability Rule: A Better Solution for Developing Countries in Promoting and Protecting Innovations?' was delivered at the International Conference on Trade, Science, Technology, and Justice, organized by the Institute of Technology Law, National Chiao Tung University, in Hsinchu, Taiwan, on 1 November 2011.

2 *Kaiser Aetna v. United States*, 444 US 164, 176 (1979); T. W. Merrill, 'Property and the Right to Exclude', *Nebraska Law Review* 77, 1998, 730; Shyamkrishna Balganesh, 'Demystifying the Right to Exclude: Of Property, Inviolability, and Automatic Injunctions', *Harvard Journal of Law and Public Policy* 31, 2008, 593.

3 Balganesh, op. cit. p. 593.

4 *KSM Fastening Sys., Inc. v. H. A. Jones Co.*, 776 F.2d 1522, 1524 (Fed. Cir. 1985).

5 See e.g. *Reynolds Metals Co. v. Cont'l Group, Inc.*, 525 F. Supp. 950, 972 (N.D. Ill. 1981); *W. R. Grace & Co. v. Park Mfg. Co.*, 378 F. Supp. 976, 986 (E.D. Ill. 1974). See also G. M. Sirilla, W. P. Atkins and S. F. Goeller, 'Will eBay Bring Down the Curtain on Automatic Injunctions in Patent Cases?', F. Cir. B. J. 15, 2005, 587.

6 *EBay Inc. v. MercExchange LLC*, 547 US 388 (2006).

7 Consignment Nodes, US Patent No. 5,845,265 (filed July 11, 1995).

8 *EBay*, 547 US at 390.

9 *MercExchange, LLC. v. EBay Inc.*, 401 F.3d 1323, 1339 (Fed. Cir. 2005).

10 35 USC. § 261 (2012).

11 35 USC. § 154(a)(1) (2012).

12 35 USC. § 283 (2012).

13 *EBay*, 547 US at 391–2.

14 See E. D. Munzo, 'Injunctions in Patent Cases After eBay', John Marshall Review of Intellectual Property Law 7, 2007, 44; J. Mulder, 'Note, The Aftermath of eBay: Predicting When District Courts Will Grant Permanent Injunctions in Patent Cases', *Berkeley Technology Law Journal* 22, 2007, 67; Engey Elrefaie, 'Note, Injunctive Relief Post EBay and the Various Applications of the Four-Factor Test in Differing Technological Industries', *Hastings Science and Technology Law Journal* 2, 2010, 219.

15 *EBay*, 547 US at 396–7 (Kennedy, J., concurring, joined by Stevens, Souter and Breyer, JJ).

16 *Amgen, Inc. v. F. Hoffman La Roche Ltd*, 581 F. Supp. 2d 160, 166 (D. Mass. 2008); G. M. Newcombe, J. E. Ostrow, P. E. King and G. N. Rubin, 'Practitioner Note: Prospective Relief for Patent Infringement in a Post-eBay World', *New York University Journal of Law and Business* 4, 2008, 549. Cf. R. J. Schutz and P. M. Arenz, 'Non-Practicing Entities and Permanent Injunctions Post-eBay', *Sedona Conference Journal* 12, 2011, 203 (arguing there are still cases where NPE successfully obtain permanent injunctions).

17 *Transocean Offshore Deepwater Drilling, Inc. v. GlobalSantaFe Corp*, No. 03–2910, 2006 US Dist. LEXIS 93408, at *13 (S. D. Tex. 2006); *Advanced Cardiovascular Sys. v. Medtronic Vascular, Inc.*, 579 F. Supp. 2d 554, 558 (D. Del. 2008); *Power Integrations, Inc. v. Fairchild Semiconductor Int'l, Inc.*, 2008 WL 5210843, at *1 (D. Del. 2008). See also E. Pesses, 'Patent and Contribution: Bringing the Quid Pro Quo into eBay v. MercExchange', *Yale Journal of Law and Technology* 11, 2009; Elrefaie, op. cit., p. 242; Newcombe *et al.*, op. cit. pp. 558–9.

18 *Smith & Nephew, Inc. v. Synthes (USA)*, 466 F. Supp. 2d 978 (W. D. Tenn. 2006).

19 Ibid. at 983.

20 *Wald v. Mudhopper Oilfield Servs.*, No. 04–1693, 2006 US Dist. LEXIS 51669 (W. D. Okla. July 27, 2006); Z4 *Techs., Inc. v. Microsoft Corp.*, 434 F. Supp. 2d 437, 440–41 (E. D. Tex. 2006).

21 D. Ellis, J. Jarosz, M. Chapman and L. S. Oliver, 'The Economic Implications (and Uncertainties) of Obtaining Permanent Injunctive Relief After eBay v. MercExchange', F. Cir. B. J. 17, 2008, 437.

22 G. Calabresi and A. D. Melamed, 'Property Rules, Liability Rules, and Inalienability: One View of the Cathedral', *Harvard Law Review* 85, 1972, 1089.

23 Ibid. at 1092.

24 H. E. Smith, 'Property and Property Rules', *New York University Law Review* 79, 2004, 1719.

25 E.g. R. P. Merges, 'Of Property Rule, Coase, and Intellectual Property', *Columbia Law Review* 94, 1994, 2655; M. A. Lemley and P. J. Weiser, 'Should Property or Liability Rules Govern Information?', *Texas Law Review* 85, 2007, 783.

26 Smith, op. cit. pp. 1720–3; Merges, op. cit. pp. 2655, 2664–7.

27 Lemley and Weiser, op. cit. pp. 784–5; Pesses, op. cit. pp. 336–44.

28 T. M. Sichelman, 'Purging Patent Law of "Private Law" Remedies', 1, 9, 11, 38–9 (San Diego Legal Stu. Paper No. 11–077, 2011), available at http://ssrn.com/abstract=1932834 (accessed 6 August 2013).

29 M. A. Lemley, 'Property, Intellectual Property, and Free Riding', *Texas Law Review* 83, 2005, 1031.

30 Sichelman, op. cit. p. 5.

31 B. M. Frischmann and M. A. Lemley, 'Spillovers', *Columbia Law Review* 107, 2006, 257; R. A. Epstein, 'The Allocation of the Commons: Parking on Public Roads', *Journal of Legal Studies* 31, 2002, S515.

32 Lemley, op. cit. pp. 1046–65.

33 *Diamond v. Chakrabarty*, 447 US 303, 309 (1980); *Le Roy v. Tatham*, 14 How. 156, 174–5 (1853); *Diamond v. Diehr*, 450 US 175 (1981).

34 The courts use the doctrine of unpatentable subject matter to confine the scope of patents to specific applications of a natural rule, rather than covering an algorithm or other law of nature as a whole. *Diamond v. Diehr*, 450 US 175 (1981); *Gottschalk v. Benson*, 409 US 63 (1972).

35 Innovation in business methods demands relatively few investments in R&D. In the Bilski case, the US Supreme Court almost categorically denies the patentability of business methods. *Bilski v. Kappos*, 561 US, 130 S.Ct. 3218, 3228–9 (2010); ibid. at 3255–7 (Stevens, J., concurring).

36 See e.g. J. Hughes, 'The Philosophy of Intellectual Property', 77 *Georgetown Law Journal* 77, 1988, 287.

37 *EBay Inc. v. MercExchange L.L.C.*, 547 US 38, 396–7 (2006) (Kennedy, J., concurring).

38 Pesses, op. cit. pp. 325–6.

39 Sichelman, op. cit. pp. 32–4.

40 I. Ayres and P. Klemperer, 'Limiting Patentees' Market Power Without Reducing Innovation Incentives: The Perverse Benefits of Uncertainty and Non-Injunctive Remedies', *Michigan Law Review* 97, 1999, 985.

41 T. M. Sichelman, 'Quantum Game Theory and Coordination in Intellectual Property', 33 (San Diego Legal Stu. Paper No. 10–035, 2010), available at http://ssrn.com/abstract=1656625 (accessed 6 August 2013).

42 A tentative thought is to distinguish inventions particularly developed for the developing world from the ones primarily focusing on the market in the developed countries, and to treat them in different manners.

43 Commentators have criticized the philosophical underpinning of recognizing intellectual property as private rights – the natural right theory; see A. S. Oddi, 'TRIPS – Natural Rights and a "Polite Form of Economic Imperialism"', *Vanderbilt Journal of Transnational Law* 29, 1996, 415.

13 From science to the law of subsidies

An empirical and political analysis of fisheries international trade

Debashis Chakraborty, Julien Chaisse and Animesh Kumar

13.1 Introduction

Ensuring a vibrant fisheries sector is extremely important for the developing and less developed countries ('LDCs'), as the sector is a major source of income, employment and foreign exchange earnings for these economies.[1] It has been reported that approximately 40 per cent of global fishery production is exported, and nearly half of the international trade is attributed to developing countries' exports.[2] Moreover, the small-scale fisheries play a considerable role in developing countries, unlike their developed counterparts.[3]

Nevertheless, reaping the natural comparative advantage may not always be possible for a developing country/LDC, given the provision of fishery export subsidies from their developed counterparts for the following reasons. First, subsidies to capital or variable costs and other subsidiary activities (e.g. equipment and labour, subsidization of vessels, price supports, etc.) provide unfair cost advantages to the recipients.[4] Second, the huge subsidies provided by several developed countries to their fishing fleets create overcapacity and may lead to overexploitation of the fish stocks in the long run[5] or harmful emissions.[6] This overexploitation may take place in the home country as well as other country waters affected by the transfer of access rights.[7] The evidence from literature indicates that access right transfers may lead to environmental consequences if the home country lacks the requisite regulatory mechanism.[8] Case studies undertaken in this regard have shown that in Senegal and Argentina, environmental overexploitation from access right transfers led to injuries to local fisheries in their own waters.[9]

It has been observed that certain varieties of fisheries subsidy provided in developed countries significantly affect production and trade patterns. For instance, the fishermen in a developed country, aided by access right transfers, fuel subsidies and subsidized fishing gear, would always be privileged enough to catch more fish and market their catch at a lower price, as compared to their developing country and LDC counterparts. The lower price becomes a reality, given the (subsidized) lower marginal cost of operation, which results in overconsumption of fish. On one hand, this trend, unless abated, might lead to the depletion of natural resources.[10] On the other hand, liberalization of the fish trade would considerably benefit the developing countries.[11] Therefore the major focus of the ongoing WTO negotiation on fisheries subsidies, as a part of the Doha Development Agenda (DDA), is to identify and prohibit the subsidies that distort production and trade most. However, the slow progress of the Doha Round negotiations on this front is likely to end up hurting the interest of developing countries.

This chapter intends to analyse to what extent the provision of subsidies in the developed countries affects the market access for major developing country exporters, and is arranged along the following lines. First, a literature survey on fisheries subsidies in developed countries is discussed, followed by the highlighting of key trends in the WTO discussions on the same. Then, an analysis of the fishery exports from developing countries is undertaken, before performing an empirical exercise to analyse the exports of select developing countries in their developed counterparts. For the sake of better comparability, OECD (Organization for Economic Co-operation and Development) data has been used for the empirical analysis.[12] Finally, on the basis of the findings, conclusions on [future] policy considerations are drawn.

13.2 The practice of fisheries subsidies: trends and consequences

The problem of fisheries subsidies became prominent in the 1990s and the increased focus on sustainable fisheries facilitated discussion on this front.[13] Historically, developed countries have supported their local players through various financial transfers. However, recently, a number of developing countries such as South Korea, Mexico and Turkey have also been actively involved in this regard. It is observed from the OECD Factbook (2009)[14] on Government Financial Transfers ('GFTs') that the major subsidy-providing countries are spread across North America (Canada, Mexico and the US), Europe (Belgium, Denmark, Finland, France, Germany, Greece, Ireland, Italy, the Netherlands, Norway, Portugal, Spain, Sweden, Turkey and the UK), Asia (Japan and South Korea) and Australia and New Zealand.[15] As seen in Table 13.1, the aggregate fisheries subsidies provided by these countries have increased from US $6,503.83 million to US $7,117.45 million over 1996 to 2006. Although fisheries subsidies declined in 1998 from the 1996 level, the same has increased in the subsequent period.[16]

The relative contribution of the major subsidy-providing countries in aggregate fishery subsidies before the Doha Ministerial (i.e. 1996–2001) and the subsequent period (i.e. 2002–06) can be observed from Figure 13.1. The relative contribution of Japan went down considerably, while the same for Germany, Ireland, Italy, Norway and the UK declined only moderately. All the other countries witnessed an increase in their share in fisheries subsidies

Table 13.1 Government financial transfers to the fishery sector (US $ Million)

Country	*1996*	*2000*	*2003*	*2006*
Australia	37.39	82.27	95.56	89.99
Belgium	4.97	6.85	1.67	7.76
Canada	545.30	564.50	589.98	591.00
Denmark	85.77	16.32	37.66	113.21
Finland	28.98	13.91	20.23	23.40
France	158.20	166.15	179.74	113.78
Germany	81.57	29.83	33.89	30.74
Greece	52.31	87.32	119.05	79.59
Ireland	112.67	116.67	64.96	29.43
Italy	162.63	217.68	149.27	119.24
Japan	3,186.36	2,913.15	2,310.74	1,985.07
South Korea	367.79	320.45	495.28	752.15
Mexico	14.20	96.90	177.00	89.07
Netherlands	39.93	1.39	6.57	21.35
New Zealand	37.24	27.27	38.33	38.57
Norway	172.69	104.56	139.20	159.52
Portugal	71.85	25.58	26.93	29.34
Spain	246.47	364.10	353.29	425.36
Sweden	62.32	25.19	30.65	41.53
Turkey	28.67	26.37	16.30	133.88
United Kingdom	115.36	81.39	82.69	114.66
United States	891.16	1,037.71	1,290.44	2,128.81
Total	6,503.83	6,325.55	6,259.42	7,117.45

Source: OECD (2009).

in the second period, whereas the increase was considerable for the US and South Korea. In aggregate, over 1996–2006, the provision of subsidy was highest in Japan (40.43 per cent), followed by the US (19.22 per cent), Canada (8.93 per cent), South Korea (7.51 per cent) and Spain (5.58 per cent).

The OECD database classifies fisheries subsidies under four categories, namely: (1) direct payments; (2) cost reducing transfers; (3) general services; and (4) cost recovery charges.[17] It is difficult to classify these subsidies under Article 1 and Article 2 subsidies, as classified by WTO, owing to overlap between categories.[18] The relative importance of these subcategories varies across the above-mentioned countries. For instance, while direct transfers are considerably important in the Canadian fisheries subsidies programme, general services hold a similar position for Japan and the US. It has been noted that in the post-Doha Ministerial period, the proportion of direct payment and cost reducing transfers subsidies in total subsidies has marginally increased vis-à-vis the late 1990s, while the same for general services has decreased.

For most of the countries, the highest proportion of the fisheries subsidies was provided under the general services category. During 1996–2003, Turkey topped in this category (99 per cent), followed by Japan (98 per cent), the UK (90 per cent), the US (89 per cent), France (76 per cent), Norway (74 per cent)

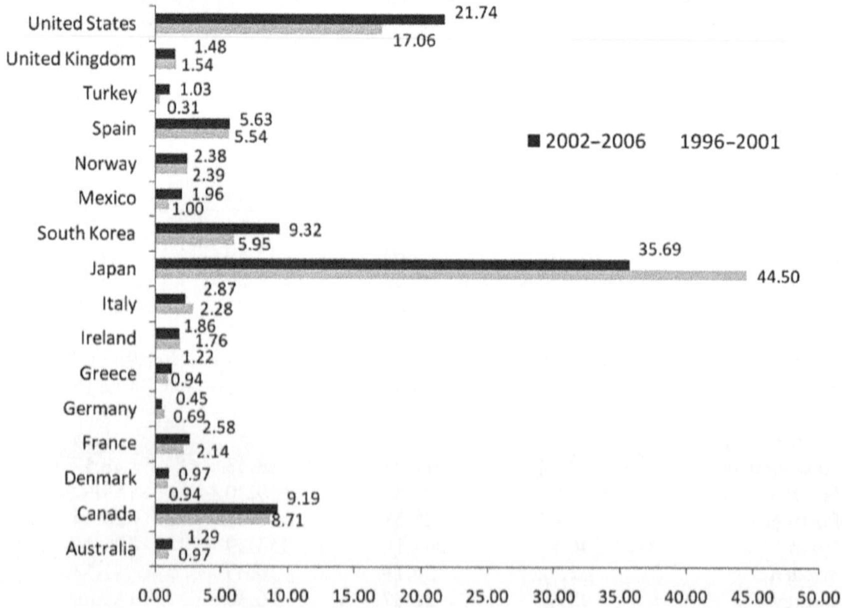

Figure 13.1 Comparing the proportional contribution (%) of the major subsidizing countries before and after the Doha Round

Source: Constructed from data obtained in OECD (2009).

and Korea (66 per cent) etc. On the contrary, the countries providing the lowest proportion of the subsidies as general services included Spain (22 per cent), Australia (32 per cent) and Italy (32 per cent). For the US, Spain, Korea and Canada the subsidies provided under general services increased considerably over this period.[19]

Among the constituents of fisheries subsidies, fuel subsidies play a considerable role. One problem with estimation of fuel subsidies is that the same can be provided both by the central as well as the provincial governments, with potential concerns for underreporting. Several studies have attempted to estimate the actual volume of fuel subsidies. The major fuel subsidy-providing countries include Japan, South Korea, the US, Spain, Norway, Canada and France.[20] It has been observed by the Fishery Centre Research Report (2006) that Japan, Russia, South Korea and Spain are at the top in terms of fuel subsidy outlay provided to high seas bottom trawl ('HSBT') fleets. Given the fact that the HSBT catches are also highest for these four countries, the possibility of overfishing cannot be ruled out.[21] It has been noted that the fuel subsidies in the US did not decline over 1996–2004, but the US continues to provide a huge volume of fisheries subsidies.[22]

The subsidies provided to the fisheries sector in the form of tax exemptions also pose a major challenge. While the major countries providing tax exemptions include Japan and the US, the exemptions provided by Norway, France and South Korea are not significant.[23]

It is to be noted that fuel subsidies and tax exemptions fall under cost reducing transfers, as per the OECD database.[24] Chakraborty and Kumar (2010) state that the level of subsidies under this category increased over 1996–2003 for Canada and Spain, while the same decreased for Belgium, Norway, the UK and the US in the recent period. Italy and Turkey have not provided this particular type of subsidy in the recent period. Looking at the percentage composition of the data, it is observed that the average contribution of this segment in total subsidies at the national level was quite significant in the cases of Australia (67 per cent), Spain (36 per cent), Norway (22 per cent), Korea (15 per cent), Canada (8 per cent) and France (7 per cent).[25]

It has been observed that in addition to the direct subsidies, indirect supports (e.g. access right transfer agreements) might play an equally significant trade-distorting role.[26] For instance, during the early 1990s, the US fleet was paying a low access charge (US $72,000 per vessel) in the Pacific island states, as compared to other vessels (US $250,000 per vessel). The remainder cost of access was paid for by the US government through a US $15 million grant to the host countries.[27] Similarly, in the EU trade agreements with LDCs (so-called European Partnership Agreements (EPAs)), the access fee for the ship-owners generally varies from 25 €/ton to 35 €/ton, which could be highly subsidized.[28] Although access payments might confer a direct benefit to the industry, this concern has not yet featured in any complaint at the WTO dispute settlement body.[29] Presently, access right transfer payments are not considered as subsidies at the negotiations.[30] It has been argued that since access payments are in the form of government-to-government transfer rather than government-to-industry transfer, they constitute indirect subsidies, and hence are non-actionable.[31] Nevertheless, access transfer payments might pose serious challenges for the developing country exporters.

13.3 WTO negotiations on fisheries subsidies: present and the future

Keeping in view the livelihood issues and food security concerns of developing countries and LDCs, the DDA emphasized the need to incorporate their interests by ensuring a fair deal within the WTO framework.[32] Given the importance of the fisheries sector for developing countries, negotiations on this front started subsequently under the wings of the Negotiating Group on Rules, with active participation of developed as well as developing countries.[33] A major focus of the current negotiations is on identifying the harmful subsidies.

Two approaches have been proposed by WTO members at the fisheries subsidies negotiations. On one hand, the 'Friends of Fish' group support a top-down approach that calls for prohibition of all fisheries subsidies barring certain exemptions. The proponents of this standpoint include Australia, Chile, Ecuador, Iceland, New Zealand, Peru, Philippines and the US. On the other hand, Japan, South Korea, Taiwan and the EU favour a bottom-up approach, arguing that all subsidies should be allowed, barring the ones specifically prohibited.[34] Although the negotiation proceeded at a slow pace, a common ground has finally been reached.[35] As a result of the negotiations, a bottom-up approach has been agreed upon instead of the top-down approach.[36] Member countries have broadly agreed to prohibit subsidies on capital costs (e.g. the acquisition, modification or construction of fishing vessels) as well as to restrict subsidies on operating costs (fuel, labour, etc.).[37] The developing countries and LDCs are presently keen to ensure appropriate and effective special and differential treatment for their domestic sectors, particularly in terms of exemptions for small-scale fisheries from WTO commitments.[38] The small and vulnerable economies have also asked for inclusion of a similar provision.[39] It is often argued that the fisheries subsidies question needs to be weighed with the stages of development by differentiating the case of developed countries (suffering from overcapacity) and developing countries (still in the growing phase).[40] The flexibility on this front is of utmost importance for the developing countries and LDCs, given the contribution of this sector in their economy.[41] It is to be noted that, over time, the flexibility promised to the developing and LDC members has been improved:

> [N]ot all fisheries subsidies would be banned, and furthermore the prohibition would be modulated by certain exceptions, general and for S&D . . . the proposed approach to special and differential treatment, and indeed to all of the flexibilities in the text, is different from, and more sophisticated than, typical transitional periods, as it is embedded in the whole structure of the draft. In particular, the subsidies in question have to do with the capture of wild marine natural resources, upon which many people depend for their very survival, and whose survival in turn depends on the proper management of those resources in the long-term.[42]

The negotiations on fisheries subsidies have attempted to finalize the modalities in line with the SCM Agreement. In 2007, WTO tabled a document that attempts to classify the prohibited/actionable subsidies.[43] It was proposed that the production and trade-distorting as well as resource-depleting subsidies fall under the first category. Subsidies under this head include: subsidies aimed at acquisition, construction, repair, renewal, renovation, modernization, or any other modification of fishing or service vessels; subsidies on operating costs of fishing or service vessels (including licence fees or similar charges, fuel, ice, bait, personnel, social charges, insurance, gear and at-sea support) or subsidies to cover operating losses; subsidies to develop port infrastructure or other port facilities exclusively or predominantly related to marine wild capture fishing (for example, fish landing facilities, fish storage facilities, and in- or near-port fish processing facilities); income support for associated natural or legal persons; price support for products of marine wild capture fishing, etc.[44]

On the other hand, the subsidies creating the least distortions on production and trade in the fisheries sector have been permitted. Subsidies under this category include: subsidies for improving fishing or service vessel and crew safety; subsidies for adoption of gear for selective fishing techniques and other techniques aimed at reducing the environmental impact of marine wild capture fishing; subsidies for compliance with fisheries management regimes aimed at sustainable use and conservation; subsidies exclusively for re-education, retraining or redeployment of fish workers into occupations unrelated to marine wild capture fishing or directly associated activities; subsidies exclusively for early retirement or permanent cessation of employment of fish workers; subsidies for vessel decommissioning or capacity reduction programmes, etc.[45] However, an early conclusion of the discussions is unlikely to be reached given the incompatibility of the data reporting practices across countries with the WTO prescribed format.[46]

Presently, there are no legal consequences if a member fails to provide notification of certain fisheries subsidies. As a result, widespread underreporting of fisheries subsidies data to WTO has been noted at times.[47] For instance, the actual subsidy received by US fishing fleets through the capital construction fund,[48] fishing access payments or state subsidies is not reported in detail.[49] A considerable underreporting has been noted in the Chinese market as well.[50] Underreporting of fuel subsidies is also widely prevalent, as evident from the literature.[51] Differential reporting to various international/intergovernmental/multilateral bodies is another observed feature. For instance, the fisheries subsidies data submitted by 12 major subsidy-providing countries to OECD and APEC (Asia-Pacific Economic Cooperation) widely differs from the same provided to the WTO.[52] Hence, the focus of negotiations should cover the issue of transparency and enforcement, including how to deal with subsidies that are not being notified; to what extent notifications should include information about the management conditions of subsidized fisheries; and how rules on notification can be enforced.[53]

The fishery sector was included under the Negotiating Group on Market Access for Non-agricultural Products ('NAMA') sectoral initiative of tariff reform, but subsequently negotiation on this front has been made non-mandatory.[54] While on one hand, several developing countries termed the sectoral initiative to be a violation of the 'Less-Than-Full-Reciprocity' ('LTFR') principle promised in the DDA; on the other hand it is widely held that unless the actionable fisheries subsidies are withdrawn, setting only tariff barriers at zero level will not result in any market access improvement.[55]

13.4 Trend in fishery products trade

While developing countries have considerable interest in terms of fisheries exports, during the late 1990s fisheries imports remained concentrated in a limited number of developed countries.[56] The scenario has not changed greatly in the new millennium. It has been observed that Japan, the US, Spain, France, Italy, Germany and the UK have traditionally been the major importers of fisheries products.[57]

The export scenario can be observed from Tables 13.2 and 13.3. Table 13.2 reports the exports of fisheries products coming under the category HS 3 (i.e. fish and crustaceans, molluscs and other aquatic invertebrates, etc.) for developed and developing countries since WTO inception. Norway, the US and Canada are among the major developed country exporters. On the other hand, China, Vietnam, Thailand, Chile, etc. are among the developing country exporters. From Table 13.3, the major players in the processed fish exports market under [the category] HS 1604 (i.e. prepared or preserved fish, caviar and caviar substitutes prepared from fish eggs, etc.) can be identified. Among the developed countries, Germany, Denmark, Poland, the US and France deserve mention in this category. The leading developing country exporters of this product are Thailand, China, Ecuador, Morocco, etc. It is to be noted that all major developed countries featuring in Tables 13.2 and 13.3 are among the recipients of fisheries subsidies (as reported in Figure 13.1).

The major OECD importers of fisheries products are reported in Table 13.4. It is observed that Japan, the US and several EU counties (e.g. France, Spain, the UK and Italy) are among the major importing countries. South Korea is another major importer of fisheries products. In line with the growing income of the developing countries and LDCs, the share of the OECD countries in both fish products and processed fish products is declining.

13.5 Data and methodology

The main purpose of the econometric exercise is to identify the relationship between the subsidies provided by major developed countries and the fishery exports of select developing countries to their markets. A few control variables are also used in the model. GDP and distance have been incorporated in the model in line with standard gravity model literature.[58] The value of fishery production in the exporting country has been included in the model as a proxy of the domestic conditions. Incorporation of preferential dummy in the model (colonial and regional trade agreements) is important because preferential agreements including GSP (generalized system of preferences) cover approximately 80 per cent of trade in the fishery sector.[59]

The current empirical analysis estimates the following panel data model involving import patterns of 21[60] major fisheries subsidies provider countries over 11 years (1996–2006).[61] The regression model is estimated separately for five developing countries, namely China, India, Indonesia, Thailand and Vietnam, so as to understand whether there has been any impact of fisheries subsidies provided by developed countries on their exports.

Table 13.2 Major exporters of fishery products (under HS 3)

Developed country	*Value (billion USD) of fishery export and % share in world trade*				*Developing countries and transition economies*	*Value (billion USD) of fishery export and % share in world trade*			
	1996	*2000*	*2005*	*2010*		*1996*	*2000*	*2005*	*2010*
Norway	3.11 (11.73)	3.25 (8.69)	4.68 (8.62)	8.51 (11.25)	China	1.74 (6.56)	2.27 (6.07)	4.35 (8.01)	8.81 (11.64)
United States	2.65 (9.99)	2.52 (6.76)	3.46 (6.36)	3.79 (5.02)	Vietnam	0 (0)	1.46 (3.91)	2.44 (4.49)	4.11 (5.43)
Canada	2.02 (7.62)	2.40 (6.41)	3.05 (5.61)	3.32 (4.39)	Thailand	0 (0)	2.27 (6.06)	1.94 (3.57)	2.87 (3.79)
Denmark	1.64 (6.19)	1.48 (3.95)	2.05 (3.78)	2.05 (2.71)	Indonesia	1.58 (5.98)	1.48 (3.96)	1.52 (2.8)	2.02 (2.66)
Spain	1.15 (4.35)	1.30 (3.48)	2.07 (3.8)	2.56 (3.38)	India	1.12 (4.21)	1.37 (3.67)	1.47 (2.7)	2.16 (2.86)
Netherlands	1.06 (4.01)	1.06 (2.82)	1.86 (3.43)	2.21 (2.92)	Chile	0 (0)	1.34 (3.58)	2.22 (4.09)	2.54 (3.35)
United Kingdom	0.97 (3.67)	0.93 (2.48)	1.59 (2.93)	1.92 (2.54)	Korea, Rep.	1.08 (4.07)	1.06 (2.83)	0.84 (1.54)	1.40 (1.85)
France	0.81 (3.06)	0.79 (2.12)	1.27 (2.34)	1.29 (1.7)	Argentina	0.95 (3.57)	0.82 (2.2)	0.78 (1.44)	1.31 (1.73)
Sweden	0.19 (0.71)	0.38 (1.02)	1.06 (1.96)	2.47 (3.27)	Russian Federation	0 (0)	0.32 (0.86)	0.46 (0.84)	2.16 (2.86)
Iceland	0 (0)	0.95 (2.54)	1.47 (2.71)	1.62 (2.15)	Ecuador	0.72 (2.72)	0.35 (0.93)	0.54 (0.98)	1.09 (1.45)
Germany	0.59 (2.25)	0.58 (1.55)	0.92 (1.69)	1.31 (1.73)	Mexico	0.68 (2.56)	0.63 (1.7)	0.56 (1.04)	0.65 (0.85)
Australia	0.74 (2.79)	0.88 (2.36)	0.85 (1.57)	0.85 (1.12)	Malaysia	0 (0)	0.27 (0.72)	0.52 (0.96)	0.70 (0.92)

Note: Ranking on the basis of sum of values from 1996 to 2010.
Source: Calculated by the authors from WITS data.

Table 13.3 Major exporters of processed fishery products (HS 1604)

Developed country	*Value (million USD) of fishery export and % share in world trade*				*Developing country*	*Value (million USD) of fishery export and % share in world trade*			
	1996	*2000*	*2005*	*2010*		*1996*	*2000*	*2005*	*2010*
Germany	323.69 (8.23)	269.78 (5.59)	486.39 (5.83)	609.68 (5.26)	China	954.02 (24.26)	933.76 (19.34)	1,331.12 (15.95)	2,042.04 (17.63)
Spain	213.02 (5.42)	282.08 (5.84)	415.93 (4.98)	577.29 (4.98)	Thailand	0 (0)	713.68 (14.78)	1,468.92 (17.6)	2,410.58 (20.81)
Denmark	273.52 (6.96)	200.97 (4.16)	314.54 (3.77)	332.49 (2.87)	Ecuador	150.31 (3.82)	213.26 (4.42)	433.47 (5.19)	598.27 (5.17)
United States	214.32 (5.45)	208.95 (4.33)	274.98 (3.3)	307.4 (2.65)	Morocco	0 (0)	0 (0)	408.54 (4.9)	589.96 (5.09)
France	136.14 (3.46)	227.44 (4.71)	204.02 (2.45)	170.38 (1.47)	Korea, Rep.	274.44 (6.98)	209.05 (4.33)	98.29 (1.18)	83.76 (0.72)
Poland	59.97 (1.53)	51.79 (1.07)	165.99 (1.99)	360.56 (3.11)	Indonesia	80.79 (2.05)	90.04 (1.86)	134.26 (1.61)	213.96 (1.85)
Canada	151.58 (3.85)	138 (2.86)	131.24 (1.57)	119.67 (1.03)	Philippines	0 (0)	68.1 (1.41)	74.22 (0.89)	253.95 (2.19)
Italy	63.17 (1.61)	73.27 (1.52)	146.5 (1.76)	179.18 (1.55)	Mauritius	0 (0)	35.45 (0.73)	107.29 (1.29)	245.06 (2.12)
Portugal	107.17 (2.73)	79.21 (1.64)	109.2 (1.31)	163.42 (1.41)	Chile	0 (0)	98.15 (2.03)	148.32 (1.78)	69.05 (0.6)
Japan	98.87 (2.51)	93.27 (1.93)	99.97 (1.2)	138.52 (1.2)	Vietnam	0 (0)	6.15 (0.13)	86.17 (1.03)	211.87 (1.83)
Netherlands	91.72 (2.33)	72.66 (1.5)	81.51 (0.98)	165.77 (1.43)	Lithuania	0 (0)	16.4 (0.34)	89.82 (1.08)	191.25 (1.65)
Sweden	89.89 (2.29)	64.63 (1.34)	73.95 (0.89)	140.16 (1.21)	Malaysia	0 (0)	36.48 (0.76)	54.82 (0.66)	65.41 (0.56)
United Kingdom	98.35 (2.5)	77 (1.59)	87.97 (1.05)	85.15 (0.74)	India	1.17 (0.03)	1.69 (0.03)	33.72 (0.4)	64.19 (0.55)

Note: Ranking on the basis of sum of values from 1996 to 2010.
Source: Calculated by the authors from WITS data.

Table 13.4 Major OECD importers of fishery products

OECD country	*Value (million USD) of fishery import and % share in world trade (HS 3)*				*OECD country*	*Value (million USD) of fishery import and % share in world trade (HS 1604)*			
	1996	*2000*	*2005*	*2010*		*1996*	*2000*	*2005*	*2010*
All OECD members	36,926.66 (91.57)	39,999.4 (86.61)	50,849.04 (81.39)	62,061.43 (74.73)	All OECD members	5,159.81 (92.7)	5,036.7 (88.45)	7,284.98 (85.67)	9,301.93 (80.18)
Japan	14,247.65 (35.33)	12,805.5 (27.73)	11,537.94 (18.47)	11,623.82 (14.00)	Japan	1,617 (29.05)	1,552.49 (27.26)	1,385.18 (16.29)	1,417.82 (12.22)
United States	5,954.12 (14.76)	8,593.46 (18.61)	9,929.23 (15.89)	11,824.59 (14.24)	United States	525.24 (9.44)	637.81 (11.2)	1,066.09 (12.54)	1,442.39 (12.43)
Spain	2,885.39 (7.15)	3,178.2 (6.88)	5,242.57 (8.39)	5,679.84 (6.84)	France	591.13 (10.62)	440.2 (7.73)	689.89 (8.11)	855.07 (7.37)
France	2,456.42 (6.09)	2,329.2 (5.04)	3,571.07 (5.72)	4,643.72 (5.59)	United Kingdom	537.89 (9.66)	453.07 (7.96)	659.17 (7.75)	874.78 (7.54)
Italy	2,114.29 (5.24)	2,058.59 (4.46)	3,395.26 (5.43)	4,165.93 (5.02)	Italy	355.65 (6.39)	388.46 (6.82)	799.96 (9.41)	978.06 (8.43)
Germany	1,861.09 (4.61)	1,589.25 (3.44)	2,453 (3.93)	3,449.61 (4.15)	Germany	415.96 (7.47)	350.83 (6.16)	575.31 (6.77)	608.35 (5.24)
Korea, Rep.	879.94 (2.18)	1,229.9 (2.66)	2,030.07 (3.25)	2,775.16 (3.34)	Spain	143.35 (2.58)	143.24 (2.52)	342.83 (4.03)	597.67 (5.15)
United Kingdom	1,050.01 (2.6)	1,299.15 (2.81)	2,089.97 (3.35)	2,255.6 (2.72)	Canada	154.3 (2.77)	160.27 (2.81)	217.01 (2.55)	291.28 (2.51)
Sweden	428.54 (1.06)	554.11 (1.2)	1,349.03 (2.16)	2,923.55 (3.52)	Australia	124.28 (2.23)	120.66 (2.12)	208.1 (2.45)	336.18 (2.9)
Canada	873.52 (2.17)	1,095.29 (2.37)	1,230.09 (1.97)	1,606.65 (1.93)	Netherlands	102.16 (1.84)	131.27 (2.31)	150.88 (1.77)	223.71 (1.93)
Denmark	965.33 (2.39)	927.64 (2.01)	1,264.13 (2.02)	1,397.83 (1.68)	Belgium	–	113.49 (1.99)	164.05 (1.93)	233.35 (2.01)

Note: Ranking on the basis of sum of values from 1996 to 2010.
Source: Calculated by the authors from WITS data.

$$FEX_{it} = \alpha_i + \beta_1 GDP_{it} + \beta_2 DIST_i + \beta_3 FSUB_{it} + \beta_4 VFP_{it} + \beta_5 P_{it} + D_{COL} + D_{RTA} + \varepsilon_{it} \quad (1)$$

where,

α_i	is unobserved specific effects in country *i*
β	represents the estimated coefficients of independent
FEX_{it}	is the real value of fishery exports from the developing country/LDC to country *i* in year *t*
GDP_{it}	is the real GDP of the importing country *i* in year *t*
$DIST_i$	is the distance between the two largest or capital cities of the exporting country and country *i*
$FSUB_{it}$	is the real value of fisheries subsidies provided by the importing country *i* in year *t*
VFP_{it}	is the real value of fishery production in the exporting country in year *t*
P_{it}	is the ratio of Consumer Price Index (CPI) in the exporting country to the same for the importing country *i* in year *t*
D_{COL}	is a dummy that takes a value 1 if the exporting country and the importing country *i* have colonial linkages and 0 otherwise
D_{RTA}	is a dummy that takes a value 1 if the exporting country and the importing country *i* have regional / preferential trade agreements and 0 otherwise
ε_{it}	is an error term.

The annual data on fishery exports from developing countries were accessed from the WITS (World Integrated Trade Solution) database.[62] The GDP values of the importing countries and consumer price indices were accessed from the World Economic Outlook Database of the International Monetary Fund.[63] The data on distance was obtained from relevant websites.[64] Owing to the problem of non-comparability in the fisheries subsidies data obtained from individual countries, the current study undertakes the empirical analysis on the basis of the data reported by OECD (2009). OECD (2009) reports the data under four categories, namely: 'direct payments', 'cost reducing transfers', 'general services' and 'cost recovery charges'. For the purpose of the current analysis, the summation of subsidies under all headings is considered. The data on value of fishery production in the exporting country is obtained from the Fisheries and Aquaculture Department of Food and Agriculture Organization ('FAO'), United Nations. The value was obtained by summing the production figure of seven major categories, viz. Crustacea (2,765); Demersal Fish (2,762); Freshwater Fish (2,761); Marine Fish, Other (2,764); Molluscs, Other (2,767); Pelagic Fish (2,763) and Fish, Seafood (2,960).[65] D_{COL} and D_{RTA} and are generated whenever applicable.

13.6 Empirical results

The panel data regression analysis has been undertaken with help of the STATA software (version 10.1). To understand the working of the model for proposed relationship in equation (1), the Hausman specification test is first conducted, on the basis of which a Generalized Least Square random effect model is estimated. The heteroskedasticity and autocorrelation-corrected regression results for the five countries have been summarized in Table 13.5. It is observed from the table that GDP of the importing country has been influencing the fisheries imports positively, while the distance between the exporting and the importing country generally bears a negative influence. For China and India, the coefficient of fisheries production term is positive, which indicates that export increases when domestic production rises. However, in the case of Thailand, a negative coefficient is noted. The price ratio is found to be positive and significant in case of China and Vietnam. The colonial linkage and RTA dummy is found to be significant in certain cases.

One interesting feature is that the fisheries export of developing countries is not found to be negatively related to the fisheries subsidies provided by the developed countries. In fact for Thailand and Vietnam, the relevant coefficients are found to be positive and significant. The seemingly counterintuitive result originates from the fact that over the study period, the fisheries export of the selected countries has increased considerably towards the developed countries such as the US and the UK, in line with their growing demand potential (reflected through their GDP). It has earlier been noted that the OECD countries, despite providing fisheries subsidies, happens to be major importers of fisheries products. The result indicates that price disadvantage owing to subsidies has so far not been a major factor influencing fishery exports from the selected developing countries. Another explanation can be that the current study considers the overall fisheries subsidies data, in the absence of long-run time-series data on Article 1 (i.e. actionable subsidies) in target economies. In other words, overall fisheries subsidies being provided in the developed country markets has not been strictly impeding market access for developing countries in their domestic markets. However, the developed country subsidies may still adversely influence their exports to other developing countries, which can be an area of future research.

Table 13.5 Regression results on the relationship between fisheries subsidies and imports in developed countries

Dependent variables	*Independent variable: bilateral fishery exports*				
	China	*India*	*Indonesia*	*Thailand*	*Vietnam*
Constant	–149,141.50	–10,655.26	5,455.56	2,970.69	36,206.53
	(64,356.94) **	(4,144.92) **	(5,712.17)	(47,351.09)	14,256.37 **
GDP (importer)	57.2534	22.1189	27.1568	43.3017	43.0216
	(5.8146) ***	(2.5178) ***	(3.0678) ***	(43.3017) ***	(6.0773) ***
Bilateral distance	–18.0416	0.1861	–1.3204	–1.1565	–8.2756
	(5.7941) ***	(0.4014)	(0.3508) ***	(1.3439)	(0.9649) ***
Fishery subsidy	0.0338	–0.0007	–0.0034	0.0577	0.0455
(importer)	(0.0289)	(0.0053)	(0.0045)	(0.0110) ***	(0.0108) ***
Fishery production	0.0035	0.0008	0.0004	–0.0140	–0.0004
(exporter)	(0.0005) ***	(0.0004) *	(0.0006)	(0.0038) ***	(0.0012)
Price ratio	69,119.77	–123.3741	148.41	44,712.08	38,728.30
	(35,715.47) **	(120.6169)	(2,377.24)	(36,738.67)	(13,870.48) ***
Col dummy	40,284.28	18,680.36	8,882.31		dropped
	(9,739.65) ***	(5,188.36) ***	(12,665.77)	–	
RTA dummy	–4,588.36	dropped	–3,778.68	2,195.02	35,753.29
	(16,772.06)		(3,235.51)	(10,229.29)	(14,522.51) **
Number of observations	163	207	173	110	96
Number of groups	15	19	16	14	14
F-statistics	347.44	366.99	153.27	157.72	254.31
Prob > chi[2]	0.00	0.00	0.00	0.00	0.00

Notes: Figure in the parenthesis shows the heteroskedastic and panel-specific AR(1) corrected standard error of the estimated coefficient.
***, ** and * implies estimated coefficient is significant at 0.01, 0.05 and 0.10 level respectively.

13.7 From science to subsidies: policy implications for international trade of fisheries

The fishery exports from the developing countries are presently suffering from several problem areas. It is widely reported from the literature that narrow self-interest driven motivations are leading to lobbying for supports to the fishery sector in developed countries, thereby causing continuation of the subsidies.[66] In addition to the fisheries subsidies, stringent SPS and TBT standards act as significant barriers on the fisheries exports of developing countries.[67] In particular, the regulations on 'trade in endangered species, labeling of origin, traceability, chain of custody, and zero tolerance for certain veterinary drug residues' in developed countries are quite stringent.[68] The negotiations on fisheries subsidies have so far concentrated on the separation of the Article 1 and Article 2 subsidies from the support policies of the countries. Similarly negotiations are going on in appropriate forums to tackle the problems associated with product and process-related standards on marine products.

In this background, the findings of the present analysis have important policy considerations for both developed and developing countries. First, the absence of the negative relationship between fishery exports from developing countries and subsidies provided by developed countries show that there exist considerable export prospects for these economies. The empirical result indicates that the growing demand in developed countries can accommodate competition from the developing countries.

The analysis underlines the need for reform of fisheries subsidies in developed countries in no uncertain terms. Moreover, the trend indicates that the recent economic crisis in the OECD countries would bear adverse consequences for fisheries exports from developing countries, and the pressure on their developed counterparts to reform support measures would intensify.[69] Second, the subsidy measures in the developed countries are not having any major trade-distorting effect but simply a protectionist mechanism for local players. It can be argued that the 'overcapacity' effect in the recipient countries is actually hurting their ability to benefit from the support measures. Although reform measures are being rolled out in recent years,[70] a more proactive approach from developed countries is expected in the coming future.

Finally, given the slow progress of the fisheries subsidies reforms, the mutual recognition of standards on this sector must be fast-tracked at multilateral and other forums so as to facilitate the developing country exports further. This initiative will provide considerable respite to the fisheries exports from developing counties, until the conclusion of the fisheries subsides negotiations.

Notes

1 See World Bank, Food and Agriculture Organization and World Fish Center, 'The Hidden Harvests: The Global Contribution of Capture Fisheries', Washington, DC: Agriculture and Rural Development Department, Sustainable Development Network, 2010; M. O. Haughton, 'Fisheries Subsidy and the Role of Regional Fisheries Management Organisations: The Caribbean Experience', available at www.unep.ch/etu/Fisheries%20Meeting/submittedPapers/MiltonHaughton.pdf (accessed 9 March 2012).

2 C. Dommen and C. Deere, 'Fish for Thought: Fisheries, International Trade and Sustainable Development', International Trade and Sustainable Development Series No. 1, Geneva: ICTSD and IUCN, 1999.

3 World Bank, FAO and World Fish Center (2010), op. cit.

4 A. Ekaterina, 'Rescuing the Inexhaustible . . . The Issue of Fisheries Subsidies in the International Trade policy', *Journal of International Commercial Law and Technology* 3(3), 2008, 147–56.

5 It has been reported at times that the current size of the global fishing fleet is much larger than the sustainable limit. For details, see World Wildlife Fund, 'Underwriting Overfishing', WWF Briefing Note, available at www.worldwildlife.org/what/globalmarkets/fishing/WWFBinaryitem8633.pdf (accessed 6 March 2012).

6 A. Gunnar, 'Fuel subsidies and CO_2 emissions in the fishing fleet', *Norges Naturvernforbund*, Norway: Friends of the Earth, 2008.

7 Developing countries/LDCs generally export the fish caught by their domestic fleets operating within their own Exclusive Economic Zones ('EEZs'). However, a developed country (e.g. the EU, Japan and the US) might obtain the right for their fishing fleets to access the EEZ of the LDC for an agreed period of time in return of financial contributions. Such entry of developed country fleets in developing country/LDC waters might lead to overfishing, with environmental repercussions.

8 See V. M. Kaczynski and D. L. Fluharty, 'European Policies in West Africa: Who Benefits from Fisheries Agreements?', *Marine Policy* 26, 2002, 75–93; M. Milazzo, 'Subsidies in World Fisheries: A Re-examination', *World Bank Technical Paper* No. 406, Fisheries Series, Washington, DC: The World Bank, 1998; S. M. Mwikya, 'Fisheries Access Agreements: Trade and Development Issues', International Trade and Sustainable Development Series Issue Paper No. 2, Geneva: ICTSD, 2006.

9 United Nations Environment Programme ('UNEP'), 'Fisheries Subsidies and Marine Resource Management: Lessons learned from Studies in Argentina and Senegal', Nairobi: UNEP, 2003.

10 P. Gareth, 'Fisheries Subsidies, Overfishing and Trade', Washington DC, available at www.bdix.net/sdnbd_org/world_env_day/2001/sdnpweb/issues/environment/article/1.pdf (accessed 10 March 2012).

11 A. Tallontire, 'Trade Issues Background Paper: The Impact of Subsidies on Trade in Fisheries Products', Project PR 26109, 2004, Food and Agriculture Organization of the United Nations, Rome.

12 See D. Chakraborty and A. Kumar, 'Implications of Fishery Sector Subsidies: A Review of Issues in light of WTO Negotiations', Centre for WTO Studies Discussion Paper No. 7, New Delhi: Indian Institute of Foreign Trade, 2010.

13 'By the late 1990s, the World Bank, the OECD and others had issued studies estimating that the magnitude of subsidies to the fisheries sector was enormous, and highlighting the potential of those subsidies to contribute to overcapacity and overfishing.' Statement by the Chairman at the Informal Open-Ended Meeting with Senior Officials at the Rules Negotiating Group, WTO, 2009.

14 Organization for Economic Co-operation and Development (2009), *OECD Fact Book 2009: Economic, Environmental and Social Statistics*, Paris: OECD.

15 D. Chakraborty, J. Chaisse and A. Kumar (2011), 'Doha Round Negotiations on Subsidy and Countervailing Measures: Potential Implications on Trade Flows in Fishery Sector', *Asian Journal of WTO & International Health Law and Policy* 6(1), pp. 201–34, 2011.
16 See Chakraborty and Kumar (2010), op. cit.
17 Organization for Economic Co-operation and Development (2006), *Financial Support to Fisheries: Implications for Sustainable Development*, Paris: OECD.
18 See Chakraborty and Kumar (2010), op. cit.
19 See Chakraborty and Kumar (2010), op. cit.
20 See A. Khan, U. R. Sumaila, R. Watson, G. Munro, and D. Pauly. (2006), 'The Nature and Magnitude of Global Non-fuel Fisheries Subsidies', in U. R. Sumaila and D. Pauly (eds), *Catching More Bait: A Bottom-up Re-estimation of Global Fisheries Subsidies*, pp. 5– 37, 14(6), Fisheries Centre Research Reports, 2nd edn, Vancouver: University of British Columbia; U. R. Sumaila and D. Pauly (2006) (eds), *Catching More Bait: A Bottom-up Re-estimation of Global Fisheries Subsidies*, 14(6), Fisheries Centre Research Reports, 2nd edn, Vancouver: University of British Columbia.; P. Tyedmers, R. Watson and D. Pauly, 'Fuelling global fishing fleets', *Ambio*. 34, 2005, 59–62.
21 Fisheries Economics Research Unit ('FERU') online database, op. cit.
22 R. Sharp and U. R. Sumaila, 'Quantification of US Marine Fisheries Subsidies', *North American Journal of Fisheries Management* 29, 2009,18–32.
23 SFisheries Economics Research Unit, 'Global Fisheries Economies: Sea Around Us Project', Vancouver: University of British Columbia, available at www. seaaroundus. org/sponsor/feru.aspx (accessed at 14 January, 2013); Sumaila and Pauly (2006), op cit.
24 A. Cox and C. Schmidt, 'Subsidies in the OECD Fisheries Sector: A Review of Recent Analysis and Future Directions', Paris: Directorate of Agriculture, food and fisheries, OECD, 2002.
25 See Chakraborty and Kumar (2010), op. cit.
26 S. David, 'Healthy Fisheries, Sustainable Trade', Washington, DC: World Wildlife Fund, 2004.
27 United Nations Environment Programme, 'Analyzing the Resource Impact of Fisheries Subsidies: A Matrix Approach', Geneva: Economics and Trade Branch, UNEP, 2004.
28 See Chakraborty and Kumar (2010), op. cit.
29 M. A. Orellana, 'Towards Sustainable Fisheries Access Agreements: Issues and Options at the World Trade Organization', Commissioned by United Nations Environment Programme, Geneva: Economics and Trade Branch, UNEP, 2008.
30 WTO, 'Draft Consolidated Chair Texts of the AD and SCM Agreements', WTO Document No. TN/RL/W/213, dated 30 November 2007, Geneva.
31 G. Porter, 'The Euro-African Fishing Agreements: Subsidizing Over-fishing in African Waters', Background Paper for UNEP/WWF Workshop, 1997.
32 WTO, 'Doha Ministerial Declaration', adopted on 14 November 2001, Geneva, available at www.wto.org/english/thewto_e/minist_e/min01_e/mindecl_e.htm (accessed 10 September 2009).
33 See D. Chakraborty, J. Chaisse and A. Kumar, 'Doha Round Negotiations on Subsidy and Countervailing Measures: Potential Implications on Trade Flows in Fishery Sector', *Asian Journal of WTO & International Health Law and Policy* 6(1), 2011, 201–34, for detailed discussions of the negotiations.
34 OECD, 'Fishing for Coherence: Proceedings of the Workshop on Policy Coherence for Development in Fisheries', Paris, 2006.
35 M. Wall and D. Vis-Dunbar, 'The Standstill in Subsidies Update', Manitoba: International Institute for Sustainable Development, 2005.
36 L. Campling, 'FFA Fisheries Trade Briefing', 2008.

37 Department for International Development, 'Fisheries subsidies and the WTO Negotiations', Policy Brief No. 9, London: Marine Resources Assessment Group Ltd, DFID, 2009.

38 WTO, Negotiating Group on Rules, 'Fisheries Subsidies – Communication from Brazil, China, Ecuador, Mexico and Venezuela', WTO Document No. TN/RL/W/241/Rev.1, dated 16 October 2009, Geneva.

39 WTO, Negotiating Group on Rules, 'Fisheries Subsidies – Communication from Barbados', WTO Document No. TN/RL/W/242, dated 7 October 2009, Geneva, at 3.

40 G. Porter, 'Fisheries Subsidies and Overfishing: Towards a Structured Discussion', paper presented at the UNEP Fisheries Workshop, Geneva, 12 February 2001.

41 WTO, Negotiating Group on Rules, 'Fisheries Subsidies – Communication from Argentina, Australia, Chile, Colombia, the United States, New Zealand, Norway, Iceland, Peru and Pakistan', WTO Document No. TN/RL/W/243, dated 7 October 2009, Geneva.

42 See WTO, 'Statement by the Chairman at the Informal Open-Ended Meeting with Senior Officials at the Rules Negotiating Group', WTO Document No. TN/RL/W/246, dated 27 November 2009, Geneva.

43 WTO, 'Draft Consolidated Chair Texts of the AD and SCM Agreements', WTO Document No. TN/RL/W/213, dated 30 November 2007, Geneva.

44 For details, see Article 1 of WTO (2007).

45 For details, see Article 2 of WTO (2007).

46 See Chakraborty *et al.* (2011), op. cit., for a detailed discussion on the data incompatibility.

47 The fisheries subsidies provided by various countries in 2000 are a case in point. See OECD (2006), op. cit.; OECD, *OECD Fact Book 2009: Economic, Environmental and Social Statistics*, Paris: OECD, 2009; Fisheries Economics Research Unit, 'Global Fisheries Economies, Sea Around Us Project', Vancouver: University of British Columbia, available at www.seaaroundus.org/sponsor/feru.aspx (accessed 3 November 2009).

48 World Wildlife Fund, 'Hard Facts, Hidden Problems: A Review of Current Data on Fishing Subsidies', Washington, DC: WWF, 2001.

49 See OECD (2006), op. cit.

50 M. Milazzo (1998), 'Subsidies in World Fisheries: A Re-examination'. World Bank Technical Paper No. 406. Fisheries Series, Washington, DC: The World Bank.

51 See A. Khan, U. R. Sumaila, R. Watson, G. Munro and D. Pauly, 'The Nature and Magnitude of Global Non-Fuel Fisheries Subsidies', in U. R. Sumaila and D. Pauly (eds), *Catching More Bait: A Bottom-Up Re-estimation of Global Fisheries Subsidies*, Fisheries Centre Research Reports, 2nd edn, Vancouver: University of British Columbia, 14 (6), 2006, 5–37; U. R. Sumaila, L. Teh, R. Watson, P. Tyedmers and D. Pauly, 'Fuel Price Increase, Subsidies, Overcapacity and Resource Sustainability', *ICES Journal of Marine Science* 65, 2008, 832–40.

52 WWF (2001), op. cit., for details.

53 See DFID (2009), op. cit.

54 WTO, 'Fourth Revision of Draft Modalities for Non-Agricultural Market Access', WTO Document No. TN/MA/W/103/Rev.3, dated 6 December 2008, Geneva.

55 D. Chakraborty and A. U. Khan, *The WTO Deadlocked: Understanding the Dynamics of International Trade*, New Delhi: Sage, 2008.

56 P. Gooday, 'ABARE Report for the Fisheries Resource Research Fund', 2002, Canberra: Australian Bureau of Agricultural and Resource Research.

57 M. Ahmed, 'Market Access and Trade Liberalisation in Fisheries', *Issue Paper* No. 4, 2006, Geneva: International Centre for Trade and Sustainable Development.

58 B. Nag and A. Nandi, 'Analysing India's Trade Dynamics vis-à-vis SAARC Members Using the Gravity Model', *South Asia Economic Journal* 7 (1), 2006, 83–98.
59 M. Dey, M. A. Rab, K. M. Jahan, A. Nisapa, A. Kumar and M. Ahmed, 'Food Safety Standards and Regulatory Measures: Implications for Selected Fish Exporting Asian Countries', *Aquaculture Economics and Management*, 9(1–2), 2005, 217–36.
60 The countries included in the analysis are Australia, Belgium, Canada, Denmark, Finland, France, Germany, Greece, Ireland, Italy, Japan, South Korea, Netherlands, New Zealand, Norway, Portugal, Spain, Sweden, Turkey, the UK and the US.
61 For Thailand and Vietnam, data for 1999–2006 and 1996–2006 has been considered.
62 HS code 3 is considered for the purpose of the current analysis. The data was obtained from World Bank, 'World Integrated Trade Solution', available at http://wits.worldbank.org/wits/ (accessed 10 March 2012).
63 International Monetary Fund, 'World Economic Outlook', available at www.imf.org/external/pubs/ft/weo/2011/02/weodata/index.aspx (accessed 10 March 2012).
64 Distances between countries were accessed from www.mapcrow.info/ (accessed 10 March 2012).
65 Figures in the parenthesis represent the item code. The data was obtained from FAO, 'FAOSTAT', available at http://faostat.fao.org/ (accessed 11 March 2012).
66 J. G. Sutinen, 'Major Challenges for Fishery Policy Reform: A Political Economy Perspective', OECD Food, Agriculture and Fisheries Working Paper No. 8, 2008, Paris: OECD.
67 H. Spencer, M. Saqib and D. Rajasenan, 'Impact of Sanitary Measures on Exports of Fishery Products from India: The Case of Kerala', Agriculture and Rural Development Discussion Paper, 2005, New Delhi: World Bank.
68 L. van Hoof, A. Payne, A. Iversen, C. Cahu, G. Tserpes, J. Pinnegar, L. Antoine, M. Evrard, V. Lamblin (2008), 'The Future of Fisheries and Aquaculture: Trends and Developments', The Future of European Fisheries and Aquaculture Research Project Report, available at www.aquacircle.org/images/pdfdokumenter/ udvikling/eu/feufar_08/3_REPORT_SYSTEM_and_DRIVERS.pdf (accessed 23 August 2013).
69 World Bank, 'Global Economic Prospects: Uncertainties and Vulnerabilities', Washington, DC.
70 P. Salz, 'Towards Elimination of Subsidies in Fisheries', paper prepared for the Baltic Sea 2020 Foundation, 2009, The Netherlands: Framian BV.

14 A second extension of the transition period

Can the WTO better integrate LDCs into TRIPS?

Arno Hold and Bryan Mercurio[1]

14.1 Introduction

Concluded as part of the Uruguay Round of trade negotiations, which created the WTO, the Agreement on Trade-Related Aspects of Intellectual Property Rights ('TRIPS Agreement') sets out the international framework for protecting intellectual property rights ('IPRs'). In addition to requiring certain minimum standards, respect for core principles such as national treatment and most favoured nation and containing several procedural and administrative requirements, the TRIPS Agreement also provided least developed country ('LDC') members of the WTO with a transition period of ten years to apply the bulk of their new obligations (through Article 66.1 of the TRIPS Agreement). By 2005, however, most LDCs had neither managed to implement the TRIPS Agreement nor taken the necessary steps required to strengthen their protection and enforcement of IPRs as the Agreement required. Thus, on 29 November 2005 the WTO/TRIPS Council extended the original Article 66.1 transition period for the implementation of the TRIPS Agreement for LDCs from 1 January 2006 to 1 July 2013.[2] The same WTO Decision called on LDCs to provide to the TRIPS Council as much information as possible on their individual priority needs for technical and financial assistance from developed country members. In other words, the Decision asked LDCs to prioritize their requirements, needs and desires and communicate them to the TRIPS Council in order to facilitate technical and financial assistance from developed country members of the WTO. As of July 2013, only eight LDCs – Uganda, Sierra Leone, Bangladesh, Rwanda, Tanzania, Senegal, Mali and Madagascar – had tabled such individual priority needs assessments. Therefore, 26 of the 34 LDC members of the WTO have yet to submit any substantial response to the TRIPS Council.

With the implementation deadline of 1 July 2013 looming and after a hard-fought debate at the TRIPS Council meeting of 11–12 June 2013, WTO members granted LDCs a second extension of the transition period for another eight years – that is, until 1 July 2021. With that decision, the ultimate resolution as to the TRIPS Agreement in relation to LDCs has merely been postponed. The objective of this chapter is thus to inform the ongoing discussions on how to meaningfully integrate the poorest countries into the WTO system for the protection of intellectual property.

The chapter is structured as follows: Section 14.2 provides a comprehensive legal analysis of the various rights and obligations for LDCs, developed country members and international organizations under the transitional arrangements in the TRIPS Agreement, subsequent WTO legislation and in particular the TRIPS Council Decision of November 2005. Section 14.3 analyses the content of the latest TRIPS Council Decision of 11–12 June 2013, which grants a second extension of the transition period for LDCs for another eight years. In Section 14.4, the authors identify substantial shortcomings of the current situation following the Decision of June 2013 and propose potential avenues for WTO members to move forward. Section 14.5 presents a brief summary and the implications of our findings for the ongoing debate and makes recommendations on potential avenues to better integrate the LDCs into the global system for the protection of intellectual property. Section 14.6 concludes.

14.2 Rights and obligations of the WTO members with regard to the LDCs' implementation of the TRIPS Agreement

14.2.1 LDCs' role in the TRIPS negotiations

At the time of the negotiation of the TRIPS Agreement, most industrialized countries had long-established comprehensive domestic legislation in the field of IPRs. These same countries had also negotiated, signed and ratified several WIPO Conventions and Treaties. Thus, industrialized countries had a strong framework of IPRs in both the domestic and the international sphere. By contrast, many developing countries and most LDCs[3] had neither a comprehensive domestic system for the protection and enforcement of IPRs nor much experience in negotiating international conventions and treaties on IPRs. It is thus not surprising that a group of industrialized countries were not only the *demandeurs* but also largely dictated the shape of the negotiating text and of the final text.

More specifically, even when seeking to include IP as a negotiating topic in the Uruguay Round of trade negotiations, the US and other industrialized countries used the carrot and stick approach to achieve the objective of strengthening the global system of IP protection. The carrots for negotiating and agreeing to the inclusion of IP in the Uruguay Round were concessions in other trade areas, notably increased access to developed country agriculture and textiles markets.[4] Developing countries were also granted several important TRIPs-related concessions, most notably, deferred implementation of the substantial portions of the agreement and in promises of technology transfer and assistance.[5] The stick came in the form of a threat of continued unilateral action[6] that could potentially threaten the trade and aid flowing from developed countries to the developing world.[7]

After initial opposition, objections from developing countries waned and attention turned to negotiating the agreement.[8] The potential benefits of the sectoral trade-offs appeared too great to ignore, and there were very real concerns among both developing countries and LDCs that without involvement in TRIPS, they would miss out on technology transfer and the capacity to attract foreign direct investment in the future. Most importantly, however, the TRIPS Agreement contained many provisions that recognize the particular concerns and needs of developing countries and LDCs,[9] and the transition periods meant that there was no immediate need to implement the Agreement (and, correspondingly, that they bore no immediate economic costs as a result of the Agreement).[10]

The TRIPS Agreement is unprecedented insofar as it was the first WTO covered agreement to venture 'beyond the border' and thus to have a considerable impact upon on the internal legal system of a member. Examples of such impact can be seen through the minimum standards set out in the TRIPS Agreement, the requirement to establish certain authorities, border controls measures and domestic enforcement mechanisms, including judicial review and even criminal liability for certain IPR offences. Unsurprisingly, the implementation costs of the TRIPS Agreement for most developing countries have been considerable, in terms of both monetary and intellectual resources. This is true even of countries that had a fairly advanced IPR framework prior to the implementation of the TRIPS Agreement, but even more so for developing countries that had not fully established a domestic IPR framework prior to the TRIPS Agreement. It is therefore no exaggeration to state that for most, if not all, LDC members of the WTO, effective implementation and operation of the TRIPS Agreement was not possible in the decade following its creation.

Recognizing this reality, the TRIPS Agreement allows for transitional arrangements for both developing countries and LDCs. The special and differential treatment of LDCs begins in the Preamble itself, which not only recognizes that transitional arrangements are necessary when aiming 'at the fullest participation in the results of the negotiations' but also specifically highlights that, owing to the special developmental objectives and particular needs of LDCs, 'maximum flexibility' should be accorded in the implementation of IP laws and regulation in order for them to create a sound and viable technological base. More specific provisions relating to transitional arrangements and LDCs are made in Articles 65 and 66 of the TRIPS Agreement.

14.2.2 Transitional arrangements contained in Article 65 of the TRIPS Agreement

Part VI (Articles 65–7) of the TRIPS Agreement provides for the transitional arrangements. Articles 65 and 66 define the length of time members are given to bring their intellectual property laws and regulations into full conformity with the obligations of the Agreement. Article 65.1 stipulates a general transition period that applies to all WTO members, regardless of their development status. According to this provision, members were obliged to fully apply the TRIPS Agreement one year after the date of entry into force of the WTO Agreement (i.e. 1 January 1995), meaning that members had until 1 January 1996 to bring their laws and regulations into compliance with the TRIPS Agreement. Articles 65.2 and 65.3 provided developing country members and members with transitional economies with an additional four years to comply with the TRIPS Agreement, that is until 1 January 2000. One caveat to this transitional arrangement was that no extension was granted with regard to the compliance with the principles of national treatment and most favoured nation as contained in Articles 3, 4 and 5 of the TRIPS Agreement.[11]

Moreover, according to Article 65.4, developing country members that, prior to the enactment of the TRIPS Agreement, had not extended product patent protection to areas of technology that had not previously protected could further delay the implementation of such protection for a period of five years – that is, until 1 January 2005. Most notably, this extended transitional period applied to the pharmaceutical and agricultural chemicals sectors, which most developing countries did not previously protect. As countries manufacturing large amounts of generics (such as Brazil and India) did not previously provide product patents on pharmaceuticals, this extended period meant that manufacturers of generics in those countries could continue copying and producing drugs that would otherwise have required patent protection by the year 2000. The only caveat to this extended transitional period was that from 1995, countries were obliged to accept patent applications and keep them dormant in a patent 'mailbox' until 2005, when the mailbox was unlocked and the applications assessed.[12] Finally, Article 65.5 provides that any changes in the laws, regulations and practice of a member availing itself of these transitional arrangements shall advance the implementation of the Agreement, and must not result in a lesser degree of consistency with its provisions (the so-called 'no rollback' provision).

14.2.3 Transition periods for LDCs contained in Article 66.1 of the TRIPS Agreement

In view of the special needs and requirements of LDC members, 'their economic, financial and administrative constraints, and their need for flexibility to create a viable technological base', Article 66.1 extended the transition period for LDCs to apply the TRIPS Agreement obligations to ten years, that is until 1 January 2006 (again, with the exception of Articles 3, 4 and 5). Moreover, the last sentence of Article 66.1 provides that the 'Council for TRIPS shall, upon duly motivated request by a least developed country Member, accord extensions of this period'. Unlike the preceding transition periods set out in

Article 65, Article 66.1 does not merely focus on providing LDCs with additional time to implement the Agreement. Instead, the provision recognizes that a rapid implementation of the Agreement could create a conflict with the economic interests and development priorities of LDCs. Therefore, this extension, as well as any subsequent extension, should allow LDCs to put domestic policies in place in order to ensure that the subsequent implementation of the TRIPS Agreement will support and not hinder their socio-economic development.

Furthermore, and again unlike Article 65.5, Article 66.1 does not contain a 'no rollback' provision. In that respect, Article 66.1 could be seen as a further provision of special and differential treatment in the context of the TRIPS Agreement. Such special and differential treatment is in line with Article 7 of the TRIPS Agreement, which stipulates that IPR protection and enforcement should:

> contribute to the promotion of technological innovation and to the transfer and dissemination of technology, to the mutual advantage of producers and users of technological knowledge and in a manner conducive to social and economic welfare.

Such provisions are also in line with Article 66.2, which attempts to address the incapacity of LDCs to attract sufficient technology transfer from industrialized countries. Article 66.2 obliges developed country members to:

> provide incentives to enterprises and institutions in their territories for the purpose of promoting and encouraging technology transfer to least-developed country Members in order to enable them to create a sound and viable technological base.

The language of Article 66.2, however, is vague and there is disagreement about the nature and quantity of the incentives that should be provided to the private sector to encourage such transfers. According to a study conducted by Suerie Moon, it is unclear whether Article 66.2 has led to *any* increase in incentives for technology transfer to LDCs.[13]

14.2.4 Technical and financial assistance (Article 67 of the TRIPS Agreement)

Given the potentially far-reaching legal and economic impact of the TRIPS Agreement as well as the limited economic, financial and administrative capacity of developing country and LDC WTO Members, it became clear during the Uruguay Round that these countries would require considerable technical and financial assistance from developed country members. Therefore, Article 67 requires developed country WTO members to provide 'technical and financial assistance' in favour of developing country and LDC members 'in order to facilitate the implementation' of the Agreement. This shall include, but is not limited to:

> assistance in the preparation of laws and regulations on the protection and enforcement of intellectual property rights as well as on the prevention of their abuse, and support regarding the establishment or reinforcement of domestic offices and agencies relevant to these matters, including the training of personnel.

The language used in Article 67 is vague, and the exact contours of the obligations it contains are unclear. Official WTO documents provide little guidance as to the exact meaning or interpretation of the terms in Article 67, and to date no dispute over the transitional arrangements in Part VI of the TRIPS Agreement has been brought before the WTO's dispute settlement body.[14] What is clear is that the provision does not impose any mandatory rules or particular methods of cooperation on developed country members. That being said, the obligation on developed country members to cooperate is triggered upon the receipt of a formal request from a developing country or LDC member, followed by the conclusion of mutually agreed terms and conditions governing the cooperation activities.

Although Article 67 refers to technical *and* financial assistance, it seems clear that the assistance *could* include technical and financial assistance or only one of the two (although it also seems that the 'or' option is not the preferred course of action). The donor and beneficiary countries are free to determine the course of the negotiation process as well as the nature and scope of the cooperation. Developing country or LDC members are at liberty to choose the developed country member from which they request cooperation, but it remains unclear whether and how developed country members could prioritize their efforts aimed at particular beneficiaries under this provision.

The vagueness and ambiguity of Article 67 has hampered its effectiveness. To put it mildly, Article 67 did not fulfil the expectations of many LDC members during the first ten years of the TRIPS Agreement and instead has led to some frustration in the development community.

14.2.5 The first extension of the LDC transition period for LDCs

In response to rising awareness of the issues surrounding access to essential medicines,[15] and in accordance with the last sentence of Article 66.1,[16] members agreed in the 2001 Doha Declaration on the TRIPS Agreement and Public Health to extend the transitional arrangements for LDCs until 2016 with respect to patents on pharmaceutical products and exclusive marketing rights.[17] Therefore, LDCs are under no obligation to provide for, or to enforce patents and data protection with respect to pharmaceutical products until 2016.[18]

Prior to the expiration of the general transition period on 1 January 2006, members agreed at the Hong Kong Ministerial Conference in late 2005 to provide LDCs with a last-minute reprieve and extend the transition period under Article 66.1 for the implementation of the TRIPS Agreement for another seven and a half years to 1 July 2013.[19] This provided LDCs with additional 'breathing space' but did not fully satisfy their desires. On the contrary, most LDCs supported a proposal submitted by Zambia in October 2005 requesting the TRIPS Council to extend the transition period for an additional 15 years.[20] In its request, Zambia (on behalf of the LDCs) argued that LDCs 'continue to face serious economic, financial and administrative constraints in their efforts to bring their domestic legal system into conformity with the provisions of the TRIPS Agreement' and that there is still a 'need for flexibility to create a viable technological base'.[21] The proposal further argued that LDCs would need more time to take full advantage of the cooperation with developed country members envisaged in Articles 66.2 and 67 of the TRIPS Agreement.

Although some developed WTO members would have preferred to grant extensions to individual LDC members on a case-by-case basis while others called for a five-year extension period, the looming expiration of the transition periods, coupled with the Ministerial Conference that was to be held in Hong Kong in late November 2005, put pressure on members to resolve the issue collectively for all LDCs within a short time. The length of the extension – seven and a half years – seems merely to be the result of a bargaining process in which the LDCs originally requested 15 years and developed country members a five-year period, rather than being the outcome of any holistic reasoning.[22]

In addition to the seven-and-a-half-year extension, the Decision also called for the establishment of a process that could facilitate the efforts and the cooperation of both LDC and developed country members to integrate LDCs into the global IPR system. Therefore, the Decision contained four procedural elements:

- First, all LDCs were asked to provide the TRIPS Council, preferably by 1 January 2008, with as much information as possible on their individual priority needs for technical and financial cooperation in order to implement the TRIPS Agreement.
- Second, the provision calls on developed countries to provide technical and financial assistance to LDCs in accordance with Article 67 of the TRIPS Agreement so as to address the identified priority needs effectively.
- Third, the Decision mandates the WTO Secretariat to increase its cooperation with WIPO and other relevant international organizations to assist LDCs in the above-mentioned needs assessment process and to make technical assistance and capacity building as effective and operational as possible.
- Fourth, the Decision introduced a 'no rollback' provision that required LDCs to ensure that changes to their laws, regulations and practice made

during the extended transitional period do not result in a lesser degree of consistency with the TRIPS Agreement.[23]

The inclusion of a 'no rollback' provision for LDCs has been criticized by some LDCs and NGOs, which argue that it reduces the policy space available to LDCs during the transition period.[24] Interestingly, the TRIPS Council Decision did not make any reference to or establish any links to the technology transfer provision in Article 66.2 of the TRIPS Agreement.

14.3 State of play before the second extension of the transition period for LDCs

14.3.1 Achievements and shortcomings of the priority needs assessment process

As mentioned above, the TRIPS Council Decision of 29 November 2005 not only extended the original Article 66.1 transition period for LDCs by another seven and a half years to 1 July 2013, but also established a process in which LDCs were requested to provide information on what they consider as priorities for technical and financial assistance that would enable them to successfully implement the TRIPS Agreement.

Although all LDC WTO members were originally requested to provide the TRIPS Council with their priority needs assessments for technical and financial assistance by 1 January 2008, only 8 of the 34 LDC Members have thus far participated in the process. More specifically, the first LDCs to participate in the process were Uganda and Sierra Leone, which tabled formal submissions of their individual priority needs at the October 2007 meeting of the TRIPS Council.[25] At the request of the TRIPS Council, Uganda then followed up its original priority needs assessment with a document entitled the 'Uganda Trade and Intellectual Property Programme (UTIP)' in June 2008. Sierra Leone quickly followed suit and presented its own national IP capacity building programme at the October 2008 meeting of the TRIPS Council.[26] Bangladesh submitted its priority needs assessment in March 2010, Rwanda and Tanzania in October 2010, Senegal in June 2011, Mali in August 2012 and Madagascar in February 2013.[27] The developed country members of the WTO, as well as the WTO Secretariat, commended these LDCs on their submissions and invited others to follow suit. Unfortunately, the other 26 LDC members of the WTO have not formally submitted their priority needs assessment more than five years after the original deadline.

Some NGOs and other commentators criticized the priority needs assessment as merely a delay tactic used by developed country members to further postpone honouring their promises for assistance. These critics also claimed that the priority needs assessment would force LDCs to spend already scarce resources on collecting data and information regarding the status of their implementation of the TRIPS Agreement.[28] Most WTO members, however, considered the priority needs assessment process as an invaluable exercise that fulfils a number of purposes. For instance, the priority needs assessment allows LDCs to table concrete and specific demands that could create the political momentum needed to mobilize potential donors as well all national stakeholders in the beneficiary country. Correspondingly, the priority needs assessment also provides potential donors with the necessary information to clearly identify what support the individual LDC actually requests and to tailor its donor programmes better to meet the needs of the requesting country. Moreover, for many LDCs, such a stocktaking exercise provides a unique opportunity to create awareness and consensus among a variety of internal institutions and stakeholders, which is a necessary precursor to developing and implementing a national innovation and IP policy. Likewise, a successfully completed priority needs assessment is a strong signalling device as it demonstrates a national commitment towards IP reform, which could be seen by some as being essential for LDCs to attract technical and financial assistance. Moreover, the priority needs assessments provide potential donors with an insight into the socio-economic context and the institutional dynamics of the TRIPS Agreement implementation in the potential beneficiary country, again allowing for better targeted and tailored technical and financial assistance.

Unfortunately, the TRIPS Council Decision of 2005 did not specify any formal requirements or a particular mechanism for the conduct and submission of priority needs assessments by LDCs. Therefore, the appropriate scope, depth, breadth and quality of the priority needs assessments remain unclear. Likewise, it is not further specified who should be funding and conducting these exercises. As a result, the priority needs assessments submitted thus far differ significantly in quality, scope, analytical reasoning and structure. In the case of Uganda and Sierra Leone, the priority needs assessment process was mainly funded by the United Kingdom Department for International Development ('DFID') and both governments received considerable support and assistance from the International Centre for Trade and Sustainable Development ('ICTSD') and a specialized consulting firm. On the other hand, Bangladesh conducted its priority needs assessment on its own without any donor assistance or support. The submissions also differed substantively, and approached the issue of how to attract the attention of potential donors in a significantly different manner. For instance, Uganda complemented its needs assessment with a fully developed national capacity building programme referred to as Uganda Trade and Intellectual Property ('UTIP'), a programme that contained detailed descriptions of activities and a clear implementation timetable with a budget of a US$ 2 million. In contrast, Bangladesh submitted only a brief priority needs assessment paper of 20 pages that included a one-page rough budget requesting approximately US$ 71 million.[29]

Overall, the priority needs assessments submitted may be well considered, carefully conducted exercises that thoughtfully analysed the perceived needs of the LDC concerned. From a development aid perspective, though, many of the proposed implementation plans did not meet the standards and principles of aid effectiveness that have been developed over recent decades (e.g. in the Paris Declaration).[30] Moreover, the priority needs identified are often not compatible with the actual capacities or project management requirements of the targeted donors. Thus, it is unrealistic for the LDC concerned, or for interested NGOs, to expect that the requests stemming from the priority needs assessment will be immediately met. Instead, the formulation of requests via the priority needs assessment should be viewed as only the first step in what development cooperation experts call project-cycle management ('PCM'), not as something that will automatically trigger the implementation of the requested projects.

There also appears to be confusion, or at the very least a certain disconnect, between LDCs and potential donors, as to the purpose of the technical and financial assistance requests contained in the priority needs assessment. For instance, while some of the requests contained in the priority needs assessments go beyond achieving compliance with the TRIPS Agreement obligations and are designed to contribute to the establishment of a national IP system that is beneficial to the country's socio-economic development (e.g. Bangladesh's priority needs assessment requests US$ 14.5 million for community-based museums and for conducting research on traditional knowledge),[31] some potential donor countries believe that technical and financial assistance should be exclusively targeted at bringing LDCs' intellectual property laws and institutions into compliance with the obligations under the TRIPS Agreement.

As a consequence of these asymmetries, it remains unclear what the follow-up procedure should be once an assessment has been submitted to the TRIPS Council. The eight LDCs that have so far participated in the exercise have received little response from developed country members and insufficient funding to make substantial progress on the implementation of their national IP plans. Above all, the submission of a priority needs assessment did not trigger any substantive additional technical and financial assistance. Overall, it is fair to conclude that the priority needs assessment process has not met the legitimate expectations of LDCs.[32]

14.3.2 Impact on the provision of technical and financial assistance by developed country members

To some, the obligation to provide technical and financial assistance has mainly been a tool used by industrialized countries to convince developing countries and LDC members to accept and agree to the TRIPS Agreement.[33] While such statements and sentiment are debatable, what is clear is that neither the industrialized world nor LDCs have prioritized LDC implementation of the TRIPS Agreement over the 17 years since the creation of the TRIPS Agreement. Instead, developed country members focused their efforts on encouraging full implementation of the TRIPS Agreement in emerging market economies, such as Brazil and India, where powerful economic interests are at stake.

This being so, the TRIPS Council Decision of 2005 put the developed country members in a somewhat inconvenient position. The newly established priority needs assessment process linked the LDC obligation to implement the TRIPS Agreement at least indirectly with the provision of technical and financial assistance under Article 67 of the TRIPS Agreement. Consequently, the Decision has limited the discretion of the donor countries as to how, where or to what extent they engage in technical and financial assistance in the field of IPRs ('IPRTA'). At the same time, these submissions raised considerable expectations in the developing world and the continued failure to successfully address the LDCs' priority needs could lead to growing resistance to further progress in the international protection of IPRs.

On the declaratory level, developed country members assert that they are fully aware of the importance of technical and financial assistance in order to support LDC members in taking the steps necessary to enable them to comply with their obligations under the TRIPS Agreement. In that respect, they have commended the LDCs that have submitted priority needs assessments and invited others to follow suit.

So far, however, most industrialized countries have either not provided any such IPRTA or have concentrated their efforts mainly on middle-income countries with which they have close political or economic ties. In addition, while some national IP institutions in developed countries have certain office-to-office cooperation activities with a few partner countries, these activities focus mostly on beneficiary countries where they are already engaged in economic, trade and development cooperation. It is also clear that the classic motive for IPRTA activities includes the assumption that such IPRTA should lead to improved protection for national IP rights holders abroad. As a consequence, most IPRTA has been provided to new emerging market economies where protection for IPR holders from developed countries is a key economic interest. Selecting emerging market economies as partner countries also makes sense as they are normally at a stage of development where they could reap significant benefits from having a functional IP system in place.

Some developed country members have not made any provision for specialized IPRTA programmes in their development aid budgets (e.g. Canada), while others have either only IPRTA programmes with a strictly regional focus (e.g. Australia in the Pacific region) or they mainly conduct such activities primarily through WIPO (e.g. Japan). As a consequence, the various developed country members have approached this issue differently; some are planning to provide technical assistance on a bilateral case-by-case basis within their existing development programmes (by reshuffling their trade cooperation budgets), while others have yet to decide how best to meet their obligation under Article 67 of the TRIPS Agreement.

Most developed country members seem to recognize the need for a certain level of coordination of their efforts to provide technical and financial cooperation under Article 67, with many delegations expressing their concern, that without adequate coordination, technical assistance projects could carry both the risk of duplication of efforts that are already underway and that of having no sustainable impact.[34] More worrying, however, is that some delegations have indicated that their development aid budgets do not contain any specific budget lines earmarked for IP-related projects. Moreover, budgets for development cooperation in the field of trade are generally limited, with a substantial proportion of assistance programmes being tied to particular regions or trading partners.

Another difficulty facing several developed country members has been in attracting the interest of national development cooperation agencies in redirecting development aid to IPRs. This difficulty probably arises because the socio-economic impact of the TRIPS Agreement is still not obvious and the benefits of IP reforms will be indirect and long term.

In summary, it is fair to say that seven and a half years after the TRIPS Council Decision of 2005, most developed country members have still not managed to come up with a comprehensive (internal or external) strategy on how to position themselves with regard to the priority needs assessment process and to what extent and under what conditions they are actually intending to provide comprehensive IPRTA.

14.3.3 Efforts of the WTO Secretariat

The TRIPS Council Decision of 2005 requested the WTO Secretariat to enhance its cooperation with relevant international organizations in order to assist LDC members. In that context, the Decision made particular reference to the provisions on technical assistance and cooperation mentioned in the cooperation agreement that WIPO and the WTO concluded in1995.[35] The two organizations also launched a Joint Initiative on Technical Cooperation for Least Developed Countries in June 2001.[36]

Since the TRIPS Council Decision of 2005, the WTO Secretariat has made considerable efforts to create awareness of the issue and to organize matchmaking with potential donor countries. For example, following the publication of the priority needs assessments of Uganda and Sierra Leone, the WTO Secretariat organized informal meetings with developed country members to consider how the priority needs identified could best be met, thus facilitating initial bilateral contacts to look at potential contributions by developed country partners. In October 2009, the WTO Secretariat hosted a WTO workshop on the priority needs assessment process at the request of the LDC Group, which aimed to facilitate an exchange of views between all actors. Responding to another request by the LDC Group, the WTO Secretariat organized three regional workshops on the priority needs for these countries in 2010.[37] Furthermore, key representatives from LDCs, developed countries and interested international organizations took part in a symposium on LDCs' needs assessment in Geneva in October 2011. This review session concluded that the existing technical assistance contact points between the partners should be used in a more systematic manner. More specifically, the participants in the review session recommended the establishment of small coordination groups in order to respond comprehensively to the priority needs assessments tabled. The participants also recommended increased coordination to support further priority needs assessments and to respond to the needs that have already been identified. Finally, the participants agreed on the need for practical tools and common resources that could provide methodological advice to LDCs on how to participate in the priority needs assessment process.[38]

As a result of the review session, Switzerland requested that the WTO Secretariat contact the Secretariat of the Enhanced Integrated Framework ('EIF') and the coordinator of the Aid for Trade initiative ('AfT')[39] with a view to gathering and presenting information on how these existing multilateral mechanisms, including their expertise and funds, could be used to assist in the implementation of the priority needs requested under Article 67 of the TRIPS Agreement.[40] Finally, LDCs recently requested developed country members to state more concretely how they intend to respond to the LDCs' priority needs assessments.[41] In that respect, Nigeria, on behalf of the African Group, proposed in the TRIPS Council that the Secretariat prepare a note aimed at indicating areas that had been implemented as well as areas still needing attention in each of the LDC members that have submitted their priority needs assessment.[42]

In October/November 2012, the WTO Secretariat, supported by the Swedish government, hosted a symposium with a variety of stakeholders to better coordinate the assistance to those LDCs that have yet to submit their priority needs assessments. Among other things, the participants agreed that further considerations should be given to identifying centralized or country-specific coordination mechanisms as well as to the idea of establishing a dedicated fund to support the priority needs assessment process.[43]

14.3.4 The need for enhanced coordination on various levels in order to make the priority needs assessment process work

To date, developed country members' response to the priority needs assessments submitted has been somewhat disappointing. Except for informal talks among industrialized countries and a few matchmaking workshops and meetings with LDCs, no comprehensive and coordinated follow-up has taken place and only very limited IPRTA has been provided. There is a variety of reasons for this lack of coordination.

Foremost is that IPRTA is a relatively new topic in the field of development cooperation and the track record of IPRTA in LDCs is very limited. There is still a lack of research and best practices when it comes to the implementation and the impact assessment of the TRIPS Agreement in LDCs.[44] While the commitment and the ability to absorb IPRTA are usually relatively high in emerging markets, the conditions in LDCs are very different. LDCs have a limited absorption capacity as their legal and institutional framework for IP protection is usually in an embryonic stage and they lack educational and professional capacity in the field of IP. Additional obstacles normally associated with working in LDCs (e.g. remote rural areas, digital gap and brain drain) also are known to affect the efficiency of such IPRTA projects.[45]

Another important reason for the slow progress in the priority needs assessment process and in the provision of IPRTA is the abundance of actors within the LDCs. On one hand, various government agencies are involved in or affected by the implementation of the TRIPS Agreement (the national IP offices, the ministries of industry, trade, finance, foreign affairs, justice, science and technology, culture, education, health and agriculture, as well as enforcement agencies such as customs, police and courts).[46] On the other hand, a myriad of non-governmental stakeholders also have to be included in the decision-making process in order to effectively strengthen the national IP system (IP professionals, industry, inventors, collecting societies, academics, chambers of commerce, teachers and the media as well as the public). The inclusion of such large and diverse groups inevitably affects the speed and efficiency of IPRTA projects.

As hinted at earlier, there is also a great need for internal national co-ordination on the donor side. The starting point is the inclusion of national IP offices. Many developed country members, however, still have separate national offices for industrial property and copyrights, and these national IP offices normally have neither experts nor spending power when it comes to technical assistance activities. Thus, even the inclusion of national IP offices has proven to be more difficult than might be assumed. Moreover, as the TRIPS Agreement is only one part of a wider framework of trade relations, the national trade ministries as well as the trade diplomats negotiating in Geneva must also be included in the process. As the budgets for development cooperation are normally managed and controlled by national development cooperation agencies, these agencies must also play a role in the process. Furthermore, since the foreign affairs ministry is usually in charge of the official relationship with a potential beneficiary country (and likely has some representation in that country) it too should be included in the process. Again, with so many agencies and interests represented it has proven difficult to effectively coordinate IPRTA projects.

Further complicating the matter is that IP is extremely controversial in the development cooperation community and most representatives of development agencies have only a limited understanding of the underlying legal and socio-economic mechanisms. Put bluntly, there is widespread distrust among many of the above-mentioned stakeholders concerning the fundamental issue of whether increased IP protection is actually beneficial for LDCs or whether it simply takes away 'policy space' in a manner detrimental to meeting the needs and desires of LDCs. In light of this tension, development agencies often do not view the modernization of IP laws and institutions as a priority, given the many other competing interests of LDCs, thus making them reluctant to fund these sorts of initiatives and programmes.

Another set of problems can be attributed to the vagueness of the TRIPS Agreement provisions and the design of the priority needs assessment process. As stated above, the exact nature and scope of the obligation contained in Article 67 of the TRIPS Agreement remain unclear. Unanswered questions include whether the obligation merely requires a certain financial or technical input or whether it is an outcome-oriented obligation. In other words, it remains unclear whether a developed country member is in compliance with its obligations under Article 67 when it provides a certain level of IPRTA or whether it is only in compliance when an LDC has finally managed to implement the TRIPS Agreement. This ambiguity also creates a certain liability problem for developed country members; thus, by agreeing to provide technical and financial assistance, it is also unclear whether the developed countries have moved away from a position of merely demanding implementation of the TRIPS Agreement to a position where they have at least partly taken some responsibility for LDCs' implementation of the TRIPS Agreement.

As mentioned above, the quality and the scope of the priority needs assessments are very heterogeneous. Moreover, the implementation plans attached to some of the priority needs assessments do not follow standardized development cooperation procedures and principles, which normally provide for the inclusion of the donors' capacities and preferences in the project design. As a result, it is highly unlikely that potential donors would support these implementation plans in an integral and comprehensive manner. Instead, a donor country will first have to assess the feasibility of a project and conduct its own project design to fulfil the requirements of its national development cooperation agency in terms of measurable outcomes, monitoring, accountability, ownership and sustainability.

From a procedural point of view, it is unclear what the follow-up process to LDCs' priority needs assessments should be. The present situation creates uncertainty for all LDCs as it is not clear that investing already scarce resources into conducting an IP priority needs assessment will eventually result in the receipt of substantial technical and financial assistance in the identified priority areas. Some developed countries believe members should respond to LDCs' requests on a first-come, first-served basis; others favour a case-by-case approach; and some believe that a transparent and predictable process should be developed within the existing coordinating structures. It is also unclear how technical and financial assistance provided to LDCs under Article 67 could be coordinated with other existing mechanisms and initiatives in this area in a manner that is useful and avoids unnecessary duplication.

This chapter argues that increased coordination at various levels, including within the donor countries and the beneficiary LDCs, as well as within the international development community would resolve some of the above-mentioned dilemmas. On the one hand, greater coordination in the funding of technical assistance could range from opening new funds and creating joint initiatives to attempts to tap into existing funding mechanisms (e.g. funding through the EIF). On the other hand, cooperation is also essential in the actual provision of technical assistance. This could range from mere information exchange between the developed country members about which donor is implementing a particular activity (checklist approach) to outsourcing the implementation of entire projects to a central coordination body.

Again, the difficulty lies in actually creating a mechanism to increase coordination efforts. Many developed country members emphasize the need to identify a central coordination body – e.g. to set up a sort of 'clearing house' mechanism – while others would like WIPO and/or the WTO to assume an essential role in this regard. Those favouring WTO involvement point to the WTO/WIPO Cooperation Agreement and the Joint Initiative as evidence of its interest in the subject matter. In contrast, several other developed country members oppose WTO involvement for systemic reasons; they argue that the WTO should not assume the role of a development organization and that this type of activity could set a precedent for other trade sectors. As mentioned before, several developed country members have identified the EIF as a possible channel of cooperation. In the following paragraphs we will further analyse this option.

14.3.5 The Enhanced Integrated Framework (EIF) and Aid for Trade (AfT) as potential coordinating bodies

In order for members to agree on a coordinated, efficient and expeditious response to the priority needs identified by LDCs in their assessments, the role of existing multilateral mechanisms or frameworks that could come into play to address these needs merit further consideration.

In response to requests from a number of delegations, the WTO Secretariat compiled information on potential coordinating roles of the EIF and AfT in the needs assessment process for LDCs, with a particular focus on how the expertise and monetary resources of these two existing multilateral mechanisms could be made use of to assist LDCs in establishing their individual priority needs assessments and receiving IPRTA.[47]

The EIF is a multi-donor programme that strengthens cooperation among donors, six core partner agencies (the International Monetary Fund ('IMF'), the International Trade Centre ('ITC'), the United Nations Conference on Trade and Development ('UNCTAD'), the United Nations Development Programme ('UNDP'), the World Bank and the WTO), observer agencies, and other development partners that are supporting the LDCs' trade agenda. Both beneficiaries and donors benefit from the EIF: LDCs can use the EIF as a vehicle to assist in coordinating donor support and to attract additional AfT resources, whereas donors can sign up to the EIF as a vehicle to deliver on their initial AfT commitments. The EIF process might be considered cumbersome, but is thought to be essential to ensure proper use of funds and to maximizing the effectiveness of the aid in LDCs. In order to receive funding from the EIF,

LDCs must first undertake a so-called Diagnostic Trade Integration Study ('DTIS') to identify a list of priority reforms in the field of trade. These reforms must be validated by national stakeholders and the national government. The EIF then supports the integration of these trade priorities into national development strategies and identifies sources of adequate funding for key priorities. Of course, using the EIF as a tool to fund IP priorities identified in the priority needs assessment can occur only when an LDC identifies IP-related needs as a priority in its DTIS framework. In summary, using the EIF mechanism in the coordination of the priority needs assessment process would require LDCs to further align all national stakeholders towards improving the legal and institutional IP framework. When such alignment occurs, LDCs gain greater access to substantial multilateral or bilateral funding opportunities.

14.4 The TRIPS Council Decision of June 2013 granting a second extension of the transition period for LDCs

A few months before the expiration of the extended transition period for LDCs on 1 July 2013, discussions concerning LDCs' implementation of the TRIPS Agreement resumed in the TRIPS Council. Unfortunately, but perhaps not unexpectedly, the discussions did not start positively. Instead, the initial discussions quickly became a blame game and finger-pointing exercise. Fortunately, the discussions slowly progressed and many members began to realize that there is a need for a more constructive and comprehensive approach to what has now become a pressing issue.

At the November 2011 meeting of the TRIPS Council, Bangladesh submitted a proposal on behalf of the LDC Group requesting a further extension of the transition period.[48] The proposal instructed the TRIPS Council 'to take a favourable decision in this regard and report thereon to the WTO Ninth Ministerial Conference to be held in December 2013'.[49]

The proposal found support in the TRIPS Council, and the members agreed to recommend the following text to the General Council to be forwarded to the Eighth Ministerial Conference, held in Geneva in December 2011, for consideration:

> Ministers invite the TRIPS Council to give full consideration to a duly motivated request from Least Developed Country Members for an extension of their transition period under Article 66.1 of the TRIPS Agreement, and report thereon to the WTO Ninth Ministerial Conference.[50]

In their Decision of 17 December 2011, the ministers invited the TRIPS Council 'to give full consideration to a duly motivated request from Least-Developed Country Members for an extension of their transition period under Article 66.1 of the TRIPS Agreement, and report thereon to the WTO Ninth Ministerial Conference'.[51]

Curiously, the length of the second extension period had not yet been agreed, and informal discussions with LDC delegations suggested that the requested period was 15 years; thus, the transitional period would extend until the year 2028. The length of the extension has been controversial, and it was expected that several developed country members would insist on a considerably shorter time. With this important decision likely to remain contentious for some time, it was likely that another extension of the transition period for LDCs would be granted in the final TRIPS Council Meeting taking place before the expiration of the current transition period on 31 June 2013. At this stage, neither LDCs nor developed country members seemed interested in discussing even more contentious alternatives to a simple extension of the transitional periods.

On 5 November 2012, however, Haiti briefly presented, under 'Other Business', a communication to the TRIPS Council on behalf of the LDC Group requesting that 'the transition period should remain in force while the Member is considered a least developed country in the WTO'.[52]

In the following month, a variety of NGOs and some academics voiced support for the LDCs' request for an unconditional extension with an unlimited time frame.[53]

At the request of Nepal acting on behalf of the LDC Group, the LDCs' draft decision was tabled for discussion at the TRIPS Council meeting on 5–6 March 2013.[54] During this meeting, most developing countries who took the floor supported the LDCs' request as drafted in the communication by Haiti and argued that an artificial deadline would not support LDCs' efforts to create a sound technological base. Some of them also argued that a linkage with technical and financial assistance under Article 67 of the TRIPS Agreement was unnecessary, had created confusion and should therefore be omitted. Furthermore, they stated that the inclusion of a 'no rollback' provision as in the 2005 Decision would only reduce the policy space for LDCs in using the flexibilities provided under the TRIPS Agreement.[55] In order to acknowledge the special needs and challenges of LDCs, these countries argued that the extension should be granted automatically and without any conditions.[56]

Developed country WTO members showed broad support for a further extension of the LDC transition period, but took a more precautionary approach and raised concerns about the idea of an open-ended time frame. For instance, the US emphasized that many LDCs already had IP laws and enforcement mechanisms in place and had taken significant steps to implement the TRIPS Agreement so it would be important to recognize and to preserve those accomplishments, and to continue that progress towards full implementation.[57] The EU stated that it is important to have more clarity on where the LDCs members stand with regard to the implementation of the Agreement and in what direction they are intending to go. In that respect, the LDC Group's proposal lacked a clear and predictable perspective. Furthermore, the EU raised concerns that the proposal does not contain any provisions that mention any need for cooperation or that take into account that IP and the TRIPS Agreement also contribute to the establishment of a viable technological base.[58] Switzerland also expressed concerns about the systemic implications of an open-ended non-application of the substantive provisions of the TRIPS Agreement for LDCs within the WTO.[59] The members requested the Chair to hold further consultations with a view to resolving the matter at the TRIPS Council meeting of 11–12 June 2013.

On 7 June 2013, the WTO members finally reached a draft decision on how to extend the LDC transition period and this draft decision was subsequently confirmed during the TRIPS Council meeting of 11–12 June 2013. Under the terms of this decision, LDCs

> shall not be required to apply the provisions of the Agreement, other than Articles 3, 4 and 5, until 1 July 2021, or until such a date on which they cease to be a least developed country Member, whichever date is earlier.[60]

The LDCs did not succeed with their request for an open-ended extension. In return for accepting an additional eight years of extension, the industrialized country members agreed not to include an explicit and binding 'no rollback' provision. The new decision nevertheless refers indirectly to the principle of 'no rollback' as LDCs will now 'express their determination' to preserve and continue the progress towards implementing the TRIPS Agreement to preparing for eventual full compliance. LDCs, however, can still make full use of the flexibilities provided under the TRIPS Agreement and retain the right to request further extensions of the compliance deadline:

> Recognizing the progress that least developed country Members have already made express their towards implementing the TRIPS Agreement, including in accordance with paragraph 5 of IP/C/40, least developed country Members express their determination to preserve and continue the progress towards implementation of the TRIPS Agreement. Nothing in this decision shall prevent least developed country Members from making full use of the flexibilities provided by the Agreement to address their needs, including to create a sound and viable technological base and to overcome their capacity constraints supported by, among other steps, implementation of Article 66.2 by developed country Members.[61]

Interestingly and in sharp contrast to the preceding Decision of 2005, the new Decision did not contain any references to the priority needs assessment process or any substantive obligations on technical and financial assistance. The preamble of the Decision of 2013 only recognizes '[t]he continuing needs of least developed country Members for technical and financial cooperation so as to enable them to realize the cultural, social, technological and other developmental objectives of intellectual property systems. . . .'

14.5 After the second extension of the transition period: potential avenues for WTO members to better integrate LDCs into the international IP system

14.5.1 Advantages and shortcomings of the June 2013 decision

Considering the current state of the discussion on how to meaningfully integrate LDCs into the international IP system, agreeing on another extension of the transition period did not come as a surprise and seemed to be the pragmatic next step. This is particularly the case as the vast majority of LDCs have not made substantial progress in the implementation of the TRIPS Agreement. Indeed, most of the LDC WTO members have not yet addressed the issue domestically or considered it a priority within their national development policies. Thus, it seemed premature to expect these countries to be ready to implement the TRIPS Agreement by mid-2013. Conversely, developed country members have to date mainly focused on shielding themselves from unspecified IPRTA requests and the submission of the first priority needs assessments has revealed the extent of their unpreparedness. Granting a merely unconditional extension of the transition period for all LDCs for another eight years was therefore a convenient way for both parties to buy time and to avoid any potential conflicts in the TRIPS Council.

If no further extension had been granted, it was clear to all that from 1 July 2013 most LDCs would not have been in compliance with the TRIPS Agreement. Without denigrating such important obligations, practically speaking it seemed very unlikely that another WTO member (whether it be an industrialized country member, a developing country or an LDC) would bring an IP-related WTO claim against an LDC; put simply, LDC markets are too insignificant to warrant such a claim and such an attempt would most likely be a public relations disaster for the complainant country and the affected industries. As bringing a claim against a non-compliant LDC is neither desirable nor feasible, WTO members could have agreed on a dispute settlement moratorium whereby members commit themselves not to institute proceedings against LDCs for a set period. This approach has a number of advantages over another extension of the transitional period. First, a moratorium is a more intellectually honest way of dealing with the inability of LDCs to comply with the TRIPS Agreement. Formally admitting that the LDCs are not in compliance with the TRIPS Agreement is not only truer to the 'single undertaking' model of WTO governance that members appear to cherish but also more realistic than simply providing multiple extensions in the false hope that implementation will at some point miraculously occur.[62] For this reason, a moratorium might have been a more credible approach. Moreover, a moratorium could also be more effective than another extension of the transitional period as it would not exempt LDCs from compliance nor technically excuse the non-compliance. It would simply recognize the inability of LDCs to comply with the TRIPS Agreement and therefore grant them special and differential treatment. Furthermore, it would put constant pressure on all WTO members to take action and would offer incentives to those LDCs that have so far undertaken the priority needs assessment and are making progress in the implementation of the TRIPS Agreement. However, the introduction of such a moratorium alone would neither resolve most of the above-mentioned dilemmas with regard to unlocking IPRTA nor would it actually improve LDC's de facto compliance.

Although granting a second extension of another eight years seems to be a pragmatic solution, there are some significant potential downsides to this decision. Foremost, the experience of the last decade strongly indicates that an extension alone will not lead to any IP-related improvements in LDCs. On the contrary, an unconditional extension will not resolve anything but will only further postpone the implementation of the TRIPS Agreement by LDCs. At the same time, it undermines to a certain degree the credibility of the TRIPS Agreement regime, inevitably leading some – including these authors – to question whether LDCs will ever have to comply with the TRIPS Agreement. More generally, the new extension undermines the credibility of a multilateral system that is premised on the belief that the protection and enforcement of IPRs are beneficial for the growth and development of members, including LDCs.[63]

Instead, it is proposed that what is needed is to increase the efficiency, transparency and predictability of the priority needs assessment process so that it creates enough incentives for both LDCs and developed countries to engage more effectively in integrating LDCs into the international IP system. As mentioned earlier, the submission of a priority needs assessment seems to be the crucial first step for LDCs and without it, no progress towards improved implementation of the TRIPS Agreement can be expected.

The TRIPS Council Decision of 2005 linked the rights and obligations contained in Articles 66.1 and 67 of the TRIPS Agreement. Under the setting created by the 2005 Decision, however, each of these two provisions blocked the realization of the other: LDCs argued they could have implemented the TRIPS Agreement had they received substantial IPRTA while developed country members claimed that they would be willing to provide IPRTA if LDCs were to consider implementation as an important development priority and participate more actively in the priority needs assessment process.

Synergy between these two provisions can be achieved only if all members manage to agree on an efficient, transparent and predictable process that ensures not only that LDCs will actively participate in the process but also that they will receive substantive support for embarking on a path of IP reform. Conversely, developed country members require assurances of LDCs' commitment to the process and that IPRTA will be spent effectively. Unfortunately, the new TRIPS Council Decision of June 2013 does not remedy this dilemma. On the contrary, it is very likely that the new extension will not only lead to a further postponement of LDCs' integration into the international IP system for another eight years without resolving any of the underlying issues, but also cause a stagnation (if not a reduction) in the fulfilment of developed country obligations to provide IPRTA. The previous extension from 2006 till 2013 has clearly demonstrated that both LDCs and industrialized countries have been reluctant to engage constructively in this process if there is no imminent deadline.

In this section, the authors present three potential avenues to remedy some of the above-mentioned disadvantages of the current situation after the Decision of June 2013:

- reform of the priority needs assessment process;
- additional incentives for LDCs and developed countries to cooperate more actively towards LDCs' integration in the global IP system; and
- a more gradual and development-oriented concept of TRIPS-implementation for LDCs.

While admittedly none of these remedies provides the proverbial silver bullet we argue that they would all contribute to a more meaningful integration of LDCs.

14.5.2 The need to reform the priority needs assessment process

Most members of the TRIPS Council seem to agree that the priority needs assessment process is an essential stocktaking exercise for all LDCs, not only in order to attract IPRTA but also simply as a developmental and governance exercise. Undertaking this process not only identifies the major shortcomings of an LDC's legal and institutional framework for the protection of IP, but it also has the potential to create political momentum for the LDC to actively engage in the multilateral system and improve its IP systems. Therefore, undertaking a priority needs assessment is viewed as having an essential role to play in encouraging LDCs to implement the TRIPS Agreement.

The TRIPS Council Decision of 2005 introduced the quasi-requirement for LDCs to submit their priority needs assessments 'preferably by 1 January 2008' and the requirement was virtually ignored by most LDCs.[64] The latest TRIPS Council Decision of 2013 does not contain any provision referring to these priority needs assessments. We therefore advocate that the WTO members should revitalise the priority needs assessment process. Although it will not have an immediate impact on the 26 LDCs that have not yet submitted their priority needs assessments, it might be an important signal to set a new deadline for submission (as the completion of a priority needs assessment takes a considerable time, the deadline should be reasonable, e.g. at least two to three years). The conduction of a priority needs assessment should be more closely linked to the individual LDC's entitlement to request IPRTA under Article 67. This would ensure that as many LDCs as possible will undergo an internal stocktaking exercise within a reasonable period. Furthermore, it would also deprive some developed countries from making the well-worn argument that they cannot provide IPRTA as the LDC has not yet prioritized or even thoroughly internalized its IP management system.

However, the situation cannot be resolved simply through the introduction of a requirement for LDCs to submit a priority needs assessment. As mentioned above, at present, the scope and quality of the priority needs assessment process are varied and results of priority needs assessments differ in their scope, depth, breadth and quality. Therefore, the WTO members should also consider establishing minimal assessment standards and best practice guidelines for the conduct and submission of priority needs assessments. The WTO Secretariat has already commissioned a guidebook for LDCs on how to use technical and financial assistance for implementation of the TRIPS Agreement.[65] Such initiatives should be further strengthened.

Another issue to be addressed is the human capital and financial resources required to complete a priority needs assessment. It is clear that many LDCs would need considerable expert advice and financial support in order to undertake a priority needs assessment, provision of which the TRIPS Council should also discuss.

In addition to the requirement to undertake and submit a priority needs assessment, we also propose that LDCs should include the establishment of an adequate IP system within their national development plans (in particular within the DTIS of the EIF). While some commentators may view this requirement as unnecessarily intrusive or merely a tool for developed country monopolizers, we include this requirement for a practical reason. The reality of technical and financial cooperation is that international donors and development agencies now focus development aid only on certain areas that are also considered key priorities from a beneficiary country perspective. Failure to link the assistance requests contained in the priority needs assessment with national development plans will result in a significant decrease in the IPRTA available. In turn, this requirement is significant in the overall success or failure of the request. By contrast, aligning the requests contained in the priority needs assessment with the national development plans and strategies of the beneficiary country should strengthen the sustainability and ownership of cooperation projects and ensure the commitment and participation of all national stakeholders. Furthermore, as the establishment of IP laws and institutions requires a broad national consensus among various intergovernmental agencies and an abundance of other national stakeholders, it would seem that such an ambitious objective can be achieved only if it is backed by a national development plan.

14.5.3 Identifying additional incentives for LDCs and developed countries to engage and cooperate more actively

The low number of priority needs assessments is evidence that the current process offers neither sufficient carrots nor sticks to encourage LDCs' participation. On the one hand, the approaching deadline of a transition period does not serve as a stick because it is obvious that most LDCs do not have the capacity to make any progress towards TRIPS compliance and that all of the LDCs simply expect a further extension, and probably another one after that. It is not even a stretch of the imagination to say that some, if not most, LDCs assume that they will never have to comply with the TRIPS Agreement. On the other hand, it is not easy to identify further incentives to encourage LDCs to participate in the TRIPS Agreement. This is particularly the case as the Agreement does not deal with trade concessions, but merely requires the implementation of minimum standards, procedural requirements and the like. One option for encouraging participation would be to further improve the conditions for technology transfer for those LDCs that actively participate in the priority needs assessment process. While the TRIPS Council Decisions of 2005 and 2013 did not link TRIPS implementation to the provision of further incentives with regard to technology transfer, it may be worthwhile considering the benefits and disadvantages of such a link in the future.

If no additional incentives to encourage LDC implementation can be found within the TRIPS Agreement itself, the WTO could also consider 'cross-incentives' for LDCs that make progress in the implementation of the TRIPS Agreement through additional benefits in other sectors of trade. Similar to the strategy of cross-retaliation found in the area of WTO dispute settlement, providing additional incentives in other sectors could serve as a useful tool for encouraging LDCs to make progress in implementing the TRIPS Agreement. However, such cross-incentives would involve several sectors of trade and thus would require a more comprehensive discussion within the current Doha Round of trade negotiations or in a future trade round. In the current atmosphere of the Doha Round, this is perhaps a longer term option rather than one for the immediate future.

Another more feasible and easily operational incentive would be to reward the efforts of those eight LDCs that have already submitted priority needs assessments with swift and comprehensive IPRTA. This would provide others who may follow suit with the necessary certainty that they will also receive an appropriate level of support from developed country members. As mentioned previously, the establishment of a coordination mechanism as well as the creation of a multilateral fund for IPRTA would play a crucial role in this process. In this regard, the efforts of the WTO Secretariat have thus far been important and should be continued. Therefore, we propose that the TRIPS Council should further strengthen the role of the WTO Secretariat in promoting the realization of Articles 66.1 and 67.

As mentioned in Section 14.3 of this chapter, the provision of IPRTA is a relatively new phenomenon in the field of development cooperation, and the track record of IPRTA in LDCs is still extremely limited. Additional research on the impact of TRIPS in LDCs and the development of best practices in IPRTA is therefore crucial. Moreover, future research should also focus on collecting empirical data about the intellectual property systems of the world's poorest countries as well as adapting existing IP policies to serve the needs of LDCs.

14.5.4 Applying a more gradual and development-oriented concept of TRIPS implementation for LDCs

Taking into account that most LDCs do not have the resources to implement the TRIPS Agreement in its entirety, and the legitimate question of whether this would even be useful or desirable given their limited innovative and administrative capacity, it is unrealistic to expect LDCs to establish a functioning fully fledged IP system similar to the ones operating in developed or even middle-income developing countries. Therefore, it might be more practicable to apply a more gradual and development-oriented concept of TRIPS implementation for LDCs.[66] Such an approach should focus first on reforms in those areas of IP that are essential for the LDCs' socio-economic development and that pave the way to a more stable, more innovative and more productive economy (e.g. establishing a basic but efficient system for the protection of national trademark holders). Setting a different standard for LDCs obviously creates certain asymmetries among WTO members, which may challenge the WTO single undertaking approach, but it could be argued that continuous extensions of the transitional period do exactly the same, but without the added benefit of offering even a gradual integration into the global IP system. Additionally, the TRIPS Council Decisions of 2005 and 2013 already required LDCs to comply with certain core principles such as national treatment and most favoured nation (although the so-called 'no rollback' provision was no longer included in the Decision of 2013). We thus propose that the future extension should be used to gradually introduce further provisions of the TRIPS Agreement that do not cost a lot but are highly relevant to strengthen LDCs' national economies and support a better integration into the global knowledge economy. Such a gradual approach would allow LDCs to integrate more smoothly into the global IP system.

14.6 Conclusion

This chapter demonstrates that the vast majority of LDCs did not achieved substantial progress in the implementation of the TRIPS Agreement during the first extension of the transition period from 2005 to 2013. Developed countries have also not sufficiently supported LDC integration into the international IP system because they have failed to provide substantive and comprehensive technical and financial assistance. This lack of progress can be at least partly attributed to the shortcomings of the priority needs assessment process introduced during the last extension in 2005. Although the TRIPS Council Decision of 2005 touched upon the reciprocity between the rights and obligations of the members under Article 66.1 and Article 67 of the TRIPS Agreement, each of these provisions has been blocking the realization of the other. As a result of these deficiencies, only 8 of the 34 LDC WTO members have thus far tabled individual priority needs assessments. The subsequent reluctance of industrialized countries to respond to these initial requests for IPRTA has led to widespread frustration among developing countries about the entire exercise. Consequently, the LDC Group (unsuccessfully) requested an open-ended and unconditional second extension of the transition period.

The present chapter argues that the latest TRIPS Decision to further extend the transition period for LDCs until 1 July 2021 – although it seems a convenient and pragmatic move to 'buy time' in the face of disagreement among developing and developed country members – could lead to a further postponement of LDCs' integration into the international IP system. Moreover, repeated extensions without considerable efforts to bring LDCs into compliance with the TRIPS Agreement undermine the credibility of the WTO system and the organization's cherished principle of a 'single undertaking'. Instead, what would be required is a transformation of the priority needs assessment to make the process more efficient, transparent and predictable so that it creates enough incentives for both LDCs and developed countries to engage more effectively in the integration of LDCs into the international IP system. Furthermore, we emphasize the need for improved coordination among all actors on the national, bilateral and multilateral level. As far as the funding of IPRTA is concerned the TRIPS Council has already identified the EIF as a potential channel of cooperation and will now require much effort as well as some additional fine-tuning to further promote this promising avenue. It is also crucial that the IP community engages in a constant dialogue with all the stakeholders involved to establish IPRTA as a credible tool for economic development cooperation.

The core of this chapter is an analysis of the potential avenues for WTO members after the second extension of the transition period in order to better integrate LDCs into the international IP system. In particular, we propose reforming of the priority needs assessment process, which would make it more rewarding for all LDCs to undertake a priority needs assessment and to include the improvement of their IP system in their national development plans.

We also try to identify additional incentives for LDCs and developed countries to engage in improving the integration of LDCs into the global IP system (e.g. to look into improving conditions for technology transfer beyond the current Article 66.2 or to provide incentives for LDCs that comply in other sectors of trade). Finally, we advocate the application of a more gradual and development-oriented concept of TRIPS implementation for LDCs and further recommend that the current extension should be used to gradually introduce further core provisions of the TRIPS Agreement that would allow LDCs to integrate smoothly into the global IP system (e.g. by establishing a basic but efficient system for the protection of national trademark holders). We strongly believe that alternatives to simply offering further transition period extensions should be seriously discussed and adopted by the TRIPS Council in an effort to make the system more efficient, transparent and successful for all interested parties.

Notes

1 Arno Hold is a Research Fellow at the World Trade Institute (WTI) of the University of Berne and the Director of the WTI/CUHK Summer Programme on Intellectual Property. Bryan Mercurio is a Professor of Law and Associate Dean (Research) at the Chinese University of Hong Kong (CUHK). The views expressed here shall neither be attributed to the institutions to which the authors are affiliated nor to their member states. Research for this chapter was partly funded by the Swiss National Science Foundation under a grant to the National Centre of Competence in Research on Trade Regulation, based at the World Trade Institute of the University of Berne, Switzerland. This book chapter updates and revises a previous *NCCR Trade Regulation Working Paper* by the same authors (No. 2012/37, October 2012) that was written before the TRIPS Council decided to grant LDCs a second extension of the transition period to implement the TRIPS Agreement. Ron Marchant, Thomas Cottier and Mathias Schaeli deserve thanks for their input and for encouraging the work on this topic.

2 World Trade Organization, Extension of the transition period under Article 66.1 for least developed country members, Decision of the Council for TRIPS of 29 November 2005, 30 November 2005 (IP/C/40) ('2005 Extension Decision for TRIPS').

3 The categorization of countries as developed or developing has been a matter of uncontested self-selection; however, this is not necessarily automatically accepted in the WTO context. According to Article XI:2 of the WTO Agreement, the WTO recognizes those countries as least developed that have been designated as such by the United Nations. The United Nations Economic and Social Council ('ECOSOC') reviews the list every three years according to the following three criteria: low per capita income, weak human resources, and high economic vulnerability. Of the 48 LDCs listed to date, the following 33 are WTO members: Angola, Bangladesh, Benin, Burkina Faso, Burundi, Cambodia, Central African Republic, Chad, Democratic Republic of the Congo, Djibouti, Gambia, Guinea, Guinea Bissau, Haiti, Lao People's Democratic Republic, Lesotho, Madagascar, Malawi, Mali, Mauritania, Mozambique, Myanmar, Nepal, Niger, Rwanda, Samoa, Senegal, Sierra Leone, Solomon Islands, Tanzania, Togo, Uganda and Zambia. Furthermore, 10 LDCs are currently negotiating their accession to the WTO: Afghanistan, Bhutan, Comoros, Equatorial Guinea, Ethiopia, Liberia, Sao Tomé & Principe, Sudan, Vanuatu and Yemen.

4 See e.g. B. Mercurio, 'Reconceptualising the Debate on Intellectual Property Rights and Economic Development', *The Law and Development Review* 3(1), 2010, 65–107; E. Durán and C. Michalopoulos, 'Intellectual Property Rights and Developing Countries in the WTO Millennium Round', *Journal of World Intellectual Property* 2(6), 1999, 853–74; C. May and S. K. Sell, *Intellectual Property Rights: A Critical History*, Boulder, CO: Lynne Rienner, 2005.

5 The benefits of the concessions are subject to debate. See D. Matthews and V. Munoz-Tellez, 'Bilateral Technical Assistance and TRIPS: the United States, Japan and the European Communities in Comparative Perspective', *Journal of World Intellectual Property* 9(6), 2006, 629–53; T. P. Trainer, 'Intellectual Property Enforcement: A Reality Gap (Insufficient Assistance, Ineffective Implementation)?', *John Marshall Review of Intellectual Property Law* 8(1), 2008, 47.

6 For instance, the US began unilaterally enforcing IPRs by virtue of the authority of the United States Trade Representative ('USTR') under Section 301 US Trade Act of 1974, in which the US initiated litigation against other countries in the US Court of International Trade ('USITC') under its domestic unfair trade practices laws, even though the respondent countries had not violated any international agreement. The

US filed cases against several developing countries, most notably Brazil, Argentina, India, China and Taiwan, and extracted concessions from the respondents in a number of cases. In so doing, the US effectively promoted the linkage of IP and international trade. In 1988, the US went further and created Special 301 to examine and identify the 'adequacy and effectiveness of intellectual property rights' in other countries. If problems are found to exist, countries are monitored and can be categorized as a 'Priority Foreign Country' or included in the 'Watch List' or 'Priority Watch List'. See A. O. Sykes, 'Constructive Unilateral Threats in International Commercial Relations: The Limited Case for Section 301', *Law & Policy in International Business* 23(2–3), 1992, 263–330 at 318–19; containing a table of cases decided under Section 301. Likewise, and partly in response to the US provision, the European Union adopted Council Regulation 2641/84 to counter 'illicit' trade practices against European exporters. See W. W. Leirer, 'Retaliatory Action in United States and European Union Trade Law: A Comparison of Section 301 of the Trade Act of 1974 and Council Regulation 2641/84', *North Carolina Journal of International Law & Commercial Regulation* 20, 1994–95, 41–96. The EC repealed the Regulation upon the creation of the WTO. See Council Regulation 3286/94, available at http://eur-lex.europa.eu/LexUriServ/LexUriServ.do?uri=CONSLEG:1994 R3286:20080305:EN: PDF (accessed 18 June 2013). The US did not, and Section 301 was subject to WTO dispute settlement. See also Panel Report, United States – Section 301–10 of the Trade Act of 1974, WT/DS152/R (22 December 1999).

7 After initially listing China, India and Thailand on the Special 301 Watch List in 1991, the US first implemented sanctions and withdrew generalized system of preferences ('GSP') concessions on Indian pharmaceutical products a year later. See M. Blakeney, *Trade-Related Aspects of Intellectual Property Rights: A Concise Guide to the TRIPs Agreement*, London: Sweet & Maxwell, 2006, p. 6. Developing country opposition to the inclusion of IPRs into GATT weakened as the US continued to threaten and implement Section 301 and Special 301 sanctions. This was especially true of larger developing countries, notably Brazil and South Korea. Perhaps more importantly, continued use of the unilateral retaliatory measures prevented the formation of effective coalitions against IPRs as a negotiating topic. D. Matthews, *Globalising Intellectual Property Rights: The TRIPs Agreement*, London: Routledge, 2002, p. 33. The 'stick' of Special 301 thus succeeded in convincing developing countries to adopt higher levels of domestic IP protection in exchange for continued preferential access to the US market. See ibid.

8 Developing countries initially argued that WIPO was the appropriate forum and then that the agreement should be limited to measures aimed at eliminating trade in counterfeit goods. The US, the EC, Japan and Switzerland, however, successfully proposed a more ambitious agreement regulating a broad range of IP-related interests. For a succinct history of the origins of the TRIPS Agreement and its negotiating process, see D. Matthews, *Globalising Intellectual Property Rights: The TRIPs Agreement*, London: Routledge, 2002, Chapter 1 (origins) and 2 (negotiations). For more detailed background on the TRIPS Agreement, see S. K. Sell, *Power and Ideas: North-South Politics of Intellectual Property and Antitrust*, New York: State University of New York Press, 1999.

9 See B. Mercurio (forthcoming), 'TRIPS and Access to Essential Medicines', in D. Prévost and G. Van Calster (eds), *Research Handbook on Environment, Health and the WTO*, Cheltenham, UK and Northampton, MA: Edward Elgar, forthcoming 2013.

10 TRIPS is the only covered agreement containing such transitional implementation periods.

11 See Article 65.2 TRIPS Agreement.

12 Several thousand applications that accumulated in India's 'mailbox' have yet to be assessed and are likely to be rejected.

13 For a more detailed analysis, see S. Moon, 'Does Article 66.2 Encourage Technology Transfer to LDCs? An Analysis of Country Submissions to the TRIPS Council (1999–2007)', UNCTAD/ICTSD Project on IPRs and Sustainable Development, Policy Brief Number 2 (2008).

14 For a review of the WTO dispute settlement system, see Y. Guohua, B. Mercurio and L. Yongjie, *WTO Dispute Settlement Understanding: A Detailed Interpretation*, The Hague: Kluwer Law International, 2005.

15 For an overview on access to essential medicines, see above note 9.

16 The last sentence of TRIPS Agreement Article 66.1 reads: 'The Council for TRIPS shall, upon duly motivated request by a least-developed country Member, accord extensions of this period.'

17 WTO Ministerial Conference, Declaration on the TRIPS Agreement and Public Health, WT/MIN(01)/DEC/2 (Nov. 20, 2001), para 7. The Declaration likewise granted LDCs an extension until 2013 to implement TRIPS, more generally. This extension remains in force and has now been extended at least until the next Ministerial Conference.

18 See World Trade Organization, Extension of the transition period under Article 66.1 of the TRIPS Agreement for least-developed country members for certain obligations with respect to pharmaceutical products, Decision of the Council for TRIPS of 27 June 2002, 1 July 2002 (IP/C/25).

19 2005 Extension Decision for TRIPS.

20 World Trade Organization, Request for an extension of the transitional period under Article 66.1 of the TRIPS Agreement, Communication from the Delegation of Zambia on behalf of the Least-Developed Country Members, 21 October 2005 (IP/C/W/457).

21 See ibid. paras 4 and 5.

22 See World Trade Organization, Minutes of TRIPS Council Meeting held on 25–26 and 28 October, 29 November and 6 December 2005, 31 January 2006 (IP/C/M/49) ('WTO Minutes of TRIPS Council Meeting'), paras 243–85.

23 Similar to the 'no rollback' provision in Article 65.5 TRIPS.

24 See WTO Minutes of TRIPS Council Meeting, Statement by Rwanda, para. 280.

25 World Trade Organization, Council for TRIPS, Priority Needs for Technical and Financial Cooperation: Communications from Uganda, 9 October 2007 (IP/C/W/500) and 27 May 2008 (IP/C/W/510); Communications from Sierra Leone, 3 October 2007 (IP/C/W/499) and 22 October 2008 (IP/C/W/523).

26 See second submissions of Uganda and Sierra Leone in ibid.

27 Communication from Tanzania, 21 October 2010 (IP/C/W/552); Communication from Senegal, 27 June 2011 (IP/C/W/555); Communication from Mali, 31 August 2012 (IP/C/W/575); Communication from Madagascar, 22 February 2013 (IP/C/W/584).

28 See for instance The South Centre/Center for International Environmental Law, 'Extension of the transition period for LDCs: flexibility to create a viable technological base or simply (a little) more time?', IP Quarterly Update, First Quarter 2006, at 6.

29 Council for TRIPS, Priority Needs for Technical and Financial Co-operation, Communication from Bangladesh, 23 March 2010 (IP/C/W/546), para. 39.

30 The Paris Declaration on Aid Effectiveness had been endorsed in 2005 by more than 100 signatories (from donor and recipient country governments, multilateral donor agencies, regional development banks and international agencies) in order to address the fact that development aid had become increasingly fragmented, less predictable, less transparent and more volatile. The Declaration represented a broad consensus within the international community on how to make development cooperation more effective by introducing new mechanisms such as conditionality, capacity building and support for governance. Furthermore, it focused on five principles: ownership, alignment, harmonization, managing for results, and mutual accountability. For an

overview on aid effectiveness, see B. Killen and A. Rogerson, 'Global Governance for International Development: Who's in Charge?', Development Brief, 2010, Issue 2 or H. Kharas, 'The Evolving International Architecture for Development Cooperation', Policy Paper 2011/11, The Brookings Institution.

31 Council for TRIPS, Priority Needs for Technical and Financial Co-operation, Communication from Bangladesh, 23 March 2010 (IP/C/W/546), para. 39.

32 Some of the participants expressed their disappointment about the exercise. See for example, World Trade Organization, Council for TRIPS, Minutes of Meeting on 8–9 June 2009, 28 September 2009 (IP/C/M/60), Statement by Uganda, paras 71–2.

33 See World Trade Organization, Council for TRIPS, Minutes of Meeting on 21 September 1995, 20 October 1995 (IP/C/M/3), para. 54.

34 See for example World Trade Organization, Council for TRIPS, Minutes of Meeting on 8–9 June 2009, 28 September 2009 (IP/C/M/60), Statement by Switzerland, paras 74–8.

35 See World Trade Organization, Council for TRIPS, Agreement Between the World Intellectual Property Organization and the World Trade Organization, 13 December 1995 (IP/C/6). In Article 4 of the said Agreement, WIPO and the WTO committed themselves to enhance their technical assistance relating to the TRIPS Agreement and to make it available also to those developing countries that are members of the partner organization. This is particularly relevant for LDC WIPO members such as Laos that are currently in the process of acceding to the WTO, as it puts them in a position to profit from IPRTA under Article 67 TRIPS. Furthermore, the two organizations agreed to keep in regular contact and to exchange information on this matter.

36 See World Trade Organization, 'WIPO and WTO Launch New Initiative to Help World's Poorest Countries Press Release', 14 June 2001 (Press/231).

37 See therefore World Trade Organization, Council for TRIPS, Minutes of Meeting on 8–9 June 2009, 28 September 2009 (IP/C/M/60), Request from the LDC Group, paras 67–8.

38 See World Trade Organization Council for TRIPS, Minutes of Meeting on 24–5 October and 17 November 2011, 15 February 2012 (IP/C/M/67), paras 330–5.

39 Both the Enhanced Integrated Framework ('EIF') and the Aid for Trade initiative ('AfT') will be further explained in section 5 of this chapter.

40 See World Trade Organization, Council for TRIPS, Minutes of Meeting on 8–9 June 2009, 28 September 2009 (IP/C/M/60), Statement by Switzerland, paras 74–8.

41 The EU and Japan have already provided such a report. See World Trade Organization, Council for TRIPS, Technical Cooperation Activities and Assistance for Least Developed Countries, Communication from the European Union, 20 February 2012 (IP/C/W/568) and Complementary Report on Technical Cooperation Activities for Least Developed Countries, Communication from Japan, 19 July 2012 (IP/C/W/572).

42 See World Trade Organization Council for TRIPS, Minutes of Meeting on 24–5 October and 17 November 2011, 15 February 2012 (IP/C/M/67), para. 339.

43 The presentations of this symposium can be downloaded on the following WTO website: www.wto.org/english/tratop_e/trips_e/ldc_e.htm.

44 There is a consensus among practitioners that IPRTA should be in alignment with best practices and general principles of development cooperation as stated for example in the Paris Declaration on aid effectiveness. In 2010, the WTO commissioned a consulting firm to draft a Guidebook for LDCs on how to implement TRIPS. This document has not yet been published. See T. Pengelly and J. Engel (forthcoming), 'Using Technical and Financial Assistance for Implementation of the TRIPS Agreement: A Guidebook for LDCs'. For the best available source of information on IPRTA best practice, see M. Leesti and T. Pengelly, 'Assessing

Technical Assistance Needs for Implementing the TRIPS Agreement in LDCs, ICTSD Programme on Intellectual Property Rights and Sustainable Development LDC – A Diagnostic Toolkit', International Centre for Trade and Sustainable Development ('ICTSD'), Geneva, Switzerland, 2007.

45 M. Leesti, 'Special Challenges for IP TA in Capacity Building in an LDC', 2006, available at www.iprsonline.org/ictsd/docs/LDCToolkit-final.pdf (accessed 18 June 2013).

46 ICTSD, 'LDC Needs Assessment under TRIPS: The ICTSD Experience (2007–11)', Information Note No.19, International Centre for Trade and Sustainable Development, Geneva, 2011.

47 See WTO Secretariat, *Note on the Aid for Trade Initiative and the Enhanced Integrated Framework* (IP/C/W/544). The note provides an overview on the funding mechanisms of both initiatives.

48 World Trade Organization, Elements Paper on the Extension of the Transition Period under Article 66.1 of the TRIPS Agreement, Communication by Bangladesh on behalf of the LDC Group, 11 November 2011 (IP/C/W/566).

49 See World Trade Organization, Annual Report (2011) of the Council for TRIPS, Addendum, 17 November 2011 (IP/C/59/Add.2).

50 See World Trade Organization, Transition Period for Least-Developed Countries under Article 6.1 of the TRIPS Agreement, Decision of 17 December 2011, 19 December 2011 (WT/L/845).

51 See World Trade Organization, Council for TRIPS, Communication from Haiti on behalf of the LDC Group, 5 November 2011 (IP/C/W/583).

52 See for example F. M. Abbott, 'Technical Note: The LDC TRIPS Transition Extension and the Question of Rollback', Policy Brief No. 15, International Centre for Trade and Sustainable Development (ICTSD), Geneva, 2013.

53 See World Trade Organization, Council for TRIPS, Minutes of Meeting on 5–6 March 2013, 13 May 2013 (IP/C/M/72).

54 See for example ibid. Statement by India, paras 11.38–40.

55 Ibid. Statement by Nepal, para. 11.87.

56 Ibid. Statement by the United States, paras 11.64–6.

57 Ibid. Statement by the EU, paras 11.69–76.

58 Ibid. Statement by Switzerland, paras 11.60–2.

59 World Trade Organization, Extension of the transition period under Article 66.1 for least-developed country members, Decision of the Council for TRIPS of 11 June 2013, 12 June 2013 (IP/C/64).

60 Ibid. para. 2.

61 For discussion of some of the problems with the 'single undertaking' model, see B. Mercurio, 'The WTO and its Institutional Impediments', *Melbourne Journal of International Law* 8, 2007, 198–232

62 Indeed, similar concerns were raised in 2005 at the time of the first extension of the transition period. See for example K. Kennedy, 'The 2005 TRIPS Extension for the Least-Developed Countries: A Failure of the Single Undertaking Approach?', *International Lawyer* 40, 2006, 683–700.

63 See 2005 Extension Decision for TRIPS, para. 2.

64 T. Pengelly and J. Engel (forthcoming), 'Using Technical and Financial Assistance for Implementation of the TRIPS Agreement: A Guidebook for LDCs', forthcoming from the World Trade Organization, Geneva.

65 For an overview of the concept of graduation in WTO law, see T. Cottier, 'From Progressive Liberalization to Progressive Regulation in WTO Law', *Journal of International Economic Law* 9, 2006, 779–821.

Index